THE CITY
OF MARVELS

THE CITY
OF MARVELS

EDUARDO
MENDOZA

*Translated from the Spanish
by Bernard Molloy*

Harcourt Brace Jovanovich, Publishers
SAN DIEGO NEW YORK LONDON

Requests for permission to make copies of any part of the work should be mailed to:
Permissions, Harcourt Brace Jovanovich, Publishers, Orlando, Florida 32887.

Library of Congress Cataloging-in-Publication Data

Mendoza, Eduardo, 1943–
  [Ciudad de los prodigios. English]
  The city of marvels / Eduardo Mendoza : translated from the Spanish by Bernard Molloy. — 1st ed.
     p.   cm.
  Translation of: La ciudad de los prodigios.
  I. Title.
PQ6663.E54C513 1988
863'.64—dc19   87-33700

Designed by Colleen Vásquez

Printed in the United States of America

First edition

A B C D E

To Ana

When the unclean spirit is gone out of a man, he walketh through dry places, seeking rest; and finding none, he saith, I will return unto my house whence I came out. And when he cometh, he findeth it swept and garnished. Then goeth he, and taketh to him seven other spirits more wicked than himself; and they enter in, and dwell there: and the last state of that man is worse than the first.

Saint Luke 11:24–26

The City
Of Marvels

CHAPTER ONE

1

Renovation fever was running high in the city the year Onofre Bouvila arrived in Barcelona.

This city is situated in the valley between Malgrat and Garraf left behind by the coastal mountain range as it withdraws inland, forming a kind of amphitheater on the coast. The climate there is mild and dependable, the sky is usually clear and bright, and the few clouds that pass over are white. The atmospheric pressure is stable, but rain, though a rare occurrence, can be treacherous and torrential. Although subject to debate, the prevalent view attributes both the first and the second foundings of Barcelona to the Phoenicians. We know at least that Barcelona makes its entrance into history as a colony of Carthage, being allied in turn to Sidon and Tyre. It has been established that Hannibal's elephants stopped to drink, romp, and rollick on the banks of the Besós and the Llobregat on their way to the Alps, where they were to be decimated by the cold and the arduous terrain. The earliest citizens of Barcelona were astonished at the sight of the animals. "Just look at those tusks, those ears, that trunk or proboscis," they remarked. This shared astonishment and the deliberations it gave rise to over the course of many years thereafter did much to foster Barcelona's sense of identity as an urban unit. In the nineteenth century the people of Barcelona would strive to regain that identity, which faded over the intervening centuries.

The Phoenicians were followed by the Greeks, the Greeks by the Iberian Layetanos. The passage of the former left traditions of craft, of the latter, the distinctive features of the race, according to ethnologists: the leftward tilt of the head to indicate interest when being spoken to, and the uncommonly luxuriant growth of hair in the nasal orifices of the Catalan menfolk. The main element in the diet of the Layetanos, of whom little is known, was a dairy product which differed little from our present-day yogurt.

But it was the Romans who made a true city of Barcelona, laying down its definitive structure. That structure, which need not be examined in detail here, was to have a significant influence on the city's later development. Everything seems to indicate, however, that the Romans felt a haughty disdain for Barcelona. Neither strategic value nor any other reason aroused their interest in it. In the year 63 B.C. one Mucious Alexandrinus, a praetor, wrote to his father-in-law, bemoaning having been sent to Barcelona; he had been seeking a post in the resplendent city of Bilbilis Augusta—today Calatayud.

The king of the particular band of Goths who later conquered the city answered to the name of Ataulfo, and the city was to remain in the power of the Goths until the Saracens took it without a struggle in the year 717 A.D. As was their custom, the Moors limited their attention to the cathedral (not the one admired today, but another, more ancient cathedral, built on a different site, the scene of many conversions and martyrdoms); they changed it into a mosque, and called it a day. The French won the city back for the faith in the year 785, and exactly two centuries later, in 985, it was taken again for Islam by Almanzor or al-Mansur, the Righteous One, the Pitiless One, or the Three-Toothed One.

The shape of the city walls was not unrelated to these conquests and reconquests. Within their complex corset of bulwarks and concentric fortifications, the streets grew ever more twisted. This attracted the cabbalistic Hebrews of Gerona, who founded branches of their sect therein, digging underground passageways leading to the Sanhedrins and the healing baths discovered in the twentieth century during work on the Metro. It is still possible to read words scrawled on the stone lintels of the old quarter— secret signs for the initiated, formulae for achieving the unthinkable, etc. The city then experienced years of splendor, centuries of obscurity.

"You'll be most comfortable here, you'll see. The rooms are none too spacious, but they are well aired, and as for cleanliness, one could not ask for more. The meals are plain but wholesome," said the owner of the boardinghouse. This establishment, in which Onofre Bouvila found himself shortly after his arrival in Barcelona, was situated on the Carreró del Xup, a back alley whose Catalan name might be rendered as Water-Tank Alley. The alley began level but sloped up almost immediately, at first gently, then more and more steeply, rising to form two steps. The steps were followed by another level section, but that soon ended in a wall built on the remains of an ancient wall dating perhaps from the Romans. From this wall seeped, constantly, a thick black liquid that over the centuries had rounded off, smoothed, and polished the steps in the alley, making them slippery underfoot. The liquid oozed its way down the slope, in the gutter, and finally, with a gurgle or two, disappeared into the drain where the alley crossed Calle de la Manga (formerly Calle de la Pera). This street provided the only access to the alley and, despite rival claims to the

3

dubious honor from other corners of the neighborhood, it could boast having been the scene of a certain grim incident: the execution of Saint Leocricia. This saint, predating the other Saint Leocricia (the Saint Leocricia from Córdoba), is listed in hagiographies sometimes as Saint Leocricia and sometimes as Saint Leocratia or Saint Locatis. She was born and bred in or around Barcelona, was the daughter of a wool carder, and became a Christian convert at an early age. Disregarding her wishes, her father married her off to one Tiburcio or Tiburcino, a quaestor. Spurred by her faith, Leocricia distributed her husband's possessions among the poor and freed his slaves. She acted without her husband's consent, however, and he was furious. For this, and for refusing to renounce her faith, she was publicly executed at the said spot. Legend has it that her head rolled down the slope and went on rolling, turning corners, crossing streets, and generally frightening the life out of unsuspecting bystanders, until at last it fell into the sea, where a dolphin or some other large fish made off with it. Her saint's day is observed on January 27.

Toward the end of the last century there was a boardinghouse on the upper level of the alley, an unprepossessing establishment, though its owners were not without fond illusions regarding its merit. The reception area was small, having room only for a pine desk (complete with brass tray for papers and the hotel register, the latter always left open and dimly illuminated by an oil lamp to enable those who wished to see for themselves the respectability of the concern to pore over the list of pseudonyms and *noms de guerre* that constituted the hostelry's clientele), a barber's cubbyhole, a porcelain umbrella stand, and an effigy of Saint Christopher, one-time patron saint of wayfarers as he is now of motorists. Invariably to be found seated behind the reception desk was Señora Agata. She was an obese lady, worn out and half bald. Her ailments obliged her to keep her feet soaking in a basin of warm water and to call out every now and then, "Delfina, the washbasin." Each time the water began to cool, she would revive just enough to utter those words. Then her daughter would bring a saucepan filled with steaming water and empty it into her basin. With so many saucepanfuls going in, the reception area was in constant danger of being flooded. This peril, however, seemed not to trouble the owner of the boardinghouse, known to all as Señor Braulio. It was with him that Onofre Bouvila had his initial interview. "Indeed, if the establishment were in a better location, it could pass as quite a reputable little hotel," the owner continued. Señor Braulio, husband to Señora Agata and father to Delfina, was a distingué gentleman of considerable stature and clean-cut features. He delegated everything to do with the running of the boardinghouse to his wife and daughter. The greater part of his day was devoted to reading the daily papers and discussing the news with the lodgers. He was riveted by all the latest inventions, and since inventions abounded in that period, his oohs and aahs filled many a long hour. From time to time, as if in response to a vehement exhortation, he would fling aside the newspaper and exclaim, "I'll go and see what the weather's up to." Out in the street he would scrutinize the heavens, then come back inside and announce, "A clear sky," or "Cloudy," or "A nip in the air." Such were his only known occupations. "It's this wretched neighborhood that forces us to set our prices so far below the true worth of our establishment," he grumbled. Then, raising an admonitory finger, he added, "Mind you, we are very careful about the admission of new clients."

"Is he referring to my personal appearance?" Onofre Bouvila wondered as he listened to Señor Braulio. Although the boardinghouse owner's cordiality seemed to rule out such an interpretation, Onofre's suspicion was well grounded: despite his tender age, and though he had broad shoulders, it was obvious that he was of less than average height. His complexion was sallow, his features small and rough-hewn, and his hair black and curly. His clothes, patched up and crumpled, were none too clean—indicating that he had been on the road for several days in those same clothes, and that he had nothing else to wear, unless there was a change of clothes in the little bundle which he put on the reception desk when he came in. The boy kept stealing furtive glances at this bundle, then would fix his gaze on Señor Braulio once more, which made the boardinghouse owner feel uneasy. "There's something in his look that puts me on edge," Señor Braulio said to himself. "Bah, it's probably just the usual story: he's hungry, mixed up, and nervous," he concluded. He had seen many arrive in that same state: the city was growing incessantly. "One more," he thought. "Another tiny sardine for the great whale to swallow without even noticing." His unease changed to pity. "He's practically a child, and feeling desperate."

"And if you will allow me the liberty of putting this question to you, Señor Bouvila, what might the motive of your stay in Barcelona be?" he said finally, hoping to impress the lad with his locution, and the lad in fact was momentarily tongue-tied, not sure he understood what had been asked.

"I'm looking for a job," he answered diffidently. A moment later his gaze was once more fixed on the establishment's owner, in case the latter said something disparaging. But Señor Braulio's thoughts had already moved on to other matters, and he was scarcely paying attention to his guest. "Ah, splendid," was all he said, flicking a speck of dust off the shoulder of his frock coat. Onofre was relieved at this lack of interest. His origins were a source of embarrassment to him, and for nothing in the world would he have revealed just what it was that had prompted him to drop everything and come running to Barcelona in desperation.

Onofre Bouvila had not been born, as some later claimed, in the prosperous, bright, jovial, and somewhat garish Catalonia that basks on the Mediterranean coast but, rather, up in the harsh, grim, brutal Catalonia that lies to the southeast of the Pyrenees and slopes down on either side of the Cadí Mountains. Irrigated by the upper reaches of the river Segre and its main tributaries, the land flattens out where that river meets the river Noguera Pallaresa, to undertake the last part of its journey, ending in the river Ebro at Mequinenza. In the lowlands the rivers run fast, and very high in spring; when the flood waters subside, they leave in their wake unhealthy, snake-infested, but fertile marshland, good for hunting. These regions of thick fog and dense forests lend themselves to superstition. Indeed, no one will set off into that murky mist on certain days of the year, when bells can be heard tolling where no church or hermitage stands, as well as cries and guffaws from among the trees, and where occasionally dead cows may be seen dancing the traditional *sardana*.

He who sees or hears such things will go mad for sure.

The mountains around these valleys were steep, and the mountain men, rough and surly, still wore skins as part of their dress. They only came down to the valleys with the thaw, to seek out wives for themselves in the festivities associated with the grape harvest or the pig slaughter. On such occasions they would play on their bone flutes and perform a dance that mimicked the gambols of sheep. They were forever chewing bread and cheese, and they drank wine mixed with water and oil. Living on the mountaintops was a still more outlandish people: they never came down to the valleys at all, and their only pastime seems to have been wrestling.

The valley dwellers were more civilized; they lived on the fruits of the vine and the olive tree, along with corn (for their animals), a few vegetables, cattle, and honey. In that region twenty-five thousand different types of bee were listed at the beginning of this century, of which only five or six thousand survive today. The wild boar and the rabbit, the fallow deer and the partridge were all hunted, as were foxes, weasels, and—to check their constant incursions—badgers. The valley dwellers fly-fished for trout in the rivers, demonstrating great skill in that art. They ate well, and as a result of a balanced diet were a tall, strong, and energetic race, physical characteristics that played a part in the history of Catalonia. One of the arguments used by the central government against the separatist aspirations of that land was that Catalan independence would mean a lowering of the average height of Spaniards.

In his report to Carlos III, who had just arrived in Spain from Naples, R. de P. Piñuela called Catalonia "the stool of Spain." Wood was in plentiful supply in Catalonia, and there was cork and one or two minerals as well. The Catalans lived in large farmhouses, *masías*, widely scattered up and down the valleys, and the parish or rectorate was the only cohesive force among them.

This gave rise to the tradition of giving the name of the parish or rectorate as the place of birth. Thus we find Pere Llebre from Sant Roc, or Joaquim Colibròquil from Mare de Deu del Roser, etc. Consequently, a great responsibility came to rest on the shoulders of the clergy. They preserved the religious, cultural, and even the linguistic unity of the area. Also falling to them was the crucial task of keeping the peace within each valley and between neighboring valleys, averting outbreaks of violence and the interminable bloodshed of vendettas. A type of clergyman emerged, whose praises were later sung by poets: shrewd, stouthearted men capable of braving the worst the weather had to offer, and who could cover astonishing distances on foot with the sacraments in one hand and a blunderbuss in the other. It was probably thanks to the clergy, too, that the region managed to avoid becoming mixed up in the Carlist civil wars to any significant extent. Toward the end of the conflict, bands of Carlists used the area as a refuge, winter quarters, and a source of provisions. The people there went about their own business. From time to time a body would appear, half buried in a furrow or among the bushes, with a bullet in the chest or in the back of the neck. Everyone pretended not to notice. Sometimes the body was not a Carlist but the victim of some personal quarrel settled under the cover provided by the war.

All that is known for certain is that Onofre Bouvila was baptized on the feast of Saint Restituto and Saint Leocadia (December 9) in the year eighteen hundred and seventy-four, that he received the baptismal waters from the hands of the Reverend Dom Serafí Dalmau, and that his parents were Joan Bouvila and Marina Mont. It is not known, however, why he was given the name Onofre and not the name of the saint whose feast fell on that day. In the certificate of baptism, the source of this information, he is identified as being a member of the parish of San Clemente and the firstborn son of the Bouvila family.

"Splendid, splendid, you'll be like a king in here," Señor Braulio said, taking a rusty key from his pocket and making a grandiose sweep of his arm in the gloomy, evil-smelling corridor of the boardinghouse. "The rooms, as you will see . . . Ah, Good Lord, what a fright you gave me!"

This exclamation was prompted by the sudden opening of the door from the inside, just as he was about to insert the key in the lock. Delfina's silhouette in the doorway stood out against the light coming from the balcony.

"This is my daughter," said Señor Braulio. "No doubt she has put the finishing touches to your room, so you'll find it even more to your liking. Isn't that so, Delfina?" Seeing that she made no answer, he turned again to Onofre Bouvila and added, "Since the health of her poor mother—my wife—is not as good as it might be, all the work of running the establishment would fall upon my shoulders were it not for Delfina's help. She is a godsend."

Onofre had seen Delfina a moment before, in the reception area, when she came to replenish Señora Agata's basin with hot water. He had scarcely noticed her then. Now, examining her more closely, he found her thoroughly repulsive. About the same age as he was, she was skinny and awkward, with protruding teeth, rough skin, and shifty eyes that were also unusual in having yellow pupils. Onofre soon learned that in fact all the chores of the boardinghouse were left to Delfina. Sullen, dirty, disheveled, raggedly dressed, and barefooted, she would be seen scurrying day and night from the kitchen to the rooms and from the rooms to the kitchen, carrying a bucket or a broom, or rags. In addition to all that, she looked after her mother, who required constant attention, since she was unable to do anything for herself, so Delfina served at the table—breakfast, lunch, and dinner. She would go shopping first thing in the morning with two large wicker baskets, which she could scarcely carry on the way back. She never spoke to the guests, and they in their turn ignored her. And apart from her sullen manner, there was the black cat that followed her everywhere. Not tolerating any other human presence in its vicinity, it would attack with tooth and claw anyone who ventured within striking range. This cat's name was Beelzebub. Deep gouges on the walls and furniture bore witness to its ferocity.

For the time being, however, Onofre knew nothing of this. He entered the room assigned to him, a small, austere cubicle. "It's my room," he thought with a kind of tenderness stirring in him. "I am now an independent man, a citizen of Barcelona." Like every other newcomer, he was fascinated by the big city. He had always lived in the country, only once visiting a decent-sized town, and that visit was by now a faded memory.

The town was called Bassora, eighteen kilometers from San Clemente (or Sant Climent). When Onofre Bouvila visited Bassora, it had just undergone a rapid transformation. Originally a center of agriculture and especially livestock, it was now an industrial city. According to the statistics, thirty-six industries were established in Bassora in 1878; of these, twenty-one belonged to the textile sector (processing cotton, silk, and wool, fabric printing, carpet manufacture, etc.), eleven to the chemical sector (phosphates, acetates, chlorides, dyes, and soaps), three to iron and steel, and one to lumber. A railroad linked Bassora to Barcelona, from whose port Bassora's shipments were dispatched. Horse-drawn coaches still provided transportation, but people generally preferred the railroad. There was gas lighting on several streets, four hotels or inns, four schools, three casinos, and a theater. Between this town and Sant Climent a road, stony and uneven, crossed the mountains through a pass usually blocked by snow in winter. A horse-and-trap used to go back and forth along this road, weather permitting. The trap, covering the eighteen kilometers between Sant Climent and Bassora on an irregular basis, with no timetable or fixed stops, brought equipment, supplies of all kinds, and letters, if there were letters, to the farmhouses; on the way back, it loaded up with whatever agricultural surplus there happened to be at the time. These surpluses were consigned by the rector of Sant Climent to a priest in Bassora, a friend of his, who sold them and sent back the profits, along with detailed accounts that nobody asked for, understood, or bothered to check. The owner of the trap was known as Uncle Tonet. When he reached Sant Climent, he would spend the night on the floor of a tavern adjoining the church. But before turning in, he recounted what he had seen and heard in Bassora, though few believed him. Uncle Tonet had the reputation of a drinker and a spinner of yarns. In any event, nobody could see how such a catalogue of marvels, even if they were true, could affect life there in the valley.

But now, for Onofre Bouvila, even Bassora dwindled into insignificance compared with the Barcelona he was seeing for the first time. This attitude, in many ways ingenuous, was not entirely unjustified: according to the 1887 census, what is now referred to as the "metropolitan area" (the city and its peripheries) had some 416,000 inhabitants, and that figure was growing at the rate of twelve thousand souls a year. Of the figure quoted in the census (an overestimation, some would say), Barcelona itself— what was then the "municipal area"—accounted for 272,000 inhabitants. The remainder lived in the towns and suburbs outside the ancient city walls. As the nineteenth century wore on, it was in these outlying districts that the larger industrial concerns established themselves. Throughout that century, Barcelona was always at the forefront of progress. In 1818 the first regular stage-coach service in Spain went into operation between Barcelona and Reus. The first experimental gaslight system was installed in the courtyard of the Palace of La Lonja, housing the Chambers of Commerce, in 1826. In 1836 the first steam-powered motor went into operation, a first step toward mechanization. Spain's first railroad was built to link Barcelona and Mataró, dating from 1848. The first electric power station in Spain was likewise built in Barcelona, in the year 1873. The gap between Barcelona and the rest of the peninsula was enormous, and the city made an overwhelming impression on the newcomer. But all this progress had demanded a colossal effort. Barcelona, like the female of some giant species who had just given birth to numerous offspring, lay drained, exhausted. Foul emanations seeped from cracks, rancid exhalations rendered unbreathable the air in the streets and homes. Weariness and pessimism held sway among the population. Only a few simple souls like Señor Braulio still saw life through rose-colored glasses.

"There are plenty of opportunities in Barcelona for people with imagination and enterprise," he told Onofre Bouvila that same night in the boardinghouse dining room, as the latter sipped at the colorless pungent soup Delfina served him. "Now, you seem honest, wide awake, and hard-working. You will make your mark, I am quite certain. Bear in mind, young man, that there has never in the history of humanity been an epoch such as this: electricity, telephones, the submarine. . . . But why enumerate these wonders? God only knows where it will all end. By the way, would you mind paying in advance? My wife, whom you have already had the honor to meet, is very particular about the accounts. Since the poor lady is so ill . . . ?"

Onofre handed over all he had to Señora Agata. That paid for a week, but left him penniless. The following morning, at the crack of dawn, he took to the streets in search of a job.

2

   That Barcelona went about its business "turning its back on the sea" was already a well-worn phrase by the end of the nineteenth century, though in fact daily life in the city gave the lie to that cliché. Barcelona had always been and continued to be a maritime city: it had lived off and for the sea; it was nourished by the sea, and gave back the fruits of its endeavors to the sea; the streets of Barcelona guided the wanderer's steps down to the sea, and that sea linked the city with the outside world. From the sea came the wind and the weather, the smells, sometimes pleasant and sometimes not so pleasant, and the salt, which ate away at walls; sea noises lulled the people of Barcelona to sleep at siesta time, ship sirens marked the passing hours, and the sad, sour squawking of seagulls was a constant reminder that the cheering sun-spangled shadows of trees along the city's avenues were a fond deception. The sea peopled the back alleys with twisted characters speaking foreign tongues and producing knives, pistols, or clubs at the drop of a hat; the sea covered the tracks of evildoers who fled to the open waters, leaving behind bloodcurdling cries in the night and crimes unpunished. The streets and squares of Barcelona were blinding sea-white in fair weather and dull sea-gray on stormy days. Onofre Bouvila, a landlubber, was bound to feel the lure of that world. The first thing he did that morning was to make his way down to the port to look for work on the docks.

   Barcelona's economic development had begun at the end of the eighteenth century and was to continue until the second decade of the twentieth, but that development was not a continuous process. Booms were followed by recessions. During the recessions, the influx of new immigrants would continue unabated, regardless of the falling demand, and finding work became well-nigh impossible. Despite what Señor Braulio had said the previous evening, Barcelona had been going through just such a depressed period for some years when Onofre Bouvila took to the streets in search of a living.

Finding that police constables had cordoned off the docks, he asked the reason, and was told that several cases of cholera morbus had been detected among the dockworkers, the disease having no doubt been brought by some vessel returning from distant shores. Peering over a uniformed shoulder, he beheld a tragic scene: some workers were putting down their loads to vomit on the quayside flagstones; others, crouched, were defecating a thin ocher liquid. Once over the attack, they would return shakily to their chores, anxious not to lose their day's wages. Those free of the disease drew away whenever a sick man passed, and brandished chains or hooks if he came too close. A group of women were trying to force their way into the cordoned-off zone to go to the aid of their husbands or friends; they were unceremoniously driven back.

Onofre Bouvila walked on, following the seafront to the Barceloneta district. At that time the great majority of the vessels still had sails. The port itself was antiquated, too: ships could only tie up stern-on because of the layout of the wharves, and this made loading and unloading difficult operations, having to be performed by launches and barges. Swarms of these craft laden with goods plied to and fro across the waters all day. Old sailors with weather-beaten faces thronged the quays and adjacent streets, wearing trousers rolled up to the knee, loose-fitting shirts with horizontal stripes, and Phrygian caps. They smoked cane pipes, drank hard liquor, ate cured meat and a kind of biscuit they would leave out to dry for weeks on end, and sucked avidly at lemons; they were terse with others, but would talk nonstop to themselves; they shunned company and were quarrelsome, but would carry with them a dog, a parrot, a turtle, or some other little creature, upon which they lavished much attention. Their lot was in fact an unhappy one: originally taken aboard as cabin boys, they would not return to their homeland until old age.

Their continual wanderings ruled out a family or any lasting friendship. Then, on their return, they would be strangers in their own land. Yet, unlike real foreigners, who can always more or less adapt themselves to the ways of a new country, these old salts were handicapped by memories that had become distorted over the years, as they whiled away their idle hours in the forging of dreams and schemes, unable to face a different reality. Some of them, precisely to avoid the unpleasantness of such a home-coming, chose to live out their last years in some foreign port far from their native land. That was the case of an old sea dog, nearly a hundred years old and of unknown origins, called Sturm, who had achieved a certain notoriety around that time among his neighbors in La Barceloneta. He spoke a language unintelligible to all, even to the professors of the Faculty of Arts, to whom he was taken, in vain, by those neighbors of his. His sole capital was a wad of notes no bank in Barcelona would change for him; but since it was a sizable wad, he was considered rich and was given credit in all the shops and bars. He was said not to be a Christian but a sun worshiper, and it was also said that he kept a seal or a manatee in his room.

La Barceloneta was a fishermen's district that in the eighteenth century had grown outside the city walls. Later it became absorbed by the city and underwent rapid industrialization. By this time the great shipyards had established themselves in La Barceloneta. As he walked around that district, Onofre came across a group of stout, cheery women sorting out fish and cackling merrily all the while. Encouraged by these outward signs of good nature, he went over to them to ask a few questions. "Maybe these women know where I can find a job," he thought. "Women are more likely to be friendly to a young man like me." He soon discovered that their good humor was really a nervous disorder that made them laugh spasmodically and uncontrollably for no apparent reason. Deep down, they were bitter, seething with suppressed rage: they would brandish knives or throw crabs and lobsters at one another over any trifle. Seeing how things stood, he took off in a hurry. He fared no better in his attempts to enlist as a seaman on board one of the vessels anchored there not affected by the quarantine. When he approached one boat, the seamen leaning on the ship's rail said, "Don't come aboard if you value your life, my boy." They had scurvy; their bleeding gums could be seen as they talked. At the railroad station the porters—who could scarcely walk, so bad was their rheumatism—told him that only members of a certain association stood any chance of being taken on for that particular kind of slavery.

And so it went. At nightfall Onofre went back to the boardinghouse, utterly exhausted. As he gobbled down his meager dinner, Señor Braulio, who was fluttering from table to table, inquired as to the outcome of his exertions. Onofre informed him that he had had no luck. The man who ran the barber shop in the reception area overheard this exchange and took it upon himself to make a suggestion. "It's obvious you're a country boy," he told Onofre. "Try the market—you might find something there." Though stung, Onofre thanked the barber for his advice—and kicked Delfina's cat for sticking its claws into his leg. He answered the girl's look of hatred with a scornful glance. Although he would not have admitted it, the day's setbacks had shaken him. "I never thought things would be so bad," he said to himself. "Bah, so what? Tomorrow I'll have another go. If I keep at it, something will turn up. Who cares what, as long as I don't have to go back home?" It was that prospect that worried him most.

Taking the barber's advice, he paid a visit the following day to the Borne, as the main fruit-and-vegetable market was called. His visit, however, was to no avail. It was the same story everywhere. Thus the hours and the days went by, with no results, nor even any hope of results. Come rain or shine, he was out footing it around the city. He left no stone unturned. He tried to get into trades he had never heard of before: making and selling cigarettes or cheeses, diving, marble cutting, well-digging, etc. Most places he tried had no jobs open; others demanded experience. In a confectioner's they asked him if he knew how to make rolled wafers, in a shipyard if he could caulk. He had no choice but to answer no.

He soon found out things that he had never suspected — that the least onerous job of all, for instance, was domestic service. A total of 16,186 people were employed in that sector in Barcelona. Conditions prevailing in other jobs were awful. Hours were long, workers had to get up every day at four or five in the morning to get to work on time, and wages were very low. Children five and up would be put to work in construction, transport, and even in graveyards, as assistant gravediggers. In some places Onofre was treated in a friendly enough way, in others with open hostility. He was nearly gored by a cow in a creamery, and a group of coalmen set a mastiff on him. Everywhere there was squalor and disease. Whole districts were afflicted with typhus, smallpox, scarlet fever. He came across cases of chlorosis, cyanosis, amaurosis, necrosis, tetanus, palsy, afflux, epilepsy, and croup. Malnutrition was rife among the child population, tuberculosis among the adults, and syphilis among all.

Like all cities, Barcelona was visited periodically by terrible plagues. In 1834 an epidemic of cholera left 3,521 dead in its wake; twenty years later, in 1854, the same illness claimed 5,640 lives. In 1870 yellow fever brought over from the Spanish West Indies spread throughout La Barceloneta. The whole district was evacuated, and the Riba wharf burned to the ground. On such occasions the initial panic that gripped the population would be followed by despondency. Processions and public acts of atonement to beg for God's forgiveness would be organized. Everybody attended these religious events, even those who only a month before had had a hand in the burning down of convents during public rioting. The most contrite would be precisely those who, not long before, had gleefully applied the torch to some poor priest's chasuble, played skittles with the sacred statues, and made broth with the bones of the saints. The epidemics waned and moved away, but they never entirely died out: pockets always remained where the disease seemed to make itself at home, putting down roots. Thus one epidemic would arrive before the previous one left, overlapping it. Doctors had to abandon to their fate the last cases of one wave in order to attend to the first cases of the next, and their work was never done.

As a result, charlatans, healers, herbalists, and quacks of all kinds proliferated. In every square, men and women were to be found preaching obscure doctrines, announcing the coming of the Antichrist, the Last Judgment. Self-styled messiahs showed a suspicious interest in people's wallets. The cures offered were quite useless if not actually counterproductive: howling at the full moon, tying little bells to one's ankles, or having signs of the zodiac or a Saint Catherine's wheel tattooed on one's chest. Unnerved by and defenseless against the ravages of the epidemics, people bought the talismans and dutifully swallowed the potions and draughts, and made their children swallow them, believing they were doing what was best for them. The City Council boarded up the houses of those who had died of the disease, but the shortage of accommodations was such, that before long somebody preferring the risk of contagion to roughing it on the streets would move in — and contract the illness forthwith.

But there were examples, too, of selfless dedication, as usually can be found in great extremity. One frequently recounted was that of a nun, getting on in years and with a hint of a mustache, by the name of Tarsila. No sooner would it come to Sister Tarsila's attention that such-and-such a person had taken to his bed stricken with an incurable ailment, than she would run to that person with her accordion under her arm. She kept this up for decades without once contracting an illness herself, despite all the coughing and sneezing over her and her accordion.

The night when the agreed time was up, Señor Braulio called Onofre to account. "Payments, as you know, are made in advance," he said. "Your weekly payment is due."

Onofre sighed. "I have not yet managed to find work, Señor Braulio. Allow me a week's grace, and I'll pay you in full out of my first earnings."

"You must not think that I am unaware of your predicament, Señor Bouvila," replied the owner, "but you must also be aware of ours. Not only does it cost us to provide for your daily sustenance, but we also lose what another client would be paying us if you vacated your room. I have no choice but to request that you leave first thing in the morning. Believe me, it hurts to have to take this course, for I have grown to like you."

Onofre scarcely ate a bite that evening. The accumulated fatigue of the day caught up with him, and he fell asleep almost as soon as he got into bed, but after an hour he woke up again with a start. The blackest thoughts began to assail him. To be rid of them, he went out onto the balcony; there he breathed in the humid, salty air redolent of fish and pitch from the port. From the same direction came a phantasmagoric glow: the light from the gas streetlamps in the mist. The rest of the city was plunged in darkness. After a while the cold got into his bones, and he decided to go back to bed. Tucked in again, he lit a stump of candle left on the bedside table and took from under his pillow a sheet of carefully folded yellow paper. Painstakingly he unfolded it and read its contents in the flickering light. As he read the words he knew by heart, his lips began to twitch, his brows to knit, and his eyes took on an expression of both sadness and resentment.

In the spring of 1876 or 1877 his father emigrated to Cuba. At the time, Onofre Bouvila was eighteen months old, and the couple had as yet no other offspring. His father was full of talk and fun, a good hunter, and, according to those who had known him before he set off on his adventures, somewhat starry-eyed. Onofre's mother came from the mountains, and had descended to the valley to be married to Joan Bouvila. A woman of few words, she was tall and lean, restless, and tended to be abrupt in her manner; her hair had been brown before it went gray, and her eyes were bluish-gray, like Onofre's—though he took after his father in all other physical respects.

Before the eighteenth century, the Catalans had rarely set off for the American colonies, and then always as government administrators sent by the Crown; from the eighteenth century on, however, many Catalans emigrated to Cuba. The money they sent back from that colony produced an unexpected accumulation of capital. With the help of that capital, the process of industrialization got under way, and new life was injected into the Catalan economy, which had been languishing since the time of the Catholic monarchs, Ferdinand and Isabella.

Some of these emigrants not only sent back money, but also ended up coming back themselves with their newly acquired riches. They were called *indianos*, and had extravagant mansions built in their native villages. Some even brought their slaves with them— black or mestizo women with whom they were obviously on intimate terms. That caused quite a scandal, and they were eventually persuaded by relatives and neighbors to marry these slaves off to wide-eyed country bumpkins. Issuing from such unions were darker-than-usual offspring who, socially rejected, usually ended up donning the cloth and being sent to missionary outposts in the Mariana or the Caroline Islands, which were still under the Archbishopric of Cadiz or Seville.

Later, such migration waned. A few men still crossed the ocean seeking their fortune, but they were isolated cases: a second son disinherited by the tradition of primogeniture, or a landowner brought to ruin by aphids, etc. Joan Bouvila did not fit into either of those categories: nobody knew at the time, and nobody learned afterward, what it was that had prompted him to emigrate. Some said ambition, others marital problems. According to one story, shortly after their wedding Joan Bouvila discovered a terrible secret concerning his wife. Awful screams and blows came from his house at night, and the baby would cry until the early hours of the morning, when the din finally died down. But the story wasn't true. After Joan Bouvila's departure, the rector of Sant Climent went on welcoming his wife, Marina Mont, into his church, administering the sacraments to her as to any other member of his flock, and treating her with particular deference.

Soon after he left, Joan Bouvila wrote a letter to his wife. The letter, sent from the Azores, where his ship had stopped off, was taken to the parish by Uncle Tonet in his pony-and-trap. The rector had to read it for her, since she could not read. To put an end to the gossip once and for all, he read it aloud from the pulpit before giving his sermon one Sunday. "When I've got work and a house and a bit of wampum together, I'll be sending for you," the letter said. "It's a fine crossing; today we saw sharks. Great shoals of them follow the boat, waiting for someone to fall overboard, to hack him to pieces with their three rows of teeth. Nothing of what goes into those jaws is ever given back to the sea." That was his first and last letter.

Onofre Bouvila folded the letter again with care, put it back under his pillow, snuffed the candle, and closed his eyes. This time he slept soundly, oblivious to the hardness of the mattress and the rabid attacks of the bedbugs and fleas. Just before dawn, however, he was wakened by the sensation of a weight on his stomach and the unpleasant feeling that he was being watched. The room was lit by a candle, not the candle he had put out a few hours previously but another, held by a person he could not identify, since his attention was riveted by something else: there on the bedspread was Beelzebub, Delfina's savage cat, its back arched, its tail on end, and its claws at the ready. Onofre's arms

21

were far from at the ready, being trapped under the sheets, and he dared not move them up to protect his face, lest that provoke the beast. He froze; beads of sweat formed on his forehead. "Don't be afraid, he won't go for you," whispered Delfina. "Unless you try anything on me—then he'll tear your eyes out." But Onofre didn't take his eyes off the cat or utter a word.

"I know you haven't found work," Delfina went on. There was a hint of satisfaction in her voice, perhaps because Onofre's failure had confirmed her opinion of him, or because she generally took pleasure in the misfortunes of others. "People think I don't know what's going on around here, but I hear everything. They treat me like a stick of furniture, they don't even nod or say hello when they meet me in the corridor. The wretches would give anything to get me into bed. . . . You know what I mean. Ah, but if they try anything, Beelzebub here will rip them to pieces. That's why they pretend not to notice me."

On hearing its name, the cat let out a wicked hiss. Delfina couldn't help a boastful laugh, and Onofre realized then that the chambermaid wasn't quite right in the head. "This is all I need," he thought. "Lord, just as long as I don't lose my eyes . . ."

"You seem different from that bunch," the maid went on, suddenly serious. "Perhaps because you're still just a kid. But you'll turn bad soon enough. Tomorrow you'll be out on the street. You'll have to sleep with one eye open all the time. You'll wake up frozen and starving, and there won't be a bite to eat. You'll fight over scraps from the garbage. You'll pray for it not to rain and for the summer to come quickly. And little by little you'll turn into a thug like all the rest. Well, what do you have to say for yourself? You can speak quietly—but don't move."

"Why did you come here?" Onofre croaked. "What do you want from me?"

"They think I'm only good for scrubbing floors and washing dishes," said Delfina, her contemptuous smile reappearing, "but I have my means. I could help you if I wanted to." She took a step toward the bed and said, "Listen to what I'm going to tell you. I have a boyfriend. Nobody knows this, not even my parents. One day, I'll run off with him. They'll search high and low for us, but we'll be far away by then. We'll never marry, but we'll live together forever, and they'll never get me here again. If you give away my secret, I'll tell Beelzebub to do his worst on your face—understand?"

Onofre swore by God and his mother that he would keep the secret.

This satisfied Delfina, who went on: "My boyfriend belongs to a group made up of brave, noble men determined to put an end to the poverty and injustice all around us." She paused to see what effect her words had on Onofre. Seeing no reaction from him, she added, "Have you heard of anarchism?" Onofre—carefully—shook his head. "What about Bakunin?" No again, but instead of flying into a rage, as he had feared, she shrugged. "That's to be expected. These are new ideas. Very few people know about them. But don't worry—soon everybody will be hearing about them. Things are going to change around here."

In the 1860s the Italian anarchist groups that had flourished during the years of struggle leading to the unification of Italy decided to send some of their people to other countries, to spread their doctrines and win disciples. The man sent to Spain, whose anarchist ideas were already known and enjoyed great favor, was named Foscarini. A few kilometers from Nice, however, the Spanish police, in connivance with their French counterparts, stopped the train Foscarini was on and boarded it. "Hands up," they said, aiming their rifles at the passengers. "Which one of you is Foscarini?" Every passenger claimed that he was Foscarini. There was no greater honor than to be mistaken for the great apostle. The only one who said nothing was Foscarini himself. Years of clandestine activity had taught him to dissemble; he looked out the window and whistled cheerfully, as if the boarding meant nothing to him. Thus the police were able to identify him without any difficulty. They dragged him off the train, stripped him to his underwear, tied him across the track with his head on one rail and his feet on the other. "When the nine o'clock express comes along," they told him, "it'll make sausage of you." One of the policemen put on Foscarini's clothes and boarded the train again. The passengers thought that it was Foscarini returning, that he had given his captors the slip, and they cheered him long and loud. The false Foscarini smiled away and jotted down the names of those who cheered with the greatest enthusiasm. Once in Spain, as an *agent provocateur*, he incited people to all kinds of violent acts, thereby predisposing people against the workers and justifying the terrible repressive measures the government was imposing.

Meanwhile, a man who was the opposite of both Foscarinis—the real and the fictitious—was coming ashore in Barcelona harbor. His name was Conrad de Weerd, and in the United States, where he came from, he was a well-known sports columnist. Scion of a vaguely aristocratic, propertied family from South Carolina that lost its entire fortune in the Civil War, de Weerd had tried his hand at journalism, to which he was inclined by nature, but as a Southerner found his path barred at every turn, in Baltimore, New York, Boston, and Philadelphia. The sports pages were his only remaining option. Though personally acquainted with the most prominent figures of his time, such as Jake Kilrain and John L. Sullivan, he was obliged to eke out a humble existence as a columnist.

In the middle of the last century, sport was little more than a pretext for betting and giving free rein to man's baser instincts. De Weerd covered cockfights, dogfights, and rat fights, as well as mixed fights of bulls against dogs, dogs against rats, rats against pigs, etc. He also had to witness exhausting, bloody boxing matches, which could go on for eighty-five rounds and usually ended in a shoot-out. Concluding at last that human nature was essentially brutal and vindictive, and that only through public education could individuals be knocked into something resembling acceptable creatures, he abandoned the world of sports and devoted himself to founding workers' associations, using money lent to him by a group of Jews with liberal tendencies. The aim of these associations was educational betterment and the cultivation of the arts, especially music. De Weerd wanted to create great choral groups of workers. "That way they'll lose interest in rat fights," he thought. He lived from hand to mouth; whatever he earned went into the choirs. But, drawn by the money, gangsters began to infiltrate the choirs. To be rid of de Weerd, they sent him off to Europe to do his proselytizing there. Hearing of the Clavé Choirs, he disembarked in Barcelona on Ascension Day in the year 1876. There he found the spurious Foscarini's crazed followers advocating the indiscriminate slaughter of children as they left school. His indignation was aroused.

Another character of interest—Delfina told Onofre—was Remedios Ortega Lombrices, alias Tagarnina. This intrepid female syndicalist happened to be working in the Seville tobacco factory. Orphaned at the age of ten, she had had to take charge of her eight younger brothers and sisters. Two succumbed to illnesses, but she managed to raise the others and still found it in herself to bring up eleven children of her own by seven different fathers. Twisting and rolling cigars, she acquired a solid grounding in economic and social theory. It happened in this way. Since each cigar girl had to roll a certain number of cigars each day, the workers decided to cover between them the quota of one roller, freeing her so she could read aloud to the others. Thus they became acquainted with Marx, Adam Smith, Bakunin, and Zola. Tagarnina's position was more left-wing than de Weerd's but less extreme than that of the Italians. She did not advocate the destruction of the factories, which in her opinion would only lead to conditions of appalling poverty throughout the land, but, rather, their takeover and collectivization.

Each leader had a following, but the various groups respected one another, no matter how wide their differences on theoretical grounds. They were always willing to cooperate, to lend a helping hand, and had never come into conflict. They were all staunchly allied to socialism, and indeed, Delfina admitted, sometimes it wasn't easy to tell one doctrine from the other.

While she was engaged in this exegesis, her yellow pupils shone with a crazed brilliance that Onofre found, if not exactly attractive, at least fascinating. The maid held her candle high like a torch, heedless of the hot wax dripping on the floor, and in her coarse shirt that covered her scrawny figure she looked like a proletarian Minerva. Finally the cat showed signs of impatience, and Delfina cut short her lecture.

"You'll find out all the rest later on if you do as I say," she told him. Onofre asked what he was supposed to do. Spread the message, she said, rouse the sleeping masses. "You're new in Barcelona," she went on. "Nobody knows you, you're young and look innocent. You can contribute something to the cause and earn a penny or two while you're at it. Not much, mind you—we're very poor—but enough to pay for your keep. We're not the bunch of dreamers some make us out to be: we know that people have to live. Well, what do you say?"

"When do I start?" said Onofre. Although he was not too enthusiastic about the whole business, Delfina's offer did at least give him a breathing space.

"Tomorrow morning, go to number 4, Calle del Musgo," said Delfina, dropping her voice to a whisper. "Ask for Pablo. He isn't my boyfriend, but he already knows about you. He'll be expecting you. He'll tell you what to do. Be careful, make sure nobody's following you. The police are always on the lookout. As for my father and your week's rent, don't worry, leave that to me. Beelzebub, let's go."

Saying no more, she blew out the candle, plunging the room into darkness. Onofre felt the cat's weight lift off and heard the soft thud of four paws on the floor tiles. Then he saw two terrible eyes glowing near the door. Finally the door closed slowly.

3

Asking people on the street, Onofre learned that the address Delfina gave him was in Pueblo Nuevo, relatively close to Barcelona. A mule-drawn streetcar went there, but it cost twenty centimos; since that was twenty centimos more than he had, he was obliged to walk, following the streetcar rails. Calle del Musgo was a dingy, godforsaken street that ran along the wall of a municipal cemetery reserved for suicide cases. The street was full of cowering dogs with thin, patchy coats and long, pointed muzzles. It had rained the night before, and the sky was overcast; the pressure was low, the air humid and clammy. But Onofre Bouvila was in a good mood: that same morning, over breakfast, Señor Braulio had come over to him and said, "Last night my wife and I had a talk, and we agreed that you should be granted a week's credit." Señor Braulio scratched his ear until it turned carnation red. "Times are hard and you are very young to be wandering alone on the face of the earth," he added. "We are likewise confident that you will presently find the job you are so tenaciously seeking, and we are of the opinion that, armed with your integrity and dedication, you will one day carve out for yourself an honorable future." Onofre had thanked him and glanced at Delfina out of the corner of his eye. The chambermaid, crossing the dining room with a pail of dirty water, didn't see him, or pretended not to.

He knocked on the door of number 4, which was promptly opened by a haggard man with a prominent forehead and thin lips.

"I'm Onofre Bouvila and I'm looking for someone called Pablo," he told him.

"I'm Pablo," the man said. "Come in."

Onofre stepped into what looked like an abandoned warehouse. There were mildew and saltpeter on the walls, and oil stains, coils of rope, and crates on the floor. Pablo took a parcel out of one of the crates. "These are the pamphlets you're to distribute," he said, handing it over to Onofre. "Are you familiar with the Idea?" Onofre noticed how both Pablo and Delfina said "the Idea," as if there were only one: that amused him. Sensing that with people like Pablo honesty was the best policy, he admitted that he was unenlightened. Pablo grimaced. "Read one of the pamphlets carefully," he said. "I haven't time to initiate you, and anyway the pamphlets spell it all out very clearly. You'd better familiarize yourself quickly, in case you're asked to explain some point." Onofre nodded. "Have they told you where your territory is?" asked the apostle. Onofre admitted that they had not. "What, not even that?" said Pablo, sighing to express how all the work involved in preparing for the revolution always fell on his shoulders. "All right, I'll tell you, then. Do you know where the World's Fair construction site is?" Onofre again confessed that he did not. "But, for heaven's sake, boy," said the apostle, shocked, "did you just drop down from the moon, or what?" Grumbling, he told Onofre how to get there and then pushed him out into the street.

Before Pablo could shut the door, Onofre asked, "What do I do when I run out of pamphlets?"

The apostle smiled for the first time. "Come back for more," he replied almost gently. He told Onofre to come to the warehouse in the mornings, between five and six o'clock—never at any other time. "If we bump into each other anywhere else, act as if we've never met," he went on quickly. "Don't give anyone this address, and never talk about me or the person who sent you here, even if your life is at stake. If they ask for your name, say 'Gaston': that will be your cover. Now, off with you: the briefer our meetings, the better."

Onofre left that strange place. When he came to a small

square, he sat on a bench, opened the parcel, and began reading one of the pamphlets. Some children were running in the square, and from a locksmith's workshop, out of sight but close at hand, came a constant clanging, which made concentration difficult. His reading ability was not good: he needed silence and time to grasp the sense. And he found half the words incomprehensible. The prose style was so convoluted, even going over the text several times did not help. "And for this gibberish I'm supposed to risk my neck?" he said to himself.

He tied up the parcel again and headed for the place Pablo had told him about. Walking, he viewed with a farmer's eye those acres that only a few years before had been carefully cultivated. Now, hemmed in by the advance of industry, the land, blackened and fetid, poisoned by the sewage from nearby factories, awaited an uncertain destiny. As the thirsty earth swallowed up those effluents, a layer of slime was formed on the surface, and it adhered to the walker's canvas shoes, hindering his progress.

At some point he must have mistaken the railroad tracks for the streetcar rails, for he got lost. Since there was nobody around to help him out, he scrambled up a rise, hoping to sight his goal or at least find out where he was. The sun's position and a rough reckoning of the time of day enabled him to determine the four cardinal points. In the east the clouds had parted and the sun's rays were finding a way through; the sea glimmered with a silver sheen in response. Turning his back on the sea, he saw, in the heavy atmosphere, the diffuse silhouette of the city, the belfries and towers of the churches and convents, the chimneys of the factories. A locomotive with no carriages in tow was maneuvering onto a siding. The billows of smoke it discharged were soon checked in their upward path by the dense, damp air, which pushed them down again. Onofre resumed walking. Whenever he saw a rise, he scaled it and scanned the horizon. At last he spotted, beyond the railroad tracks, an open level site where men, beasts, and carts were swarming. Buildings under construction could be seen there, too. This had to be the place he was looking for. "Or, if not, they'll be able to put me right," he said to himself. He clambered down the hillock and set out for the site, the parcel of pamphlets under his arm.

The Citadel—Ciudadela—the shameful memory of which still lingers on and whose name is synonymous with oppression, appeared and disappeared in the following manner.

In 1701 Catalonia, jealous of her liberties and feeling them to be under threat, embraced the cause of the Archduke of Austria in the War of Succession. After the defeat of that party and the enthronement of the House of Bourbon in Spain, Catalonia was severely punished. The war had been long and bitter, but its aftermath was worse. Bourbon armies sacked Catalonia; the commanders looked the other way as the soldiers took their revenge. Then came the official punishment: Catalans were executed by the hundreds, and their heads were put on lances and exhibited at prominent points up and down the principality. Thousands of prisoners were sent to do hard labor in remote regions of the peninsula and even in the American colonies; they died in their chains, far from their native land. The younger women were used for the pleasure of the soldiery, which resulted in a scarcity of marriageable ladies, still felt in Catalonia. Large areas of farmland were devastated and strewn with salt to render the soil infertile; fruit trees were torn up by the roots. An attempt was made to wipe out livestock, especially the much-prized Pyrenean cow. That extermination—by artillery and bayonets —was thwarted, since a few head of these cattle fled to the mountains, where they survived in the wild until well into the nineteenth century. Castles were pulled down, the hewn stone used to wall in certain towns, making them penitentiaries in all but name. Monuments and statues adorning boulevards and squares were smashed. The walls of palaces and public buildings were first whitewashed and then covered with obscene illustrations and offensive expressions. Schools were turned into stables, stables into schools. Barcelona University, where revered figures had studied or taught, was closed, and the building that housed it was dismantled stone by stone; these stones were then used to block the aqueducts, canals, and irrigation ditches that carried water to the city and the cultivated land around it. The port of Barcelona was strewn with deliberate hazards to shipping: sharks were brought specially from the West Indies in large tanks and dumped into the surrounding sea. Fortunately, the Mediterranean did not suit them; those that did not succumb emigrated to warmer latitudes through the Straits of Gibraltar, which were already in English hands at that time.

The king was kept informed of all these measures. "Maybe," he said, "the Catalans still have not learned their lesson." Philip V, duke of Anjou, was a monarch of the Enlightenment. A French writer has described him as a *"roi fou, brave et dévot."* He married an Italian woman, Elizabeth Farnese, and died insane. Though he was not by nature bloodthirsty, malevolent advisers filled his ear with all manner of horrors concerning the Catalans, not to mention the Sicilians and Neapolitans, and overseas the Creoles, Canary Islanders, and the peoples of the Philippines and Indochina, all subjects of the Spanish Crown. So he had a huge fortress built in Barcelona in which he lodged an army of occupation ever ready to issue forth and quell an uprising. From the beginning this fortress was known as the Citadel. The governor lived inside, completely cut off from the people. In every respect, the most extreme systems of colonial rule were reproduced. Those found guilty of sedition were hanged in the courtyard and their bodies left for the vultures.

Under the shadow of that bastion, the people of Barcelona lived out their servility, shedding tears of rage and regret. Once or twice they attempted to take the fortress by storm, but were easily driven back, forced to abandon the field of battle strewn with their casualties. The soldiers, jeering, would appear in the

31

fortress loopholes and urinate on the dead and wounded lying below. But offsetting such heinous entertainment was their isolation: they could not set foot outside the fortifications or mix with the civilian population, who hated them; all forms of amusement were off limits to them; they were like prisoners. Denied the company of women, they resorted to sodomy and neglected personal hygiene: the Citadel became a breeding ground for disease of all kinds.

Petitions from both sides to put an end to that symbol of hostility and infamy were sent to each new monarch in turn. Only a handful of fanatics argued for its continued necessity. Each new monarch would agree to all that was said, but do nothing about it, such being the usual practice of those wielding absolute power.

By the middle of the nineteenth century the Citadel had lost its *raison d'être*, developments in the technology of warfare having made it redundant. In 1848, on the occasion of a popular uprising, General Espartero had deemed it more expedient to bombard Barcelona from the top of the Montjuich hill.

At long last, after a century and a half of existence, the Citadel's great walls were pulled down. The site and the buildings that went with it were given to the city, as if to efface the memory of so much accumulated suffering. Some of these buildings were justifiably razed to the ground; others still stand today. It was decided to put a public park in the precinct, for all to enjoy. What a moving contrast it was to observe how trees now took root and flowers blossomed in a place where so many atrocities had been committed, where, not long before, the gallows had stood. A lake was made there, too, and a colossal fountain bearing the name Cascada. This park was called, and still is called, Citadel Park.

In 1887, when Onofre Bouvila first set foot in the park, work was in progress on what was to be the site of the World's Fair. This was in early or mid-May of that year, and the work was well under way. The work force had reached full strength, some four thousand men—an unprecedented number. Add to that an equally large number of donkeys and mules. Cranes, steam engines, and wagons were also in operation. Dust was everywhere, the noise was deafening, the confusion absolute.

Don Francisco de Paula Rius y Taulet was then in his second term of office as mayor of Barcelona. He was getting on at fifty years of age and wore a permanent frown, his bald head hinting at the sweep of his imagination, and his remarkably bushy side whiskers effectively concealing the lapels of his frock coat. Said by columnists to have a patrician air, he was most careful of the prestige of the city and his management of its affairs.

In the sultry summer days of 1886 he faced a thorny dilemma. A few months previously he had been visited by a gentleman named Eugenio Serrano de Casanova. "I wish to bring a matter of the utmost gravity to the attention of Your Excellency," the visitor said. Originally from Galicia, Don Eugenio Serrano de Casanova had settled in Catalonia, brought as a young man by his fervent espousal of the Carlist cause. The passing years had dampened his fervor for the cause but not his energy: he was an enterprising man with a taste for travel. His journeys had afforded him the opportunity to visit and marvel at the World's Fairs of Antwerp, Paris, and Vienna. Not one to let an idea go to seed, he drew up plans of his own and asked the Barcelona City Council to allow him to do there what he had seen done in those other cities. The council granted him the use of Citadel Park. "If he wants to get mixed up in such harebrained schemes, the best of luck to him," was the attitude of the authorities—an attitude both negligent and perilous.

In point of fact, no one sat down and worked out just what was involved in organizing a World's Fair. These World's Fairs were a recent phenomenon. Although the idea was conceived in France, the first such event was held in London in 1851. The Paris fair followed in 1855. Much was left to be desired in its

33

organization: the doors of the great precinct opened fifteen days after the date originally fixed, and many of the items to be exhibited were still in their crates even then. Among the illustrious personalities who visited it was Queen Victoria herself, then at the peak of her power. *"Pas mal, pas mal,"* muttered the queen as she went along, a hint of wryness in her tone, probably pleased at this display of incompetence on the part of the French. Behind her was a Sepoy, well over six feet tall not counting his turban; he carried a crimson silk cushion upon which lay the Koh-i-noor, then the largest known diamond in the world—as if Queen Victoria wished to imply, "Just one of my belongings is worth more than all here displayed." A mistaken attitude, since the point of the whole thing was for countries to vie with one another in ideas and progress.

Further conventions were held in Antwerp, Vienna, Philadelphia, and Liverpool. London had already organized its second World's Fair in 1862, and Paris in 1867, when Serrano de Casanova launched his scheme in Barcelona. If his enthusiasm was not in short supply, capital was. Barcelona was undergoing a severe financial crisis, and the promoter's pleas went unheeded. The initial funds were soon used up, and the scheme had to be abandoned.

Serrano de Casanova arranged to see Rius y Taulet, the mayor. Softly, as if he were imparting a secret, he said, "I deeply regret to tell you, Your Excellency, that I have decided to give up." Work on the preparation of the park had already begun, and had received wide publicity.

"Confound it and confound it again!" exclaimed Rius y Taulet. He seized a little bell of crystal and gold that was on his desk in his town-hall office and rang it long and loud. When a clerk finally answered his call, the mayor instructed him to summon all the prominent citizens of Barcelona to a meeting without delay: the bishop, the governor, the field marshal, the president of the City Council, the rector of the university, the president of the Athenaeum, etc. The clerk fainted on the spot, and the mayor himself had to bring him around, fanning him with his handkerchief.

Once assembled, these worthies evinced more of a desire to display eloquence than a willingness to act; all were ready to venture an opinion, but none would commit himself or the institution he represented, and would certainly not offer financial backing for Serrano de Casanova's wild undertaking. Finally Rius y Taulet gave an enormous thump on the table with a leather folder. "Jesus Christ, for the love of God!" he roared. This exhortation was heard as far as the Plaza de San Jaime, became public property, and stands today, along with other famous utterances of his, engraved on that indefatigable mayor's monument. The bishop made the sign of the cross.

A mayor is not somebody to be fooled with. In less than an hour he had extracted from all present their promise to back the project. "To pull out now would be a blot on the reputation of Barcelona," he told them. They agreed to form a board of directors. A trust was also set up, to be composed of civil and military authorities, presidents of associations, bankers, and leading figures from the worlds of commerce and industry. A technical committee of architects and engineers was formed. As time went by, such committees proliferated—committees dealing with Spanish firms, committees for potential foreign exhibitors, committees to adjudicate competitions and award prizes—all of which generated confusion and much treading on toes.

The project was unanimously deemed "viable." Whether public opinion accepted the viability of the project was, however, another matter. "Other considerations apart," noted a contemporary newspaper, "the attractions offered by the municipality are neither sufficient nor so numerous as to render agreeable to the visitor a brief sojourn here." Everybody thought that Barcelona would offer a sorry spectacle if it tried to put itself on the same footing as Paris or London. (Nobody gave a thought to what cities like Antwerp or Liverpool had to offer at that time, both cities having organized their respective fairs with much less fanfare.) "In Barcelona, notwithstanding the gentleness of the climate, the excellence of the location, the ancient monuments, and the few (all too few) private enterprises on view, we fall short of other European municipalities of comparable population," said a letter appearing in a newspaper around that time. "Everything touching public administration," the letter went on, "is of an inferior nature. The city's constabulary is generally disgraceful; a great deal is left to be desired with regard to law and order. Numerous services necessary in a city of some 250,000 inhabitants are badly organized when not entirely lacking. The narrowness of the streets in the old quarter, and the lack of large squares there, and in the new districts as well, hinder traffic and preclude recreation. We are without pleasant promenades. We are deficient in libraries, hospitals, poorhouses, prisons, etc."

This letter, occupying a number of pages, also said: "We have gone to great expense over Citadel Park, yet it is of mean dimensions; a vast forest and a lengthy promenade are wanting there, and that paltry lake is an absurdity." The author of this letter must have had in mind the celebrated parks of the time— the Bois de Boulogne and Hyde Park. To these invectives the letter added: "Stunted imagination coupled with swollen vanity all too frequently characterizes our local administration's actions. Of late, Barcelona has become a dirty city. The façades of houses of antiquity are in a repugnant state!"

Such letters were common in local newspapers at the time. An editorial appeared September 22, 1866, bearing this headline: "Commercially Speaking, Is the World's Fair to Be Considered a Blessing or a Curse?"

Even so, opposition to the project was subdued. Generally the citizens seemed willing to face up to the risks entailed in the venture. And they knew from experience that whatever the authorities decided to do would be done; centuries of absolute rule had taught people not to waste their energy over such matters. But the most important thing was that the first World's Fair to be held in Spain would be held in Barcelona, not in Madrid. This had been commented upon in the capital's press; the Madrid journalists were uncomfortable but resigned themselves. "Communications between Barcelona and the rest of the world, by land and sea, render it more suitable than any other city of our peninsula for the purpose of attracting foreign visitors," they wrote. One would think *they* were responsible for the choice of Barcelona as the setting for the event. But would Madrid help pay? The government's attitude was basically: "You got yourselves into this, now you can fork out for it."

At that time the country's economy was as centralized as everything else; the wealth of Catalonia, as that of every other part of the kingdom, went straight to the state coffers in Madrid. Town halls met their expenses through the collection of local taxes, but for any out-of-the-ordinary expenditure they had to turn to the government to obtain a subsidy, a loan, or—as in the present case—a deaf ear. This created a sense of solidarity among the Catalan people.

"They are giving us," observed Rius y Taulet, "a flying boot in the breeches." There was no disagreement on that point. "With Madrid, we end up at loggerheads; without Madrid, we end up nowhere at all," said Manuel Girona, a noted financier who at that time was serving as president of the Athenaeum. He had a reputation for never losing his temper. "Let us leave for another day all outbursts of spleen and concentrate instead on realities," he advised. "We must bargain with Madrid; it will be humiliating, but the cause amply justifies it."

This put an end to the argument and to that particular meeting, which was being held, Wednesday, in the restaurant called Las Siete Puertas. On Sunday, after hearing High Mass, two board delegates set off for the capital. They traveled in a carriage specially designated for the purpose by the City Council itself; this carriage bore on both doors the emblem of the Ciudad Condal—the Count's City, as Barcelona was and still is known. With them they took, in two huge crocodile portfolios, all the papers relating to the project, and, in several trunks lashed onto the back of the carriage, a good supply of clothes, for they anticipated a long absence. And they were not mistaken.

They registered in a hotel as soon as they got to Madrid, and the following morning they reported to the Ministry of Development. Their arrival caused quite a stir: the clothes and capes they were wearing had once belonged to Joan Fivaller, the legendary protector of Barcelona and champion of municipal liberties in the Middle Ages. Over the centuries the wool of those garments had changed into flock, the silk into a kind of cobweb. As the delegates passed by, holding the portfolios before them in both hands like an offering, a layer of fine brown dust was deposited on the ministerial carpets. These two delegates were called, respectively, Guitarrí and Guitarró, names that, had they not been genuine, would have seemed especially invented for the occasion.

Guitarrí and Guitarró were shown to a room with an extraordinarily high coffered ceiling, furnished only with two chairs in the Renaissance style (and quite uncomfortable they were, too) and a painting three meters high by nine meters long from the studios of Zurbarán depicting a scrofulous old hermit surrounded by skulls and tibias. There they were made to wait for more than three hours, after which time a half-concealed side door was opened and in came a fellow with puffed-up features and muttonchop whiskers, wearing a heavily braided dress coat. The two delegates leaped to their feet. Guitarrí whispered into Guitarró's ear, "One glance from him is enough to put the fear of God in one!"—the long wait had taken its toll on his nervous system. They both bowed long and low. The man, who was no minister but an usher, dryly informed them that the Right Honorable Minister was unable to receive them that day but bade them be so kind as to return to the ministry the following day at the same hour.

The confusion over the usher's showy uniform was only the first of a long series of such *faux pas*: the board delegates were moving in unfamiliar circles; they never knew what attitude to adopt in that city of taverns and convents, street vendors, pimps and procuresses, ragged paupers and beggars; in the ministry there existed an even stranger world of pomp and ceremony, saber rattling and sinecures, with scheming generals, crooked dukes, miracle-touting priests, court favorites, *toreros,* dwarfs, and court jesters who made fun of Guitarrí and Guitarró, of their Catalan accents and their peculiar syntax. Three months were spent going back and forth between the hotel and the ministry, after which time they sent back to Barcelona an account of what was happening and a request for further instructions. A package reached them by return post, sent by Rius y Taulet himself, containing money, a plaster cast of Our Lady of Montserrat, and a message saying, "Courage—one party or the other must give way, and, by God in all His glory, it will not be *this* party." The poor delegates rarely ventured out of their hotel. The staff, accustomed by now to their presence and persuaded that little was to be hoped for in the way of tokens of generosity from that quarter, had dispensed with such amenities as changing towels or sheets, or dusting the Spartan, broken-down pieces of furniture. In the interests of economy, the two shared the same room, a great inconvenience, and in making their breakfast and evening meals they used the hot water from the bathtub.

Their greatest trial continued to be not these privations but their morning visits to the ministry. The swarm of loafers and scroungers who hung around its corridors and antechambers had composed a malicious little ditty in their honor, and the delegates heard it hummed or whistled at every turn. More vexatious still were the practical jokes played on them by the ministry minions, such as balancing buckets of water on doors along their path, laying trip wires to make them stumble, or singeing the tails of their coats with candles. Some days Guitarrí and Guitarró would go in and find their seats occupied by other petitioners, earlier birds than themselves, veterans hardened by a lifetime of bureaucratic mistreatment, who pretended not to notice their presence and monopolized the seats throughout the ritual three-hour wait.

The minister still showed no signs of receiving them. Every day—after their wait in that room, whose every detail was by now utterly familiar to them—the half-concealed door would open and the usher with the side whiskers would enter, handing them a tray bearing a hurriedly written note from the minister, in which he informed them that much to his regret he was unable to attend to them that day. The liberal sprinkling, in these notes, of terms from the gutter end of the vernacular sometimes rendered them completely unintelligible, which only increased the delegates' anxiety, straining as they did always to guess the minister's meaning and mood from the slightest scrap of evidence.

From time to time, and after much discussion and vacillation, they would reply to his notes with a note of their own. For that purpose they had printed, at an establishment on Calle Mayor specializing in such things, letterheads, but with the coat of arms of Valencia—an error or sabotage?—instead of the requested coat of arms of Barcelona. But ordering new stationery would have meant a month's delay, so they resigned themselves. They might write: "We are highly sensible of the great demands made upon the time of the Right Honorable Minister, may God save him, yet with all due respect we make so bold as to persist, in view of the great importance of the mission entrusted to us," etc. To which the minister might reply the following day with such expressions as "have a clock up my ass" (meaning he was pressed for time), "knocking the shit out of me" (meaning he was overworked), or "sit on your dicks" (an exhortation to be patient). "The Right Honorable Minister might have more time at his disposal," the delegates eventually rejoined, "were he to spend less of it on witticisms." At night they wrote to their families in Barcelona—long, troubled, homesick letters. Sometimes the ink would be smeared, where the writer was unable to hold back a tear.

Meanwhile, in Barcelona, the World's Fair board of directors, presided over by Rius y Taulet, had not been idle. "As for Madrid, we'll present them with *faits accomplis*," was their motto. Plans for the buildings, monuments, equipment, and outbuildings that were to make up the precinct for the fair were commissioned, presented, and approved, and work began at a pace that could not be sustained long with the funds available. When the entire Citadel Park was turned upside down, the City Council invited journalists to come visit it. As a further inducement, the journalists were regaled with a banquet whose menu testifies to the cosmopolitanism of the hosts: *Potage: Bisque d'écrevisses à l'américaine. Relevés: Loup à la génevoise. Entrées: Poulardes de Mans à la Toulouse, tronches de filet à la Godard. Légumes: Petits pois au beurre. Rôtis: Perdreaux jeunes sur crustades, galantines de dindes truffées. Entremets: Bisquits Martin decorés. Ananas et gâteaux. Desserts assortis. Vins: Porto, Château Iquem, Bordeaux, et Champagne (Ch. Mumm).*

The speeches that brought the banquet to a close confirmed the official opening date (spring 1887); appreciative reviews of the event appeared in many publications. Posters were also printed and displayed in railroad stations throughout Europe; corporations and firms both home and abroad were sent invitations to participate; and, as was the practice at the time, several literary competitions were held. The response from future participants was lukewarm, but it was a response nonetheless.

At the end of 1886 the first officially accepted bids were reported in the press: "Lavatory facilities are to be supplied, subject to the conditions already stated, by Señor Fraxedas y Florit. This farsighted purveyor intends to install in the said facilities a complete grooming service, with rooms furbished with toiletries, towels, and cosmetic items. A room will be set aside for the care of footwear, and a suitable number of errand boys will be made available to members of the public and exhibitors alike for the purposes of dispatching messages and conveying articles purchased in the fair to the customer's abode. May we congratulate Señor Fraxedas y Florit on his acumen in not remaining indifferent to this commercial opportunity, which otherwise would have fallen into the hands of foreigners."

The minister of development eventually gave in. A corpulent, fierce man, barely human in appearance, he was called "*el africano*" behind his back. He had never set foot in Africa, nor had he the remotest connection with that continent; it was his bearing and general disposition that earned him the epithet. Far from taking offense on learning of his nickname, he started wearing a ring in his nose. His reception of the two board delegates was hostile, yet, unbeknown to them, time had been working in their favor and the minister had no cards left to play. The countless hours spent waiting, the anguish, and the humiliation had given Guitarrí and Guitarró the advantage: after so many hours in each other's company day and night, they had become like two peas in a pod, and were the very image of the saintly hermit in the painting from the studios of Zurbarán that they had been contemplating, day in and day out, for months on end. In their presence the minister felt overcome by a sudden fatigue, all the weight of the vast power invested in him pressed down upon his shoulders. The confrontation, when it came, was no titanic clash but a listless exchange shot through with weariness and melancholy.

4

The area in Citadel Park had been fenced off to protect the site from the curious. This perimeter, however, had been breached at numerous points; its effectiveness was further diminished by the continual traffic moving through its gateways as people came and went unchallenged. Onofre Bouvila stuffed five pamphlets down his shirtfront, hid the rest between two granite slabs by the wall flanking the railroad tracks, and slipped unnoticed into the precinct. It was only then, as he beheld that pandemonium for the first time, that the magnitude of his task dawned upon him. Apart from helping his mother around the farm, he had never had a regular job and therefore had no idea how difficult it was to deal directly with one's fellow human beings. "I've gone straight from feeding chickens," he thought, "to spreading the revolution. But so what? If you can do one, you ought to be able to do the other." Cheered by that reflection, he made his way over to a group of carpenters who were busy nailing planks onto the framework of a pavilion. To attract their attention, he went through his repertoire of greetings: "Hello! How's it going there? Good morning!" and so on.

Finally one of the carpenters noticed him out of the corner of his eye; a raised eyebrow served to ask him what he wanted.

"I have some interesting pamphlets here!" Onofre shouted, taking one out and showing it to the carpenter.

"What's that you said?" the carpenter shouted back. The hammering either prevented him from hearing anything just then or else it had deafened him for good. Onofre was about to repeat himself, but was not given a chance: a wagon drawn by three mules forced him to leap back out of the way. The muleteer cracked his whip in the air as he leaned back, digging in his heels and pulling at the reins. "Make way, make way!" he called out. Rubble was piled on the wagon, sending up clouds of white dust as the wheels bumped their way over stones and ruts, giving off deep metallic sounds, like some mighty door knocker. "Giddyap there, mule, get on out of that!" the driver was shouting. Onofre thought it best to move off. For a moment or two he toyed with the idea of dumping the whole pack of pamphlets on some rubbish heap and telling Pablo he'd distributed them all, but he soon thought better of it: the anarchists might be keeping watch on him, for the first few days at least.

"What's that you have there, boy?" a bricklayer asked him.

The bricklayer was one of a small group of workers sneaking a break. They had a lookout man; if he saw the foreman coming, he would whistle, and they would hurriedly go back to their places.

"It's for you, about joining the revolution," Onofre answered, handing him a pamphlet. The bricklayer crumpled it into a ball and tossed it onto a pile of rubble. "Around here nobody knows how to read," he told Onofre. "Besides, what's all this about revolution? That's serious business. You'd better beat it before the foreman comes along and sees you."

Put on his guard by the bricklayer, Onofre spent a while going carefully over the site, from one end to the other. He soon learned to spot the foremen, and found that they were more interested in having their orders carried out than in the ideological aberrations among their subordinates. "Even so, I'd better be careful," he said to himself.

Coming and going around the grounds, in addition to the foremen, were men wearing dust coats, caps, and goggles. They inspected the progress of the work, measured with rules and theodolites, consulted plans, and gave instructions to the foremen, who listened attentively, as if understanding the whole thing perfectly. "Don't you go worrying yourself, sir, we'll do it just like you say," was the message they conveyed with their nodding and bowing—"down to the last detail." These important individuals were the architects, their assistants, and their associates.

Yet, for all this show of coordination, each group of workers seemed to go its own way, heedless of the others. One group would erect a scaffolding that another would pull down; one would dig a trench that another would fill in; one would lay brick, and another would tear down the wall just built. All this was punctuated by orders and counterorders, shouts, whistles, neighing, braying, boilers whining, metal screeching, boulders clattering, planks rending, tools clashing, as if all the lunatics in the land had assembled there to give vent to their madness.

Work on the fair had acquired a momentum that nothing

could stop. The technical know-how was not lacking: Barcelona at that period could boast some fifty architects and 146 master builders, with several hundred furnaces, foundries, sawmills, and metallurgical factories at their disposal. Labor was also in plentiful supply, given the growing unemployment as the recession dragged on. The only thing that was not available in abundance was the money to pay all those people and the suppliers of raw materials. And Madrid, according to a phrase coined by a satirical periodical of the time, "kept the purse strings between clenched jaws." "We'll sidestep the problem," said Rius y Taulet with a shrug, "by not paying." Applying that principle, the City Council contracted huge debts. "Only two things make me feel like a real mayor," he used to say, "spending money right and left, and playing the wild rover." His successors in the position adopted that motto, too.

But all this was still way above Onofre Bouvila. As he wandered around the grounds, trying to familiarize himself with their layout, he got an unpleasant surprise: the sudden appearance of the much-feared Civil Guard. But the Civil Guard, he decided, had their hands full with brawls, mutinies, and other disturbances of the peace, and a little caution on his part would allow him to go unnoticed. Comforted by these reflections, he went back on the offensive, but at the end of the day still had not succeeded in placing a single pamphlet. Worn out, dusty, and having eaten nothing since breakfast, he made his way back to the boardinghouse.

"How can it be that such a simple thing as giving away a piece of paper to somebody is beyond me?" he wondered as he walked along. "But I'm not giving up," he told himself, "even though it's plain that things are more complicated than they seemed at first. Before getting down to any job, it's a good idea to get the lay of the land. Yes, I still have a lot to learn, but I must learn quickly, because although I'm still young, I have to make a start now if I want to be rich."

Being rich was the goal he had set himself in life. After his father emigrated to Cuba, he and his mother struggled on, suffering great deprivations; they often went hungry, and every winter brought the renewed torture of the cold. Ever since he could think for himself, Onofre had lived on the hope that one day his father would come back laden with money. "Then everything will be all right," he would tell himself, "and the good times will never end." Although his mother did nothing by word or deed to encourage that fantasy, she did not discourage it, either—she simply never brought up the subject—and he had gone on dreaming to his heart's content. He never wondered why his father didn't send back a little money once in a while if he was indeed rich, or why he allowed his wife and child to subsist in the direst of straits while he lived in luxury. When Onofre, in his innocence, told others of his fantasy, he was hurt by their reaction, so now he, like his mother, avoided the subject.

Thus they lived year after year, until the day Uncle Tonet came with the news that Joan Bouvila was on his way back from Cuba—and rich, too. Nobody knew how that news had reached the driver's ears. Many cast doubt on the truth of it, but they were forced to eat their words a few days later, when he arrived with Joan Bouvila in person seated in his trap. Ten years before, Uncle Tonet had taken Joan down to Bassora, to the railroad station, from where Joan had left for Barcelona and the ship that was to take him far away. Now Uncle Tonet was bringing him back. People from all around gathered in front of the church to watch; they searched the hill and the rough road that came down through the holly oaks. An altar boy was poised to set the church bells pealing at a sign from the rector.

Onofre was the only one who failed to recognize his father when the trap rounded the bend in the road. The others saw that it was Joan right away, despite the physical changes wrought by those ten years of climatic extremes and varying fortunes. He was wearing a white linen jacket almost dazzling under the autumn sun and a broad-rimmed Panama hat. On his knees he had a square package wrapped in a checkered handkerchief. "You must be Onofre," was the first thing he said as he jumped down from the trap. "Yes, sir," Onofre answered. Joan Bouvila fell to his knees and kissed the dust. He would not get up until the rector had given him his blessing. He looked at his son, his eyes glazed with emotion. "You've grown," he said. "And who do they say you take after?" "After you, Father," Onofre unhesitatingly replied, conscious of the curiosity focused on them from all sides, and of the conjectures that would be going through the heads of all present. Joan Bouvila took the square package out of the trap. "Look what I've brought you," he said, removing the checkered handkerchief. It was a wire cage containing a monkey a little larger than a rabbit, thin, and with a very long tail. The monkey, apparently annoyed, bared its teeth with a ferocity not at all in keeping with its small size. Joan opened the cage door and put his hand inside; the monkey latched on to his fingers; then he drew out his hand and brought the animal close to Onofre's face. "Take it, don't be afraid," his father said to him. "He won't hurt you—he's yours." Onofre took it, but the monkey scrambled up his arm onto his shoulders and lashed his face with its tail.

"I've arranged for some prayers to be said to thank Our Lord for your safe return," the rector said. Joan Bouvila gave a little bow, then let his gaze wander over the façade of the church. It was a rudimentary stone building with only one nave, rectangular, and a square belfry. "This church needs a thorough restoration," he remarked. From then on everybody called him "the americano" and expected him to bring about great changes in the valley. He took off his hat and offered his wife his arm; they went into the church together. Candles shone before the altar. Nobody had ever seen such ceremony there before.

Onofre recalled those wonderful moments as he walked back tired and hungry to the boardinghouse. Whenever a carriage passed, he tried to catch a glimpse of whoever was inside, in case it was some personage, to fuel his daydreaming. Such carriages became

infrequent, however, as he drew closer to the dreary neighborhood of his boardinghouse.

Not discouraged, Onofre was back on the fairgrounds the
following day at the crack of dawn. This time, he left the pamphlets behind and simply reconnoitered, having resolved to get to
know every inch of what was to be his field of operations. He
soon learned that not all the workers there were of the same
rank.

Between craftsmen and laborers there was a world of difference. The craftsmen, skilled, were organized in hierarchies and
according to the customs of the ancient guilds; they enjoyed the
respect of their employers and spoke to the foremen almost as
equals. Their pride was not unlike that of the artist; they knew
they were indispensable and did not take readily to the principles
of trade unionism, being well paid.

The laborers or journeymen, on the other hand, were entirely unskilled. They had come to the city out of desperation,
driven from their lands by drought, the ravages of war, or plague,
or simply because local resources were insufficient for their up-
keep. They brought in tow their families, and sometimes distant
or disabled relatives they could not leave behind, assuming responsibility for the latter with the heroic loyalty of the poor. They
lived in huts of tin, wood, and cardboard along the beach between the World's Fair landing stage and the gasworks. Women
and children swarmed by the hundreds in that encampment, which
had sprung up in the shadow of girders that already outlined the
future pavilions. Some of these women were married to the laborers; others were only tagging along with them; others still
were their mothers, unmarried sisters, mothers- or sisters-in-law.
Most were in an advanced state of pregnancy. They spent all day
hanging out damp clothes in the warm sea breeze, on lines tied
between canes stuck in the sand. They would also cook over
braziers set up in the doorways of their huts, energetically fanning the embers with straw fans, or do their darning and mend-

ing. Keeping an eye, all the while, on their children, who were so dirty, it was difficult to see their faces. The children had swollen bellies, went around naked, and were forever throwing stones at people. If they came too close to the women at their cooking, they were likely to get a slap or a wallop with a frying pan. That would keep them at bay for a while, but they would soon be back, drawn by the smell of the cooking. Squabbles, yelling, and insults were common among these women, and they frequently came to blows. The Civil Guard would keep watch from a prudent distance, intervening only if knives were brought into play.

Onofre Bouvila spent his days learning all these things for himself. Turning his inoffensive air to good use, and not being tied to any fixed schedule or location, he wandered here, there, and everywhere, so that people would get accustomed to seeing him. He never made a nuisance of himself with people at their jobs; when they were taking a break, he would ask them about their trade. If there was some way he could help out, he would do so. Eventually he was tolerated by all and, by a few, welcomed.

After the first week, despite not having distributed a single pamphlet, he found on his pillow the money that Delfina had promised him. He was pleased at the honesty and understanding of his employers. "I won't let them down," he thought. "Not because I have any interest in this revolution I'm helping to spread, but to show them I can do this as well as the next man. Soon I'll be able to give out these damned pamphlets. My persistence and caution are beginning to pay off: I've overcome the distrust they all showed at first. But, then, nobody watches me now: they're all wrapped up in this crazy World's Fair business."

Indeed, in 1886, with two years still left before the official opening, a newspaper pointed out that "many persons from foreign parts, arriving in Barcelona, will form some opinion of her beauty and of her progress in matters technical," for which reason "public adornments and personal comfort and safety are under the present circumstances the subjects most pressingly requiring the attention of our authorities." Hardly a day passed without editorial suggestions. "Dig sewers in the new part of the city," proposed one newspaper; "Remove those shacks so offensive to the eye in the Plaza de Cataluña," proposed another; "Provide stone benches along Paseo de Colón, and improve outlying districts such as Poble Sech, through which the interested traveler in Barcelona must pass to ascend Montjuich, tempted to those lofty heights by the delectable springs that grace the summit," etc. Some expressed concern about the cupidity of the owners of inns, restaurants, hostelries, cafés, boardinghouses, and so on, who were reminded that "the desire for excessive gain is most often counterproductive, being harmful to one's best interests, as it offends the traveler." Of most concern to the press was not the impression the city itself might make but the impression likely to be made by its inhabitants, in whose honesty, competence, and good manners the press clearly had little faith.

"I need more pamphlets, Pablo," said Onofre.

The apostle grumbled. "It took you over three weeks to distribute the first bunch," he told him. "You must try harder." It was five in the morning; the sun had come up over the horizon and was finding its way into the den between the slats of the shutters. The sharp light of that summer morning made the room look smaller, dustier, and more ramshackle than before.

"It wasn't easy at first, but you'll see how it will go better from now on," said Onofre.

And indeed, he got through the second parcel in only six days. Pablo said to him, "Look, boy, I'm sorry about what I said the other time. I know getting started isn't easy, and sometimes my impatience gets the better of me. It's the heat, this heat, and being shut up in here—it'll be the death of me." The heat was making itself felt on the World's Fair grounds, too. Tempers would fray over nothing, and bouts of summer diarrhea soon appeared—and much feared they were, for they killed off children by the dozen.

"There'll be worse to come," said the quieter types, "when the job is done and we're all left without work."

Those more sanguine thought Barcelona would become a great city after the World's Fair inauguration; that there would be work for all; that public services would improve by leaps and bounds, and everyone would receive the assistance he needed. Many scoffed openly, hearing that. Onofre would then seize on this opportunity and start talking about Bakunin, and he always ended up giving out a few pamphlets. Meanwhile, he couldn't help thinking to himself, "Look at me, an anarchist, and a few weeks ago I never heard of all this nonsense. Now I sound like a lifelong supporter. It would be laughable if I wasn't risking my neck for it. Anyway," he always wound up, "I'll do the best I can. It's no more dangerous, surely, to do it well than to do it badly, and if I do it well, they'll all come to trust me." The idea of getting people to trust him without his having to reciprocate that trust struck him as extremely clever.

<h2 style="text-align:center">5</h2>

"So, young man, you are working at the site of the World's Fair, are you? Very good, very good indeed," Señor Braulio said to Onofre when he handed over his weekly payment. "I am of the persuasion—as I have told my good wife, who will bear me out—that this fair, unless God wills it otherwise, will elevate Barcelona to its rightful position."

"I agree entirely, Señor Braulio," Onofre replied.

Besides Señor Braulio, his wife Señora Agata, Delfina, and Beelzebub, Onofre had been getting to know the other characters in the little world of the boardinghouse. There would be eight, nine, or ten guests there, depending on the day. Only four of these were resident guests: Onofre, a retired priest called Father

Bizancio, a lady fortune-teller named Micaela Castro, and the barber who worked in the reception area, to whom everybody referred simply as Mariano. An obese, ruddy man with a malicious twist to his nature, though outwardly very congenial, he was also a great talker; it was perhaps for this reason that he was the first guest Onofre got to know.

The barber told him he had learned his trade while in military service, had subsequently been taken on in several barber shops around the city, but then, wanting to improve his lot—with an eye to marrying a manicurist—had set up shop on his own. The marriage never materialized. "When the day of our nuptials was getting close, she suddenly took to crying," Mariano explained. When he asked her what was wrong, she replied that she had been involved for quite some time with another gentleman, who had given her lots of presents and promised her a little apartment of her own. She hadn't had the heart to spurn this gentleman, but now couldn't very well get married without confessing all. Mariano was taken aback. "How long has this been going on?" was all he found to say. Was it a matter of days or months or years? But she failed to clear up that important point; upset, all she could say was, "I'm in such a state, such a state." The barber tried to get back the engagement ring he had given her, but she refused to return it, and the lawyer he went to advised him not to take the matter to court: "You'll lose if you do." By now, it was water under the bridge, and he was glad things had turned out the way they did. "Women just mean expenses and more expenses," he declared.

On the subject of his professional life, however, he always spoke enthusiastically. "One day I was in one of the barber shops down in the Raval, in the old part of town," he told Onofre, "when I heard a great commotion in the street. So out I went, saying to myself, 'What is all this about?' And I saw a whole battalion of horses lined up at the shop door. Suddenly this aide-de-camp gets off his horse and comes into the shop. I can still hear the clatter of his boots and the jangling of his spurs on the tiles. Well, he looks at me and says, 'Is the owner around?' And I say, 'He's just this minute gone out, sir.' And then he says to me, 'Is there nobody here who can cut a man's hair?' And I say, 'At your service, sir, pray be seated.' 'It is not for me,' says he, 'it is for my general, General Costa y Gassol.' Can you imagine it? No, of course you can't, you're only a kid, you weren't born then. Well, Costa y Gassol was a Carlist general, and renowned for his courage and ferocity. He took Tortosa with only a handful of men and put half the folks there to the sword, just like that. Then Espartero had him shot. He was a great man, too, Espartero; they were a match for each other, them two, if you want my opinion, and nothing to do with politics. Now, where was I? Oh, I know. So who do I see walking in the door but Costa y Gassol in person, covered with medals from head to toe. He sits himself down, looks at me, and says, 'Haircut and a shave.' And I, shitting hot bricks, say, 'At Your Lordship's command, General.' Well, to make a long story short, I do as he says, and when I've finished he asks me, 'What do I owe you?' And I say, 'For Your Lordship, no charge, General.' And with that he leaves."

Like all barbers of his time, Mariano also pulled teeth, applied ointments, mustard plasters, and poultices, and arranged abortions. A hypochondriac, he had bladder and liver problems, and avoided Micaela Castro like the plague, for she had foretold an imminent and painful death for him.

The seer was an elderly woman with one eye always half closed. She was withdrawn, speaking out only to predict woeful events. She had an unshakable faith in her own prophetic powers; calamities that failed to materialize did not dissuade her from announcing further calamities. "An all-consuming fire will sweep Barcelona, and none shall emerge unscathed from that pyre," she would say as she entered the area that served as a dining room. Nobody took any notice of her, although nearly all the guests secretly knocked wood or crossed their fingers. Nobody knew

53

how she dreamed up so many horrors—floods, epidemics, wars, famine—or why she did so. By a special concession from Señor Braulio, who was fond of her, she received her clients in her room, people of all ages and both sexes, of humble condition. They emerged from these consultations thoroughly shaken and very long in the face. Soon after, however, they would be back for another dose of doom and despair. Her ominous revelations lent a certain grandeur to their monotonous existence; perhaps that was why they came. Perhaps, too, because the prospect of imminent tragedy made the wretchedness of their daily lives seem more bearable. In any event, nothing that she prophesied ever came to pass, though other things equally unpleasant did.

Father Bizancio used to exorcise her from the other end of the dining room, his eyes fixed on the tablecloth in front of him, muttering under his breath. They never sat together. Since they both lived in the world of the spirit, there was mutual respect between them, even though they were in enemy camps. For Father Bizancio, Micaela was an opponent worthy of his ministry: Satan incarnate. For her, Father Bizancio was a constant moral prop, for he actually believed in her powers, even if he did attribute them to the devil.

Father Bizancio, who was by then very old and worn out, did not want to die without having gone to Rome to prostrate himself, as he put it, at Saint Peter's feet. He was also eager to see with his own eyes the legendary Santiago censer, which he erroneously believed to be in the Vatican. Micaela Castro said that he would indeed soon undertake that pilgrimage to Rome, but that he would die on the way without seeing the Holy City. Neighboring parishes (La Presentación, San Ezequiel, Nuestra Señora del Recuerdo, etc.) would turn to Father Bizancio whenever any solemn service required supernumerary personnel or reinforcements in the choir or in the monastery; he was also called upon to perform in plainsong, and as precentor, versicle singer, Evangelist reader, and even as a singing and dancing *seise* in the

Seville tradition, things almost passed into oblivion today, but with which Father Bizancio was well acquainted though by no stretch of the imagination adept. From such duties he earned a little money, enough to keep the wolf from the door.

The priest, the barber, the pythoness, and Onofre Bouvila himself occupied the third-floor rooms. Though neither more spacious nor better in any way than the others, these rooms did possess the advantage of having balconies onto the street, which view made them look cheerful despite the cracks in the ceiling, the bumps on the floor, the great damp patches on the walls, and the dilapidated furniture. Snow-white turtledoves, who must have lost their way or escaped from somewhere, made their nests nearby and would alight on the wrought-iron railings of these balconies. Since Father Bizancio often gave them pieces of unleavened bread broken from unconsecrated hosts, they showed up there every day.

Nonresident guests were put in the second-floor rooms, with neither balcony nor window onto the street. Señor Braulio, Señora Agata, and Delfina slept on the fourth floor, under the roof. Señora Agata suffered from a mixture of arthritis and gout, which left her glued to her chair, never wholly awake and never wholly asleep. She would perk up only when there were sweets and cakes to be had, but, since her doctor had strictly forbidden her such things, her husband and daughter seldom allowed her to indulge her sweet tooth, only on special occasions. Although she was constantly in pain, she never complained—not so much out of mental fortitude as from physical decrepitude. Sometimes her eyes would moisten and tears would slip down her smooth, chubby cheeks, but her face remained expressionless. This family misfortune seemed not to trouble Señor Braulio. He was always in a good mood, always ready to engage in polemics over anything at all, and liked to tell and hear jokes. However bad the jokes were, he would show his appreciation by long, restrained laughter. An hour later, he would still be chuckling away. He was always clean and well groomed. Mariano would shave him in the mornings and, on certain occasions, again in the afternoon. Except at meals, for which he was always impeccably dressed, he went around the boardinghouse in his drawers, in order not to wrinkle the trousers his daughter grudgingly ironed for him every day. He was on good terms with the barber, got along well with the priest, and treated the fortune-teller deferentially—though he rarely sat at her table, since whenever a trance came upon her, she would lose control of her movements, thereby endangering his impeccable attire.

Smartness apart, his most noteworthy feature was being uncommonly accident-prone: one day he would appear with a black eye; another day it would be a nasty-looking gash on his chin; another, a bruise on the cheek; another, a dislocated hand. He was never free of bandages, plasters, or dressings. In a person so particular about his appearance, this was odd, to say the least. "Either he's the clumsiest man I've ever known, or there's something funny going on here," Onofre thought. But it was Delfina who was by far the most enigmatic member of the family, and the one who most troubled Onofre, for he felt attracted to her—an inexplicable attraction, but one that grew obsessive.

Onofre was so successful in distributing the pamphlets that he was frequently obliged to go back to Calle del Musgo for more. He always saw Pablo there; as these meetings became more frequent, friendship arose between the seasoned apostle and the eager neophyte. The former constantly complained about the tenacity of the police, who had been hounding him nonstop for several years. It was this that had forced him to adopt his life of isolation; he was a man of action, and inactivity was the worst of all possible tortures for him—or so he thought at the time. At his wits' end, he envied Onofre his daily contact with the laboring masses, but believed that Onofre did not make full use of the priceless gift and yelled at him for any reason, real or imaginary.

Onofre, who was gradually getting to know him, let him have his say; Pablo, he knew, was really a creature to be pitied, was mere cannon fodder. He took offense easily, contradicted for the sake of contradicting, and would never admit that he was wrong—three unequivocal signs of a weak character.

Yet Pablo came to a worse end than he deserved. In 1896, when he had been a prisoner for several years in the dungeons of Montjuich, his jailers set to work on him over the Corpus Christi bombing. One morning they took him out of his cell, blindfolded and bound with leather thongs that cut him to the bone. They had no trouble carrying him between them: his ill-treatment had reduced him to a shadow of himself; he weighed barely thirty kilos. When they removed his blindfold, he found himself at the edge of a cliff; waves were breaking against the rocks below. A gust of wind would have sufficed to make him lose his balance and finish him. He was tempted to let himself fall and so put an end to his torment, but he didn't. "It won't be of my own accord," he thought, gritting his teeth. A lean lieutenant with the blue face of a cadaver brought the point of his saber to rest on Pablo's chest. "You are going to sign a confession," he said, "or I will kill you here and now. If you sign, you will be released eventually." He showed him a transcript of a statement supposedly made by him in which he claimed to be one of those responsible for the Corpus Christi tragedy, that his name was Giacomo Pimentelli, that he was Italian. It was totally absurd: being several years in prison, Pablo could hardly have taken part in a deed which occurred only a few days ago and out in the streets. Nor was he even remotely Italian, though thus far nobody had managed to get out of him his real name or where he came from: under interrogation he insisted that his name was Pablo, only Pablo, and that he was a citizen of the world and a brother to exploited humanity everywhere. Having failed to extract the confession from him, they took him back to his cell and hung him by his wrists from the door. He was left like that for eight hours. From time to time a jailer would come up to him, spit in his face, and savagely wring his genitals. They took him through mock executions almost every day: sometimes tying a rope around his neck, sometimes making him put his head on a block and pretending they were about to behead him, sometimes making him face a firing squad. His resolve finally crumbled and he signed the statement, confessing a guilt that was in a sense genuine, since by that time he hated all human beings and would have killed had he been given the chance. Then they shot him, this time for real, down in the castle moat, like so many others, by express order from Madrid.

The man who issued that brutal order was Don Antonio Cánovas del Castillo, then prime minister. A few months later, when Cánovas del Castillo was taking the waters at the spa town of Santa Agueda, he remarked to his wife that he had bumped into an odd character, a guest like themselves in that therapeutic establishment, and that the fellow had greeted him with great deference. "I wonder who he is," said the prime minister. A cloud of foreboding darkened his gaze, but he kept his suspicions to himself, not wishing to alarm his wife.

Cánovas dressed in black; collected paintings, porcelain, walking sticks, and ancient coins; was sparing with words; detested ostentation, such as the wearing of gold and jewelry. Concerned about the problems facing the country at home and abroad, he had taken steps to have anarchism repressed with an iron hand. "We have quite enough on our plate without letting that pack of rabid dogs add to our troubles," he figured. A tough line seemed to him to be the only way to deliver his country from the chaos he saw gathering on the horizon.

The man who troubled him that summer of 1897 was an Italian—the genuine article this time, by the name of Angiollilo—who had entered himself in the spa hotel register as a correspondent for *Il Popolo*. He was young, had ash-gray hair, a somewhat decadent air, and very polished manners. One day, as

Cánovas was reading his newspaper on a wicker chair in the shade of a tree in the spa's garden, Angiollilo approached him. "Die, Cánovas," he said. "Die, butcher, bloodthirsty, preposterous man." He took a revolver out of his pocket and shot Cánovas three times at point-blank range, killing him instantly. Cánovas's wife, beside herself, hit the assassin with a fan made of lace and mother-of-pearl that she kept hanging from her wrist. "Murderer!" she screamed at him. "Murderer!" Angiollilo replied that he was not a murderer but, rather, the avenger of his anarchist comrades. "With you, madam, I have no quarrel," he added. Men rarely explain their actions, and when they do, they generally botch the job.

So great were the quantities of materials used every day in work on the fair, reports a newspaper of the time, that "the brickyards are well-nigh depleted, likewise the cement that was brought in such vast amounts from various locations within the principality and without. In the building of the Great Palace of Industry alone, eight hundred quintals of this substance are used up with each day that passes. In like fashion, the great iron foundries of La Marítima and Girona & Co. are hard at the task of meeting their contracts for girders and summers, as indeed are numerous carpenters' shops, where work of noteworthy magnitude is under way." The site comprised 380,000 square meters. Though unfinished, the first buildings were already standing. Those that had survived from the Citadel were refurbished. What was left of the great walls was knocked down, and new barracks were being built on Calle de Sicilia for the use of the military presence still there. None of which meant that work was nearing completion. In fact, the date originally fixed for the inauguration had already come and gone. Another date was fixed, "a deadline positively not susceptible of postponement," for April 8, 1888. Even so, there was a second attempt at postponement, but it was unsuccessful: Paris was making preparations for a fair for the year

1889, and running concurrently with Paris would have been suicidal.

In the Barcelona press the initial enthusiasm had cooled off. "We wonder whether so much money and such great effort might not have been more fittingly employed in more useful ways, to address more pressing concerns, instead of being squandered on public works of conspicuous but short-lived effect and of doubtful value," argued some. Others adopted a still tougher line: "For any person conversant with such matters, it is plain that the Barcelona World's Fair, as conceived by those who presume to organize it, will either fail to take place at all, or go forward in such a fashion as to heap ridicule upon Barcelona in particular and Catalonia in general, and be the ruination of the municipality." And so on.

With affairs in this state, Rius y Taulet visited the site, accompanied by numerous dignitaries. They all did their best: they hopped from plank to plank, jumped over ditches, and wriggled between cables. The mules snapped at the tails of their morning coats.

Onofre Bouvila was making progress, too. Having explained so often the pamphlets to others, he ended up understanding them himself. He could see how right the revolutionaries were in their demands. That a spark was all that was needed to start the prairie fire. He spoke well, alternating logic with demagoguery. Some of his listeners, persuaded, helped him to spread the idea. The storms that came in early September and converted the park into a mudbath, an outbreak of typhoid fever, and delays in the wages due to the slowness with which Madrid doled out the meager subsidy it had finally granted the World's Fair—all helped the message travel. Onofre was surprised at his success. "After all," he thought, "I'm only thirteen." Pablo even honored him with one of his rare smiles. "In the early days of Christianity," he said, "children brought about more conversions than adults. Saint Agnes was the same age as you, thirteen years old, when she was put to the sword; Saint Vito was a martyr at the age of twelve. Still more surprising," he added, "is the case of Saint Quirze, Saint Julita's son: when he was only three years old, his eloquence dumbfounded the prefect Alexander, who rewarded the babe by hurling him against the proscenium steps with such force that his brains were dashed out, splattering the floor and the tribunal table."

"Where do you get all this from?" asked Onofre.

"I read it. What do you expect me to do, shut up here in this cage, except read? I spend the hours and the days reading and thinking. Sometimes my thoughts build up to such a pitch that I frighten myself. Other times, an irrational fear takes hold of me. Or I'll start crying for no reason at all, and that can go on for hours." But Onofre was not listening to him, for he, too, was deeply troubled in his mind.

CHAPTER TWO

1

"No, it can't be what they call love, and yet what is it, what's going on with me?" he wondered. All through the summer of 1887, and most of the autumn, too, his obsession with Delfina grew. They had not said a word to each other since that night when she came to his room with her cat. An occasional glance of recognition or a gesture, when their paths crossed in the board-inghouse, passed between them, that was all. Every Friday he found his money waiting on the bed, a sum that was beginning to strike him as small when measured against his efforts, his successes, his deserts. All he knew of her was that nocturnal con-versation by candlelight; now he sifted those words over and over, trying to wrest new meanings from them. His imagination ran wild, building mountains from the molehills of what he remem-bered. Unaware that this was his sexual awakening, he tried to grasp everything through reason, believing he could solve any problem with careful thought.

But eventually he realized that he was getting nowhere. "What shall I do?" he wondered. She had told him she had a boyfriend, and that for him was like an open wound. Onofre's only thought was to eliminate him, but in order to accomplish that he needed to find out certain things: who he was, where and when they saw each other, what they did when they were together, etc. Given the tight schedule of the boardinghouse and the fact that her parents were ignorant of her antics, he inferred that the meetings occurred at night.

This was exceptional in those days. Until well into the twentieth century, most activity in Barcelona came to a halt at sunset; any activity that did not could safely be assumed to be improper. In the popular imagination, the night was peopled with ghosts and filled with hazards. Some believed that the night was a living being, that it had a strange alluring power over people, and that he who set off aimlessly into the dark would never return. Night was equated with death, and dawn with resurrection. Electricity, which was to put an end to the gloom of cities once and for all, was still in its infancy and viewed with serious reservations. "Artificial light should neither dazzle nor flicker, it should be abundant, but not so abundant as to scorch the eye," said a magazine in 1886. "Bright lights should never be used without ground-glass shields on account of the concentration of light in the filament." Another Barcelona newspaper of the same year, however, states that "Electric light is preferable, according to the eminent oculist Professor Chon de Breslau, to any other form of illumination, provided it is steady and abundant."

None of this was of any concern to Onofre as yet. He imagined Delfina swallowed up in the depths of the darkest night, a transfigured being, fearsome yet attractive, seeking out her lover. Her tight-lipped manner, her lizardlike complexion, her sulphurous pupils, her mop of coarse, dirty hair like a chimney sweep's brush, and her ragged, outlandish dress that made her look like a comical scarecrow, were all transformed by the night's spell into attributes of a bewitching presence.

In his resolve to catch the clandestine lovers at their game Onofre decided to stay up every night. From that day on, when the last waking sounds in the boardinghouse died down and the last oil lamp was extinguished, he would steal from his room and take up his post on the staircase landing. "If she comes out of her room, she will have to come this way," he reasoned. "She'll pass here without seeing me, so I'll be able to spy on her and find out where she's going and why." His nightly vigils became habitual and interminable. The clock towers of La Presentación, San Ezequiel, and Nuestra Señora del Recuerdo marked the exasperatingly sluggish passing of the hours. Nothing disturbed the quiet of the boardinghouse in its repose. At around two in the morning, Father Bizancio would emerge from his room to go to the lavatory. He would come back shortly, and very soon could be heard snoring again. At three, Micaela Castro would begin talking to herself, or to the spirits, which psalmody went on till dawn. At four and again at half past five, the priest made another visit to the lavatory. The barber slept on in silence.

From his hiding place Onofre took note of everything. His boredom made the most banal detail seem important. What worried him particularly was the cat, the perfidious Beelzebub; the very thought of its prowling around the house after mice, or that Delfina might take it with her on her night excursions, chilled him to the bone. As the night wore on, he would dream up ways of getting rid of the cat without arousing suspicion. The dawn would find him lost in these meditations, stiff, tired, and in an ugly mood. He would go back to his room before the others woke up, take his bundle of pamphlets, and set off for the World's Fair. "I'll go back to the same spot tonight," he would tell himself, "and every night this year, if need be." Later his fatigue would get the better of him, and his eyes would close and his head sag in spite of himself as he kept watch.

He awoke with a start, hearing a rustle of cloth against cloth. Holding his breath, he made out the sound of careful steps coming down the stairs. "At last," he thought. As he squatted at the edge of the stairs, he felt a body go by, inches from his face. There was a powerful waft of perfume. It was incredible that Delfina would resort to such coquetry, fixing herself up like that to run off to some man. "She's doing it for his sake," he said to himself. "So this is love." He waited a moment or two, then began creeping down; the steps of the quarry and the hunter were almost soundless on the artificial marble stairway. "If she stops for any reason, I'll stumble straight into her," he thought, proceeding with redoubled caution. The distance between them grew. "At this rate, I'll lose her. She knows every inch of the house. Besides, she must have done this hundreds of times, and I'm so stupid I didn't even think to count the steps on each flight." He risked breaking his neck at every landing. Flustered, he lost all sense of space and time, not knowing whether he had already reached the ground floor or was still on the second floor, whether he had been at this foolish pursuit for a few moments or for an hour. Next he heard the front-door hinges creak. "She's giving me the slip," he said to himself, and rushed down the remaining steps; he fell in the reception area and hurt his knee on the stone floor, but he kept up his pursuit despite the limp.

It was a moonless night, and the street was as dark as the inside of the house. Out in the open, the perfume was lost after a couple of yards. Onofre hobbled as far as the first street corner. A damp east wind was blowing. There was no sound anywhere. He wandered aimlessly for a while, until it was quite clear that he had lost the trail, then limped back to the boardinghouse. There he resumed the watch in his usual spot, but the dampness had got into his bones and he was shivering.

"There's no sense at all in what I'm doing," he told himself. He was trying hard not to sneeze, for sneezing would give him away. Finally, he gave up his vigil, went back to his room, and got into bed, feeling sorry for himself. "She has made a fool of me," he thought. "Now she is in somebody else's arms and they're both laughing at me, and here I'm in bed sick."

He must have fallen asleep, for when he opened his eyes, a

man not unfamiliar to him was examining him with interest. "He died not long ago," he heard the man saying, obviously referring to him. "There is no odor, and his joints are not yet stiff," the man went on. The night light gleamed in his glasses and threw a giant shadow on the wall opposite. "Now I know who he is," Onofre thought. "But what is he doing here, and who is he talking to?" As if in reply to the question, Onofre's father moved out of the shadows. "Do you think he will be presentable?" he asked. Onofre's father was wearing the same white linen jacket, but in deference to the solemnity of the occasion had taken off his Panama hat. "Do not worry yourself over that, Señor Bouvila," the man replied. "When we deliver him to you, it will be as if you had not lost him at all."

"This is a dream for sure," Onofre said to himself. A long time before, he had lived through this scene. One winter morning, the monkey his father brought back from Cuba was found dead. His mother was always first up in the mornings; it was she who found the body hunched up in the cage. She had never shown any fondness for that dirty, high-strung, malignant creature, but when she saw it dead, she felt a sudden wave of compassion and shed a few tears. "Coming all this way to die here, so far from its own kind!" she thought. "How lonesome!" "It's all your fault," she told her husband indignantly, "for having taken the poor thing from its home. The Lord didn't put it there for nothing, you know." Onofre was awake by then and overheard this conversation between his parents. "How do you know what would have become of him if I didn't get it into my head to bring him here?" the *americano* retorted. When they had both run out of arguments, he exclaimed, "I've just had an idea! Onofre," he said, addressing his son for the first time, "would you like to see Bassora?"

Joan Bouvila often went to Bassora; he was widely believed to have invested part of his fortune there and deposited the rest in the banks of that town. On such occasions he would be away for three or four days at a time; when he returned, he never spoke about what he had been doing, what he had seen, or how the business affairs he had gone to supervise were coming along. Sometimes, though not always, he would bring back some trifling little present: ribbons, sweets, some perfumed soap, or an illustrated magazine. Other times, he would come back very excited; he never said why, but at supper he would be more talkative than usual, telling his wife that they would make the next trip together and before coming home travel on to Barcelona or even Paris. Nothing came of these promises.

On the occasion of the death of the monkey, however, Onofre and his father went to Bassora together. Winter was only just beginning then, and the road was still clear, but it was getting dark by the time they reached the town. First they went to see a taxidermist whose address they had been given by a municipal policeman. The monkey's body, wrapped in a bundle, aroused the taxidermist's professional interest. "I've never done a monkey," he said, feeling the lifeless form with his expert hands. The workshop was dimly lit; several animals had been put aside, propped against the wall, in various stages of completion: some had their eyes missing, others their horns, others their feathers. A cane framework replacing the skeleton could be seen inside most of them through an opening in the belly, from which pieces of cotton and straw stuck out. The taxidermist apologized for the lighting: the shutters had to be kept tightly closed to keep out the blowflies and the moths, he told them.

Before taking his leave of the taxidermist, the *americano* handed over a sum of money as a deposit, and the taxidermist gave him a receipt, saying that the job wouldn't be finished until after Christmas. "The hunting season is in full swing, and it has become fashionable to have specimens stuffed to decorate the dining room, the parlor, or the living room," he said, letting them know in this way that Bassora was a town of refined taste.

While the man was speaking, Onofre took a final look at

the monkey's body. The table upon which they had placed it gave off a smell of disinfectant. Lying on its back with its feet and hands tucked up, the monkey looked somehow smaller. A damp draft ruffled the grayish hair on the side of its head.

"Let's be on our way, Onofre," his father said. Night had fallen, and the sky was red like the vaults of hell in those illustrations from *Companions in Piety* the rector had occasionally shown Onofre in the hope of inspiring a holy fear of God in him. Iron foundries were responsible for this particular glow, his father explained. "Look, son, this is progress." There were cities in America, he said, where the sun never pierced the smoke from the chimneys.

Onofre had just turned twelve when his father took him to Bassora to have the monkey stuffed. They walked along gaslit streets full of workers coming and going from their homes to the factories. Factory sirens sounded, announcing a change of shift. In the middle of a road a narrow-gauge train passed, spewing cinders on the passers-by and blackening the walls of the buildings. People had soot on their faces. There were bicycles on the move, some carriages, and quite a few wagons, drawn by sturdy nags that puffed and panted along. On the main avenue the lights were brighter and the people better dressed. They were nearly all men; the time appointed for the evening stroll, the *paseo*, had come and gone, and the ladies had retired to their homes. The pavements were narrow, restaurants and cafés having encroached upon them with their canopies; through their windows the silhouettes of the customers could be seen and a general hubbub heard.

Onofre and his father went into a restaurant. Onofre noticed how people glanced derisively at the *americano*: his white linen suit, his Panama hat, and the blanket he wore over his shoulders to keep out the cold caught everybody's attention in that inland town in the middle of winter. His indifference was such that one would have thought him blind. After tucking his napkin under his chin, he studied the menu with knitted brow, then ordered pasta soup, baked fish, goose with pears, salad, and fruit and cream. Onofre was amazed: he had never before sampled such dishes.

Now, however, those memories had become a nightmare that beleaguered him, and from which he awoke drenched in sweat. At first, terrified, he did not know where he was. Then he recognized the boardinghouse room, and the familiar bells of La Presentación's clock tower reassured him.

What continued to trouble him was not the taxidermist dream but the odd feeling that he had been tricked. As he went over the events of that night, the feeling grew. "I could swear I witnessed one of Delfina's escapades," he told himself, "and yet there's something in all this that doesn't quite fit. There's more mystery here than I ever suspected." He wanted to think, but his head spun and his temples throbbed. One minute he would be gasping from the heat, and the next gripped by a chill that made his teeth chatter. Each time he dozed off, the taxidermist reappeared, and the journey to Bassora would be repeated with painful precision. And each time he awakened, Onofre would again puzzle over his recent nocturnal adventure. The two episodes seemed somehow connected. "But how?" Onofre wondered. "What of what happened back then can unlock the mystery of what took place last night?" He told himself that he would think it all out tomorrow, when his head was clearer, but his brain persisted obstinately in its futile, exhausting task, and each hour that passed was an endless torture.

"Don't be afraid, my son, it's only me," said the voice. Onofre woke up, or thought he woke up, and saw a stranger bending over him. He would have cried out had he had the strength to do so. The stranger spoke gently, as if to a child or pet dog. "Here you are, drink this down, it has quinine in it, for the fever. It will do you good." He brought a steaming cup to

Onofre's lips, and the boy drank eagerly. "Not so fast, not so fast, my son, you'll choke yourself." By now Onofre recognized Father Bizancio. The latter, seeing how the sick boy was gradually becoming lucid again, added, "You have a high temperature, but I don't think it's serious. You have been working hard and not sleeping enough lately, and on top of that you caught a whopper of a cold, but it's nothing to worry about. Illnesses are manifestations of God's will, and we should receive them with patience, even gratitude, for it is as if God Himself were speaking to us through His microbes to give us a lesson in humility. Why, I myself—although in good health, thanks be to God—suffer from all kinds of complaints, as is only natural at my age. Every night I go to the bathroom three or four times to relieve my bladder, which has been awfully touchy of late; starchy foods give my digestive system no end of trouble; and when the weather changes, my joints ache. So you see."

"What time is it?" Onofre asked.

"Half past five or thereabouts. But what are you doing?" the priest asked, seeing Onofre try to get up.

"I must be off to the World's Fair."

"The fair will have to get along without you for now. You are in no condition to be getting out of bed, let alone going outside. Besides, it is half past five in the evening, not the morning. You have been delirious and talking in your sleep all day."

"Talking?" exclaimed Onofre, alarmed. "What did I say, Father?"

"What people always say under such circumstances, my son," the priest replied, "nothing. At least, nothing I could make sense of. Now, go back to sleep and don't worry about anything."

When he recovered and was able to go back to the World's Fair with his bundle of subversive pamphlets, that strident, dusty world seemed remote to him, as if, instead of having been away for a couple of days, he had really come back from a long journey. "Here I am again, wasting my time like a fool," he told himself. He considered having a serious talk with Pablo, asking him to entrust him with a weightier task, to promote him up the revolutionary ladder. He soon realized, however, that neither Pablo nor any of the other anarchist leaders would sympathize with his request. The cause they defended was not one that you joined with a view to personal advancement; it was one for which you sacrificed everything without expecting anything in return, whether compensation or recognition. "This idealism," Onofre reasoned, "is what allows them to make use of people without regard for their personal needs. For such fanatics anything is good if it serves as an instrument for the revolution."

Onofre decided to revenge himself on the anarchists at the first opportunity, unaware that in his hatred he showed their influence on him, the extent to which he had become imbued with their spirit. Although their ends were to be very different, even diametrically opposed, he would always share with the anarchists a fierce individualism and a taste for action, risk, immediate results, and simplification. He owed his killer instinct to them. But he would never realize this. In fact, he would consider himself their irreconcilable enemy. "They preach justice but don't think twice about putting me in danger, exploiting me," Onofre now seethed. "The bosses are fairer, they exploit the worker openly, paying him for his work, allowing him to move up if he sticks at it, and listening to his demands—even if sometimes that takes a little prodding."

This last reflection referred to the unrest prevalent among the bricklayers. They had asked to have their daily pay increased by half a peseta, or the working day reduced by one hour. The board turned this down: "The budget has already been voted on," they argued, "and it is beyond our power to modify it." This was a very lame reply. Rumors of a strike alarmed the board.

Things were not going well: financial reserves were going down much faster than the buildings were going up. Of the eight million pesetas promised by the government, only two million materialized. In October 1887 the City Council of Barcelona was authorized to float a public loan for three million pesetas to cover the World's Fair deficit. At around that time the Café-Restaurant was nearly finished, the Palace of Industry well advanced, and work was beginning on what was to be the Arco de Triunfo. That same month a Barcelona newspaper published this report: "A project has been submitted to the board of directors of the World's Fair for a building in the form of a church, which will display religious objects of the Catholic faith. The project is in good taste, and is the work of the Parisian architect M. Emile Juif, from the offices of Charlot & Co., by whom the expenses will be defrayed," etc. And a few days later, another report: "It is our privilege to announce that the well-known industrialist of this city D. Onofre Caba, manufacturer of and patent holder for the purified salt distributed under the trade name La Palma, is making preparations for a magnificent and most curious contrivance destined for the coming Barcelona Fair. The said contrivance is an exact reproduction, in salt and full ten palms high, of Hercules's Fountain, situated in the former Paseo de San Juan."

At the end of November, temperatures dropped suddenly to unprecedented levels. It was a freak cold spell lasting only a few days, a foretaste of the bitter winter that was in store. Still weakened by his fever, convalescing, Onofre was miserable. For the first time since arriving in Barcelona six months ago, he felt homesick for his valley and his mountains. In addition to this was the constant agitation he suffered—caused, unbeknown to her, by Delfina. "I must do something," he told himself, "or I'll go and hang myself from the nearest tree."

One morning that November, he went to the fairgrounds with the usual parcel of pamphlets, but also carried a sack of some weight. He spent the first few hours wandering around the site, chatting with people. They brought him up to date on the bricklayers' demands, the strike plans, and the points of disagreement. "This time," they said, "we're seeing it through. We won't take no for an answer." Onofre nodded, but was thinking, instead, about Delfina's cat. Whatever he saw or heard made him think of her, as if his thoughts were tied to her by a rubber band that would stretch only so far, then snap back in an instant. But he kept nodding. He had already formed the habit which was to stay with him for the rest of his days, of always saying yes while inwardly preparing treachery.

When the sun was higher in the sky and the cold had relented a little, he got together a group of workers and began his harangue, as he did every day. For the workers, tired from their labors, any excuse was good enough, so they formed a circle around him. Things had to be done quickly: the foremen, believing that some conspiracy was being hatched, might summon the Civil Guard.

"The strike," he said in his usual tone of voice, "is not what I wanted to talk about today. No, I have gathered you here to let you in on a sensational discovery that could transform your lives as much as or more than the elimination of the state in all its forms!"

He bent down, opened the sack, and took out a flask containing a cloudy liquid, which he showed to his listeners.

"This hair restorer you see before you, of proven effectiveness and sure-fire results—I'm not asking one peseta for it, I'm not asking two reales, I'm not even asking one real. . . ." Thus began his career in the world of business. Years later, his changes of mood would have share prices in a flurry in stock exchanges all over Europe, but now he was selling hair restorer that he had stolen the night before from Mariano's little cubbyhole in the boardinghouse. Onofre had listened to the charlatans hawking their wares in the Puerta de la Paz and was doing his best to imitate their style.

When his patter was over, a dumbfounded silence reigned.

"Maybe I overdid it," he thought to himself. "Maybe I've thrown away my only livelihood. The anarchists will never forgive me. The workers, insulted, might even hand me over to the Civil Guard and I'll be shut up in Montjuich Castle."

Suddenly a tremendous roar of a voice was heard from the audience: "I'll take one!" It belonged to a giant with a snub nose and a receding hairline. Elbowing his way to the front, he held up his ten centimos to pay for the product. Onofre took the money, handed the giant a flask, and asked if anybody else was buying.

A lot did. With their ten-centimo coins they pushed and shoved their way to the front in their eagerness to obtain a flask. The sack was emptied in less than two minutes. Onofre advised the crowd to disperse, and went and hid in the narrow, little-used alley beteween the east wall of the building that was to house the Martorell Museum and the wall marking the boundary between the World's Fair Park and the Paseo de la Industria. He took the coins from his pocket and looked at them with delight. He was still admiring them when he noticed a shadow on the wall opposite. Turning, he found himself face-to-face with the giant who had bought the first flask of hair restorer, which he still had in his hand. "Remember me?" asked the giant. His eyebrows and beard gave him the look of an ogre. He was hairy from chest to chin.

"Of course," said Onofre. "What do you want?"

"My name's Efrén, Efrén Castells. I'm from Calella. Not Palafrugell Calella—the other Calella, on the coast. I've been working as a laborer here, but only for a month and a half. That's why I didn't see you before, and you didn't see me. But I know who you are. And now give me two pesetas."

"And why should I do that, if it's not too much to ask?" Onofre assumed an expression of innocent surprise.

"Because, thanks to me, you made four pesetas. If I hadn't bought the first flask from you, you wouldn't have sold one. You're a good talker, but you need more than talk to sell. I ought to know: my grandfather on my mother's side was a horse trader. Come on, give me two pesetas and we'll be partners. You'll do the talking, I'll start off the buying. And if anything goes wrong, I can look after you. I'm strong. I can split a skull with one punch."

Onofre took a good look at the giant and liked what he saw. The man was obviously honest: he was willing to settle for what he had asked—and equally willing to split Onofre's head open. Onofre didn't question the giant's strength. "What I can't figure out is why you don't just take the four pesetas from me," he said. "Nobody can see us here. And I couldn't report you to the police even if I wanted to."

The giant laughed. "You're a clever one all right. What you just said proves how clever you are. Me, on the other hand, I'm as stupid as I am strong. I can think and think, but I never get ideas. If I took your four pesetas, that's all I'd have, four pesetas. But then I said to myself: this boy will go far. I want to be your partner, with you giving me half of what you earn."

"Look," said Onofre to the giant from Calella, "this is what we'll do: you help me sell the hair restorer, and I'll give you a peseta for every day we work, regardless of whether the take is good or bad. Even if I make nothing at all. And as for our future dealings, we'll talk about that when the time comes. All right?"

The giant thought it over, then agreed. "Done," he said. He was so stupid, he admitted, that he hadn't completely understood Onofre's proposal, though he was convinced that somewhere along the line Onofre, with that cunning of his, had tricked him. "But it's no use arguing," he said. "I know my limitations." They shook hands, thus putting the seal on an association that was to last several decades.

Efrén Castells died in 1934, ennobled with the title of marquis by Generalísimo Franco in recognition of his service to the fatherland. Despite the physical decline brought on by age and infirmity, Castells was still a giant when he died, and a special coffin had to be made for him. He left a considerable fortune in securities and real estate, as well as a priceless collection of Catalan paintings, which he bequeathed to the Museo de Arte Moderno, then installed in the Citadel Arsenal. That building, to which alterations and improvements had been made with the 1888 World's Fair in mind, was situated only a few yards from the spot where he had struck his first deal with the person to whom he was to dedicate a lifetime of blind devotion, and in whose shadow he would commit many crimes.

2

That day, on his way back to the boardinghouse, Onofre bought more flasks of hair restorer at a pharmacy and put them in the barber's cubbyhole to replace the ones he had stolen. He was very pleased with himself, but after supper, alone in his room, he couldn't think where to hide his gains. All the cares money brings instantly beset him. No place seemed safe now. Finally he decided to keep the money on him always. Then his thoughts turned to Efrén Castells. The giant might prove useful. If not, Onofre would get rid of him somehow.

He was more nervous about Pablo: sooner or later the anarchists would hear of his commercial dealings carried on under the cover—and to the detriment—of the cause. He was not sure how they would react. If he dropped the revolutionary propaganda altogether and concentrated exclusively on his selling, would they accept the change? No. He knew too much. They would consider him a traitor, would resort to violence. "Nothing but problems," he thought. It took him a long time to get to sleep; he woke up several times, and had a disturbing dream in which he saw himself once more in Bassora with his father.

The persistence of that memory surprised him. "Why should it become so important all of a sudden?" he wondered. And he attempted again to reconstruct everything that had happened at that time. He first saw those three gentlemen of Bassora as he ate supper with his father in the restaurant. His father turned pale when they came in.

These gentlemen were the descendants of the men who had set industrialization in motion in Catalonia at the beginning of the nineteenth century, the men whose titanic efforts had transformed that rural, lethargic land into one that was prosperous and dynamic. These descendants, however, did not come from the land or the local workshop, they had studied in Barcelona, traveled to Manchester to acquaint themselves with the latest advances in the textile industry, and been to Paris, in which dazzling city they experienced all that was most noble and all that was most depraved. They visited the Palais de la Science et de l'Industrie, where extraordinary inventions and the most refined and complex technology were on display, and on whose façade letters of bronze spelled the motto ENRICHISSEZ-VOUS; they visited the Outcasts' Salon, where Pissarro, Manet, Fantin-Latour, and other artists exhibited turbid, sensual canvases painted in a style called "Impressionist"; they went to the Salpetrière to see the young Dr. Charcot perform exercises in hypnosis, and to the Latin Quarter to hear Friedrich Engels announce the imminence of the proletarian revolt. They drank champagne in the most stylish restaurants and absinthe in the dirtiest dives; they squandered their money in pursuit of celebrated *mondaines,* those *grandes horizontales* people were already beginning to associate with Paris; at dusk they boarded the new *bateaux-mouches* (the *Géant* and the *Céleste*) to cruise along the Seine, and from the towers of Nôtre-Dame they took in the intoxicating air and light of the magic city. Nothing now was left of that Paris: the city's very greatness had kindled the envy and greed of other nations; unbounded pride had sown the seeds of war, hatred, and discord. The aged and sick Napoleon III was living in exile in England after his humiliating defeat at Sedan, and Paris was pulling itself together painfully after the tragic days of the Commune. The old

Paris, gone forever, lived on in these representatives of the upper crust of the Catalan bourgeoisie, the unexpected heirs of the Second Empire's *chic exquis*.

"Well, bless me if it isn't old Bouvila! What are you doing here, you old dog? My, it's a small world!" boomed one of the three gentlemen, entering the restaurant in Bassora. "And how's the family? All well?" The other two gentlemen came over to the table and slapped the *americano* on the back. The latter looked uncomfortably at them. Then Onofre became the center of their attention. "And who might this boy be? Your son? He's a big fellow now! What's your name, son?"

"Onofre Bouvila, sir," he said.

When the *americano* stood up to return their greetings, his chair fell over. They all laughed, and Onofre realized that these men considered his father a fool.

"My son and I are here to perform a painful duty," said the *americano,* but the three gentlemen were no longer paying the slightest attention to what he was saying.

"Fine, splendid," they said. "We have no intention of disturbing you. We just came to get a quick bite of something and talk a little business. Then it's home for us and back to our families for a while. Except this one here, of course," added the man speaking, pointing to his companion who was the exception. "A bachelor with no ties, he will be raising hell again, I suppose." The target of this joke blushed slightly. His face betrayed the alcohol and narcotics he had consumed years before in Parisian haunts, and the debilitation from the caresses of some *demimondaine.*

When Onofre and his father left the restaurant, an icy wind was blowing and a film of frost had formed, to creak and crackle underfoot. The *americano* wrapped himself in his blanket. "The scoundrels," he muttered. "Because I come from the country, they take me for some bogtrotter. City people! They don't know a pear tree from a tomato plant. Never trust city people, Onofre, my boy."

His teeth chattered from the cold or anger as he walked; now and then Onofre had to run to keep up with him. "Who were they?" Onofre asked.

The *americano* shrugged. "Nobody. Three dandies. Three moneybags named Baldrich, Vilagrán, and Tapera. I've done a little business with them." He looked around him as he spoke, searching for the inn where they had reserved a room for the night. There was no one out in the street at that late hour except a few gray-skinned, half-starved women in the pale circles of light cast by the gas streetlamps. Whenever he saw one of them, the *americano* grabbed Onofre's arm and took him to the other side of the street. Eventually they chanced upon a swollen-faced night watchman, who gave them directions to the inn.

They were tired when they arrived: walking dark streets was not the same as walking in the country. Inside, the cold gradually left their bones. A pipe coming out of the salamander stove in the entrance hall went to all the rooms, giving off heat and—from the joints—a yellowish smoke that left a sour taste in one's mouth. Chords from a piano and muffled voices could be heard coming from down the hall or from a nearby house. They heard a train whistle in the distance. Horses' hoofs rang on the paving outside.

They got into the double bed, and the *americano* put out the oil lamp. In the dark, he told his son, "Listen, Onofre, there are women who do terrible things for money, it's time you knew that. Some day I'll take you to one of those places, meanwhile not a word of this to your mother. Now forget it all and go to sleep."

More than a year had gone by since, yet Onofre remembered clearly the dissolute, jovial faces of those gentlemen, and imagined himself cornered by the women his father had alluded to, women who, as he tossed and turned, sometimes resembled Delfina. The following morning found him exhausted, but he heaved his sack over his shoulder and set off once more for the World's Fair site. He could not retreat now, he told himself, he had taken the plunge. Besides, if he did not give Efrén Castells the promised peseta, he'd be risking a blow—possibly a lethal one. When he found himself back in his usual place and selling the hair restorer, as he had done the day before, his good spirits returned. The prospect of profit, of gain, and of acting independently were stimulating.

Business was so brisk over the days that followed that Onofre's only problem was where to hide the money. Carrying it on his person was making him a nervous wreck: the section of town in which he lived was full of robbers. It never occurred to him to open a bank account, because he had the notion that banks accepted only money that was honestly earned and his, he somehow thought, was not. But it would have made no difference: since he was a minor, no bank would have accepted his application. In the end he decided on the classic solution, a mattress—not his own, however, but Father Bizancio's. The priest was as poor as a church mouse, and nobody would dream that he was sleeping on a small fortune. The likelihood of Delfina getting it into her head to take the mattress out and beat it was so small, it could safely be ruled out. In addition, the priest left early every morning, giving Onofre easy access to his room.

But Onofre still had the anarchists to deal with. One day, receiving him, Pablo punched him without warning. Onofre went down. The apostle came at him. "Scoundrel, renegade, Judas!" he yelled, kicking him with all his might.

Onofre did his best to ward off the blows. "Pablo, take it easy, what's the matter? Have you gone insane, or what?"

"You know very well what the matter is, you blackguard," Pablo panted. "Tell me, then, what you've been up to these days. Peddling hair restorer, eh? So that's what we pay you for, is it?"

Onofre gave him time to let off steam, then began talking. When he finished, they were both laughing. They had one thing in common, ideology aside: a very low opinion of society and all its members. As far as they were concerned, any deception was acceptable, could be justified by the stupidity of the victims. Theirs was the law of the wolf.

Onofre told Pablo that selling hair restorer was just a ruse to keep the police off his trail, a cover for his real activities. He had distributed more pamphlets than anybody over those months; didn't that prove his loyalty to the cause? And when it came down to it, who was running all the risks? Pablo finally apologized. "Being shut up here has driven me mad," he said. He hadn't wanted the job of keeping tabs on the business affairs of others—it was degrading. He had wanted to plant bombs, but they wouldn't let him.

Onofre was no longer listening. He had heard Pablo's complaints before, and his mind was on other matters.

Since the night he followed a waft of perfume and footsteps into the street, only to be thwarted by the darkness, Onofre had counted and re-counted the steps in the boardinghouse staircase, calculated the angle of each flight, memorized every obstacle, and made the descent by feel alone. "If Delfina passes this way again, I won't lose her," he said to himself. "As long as she doesn't have that accursed cat with her," he then thought with a shudder. Once he asked Efrén Castells how one went about killing a cat. "It's easy," the giant answered. "You wring its neck until it's dead. That's all there is to it." Onofre did not seek his advice again.

Finally, one day shortly before Christmas, he heard the swish of fabric on the third-floor landing and the faint sound of steps descending. He held his breath and told himself, "Now or never." He let the perfume go by, waited for what seemed a prudent length of time, then went into action. He reached the foot of the stairs just as Delfina was opening the front door. The moon was out that night, revealing a woman's figure in the doorway. He had only a glimpse, but it was enough to make him realize that the woman he was following was not Delfina. Her form, blurry in the moonlight, showed more clearly when she passed under one of those niches in the walls where pious people kept oil lamps burning in honor of the Virgin or a saint. Except along the city's main arteries, this was the only form of street lighting in the city. It was a cold night in that terrible winter of 1887. The mysterious lady strode fearlessly on through the deserted streets. The woman had to be mad, to walk alone at that hour, he thought.

The area they were entering separated the foothills from the railroad in the district known as El Morrot. With a radius of only half a kilometer, El Morrot lay to the south of the ancient city walls. One could reach it only by crossing a barrier two hundred meters long, three meters wide, and eight meters high— this barrier was an enormous mound of coal imported from England or Belgium and piled up to await transportation to factories in or around Barcelona.

The coal was kept so far from the city because of the high risk of fire. Fire on the surface of the pile was easy to put out. But if it started deep inside, it would go unnoticed, until a catastrophic blaze was unavoidable. First to appear would be wisps of pale smoke rising here and there, pungent and very toxic; these emanations would then form an all-enveloping cloud, and woe betide the hapless creature who inhaled it. By the time real flames appeared, it would be too late to fight the fire.

Such fires reached heights of up to twenty meters, casting a red glow visible in the sky as far as Tarragona and Majorca on clear nights. Ships tied along the wharves would shove off and anchor out at sea, preferring the ground swell to the heat and the noxious gases given off by the blaze. These fires could last several weeks once they caught hold, and their cost was incalculable: besides the loss of the coal, all industry was brought to a standstill. Hence the vicinity was not safe for residential purposes, and hence, a slum of the lowest order had grown up, the most disreputable district of Barcelona. There were theaters there offering shows as indecent as they were stale, plus grimy, clamorous taverns, an occasional fifth-rate opium den (the better-class ones were up near Vallcarca), and sinister bordellos. Only the dregs of Barcelona ever came here, and sailors, not a few of whom would never again put to sea. Only prostitutes, pimps, thugs, smugglers, and criminals lived here. A small sum secured the services of a thug, and a little more, those of a hired killer. The police ventured into this zone in broad daylight only, and then merely to negotiate exchanges of prisoners. It was practically an independent state; IOUs circulated here like genuine currency. The inhabitants also had their own penal code, and a very strict one. Justice was summary: it was not unusual to find a man swinging by his neck from the door lintel of some house of entertainment.

When Onofre saw the place into which the mystery lady was unwittingly leading him, he began to have second thoughts. "If this woman isn't Delfina, why should I follow her? In this path through the coal, some thug might jump out and kill me, and bury me, and no one would know or even miss me." For it was known that people who met a violent death here, if they were not deliberately left out for all to see, were buried in the coal. And in the coal they remained, until such time as a crane deposited it in a barge, wagon, or cart. Stokers shoveling coal into boilers would see a boot sticking out, or fingers, or a skull with tufts of hair still clinging to the occiput. Onofre was tempted to go home.

But he did not turn back. And so he entered the shanty-town. The streets were laid out on a regular grid pattern, as is usual in such places. On the cracked and rutted strip of dry mud that was the street, drunks slept in their own excrement. The strumming of guitars and snatches of song drifted out from the taverns—salacious songs, yet conveying melancholy and anguish. "How did I end up like this?" seemed to be the theme of the liquor-hazed, torn voices. "This wasn't what I dreamed of in my youth." There were castanets, too, and heels rapping, shouts, glasses breaking, furniture being overturned, people running and quarreling.

Straight down these streets went the mystery lady. Onofre, backing into a doorway, watched her enter an establishment whose wooden door closed after her. He decided to wait and see what happened. A cold, wet wind was blowing, salty, since the sea was so close; he wrapped over his nose and mouth the scarf he had had the good sense to bring.

He did not have to wait long. A few minutes later, the woman emerged, to the accompaniment of a surge of voices. He caught a glimpse of her face for the first time, and recognized the face. "No, it can't be," he told himself. "I must be seeing things." The woman took a little envelope and sniffed some white powder into her nose, closed her eyes, opened her mouth wide, stuck out her tongue, wriggled her shoulders, hips, her whole body. She then howled like a satisfied she-wolf and made for the next tavern, which had a window facing the street. The air inside, warmed by a salamander stove, condensed on the already grimy windowpanes, veiling the goings-on within but nonetheless allowing one outside to observe unobserved—which is what Onofre Bouvila did.

The patrons were the nastiest types imaginable. Some were gambling, their sleeves stuffed with cards and their knives ready to be buried in the throat of an accuser; others danced with squalid glass-eyed hetaeras to the music of a blind man's concertina. A dog lay at the player's feet, pretending to be asleep but snapping without warning at the dancers' calves. In a corner the woman Onofre had followed was arguing with a customer who had curly hair and copper-colored skin; she fussed, he frowned. Onofre saw him take a swipe at her. She grabbed the man's hair and tugged, as if to pull his head from his shoulders, but could not get a proper grip, given the unguents he had smeared on his hair. The man punched her in the mouth; she stumbled backward and fell across a table, sending bottles, glasses, and cards flying. Now the man advanced on her with a murderous gleam in his eye and a curved sheep-shearing knife in his hand. The woman wept, and the customers jeered at both of them.

The owner of the place put a stop to this: he told the woman to leave immediately. No one doubted that she was to blame, that she had provoked the man. Back in the cover of his doorway, Onofre saw her come stumbling out. A trickle of blood from the corner of her mouth turned violet as it mixed with her makeup. She felt with her fingers to see that all her teeth were still firmly rooted in her gums, removed her wig, mopped the sweat from her brow with a polka-dotted handkerchief, set her wig back in position, and began walking home. The wind had dropped and the air was still, dry, and crystal clear, so cold that it was painful to breathe. Onofre caught up with her at the pile of coal.

"Señor Braulio!" he shouted. "Wait for me! It's me, Onofre Bouvila, from your boardinghouse!"

"Oooh, my son," exclaimed the hotelier, his cheeks still wet with tears, "I was hit in the mouth, and they would have stuck me like a pig if I hadn't left. What scum!"

"But why on earth do you come to this sickening place? Just to get beaten up, Señor Braulio? And dressed as a woman, too! That can't be normal," said Onofre.

Señor Braulio shrugged and began walking again. Suddenly large storm clouds blotted out the moon, leaving them in total darkness. They tripped, went sprawling in the coal, hurting their knees, hands, and faces. Onofre and Señor Braulio ended up arm in arm to steady each other.

"Have you noticed, Onofre?" exclaimed Señor Braulio after a while. "It's beginning to snow. It's years since it last snowed in Barcelona!"

There was a noise behind them: the inhabitants of the depraved shantytown were coming out into the street with torches and oil lamps to view the rare spectacle.

It was the coldest winter in living memory in Barcelona. It snowed around the clock, snowed for days on end. The city was buried under more than a meter of snow, traffic ground to a halt, and even the most essential public services were cut off. Temperatures dropped to several degrees below freezing: that means little in other, more northerly climes, but it meant a great deal in a city unprepared for this eventuality, and where people did not have the constitution to face such extremes. The cold claimed many victims. One morning Onofre, hardened by life in the country and nothing daunted by the rigors of the weather, opened his balcony to view the cityscape of white houses, and found still perched on the railing the stiff body of one of the turtledoves. When he tried to take hold of it, it fell and smashed to pieces in the street below, as if made of china.

The freezing water burst pipes and ducts; the taps and public fountains ran dry. Supplies of drinking water had to be brought in by carts at certain times in certain places around the city. The cart men would signal their presence by sounding brass horns, and the people would brave the cold, which penetrated their clothes, as they lined up out in the open. The police often had to intervene to stop fights and, indeed, riots resulting from the slowness of the service. Sometimes a person on the line froze in place; he would be freed by having warm water thrown over his shoes—or simply by brute force, being tugged at till he came loose. Many city dwellers obtained water by bringing buckets of snow into their houses and waiting for it to thaw. Others did the same with the icicles hanging from the eaves of their houses. All this, despite the inconvenience caused, fostered a sense of an adventure shared, of a brotherhood in adversity, among the people of Barcelona. Everyone had a story to tell.

For those working outside, the situation was agonizing. The World's Fair laborers suffered unspeakable torment, open as the site was to the sea and the winds. While at other, similar places, such as the port, work had been called off temporarily, at the fairgrounds it went on faster than ever. In addition, the bricklayers, not having received a satisfactory reply to their demands, decided to go on strike.

Pablo, whom Onofre was keeping up to date on events, flew into a rage. "This strike is idiotic." Onofre asked him to explain why. "There are two types of strike," Pablo said, "one intended to win some specific gain, and one intended to rock the established order, contributing to its eventual destruction. The first type is very much to the detriment of the worker, because in the end it consolidates the prevailing unjust system in society. The strike is the proletariat's only weapon, and it's stupid to waste it on trivia. What's more, this strike lacks organization, a base, leaders, well-defined aims. It will be an out-and-out failure, and the cause will have taken a giant step backward."

Onofre disagreed. As he saw it, the apostle was angry only because the strikers had completely ignored the anarchists, not seeking their advice or asking them to join in the collective action—much less to act as its leaders. Even so, Onofre was to learn that strikes were indeed a double-edged weapon, one that the workers would do well to use with caution, and that strikes could be of considerable benefit to the bosses who manipulated them. But for the time being Onofre simply kept a close watch on events, trying not to miss anything—or leave himself exposed should things take a turn for the worse.

The strike, as Pablo foresaw, came to nothing. One morning Onofre arrived at Citadel Park and found almost all the workers gathered in the central esplanade of the future World's Fair, the former Plaza de Armas of the Citadel, opposite the Palace of Industry. This palace was still only an immense framework of planks; it occupied an area of some seventy thousand square meters and stood twenty-six meters high at its highest point. Now, covered in snow, empty and abandoned, it looked like the skeleton of some antediluvian animal. The workers did not talk among themselves; they seemed lost, and made a restless sea of caps. The Civil Guard had taken up strategic positions. Their capes and three-cornered hats stood out on the rooftops against the sharp morning sky. A mounted detachment patrolled the area around the park.

"If they charge, remember that they can bring their sabers into play only to the right of the horse," some workers, veterans of other skirmishes, told the greenhorns. "They can't touch you if you're to the left. And if they catch you, get down on the ground and cover your head with your arms. Horses won't trample a body on the ground. It's better than making a run for it."

Some remarked that it was easy to frighten a horse, brainless jittery beast that it was, by waving a handkerchief before its eyes. This would make it rear and throw its rider. But everyone inwardly thought: Let someone else be the first to try that.

Eventually the order to begin—nobody knew where it originated—went around. The group started walking slowly, shuffling. Onofre, who followed them, noticed that the group, which initially numbered a thousand or more, thinned out to two or three hundred people almost as soon as the march began. The rest vanished. Those who stayed made their way out of the park through a gate situated between the Glasshouse and the Café-Restaurant, and started down Calle de la Princesa, heading for the Plaza de San Jaime. They did not seem threatening. It looked, rather, as if they all wanted to get it over with, sensing that the strike was pointless. The shops along Calle de la Princesa had not pulled their grilles down, and people leaned out of windows to see the demonstration go by. The mounted police kept up with the workers, their sabers in their sheaths, and seemed annoyed more with the cold than with the civil disturbance.

Onofre followed the marchers a while, then turned down a side street to rejoin them farther up. In a little square nearby he ran into a whole company of mounted Civil Guard with three low-caliber cannons on carriages. If things got hot, he realized, the demonstration would end in a bloodbath.

Fortunately nothing serious happened. When they arrived at the intersection with Calle Montcada, the marchers stopped. "We might as well call a halt here," they seemed to be thinking. One worker climbed up onto a lattice window and made a speech to the effect that the demonstration had been a success. Then another worker took his place and said that everything had gone wrong because of the lack of organization and class conscious-ness; he urged them to get back to their work without delay. "Maybe that way we can avoid reprisals," he said at the end of his address. Both speakers were heard out with attention and respect. The first of them, as Onofre found out later through Efrén Castells, had been a police informer; the second, an honest bricklayer with trade-unionist leanings. The bricklayer lost his job over the strike and was never seen again in Citadel Park.

The results of the day's proceedings could be summarized as follows: by midday all the workers had gone back to their jobs, none of their demands were met, and the event was not even reported in the local press.

"It was bound to turn out like that," Pablo grumbled, not without a glint of satisfaction in his febrile eyes. "Now we'll have to wait years before any other collective action can be considered. I'm not even sure it's worthwhile for you to continue with the pamphlets."

Onofre, alarmed at seeing that source of income endan-gered, changed the subject by telling what he had seen when he left the marchers.

"Well, naturally," said Pablo. "What did you expect? As much as they can, the authorities leave the demonstrators alone. A few police look after public order and the flow of traffic. Then the people say, 'I don't know what they're complaining about—the government is so benevolent.' But if things get out of hand, the mounted guard charges. And if that doesn't do the trick, it's cannon fire into the crowd!"

"Then why go on trying?" asked Onofre. "They have the guns. Nothing will ever change. Let's switch to something more lucrative."

"Don't say that, boy, don't say that," answered Pablo, his eyes fixed on an unseen horizon wider and brighter than the damp, cracked walls of the basement he lived in. "It's true we have only our numbers to weigh against their weapons—our numbers and the boldness born of desperation. But one day we shall be victorious. It will take much blood, much suffering, but the price paid will be small, for we shall be buying a future for our children, a future with equal opportunity for all and no more hunger, no more tyranny, no more war. I may never live to see it; nor you, Onofre, even though you're very young. Many years must pass, and there are a multitude of things to be done first: destroy the present order, bring oppression to an end, abolish the police, the army, private property, money, the church and education as we know it, and much more. That is a good fifty years' work."

The cold, which claimed so many victims that winter, did not leave the boardinghouse without its casualties. Micaela Castro, the fortune-teller, took seriously ill. Father Bizancio brought a doctor to examine her, a young man who showed up dressed in a white coat spattered with red stains. Taking some dirty and slighty rusted instruments from his bag, he started prodding and poking the patient with them. Everybody could see that the doctor knew nothing about medicine, and that the spatters on his coat were only tomato stains, but they all pretended not to notice. Despite his obvious incompetence, the doctor was clear about his diagnosis: Micaela Castro did not have long to live. Old age and complications were carrying her off, he said. He left a prescription for a sedative and left. When they were alone again, the resident guests and Señor Braulio went down to deliberate on the matter in the hall, where Señora Agata was sitting with her feet in her basin.

Mariano was in favor of having the sick woman removed from the boardinghouse as soon as possible: although the doctor had assured them that the pythoness's illness was not contagious, the barber was afraid. "Let's take her to the charity home," he proposed. "They'll look after her there till she dies."

Señor Braulio agreed with the barber. Señora Agata said nothing, as usual, and did nothing to indicate that she understood the purpose of the meeting. Onofre said he would go along with the majority.

Only Father Bizancio objected. As a priest, he had had occasion to visit one or two hospitals, and had found the patients' living conditions terrible. Even if there was a free bed there, he said, to abandon the lady to her fate in an unfamiliar place, in the hands of strangers, among others as near death's door as herself, would be an act of cruelty that ill became good Christians. Her ailments, he added, required no special attention and would inconvenience no one. "The poor old lady has lived in our boardinghouse for many years. This is her home. It is only right to let her pass away surrounded by the present company, we being, so to speak, her family, all the family she has in the world. Bear in mind," he said, looking at each of them in turn, "that this woman has made a pact with the devil. Damnation and an eternity of torment await her. Since she is faced with such a terrible prospect, the least we can do is try to ensure that what remains of her earthly existence is as free from discomfort as we can make it."

The barber began to argue, but was interrupted by Señora Agata. "The reverend father is right," she said in the hoarse voice of a miner. Nobody apart from her husband had ever heard her speak; her intervention settled the matter. The barber gave way in the end: he had no other choice. Father Bizancio promised to attend to the sick lady's needs so that she would not be a burden on anyone. The meeting concluded amicably. At suppertime, Micaela Castro's absence cast a cloud of melancholy over those present, who never again would find relief from their cares in her and her trances.

The year 1887 finally drew to a close. For one reason or another it seemed longer than other years; perhaps because, as sometimes happens, it had not brought any good luck. "Let's hope the next one will be a little better," the people of Barcelona said to one another. It is also possible that the severe cold of the last weeks contributed to the bad memory the year left. The snow, where it had not been cleared away, turned to ice, inviting falls and broken bones. The Plaza de Cataluña, dug up at the time and full of craters, mounds, and ditches, was a desolate sight, with something of the Arctic about it. On this theme, a newspaper ran the story that in a hollow in that square several eggs, uncommonly large, had been found, and that laboratory analysis revealed them to be penguin eggs. The joke is some indication of how the cold dominated city life, and more especially the lives of those who lacked the means to protect themselves from its ravages.

On the beach, where the homeless workers and their families lived, the situation became desperate. One night, the women took their children in their arms and set off. The men did not go with them, judging—correctly—that their presence in the march would give it the wrong character. The women and children crossed the iron bridge connecting the beach to Citadel Park and walked between the half-built pavilions until they came to the Palace of Fine Arts. This palace, no longer existing today, was to the right of the Salón de San Juan as one entered from the Arco de Triunfo, in the apex formed by the *salón* and Calle del Comercio—i.e., outside the park itself, though still within the World's Fair grounds. The Palace of Fine Arts was eighty-eight meters long, forty-one meters wide, and thirty-five meters high, not counting the four towers with their four domes, each dome crowned by a statue of Fame by way of adornment. Inside the palace, apart from the rooms and galleries designated for exhibiting works of art, there was a magnificent hall, fifty meters long and thirty meters wide, in which the most solemn occasions of the World's Fair program were to take place. It was in this hall that the women and children resolved to spend the night. The Civil Guard officer on duty in the park reported the fact to the authorities. "Pretend you have seen nothing," came the answer.

"But they're making bonfires in the middle of the hall," said the officer. "Smoke is coming out the windows."

"We don't want an incident on our hands and see it splashed all over the foreign press with only four months to go before the opening. Look the other way," was the reply from the authorities.

"Very well," said the officer, "but I want the order in writing, and within half an hour, or I'll clear them out, the whole pack of them, using whatever force is necessary. We have a machine gun positioned on the roof of the Café-Restaurant, and can mow them down as they come out."

The authorities sent a councillor, who, braving the cold and slipping on the ice, made it to the scene of the impending massacre, clutching the order, before the officer could carry out his threat. The following day an agreement was reached with the workers' families, though not the workers themselves: for a period of two weeks they could occupy the new barracks on Calle Sicilia, light bonfires there, and do whatever they pleased.

The reason the women got such good terms was that Efrén Castells had sold them several flasks of hair restorer and some of them had grown beards. The councillor sent to the Palace of Fine Arts in the name of the mayor, facing a committee of bearded women, hastily agreed to all their demands. Only his connections in high places saved him from dismissal from his post. And all because Efrén Castells was such a ladies' man, a satyr. On the excuse of selling hair restorer, he would slip into the huts when the menfolk were at work on the site, and once he got inside, there was no stopping him. He had a virile look that appealed to nearly all women, was jovial by nature, adept at flattery, and threw his money around with abandon, as a result of which, fortune smiled on him in matters of the heart.

Onofre took a dim view of his partner's behavior. "One of these days you're going to get us into serious trouble," he told him.

"Have no fear," Efrén answered. "I know women inside and out. They'll deceive their husbands at the drop of a hat, but let themselves be flayed alive rather than betray the fancy man who treats them right. Why is that, you ask? Search me, friend! Perhaps they like to suffer. If you want a woman to take care of you, be unfaithful to her. That's the best system."

Efrén used the pesetas Onofre paid him to buy presents for his conquests. "Apparently one has to be a big spender as well as a rogue," thought Onofre. "All that other people are worth is what you're clever enough to get out of them. That's what human beings are: grist for the mill." These thoughts and others in a similar vein would pass through his head as he stood vigil on the landing in the boardinghouse, waiting for Delfina. The cold went through him; only his youth and sound constitution saved him from serious illness. Señor Braulio now had stopped his excursions, putting his flounces and frills away for the spring. Onofre did not tell him about his plan to catch Delfina and her boyfriend *in flagrante delicto*. Señor Braulio knew nothing of his daughter's amours, nor she of his.

One night, at the stroke of two, a voice roused Onofre from his reflections. It was Micaela Castro calling out for water. Either Father Bizancio, who was supposed to be looking after her, was fast asleep, or else he had gone a little hard of hearing in his old age. Minutes ticked by and nobody answered her call. The fortune-teller's voice was so feeble that one could scarcely tell where it came from. Onofre went to the kitchen, filled a glass with water, and took it to the sick woman. Her room reeked, like seaweed rotting in the sun. Onofre groped his way to the fortune-teller, managed to find her chilly hand, and put the glass in it. He heard her avid gulping, then took the empty glass from her. The dying woman mumbled something. Onofre bent closer to hear. "May you get your reward in heaven, my son," he thought he made out, and said to himself, "Huh, that was all she was saying." But an idea began to take shape in his mind.

In mid-January the good weather returned, and the city stirred from its lethargy. At the World's Fair the ice melted to reveal the balustrades and pedestals the master builders had spent weeks trying to find. The thaw created large puddles, which were not only a nuisance but also dangerous, since they could—and indeed did—cause the ground to sink in places, which in turn caused disturbingly large cracks in walls and foundations. A section of a building collapsed, burying a bricklayer's assistant under a pile of rubble. There was no time to locate the body, so they rolled the rubble flat and started rebuilding on top of it. The incident was kept secret, and visitors to the fair never suspected there was a body under their feet. In ancient cities, this is not uncommon.

With the thaw a tribe of gypsies appeared, walking along the beach. The workers' wives stood in the doors of their huts to block entry, for it was widely believed that gypsy women stole infants. This tribe was actually just doing what it could to earn its daily bread by mending pans, clipping dogs, telling fortunes, and making bears dance. The workers, having no pans, no dogs, and no futures, were interested only in seeing the bears dance. And so it was that the Civil Guard had to intervene. They moved on the gypsies, who had installed themselves and their tambourines in the Plaza de Armas. The officer, promoted over the incident at the Palace of Fine Arts, approached the gypsy who seemed to be in charge and told him to leave and take his companions with him. The gypsy replied that they were harming no one. "I am going off to take a leak," said the officer. "If you are all still here when I get back, I'll have the bears shot, the men sent off to do forced labor, and the women shaved to the skull. Now, do as you think best." Bears and gypsies vanished in a trice.

Two or three days later, another group, every bit as exotic as the first, showed up in the fairgrounds. Leading the way was a gentleman with a top hat of green plush and a frock coat of the same color. The gentleman sported a waxed jet-black mustache. He was followed by four other men who were carrying between them a platform on which stood an object whose shape was hidden by a tarpaulin. No sooner did the Civil Guard set eyes on these five characters than they fell on them, using the butts of their rifles. It turned out that the gentleman in green was the first participant to arrive for the World's Fair, one Gunther van Elkeserio, come from Mainz with four employees. The poor participant had brought an electric spindle of his own invention and was wandering around asking people in German and English where to enroll and where to put his spindle until the fair opened its doors.

The authorities had urged exhibitors to bring what they wished to display in Barcelona in advance, to avoid last-minute bottlenecks. Several warehouses were made available for the storage of exhibits until their respective pavilions were completed.

The storage was more complicated than it at first appeared. Not only did the objects have to be protected against the elements and the damp (and they might be precision equipment, artwork, or simply things that were delicate or perishable), not to mention against the destructive inroads of rats, cockroaches, termites, etc.; they also had to be arranged so that they could be easily located later and retrieved. The authorities had made provisions for this, drawing up and publishing an exhaustive inventory classifying articles from the world over. To each item a number was given, a letter, or a combination of the two.

Onofre Bouvila soon came upon one of these lists, and he gave it his close attention. "I never dreamed that there were so many things that could be bought and sold," he said to himself. This discovery depressed him for several days. Finally, accompanied by Efrén Castells and surmounting numerous obstacles, he got inside one of those warehouses. Lighting their way with an oil lamp, they found boxes and packages of various sizes from floor to ceiling. Some were large enough to contain a carriage along with its horses, and others small enough to fit in a man's pocket. There was something in each package. Onofre consulted the list by the light of the oil lamp: mechanical furniture used in surgery and orthopedics; trusses for hernias and varicose veins; crutches, spectacles, ear trumpets, false teeth, artificial limbs, and straitjackets. "Touch wood," whispered Efrén. At Onofre's request, the giant from Calella wrenched open one of the biggest crates. Inside was a calender of the type used in pressing paper.

Being a gentle giant, Efrén had won the confidence of all the little rascals on the beach, the children of the women he spent his time seducing, making use of them to convey gallant messages to and fro, and to arrange trysts. Onofre and Efrén together organized and trained these scamps to enter the warehouses, break into the crates, and bring back articles, which would then be sold or raffled. The children were given so much for each article. Efrén's earnings burned a hole in his pocket and were soon gone; Onofre, on the other hand, who never spent any of his, was accumulating a modest fortune in Father Bizancio's mattress. "I can't understand what you want all that money for," the giant would say to his partner. "There might be sense in *my* saving— I'm stupid, so I should give some thought to the morrow. But for you to save, with all your brains—I just don't get it." The truth was that Onofre spent nothing because he had no idea what to spend his money on, having nobody at his side to teach him how to spend.

Delfina left the boardinghouse for an hour every morning, Onofre learned from his spying, to market. One morning, he took off from his business activities to follow the maid. She set out with two wicker baskets, and the cat at her side. She walked absentmindedly, as if her thoughts were far away, and stepped into puddles and through piles of refuse in her bare feet. The children running in the alleys stopped and watched her pass; they would have thrown stones at her if it hadn't been for that mean-looking cat. And the saleswomen in the market had no welcome for Delfina. She took no part in their chitchat and haggled fiercely. Whatever she wanted to buy had seen better days, and she always demanded a discount.

If a saleswoman assured her that a cabbage was not rotten but still retained something of its pristine verdure, Delfina would say that the vegetable in question stank to high heaven, was surely riddled with worms, and that she would not pay such an exorbitant price for that disgraceful excuse for food. If the saleswoman stood her ground, Delfina would scoop up Beelzebub and dump him on the counter between them. The cat's back arched, his hair stood on end, his claws emerged, and the intimidated saleswoman surrendered. "All right, then, take your cabbage and pay what you want, but don't ever come to my stall again. I won't serve you any more, and that's final." Delfina would shrug and come back the next day, not at all daunted. The saleswomen went pale with fury whenever they set eyes on her. They even turned to the market's resident witch: to give Delfina—and particularly her cat—the evil eye. Onofre learned all this with no difficulty, because as soon as the saleswomen were rid of her and her fiendish cat, they unleashed their tongues.

On the way back to the boardinghouse, Onofre approached Delfina. "I was taking a walk," the boy said to the maid, "and happened to see you. Can I help you with your baskets?"

"I can manage just fine by myself," she snapped, quickening her step, as if to show that the full baskets were no burden.

"I didn't say you couldn't manage. I only wanted to be polite."

"What for?"

"There's no what for about it," said Onofre. "Politeness has no motive. If there's a motive, then it isn't politeness, it's self-interest."

"You talk too fancy," Delfina cut him short. "Go away, or I'll set the cat on you."

He had to get rid of the cat, which meant killing it. All the methods he devised were good, but each presented some insurmountable difficulty. Finally he came up with one that seemed feasible. It involved greasing the roof of the boardinghouse: when Beelzebub went up on the roof to prowl, as cats were wont to do, he would slip and fall off. A fall from the fifth floor would surely put an end to the cat. Onofre nearly met his own end while carrying out the plan. When he had greased every square inch of the tiles, he went back to his room and lay on his bed. Nothing happened that night. The following night, he fell asleep, tired of waiting.

At two o'clock he was awakened by a noise. Moans and curses came from the balcony. He opened the balcony door, looked out, and there in the moonlight saw a man hanging from the railing, struggling in vain to get a foothold in a chink in the wall. "Please," the man begged Onofre when he saw him, "give me a hand here, or I'm done for." Onofre gripped him by the wrists, hoisted him up, and deposited him in his room. As soon as the man's feet touched the ground, he slipped and fell on his behind. "I've busted my ass in twenty places," he groaned. Onofre lit the candle and told him to keep his voice down. "What were you doing on my balcony?" he demanded.

"Some bastard," said the man, "must have greased the roof or something. A good thing I caught that railing, or I'd have had it."

"And what were you doing on the roof at this time of night?"

"What's that to you?"

"Nothing to me, but the owners of this place and the police might want to know."

"I'm no burglar," said the man, "and I was doing nothing wrong. My name is Sisinio. I'm the boyfriend of a girl who lives here."

"Delfina!"

"That's her name," said Sisinio. "Her parents are strict and won't let her see any man. We meet on the roof at night."

"That's amazing!" said Onofre. "And how do you get up on the roof?"

"With a ladder. I put it against the wall on that high place in the back, so there's not far to climb. I'm a painter by trade."

Sisinio looked about thirty-five. Narrow-chested, with thin hair, bulging eyes, and a receding chin, he had two teeth missing and made a hissing noise when he spoke. "So this is my rival," thought Onofre gloomily.

"And what do you do there on the roof?" Onofre asked.

"I don't see how that's any of your business."

"Don't worry, I'm one of you. My name's Gaston. Pablo can tell you all about me."

"Ah, I see," said Sisinio, smiling for the first time. He told Onofre that in fact they did little on the roof—they talked, once in a while they kissed, and that was it. It was difficult to go much further up there. Sisinio had suggested hundreds of times that they meet in a place more convenient, but Delfina refused. "You wouldn't love me afterward," she'd say. They had been going on like this for two years. "I don't know why I put up with it," said Sisinio.

Onofre asked him why they didn't get married.

"I'm married already. I have two daughters. I haven't worked up the courage to tell Delfina yet. She's so starry-eyed."

"And what does your wife have to say about all this?"

"Nothing. She thinks I'm doing some nightwork. Before I go home, I splash a little paint on myself, to make it look convincing."

"You stay here," said Onofre. "I'll go and get Delfina. If she goes up on the roof, she'll slip and kill herself." He went out into the corridor just as Father Bizancio was groping his way to the bathroom. The fortune-teller was moaning in pain. "All I need now," thought Onofre, "is to bump into Señor Braulio in his floozie gear. How did I end up in a place like this!"

When he knocked softly on Delfina's door and identified himself, her reply was, "Clear off, or I'll set the cat on you."

"I only came to tell you that Sisinio had an accident," said Onofre.

The bedroom door opened immediately. Four pupils smoldered in the doorway. The cat gave a snort, Onofre took a step back, but the maid said, "Don't be afraid, he won't hurt you. What happened?"

"Your boyfriend fell off the roof. He's in my room. Come on down, but don't bring Beelzebub," said Onofre.

As Delfina and Onofre made their way down the stairs, he took her arm; she did not attempt to free herself. He noticed that she was trembling.

Sisinio, stretched out on the bed, looked like a corpse in the candlelight, although he made an effort to smile.

"I'll leave you with him," Onofre said to Delfina. "Just don't let him die in my room if you can help it. I don't want trouble. I'll be back at the crack of dawn."

In the street outside the door, he hesitated, not knowing where to go. Suddenly there was a sharp meow, and a body fell, brushing his shoulder, and hit the ground. Using an iron bar, Onofre moved Beelzebub's body to the gutter and stuffed it down a drain. Thus in one night Delfina lost the twin pillars of her security.

His Holiness the Right Reverend Bishop of Barcelona had journeyed to Rome as a novice. In Milan, where he stopped for a few days, he saw His Imperial Highness the Archduke Francis Ferdinand of Austria (the same Archduke Francis Ferdinand who was to meet a tragic end many years later in Sarajevo) inspecting the guard. That spectacle remained in the illustrious prelate's memory to the end of his days.

Now the workmen were putting down their tools, straightening up, and taking off their caps as he went past to the accompaniment of the bells of the Citadel church and the blaring trumpets of the cavalry regiment following the retinue. The Right Reverend Bishop and His Excellency the Mayor passed through the Arco de Triunfo side by side. Thronging behind them came the other officials. Farther back, and for the most part not terribly excited by the affair, was the consular corps. All but treading on the ordinary's heels was a deacon bearing the stoup—a vessel of beaten silver containing holy water. The bishop had his pastoral crozier in his left hand, while his right hand shook the aspergillum, which he dipped in the stoup every now and then. In the event of a direct hit with the holy water, the workman concerned would immediately make the sign of the cross. It was pitiful to see the bishop's cope dragging in the dust. The Palace of Industry, where the official ceremony was to take place, was still only a shell, but drapes had done much to cover this deficiency, creating the effect of a marquee.

A chapel had been erected on a prominent spot. In it stood a recently restored statue of Saint Lucia of gilt silver, dating from the eighteenth century or earlier. The municipal band was ready on the left of the central nave, and played a march when the officials entered. The bishop blessed the site. He and the mayor made speeches, after which there were cheers for the king and the queen regent. The two delegates, who had traveled back and forth between Barcelona and Madrid so many times they could reel off by heart the names of all the towns and villages along the way, shed tears. They considered themselves, if not exactly parents, at least midwives of the event. Their efforts, in fact, had been poorly rewarded: the central government gave not enough to save the Barcelona City Council from ruin yet enough so that the Catalans could not take all the credit for the fair themselves.

Another peal of bells marked the end of the ceremony, and work was immediately resumed. It was March 1, 1888; there was one month and seven days to go before the official opening.

The diversification of and increase in Onofre Bouvila's commercial activity—particularly after the discovery by the boy thieves of an exhibit called "Betel, Peruvian Bark, Hashish, and Other Plants Chewed or Smoked" intended for the Pavilion of Agriculture (situated, like the Palace of Fine Arts, outside the park, by the north wall between Calle Roger de Flor and Calle Sicilia, on the main road to San Martín and France), items which fetched a very good price through a fence who was a master stucco plasterer—worried Pablo, to whom it was becoming increasingly clear that his ward, for all his outward tokens of respect toward his mentor, was taking him for a ride. Pablo did not know what to do. He was aware of Onofre's prestige among the workers at the fair, and did not have the courage to reveal to his comrades the awkward position in which his own weakness had placed him. His only contact with the outside world was Onofre; he learned only what Onofre saw fit to tell him. He was a puppet in Onofre's hands.

Since Pablo had often said that the first thing to be swept away in Catalonia was the Liceo Opera House, Onofre went to see for himself what this so-very-important institution was. "The Liceo is a symbol, like the king in Madrid or the pope in Rome," Pablo had told him. "Thank God we have no king or pope in

Catalonia, but we have the Liceo." Onofre paid what seemed to him an outrageous price and was then directed to a door in a side alley strewn with cabbage stems. The wealthy entered by the portico on the Ramblas, alighting from their carriages there. The women's dresses were so long that even after they disappeared from sight through the glass door, their trains would still be flowing from the carriages, as if some giant reptile were coming to the opera.

Onofre, climbing an endless flight of stairs, eventually arrived, puffing, at a level where the only seating was a long iron bench already occupied by music lovers who had spent whole days there, sleeping flopped over the parapet like carpets put out to air, eating crusts of bread with garlic, and drinking wine from leather wineskins. The place crawled with lice. Its occupants were armed with stumps of candles, by which light they followed the score and libretto. Some had lost their sight and their health there in the Liceo.

The rest of the opera house was very different. Its splendor was dazzling. The silks, muslins, velvets, capes covered with sequins, jewels, incessant popping of champagne corks, valets coming and going, and the continual murmur rich people generate when gathered in strength, all delighted Onofre. "That's how I want to be," he said to himself, "even if it means putting up with this insipid music that seems to be going on forever." He was unlucky enough to have attended a performance of *Trifon and Cascanti,* a mythological opera staged only once in the Liceo and very rarely elsewhere in the world.

At breakfast, Delfina approached him. Even her ugliness could not hide the ravages of sleepless nights. She asked him if by any chance he had seen Beelzebub. "He's been missing for days," she said, very upset.

"No great loss," Onofre replied.

Efrén Castells was waiting for him at the fairgrounds gate.

"There's trouble," said the giant. "The last few days, I've noticed a pair of characters who seem to be watching you. At first I thought they were just curious, but they're too persistent for that. I know for a fact they don't work here. They've been asking questions."

"Policemen," said Onofre.

"I don't think so," said Efrén. "The style isn't right."

"What, then?" asked Onofre.

"I have no idea, but I don't like the look of it. Maybe it wouldn't be a bad idea for us to take a little holiday. Things are just about sewn up here anyway."

It was true. Onofre's gaze ran over the colossal project he had seen grow almost from its birth. When he first set foot in the park a year ago, the site was like a battleground. Now it looked like a setting for a fairy tale. When the World's Fair technical board submitted its first project to the mayor, the mayor tore it to shreds with his own hands. "You bring me plans for a glorified junk sale," he exclaimed, "when what I want is a grand pageant." Now two and a half years had passed, and the mayor's vision, though certain concessions had been made in the cold light of day, was amply realized.

Onofre and the giant from Calella sat on blocks of limestone opposite a hut constructed from lengths of liana by the Philippine Tobacco Association. A half-naked native squatted in its doorway, shivering, and rolled cigars. He had been brought over from Batangas specifically for that purpose, and had been told not to budge an inch from the spot until the event was over. He was also taught to say *au revoir* to the visitors. Whenever the sky grew dark, he would look anxiously upward, as if expecting some whirlwind to pick him and his hut up and send them spinning like tops back to Batangas.

"All this," Onofre reflected, "is useless, meaningless. And for us it's the same story: our dreams, our labors all come to nothing."

"Don't take it so much to heart, boy," answered Efrén. "You're smart, you'll find some meaning in it all."

Onofre entered the fortune-teller's room without knocking. The dying woman was laid out on the bed, eyes closed, the blankets up to her chin. He saw how old she was in the light of the candle that flickered in an oil bottle attached to the headboard. He turned to go.

"Onofre, is that you?" asked the fortune-teller.

"Go back to sleep, Micaela," he said. "I only came to see if you needed anything."

"I don't need anything, my son, but you do," murmured the seer. "You are confused, you are lost."

"How do you know?" asked Onofre, taken aback—the old lady had not even opened her eyes.

"Nobody comes to me who is not lost, my son. One doesn't need to be a seer to see that. What is bothering you?"

"Micaela, tell me my future."

"Ah, my son, my powers are greatly diminished. I am no longer of this world. What time is it?" asked the fortune-teller.

"Half past one," he answered.

"I have little time left," she said. "At four-twenty I die. They have told me already. They are waiting for me, you know. I shall soon join them. I spent all my life listening to their voices, and now my own will join their chorus, and someone of this world will listen to me. We spirits have our cycles, too. I am taking the place of a weary spirit, and he will at last be able to rest in the peace of the Lord. Oh, I know Father Bizancio says it's the devil that awaits me. That is not true. Father Bizancio is a good man, but very ignorant. Give me my cards and let us waste no more time. You'll find them in the little cupboard, the third shelf."

Onofre did as the old lady bade him. The cupboard contained some crumpled black clothing, various odds and ends, and a box of rice paper tied up with silk ribbon. On the third shelf he saw an old prayer book, a rosary with white beads, and a wrist garland of herbs in an advanced state of decomposition. There was also a pack of playing cards. He took these and gave them to the seer, whose eyes were now open.

"Draw up your chair, my son, and sit beside me," she said. "But first help me sit up. . . . That's right, thank you. One must do things properly, for appearances' sake." She smoothed the bedspread and put nine cards facedown in a circle. "The circle of knowledge," she said, "also known as Solomon's Mirror. This is the center of the heavens, and here are the four constellations with their elements." She held her hand in the air, index finger extended, then brought it down on a card. "The house of dispositions," she said, turning it over, "or Oriental angle. You shall live many years and be rich. You shall marry a beautiful woman and have three children. You shall travel and enjoy good health."

"That's fine, Micaela," said Onofre, getting up. "Don't tire yourself any more. That's all I wanted to know."

"Wait, Onofre. What I have just told you was all humbug. Do not go. Now I see an abandoned mausoleum, by moonlight. That signifies fortune and death. A king. Kings signify death, too, but also power—such is their nature. Now I see blood. Blood signifies money, and also blood. And now what do I see? Three women. Onofre, bring your chair closer."

"I am here, Micaela."

"Listen carefully, my son. One of them is in the house of upsets, misadventures, and sufferings. She will make you rich. The second is in the house of heritage, which is also the house of children. She will make you powerful. The third and last is in the house of love and science. She will make you happy. In the fourth house there is a man. Beware of him—he is in the house of poison and the tragic end."

"I don't understand a word you're saying, Micaela."

"Ah, my son, oracles are always this way: true but unclear.

If they were clear, do you think I would be dying in this grubby boardinghouse? Just listen and remember. When what I have foretold comes to pass, you will recognize it right away. That is not much help, I know. But let us return to the cards. I see three women."

"You already said that."

"I have not finished. One will make you rich, one powerful, and one happy. She that makes you happy will make you miserable; she that makes you powerful will make you her slave; and she that makes you rich will curse you. Of the three, this last is the most dangerous, for she is a saint. God will hear her curse and, to punish you, create a man. He is the man of whom the cards speak, a man without luck. He does not know that God has put him in the world to carry out His vengeance."

"How will I recognize him?" asked Onofre.

"I do not know. One always recognizes these things. In any event, whether you recognize him or not will change nothing. It is already written that it will be he who destroys you. It is useless to stand up to him. His weapons and yours are different. Both of you will be devoured by the dragon. But fear not. Although dragons make a dreadful commotion, there is nothing behind their roaring and flames. Fear the goat, symbol of treachery. But do not make me toil any more, for I am very tired."

The cards slipped off the bedspread to the floor. The fortune-teller let her head drop back on the pillow and closed her eyes. Onofre, thinking she was dead, took the candle and brought it to the old woman's mouth. The flame moved—she still breathed. He gathered the cards from the floor and put them back in the cupboard, but shuffled them carefully first, so no one else would know his future. Then he tiptoed out and went back to his own room, where he lay in bed thinking, trying to make sense of what he had just heard.

Delfina still went to the market every day. Seeing her without her cat, the saleswomen vented the wrath that had been bottled up over years of terrorization: some refused to serve her; they called her names or wouldn't speak to her at all; others short-changed her and laughed in her face if she protested. Once, a rotten egg was thrown at her back. She made no attempt to wipe it off her dress. As for Sisinio, Onofre never saw him again, and had the impression that the painter and the maid parted company after the night of Beelzebub's death.

Micaela Castro died the same afternoon she read Onofre's future in the cards. Father Bizancio went into her room and, finding her dead, closed her eyelids and snuffed the candle. She was buried the following day, with prayers for the dead said in the San Ezequiel parish church. According to the papers found in her cupboard, she was not Micaela Castro but Pastora López Marrero. She was sixty-four years old when she died. There was no way of tracing any relatives, and no reason to, because there was no inheritance. Delfina changed the sheets on the bed, and the room was taken that same day by a young philosophy student.

Near one of the gates to the park from Paseo de la Aduana stood a pavilion tiled inside and out and called Pabellón de Aguas Azoadas, or Pavilion of Nitrogenated Waters. It was ready by the end of January but still empty by the middle of March. Onofre Bouvila and Efrén Castells, having obtained a key, kept their booty there. The boy thieves had hauled in a consignment of timepieces the day before. Now, Onofre and Efrén were at a loss what to do with all these watches and clocks. There were pocket watches, clocks for towers and public buildings, repeater watches, watches with second hands, navy chronometers, pendulums, astral watches, chronometers for astronomical and scientific observations, clepsydras, hour glasses, regulators, clocks that showed the solar and lunar cycles, electric clocks, clocks for gnomonic applications, equinoctial, polar, horizontal, azimuthal, right ascension, and declination clocks, meridian and septentrional watches, pedometers, and various counting devices and apparatuses to mark, register, pinpoint certain natural phenomena, and there were all kind and manner of parts. Thus read the catalogue. "Unless we get rid of these clocks," said the giant, "we'll be driven out of our minds by the tick-tocking and the chiming."

5

One of the last-minute preparations for the opening of the World's Fair made by the city authorities was to weed out all Barcelona's undesirables. "For some time now our officials have been singularly active in their efforts to rid us of the plague of loafers, ruffians, and miscreants who, finding insufficient scope for their criminal deeds in smaller communities, seek refuge in the turmoil of populous cities; and while our officials have not as yet extirpated completely these social cancers that continue to gnaw at the foundations of this refined capital, they have indeed made appreciable progress in this most onerous task," says a newspaper of the time. There were now police raids every night.

"The group is being temporarily dissolved," said Pablo.

Onofre asked him what he would do now.

"Rest assured, we will resume the offensive with redoubled vigor," the apostle said, though with little conviction.

"And the pamphlets?" asked Onofre.

The apostle's mouth twisted disdainfully. "We're finished with pamphlets."

What would happen, then, to his weekly payments, Onofre wanted to know. "You'll have to do without them," answered Pablo, a hint of satisfaction in his voice. "Occasionally circumstances oblige us to make certain economies. Anyway, this is a political cause: it is not our job to guarantee people an income."

Onofre started to ask something else but was cut short by an imperious gesture of dismissal. He turned to leave.

"Wait," Pablo said, "we may never see each other again. The struggle will be a long one." This was spoken hurriedly. Obviously it was not what he wanted to say. There was something else on his mind, but he felt too timid or embarrassed to talk about it. So he clung to his well-tried rhetoric. "In fact, the struggle will never be over. The socialists, fools that they are, think the revolution will solve everything. They think that man's exploitation of man, once society frees itself from its present rulers, will cease. But we know that the strong will always exploit the weak. This struggle is the inevitable destiny of human beings." His speech over, he embraced Onofre. "We may never see each other again," he said in a voice choked with emotion. "Good-bye, farewell."

In one of these police raids, Señor Braulio was hauled in. He had gone out all frilled up to be thrashed by young toughs. That night, for a change, it was the police who did the honors. They then demanded bail before releasing him. "Anything at all," he said, "as long as my poor wife, who is ill, and my daughter, who is still very young, never hear of this." Since he had no money on him, he sent a boy off to the boardinghouse with a message for Mariano the barber, asking him for the sum set by the magistrate. "Tell him I will repay him as soon as I can," he said. But Mariano claimed that he did not have the money. The messenger ran back to the police station and reported the barber's refusal to Señor Braulio, who, seeing that scandal was unavoidable, took advantage of a momentary lapse of vigilance on the part of the police to drive into his heart the long shell back-comb he wore in his wig.

The stays of his corset deflected the comb, leaving him with only a few cuts, which nevertheless bled profusely. His skirt and petticoat were ruined, and there were puddles of blood on the police-station floor. The police took the comb from him and kicked him several times in the kidneys and groin. "Let's see if that knocks any sense into you, you old whore."

Señor Braulio sent the messenger back to the boarding-house. "There's a young fellow there by the name of Bouvila, Onofre Bouvila," he told the boy, stretched out on a narrow bench, aching and soaked in blood. "Be discreet. I don't think he has a penny to his name, but he will know what to do to help me out."

Onofre, receiving the message, concluded that fortune was smiling on him. "Tell Señor Braulio that before dawn I myself will come to the police station with the money," he said to the boy. "And tell him not to get impatient or try any more crazy tricks tonight."

When the boy left, Onofre went upstairs and knocked on Delfina's door. "Why should I open the door to you?" came the surly reply when he identified himself.

Onofre could not help smiling. "You had better open up, Delfina," he said gently. "Your father is in trouble. The police have him locked up, and he already tried to kill himself."

The door opened and Delfina appeared, wearing the same shabby nightshirt he had seen on her twice before: once, when she came to his room to offer him work, and again, when he went up and told her that Sisinio had fallen off the roof.

Señora Agata's complaining voice came from the adjoining room. "Delfina, the washbasin."

"Don't stand there in my way," Delfina said to Onofre. "I have to take Mama her water."

Onofre did not budge. He saw fear in the maid's eyes, and that gave him the courage he needed. "Let her wait," he said, baring his teeth. "You and I have more important things to attend to."

Delfina bit her lower lip and finally said, "I don't understand."

"Didn't I tell you? Your father is in danger. What's the matter with you, have you gone crazy?"

Delfina blinked. "Ah, yes, my father," she murmured. "What can I do for him?"

"Nothing," said Onofre, angry. "I'm the only one who can help him now. His life depends on me."

Delfina paled and lowered her eyes. The San Ezequiel clock

chimed several times. "If you can help him, why don't you? What are you waiting for? What do you want from me?"

The sick woman's plaintive voice still came from the next room. "Delfina, what's going on? Why aren't you coming? Who are you talking to?"

Delfina made a move to go, but Onofre took hold of her shoulders and pulled her toward him, more in anger than passion. Through the stiff cloth of her nightshirt he could feel her angular body.

"Let me go," she pleaded. "I cannot keep my mother waiting. She may have an attack if I don't go to her."

Onofre was adamant. "You know what you have to do if you want to see your father again," he said, shoving her back into her room and kicking the door shut behind him as he fumbled with the buttons of her nightshirt.

"Onofre, for God's sake," she said.

He gave a low laugh. "You don't have the cat to defend you now: Beelzebub is dead, he fell off the roof and smashed his brains on the street. I shoved the body down the sewer myself. Damn!" he exclaimed, unable to unbutton the nightshirt because of his lack of experience with female garments and his excitement.

Seeing his predicament, Delfina dropped backward onto the bed and pulled her nightshirt up to her hips. "Come on, then," she said.

The San Ezequiel clock struck four. "The sun will be up soon now," Onofre said. "I promised Señor Braulio I would be at the police station with the money before dawn, and I'll keep my word. Business is business." Delfina looked at him with an enigmatic expression. "I don't know why you plotted and planned like this," she murmured, as if to herself. "I'm not worth all that trouble."

In the diffuse light of dawn her body, as she lay on the

rumpled sheets, looked wan, almost gray. "She's skinny," thought Onofre, mentally comparing it with the bodies of the workers' wives he had seen seeking relief from the summer heat by frolicking in the waves, most of their clothing left behind on the beach. "How different she looks now," he thought. Then he said, "Cover yourself." She did so with the edge of the sheet. Her wiry, tangled hair made a kind of nimbus around her face. "Do you have to go so soon?" she asked. He said nothing, dressing as quickly as he could. Señora Agata had stopped calling, and silence reigned in the bedroom. Onofre headed for the door, but Delfina's voice brought him to a halt.

"Wait, don't go yet. Don't leave like that. What happens now?" She waited for Onofre's reply, but he did not understand the question. She covered her face with her left hand. "What do I tell Sisinio?" she asked.

Onofre laughed. "No need to worry about him. He has a wife and children, he was fooling you all along. If you have any hopes set on that rascal, you're making a big mistake."

Delfina's eyes were fixed on Onofre. "One day I'll tell you something," she murmured. "But now, go."

Onofre went down two flights, waited for Father Bizancio to go to the bathroom, and took the required sum from the priest's mattress. With it he secured Señor Braulio's release from the police station and took him back to the boardinghouse by hackney carriage, for Señor Braulio was weak from having lost so much blood. Delfina received them clutching her stomach. She had been vomiting. Afraid of becoming pregnant by Onofre, she had had recourse to homemade remedies and seemed deathly ill.

"My dear girl!" exclaimed Señor Braulio. "What happened to you?"

"And you, Father, dressed like that—and covered with blood!"

"With blood and with opprobrium, Delfina, my dearest, as you can see. But what have you been doing?" asked the owner of the boardinghouse.

"The same thing, Father. The same as you," Delfina answered.

"Whatever happens, your poor mother must not know of this," he said.

When they went in to see her, Señora Agata had grown worse. Father Bizancio, hearing the lamentations and sobbing that came from the top floor, went up in his nightshirt to see if his services were required, and Señor Braulio had to hide in the closet so the priest would not see him dressed as he was. Onofre sent Father Bizancio away to fetch the doctor. When the priest left, Delfina took Onofre aside.

"Leave this boardinghouse and don't come back," she whispered. "Don't stop even to pick up your things. I will say no more. You've been warned."

Realizing that this warning was not made idly, Onofre fled.

The sky was red and the birds were chirping as the workers went to work, carrying their small children in their arms to allow them to sleep a little longer, until they reached the factory gates. There the children were wakened, and adults and children went their separate ways: the adults to the dangerous and more difficult jobs, the children to those that were safer and easier.

At Citadel Park Onofre saw the cables of the chained balloon above the trees. The engineers were making sure that everything was in perfect working order and firmly tied down: it would not do to have the balloon break free, with the World's Fair in full swing below, and carry off its basketload of terrified tourists at the mercy of the winds. (The "tourist," his needs and comfort, that was the chief concern during those last days. The newspapers spoke of nothing else. "Each and every visitor," they wrote, "upon his return to his own country, will be the apostle of all that he has seen and heard.") The balloon worked splendidly, but whenever that wicked wind they call the *vent de garbi* was blowing, it would get into mischief, turn upside down.

One entered the park through the Arco de Triunfo. This

arch, which can still be admired today, is of bare brick, and Mudejar in style; it has on it the coats of arms of every province of
Spain, with the province of Barcelona on the keystone. There are
two friezes as well, one on either side: of Spain participating in
the Barcelona World's Fair, and Barcelona expressing gratitude
to the foreign nations present.

The Arco de Triunfo led to the Salón de San Juan, a remarkably wide avenue with trees, mosaic paving, large lamps,
and eight bronze statues to welcome the visitor. In the Salón de
San Juan stood the Palace of Justice, which is still there, and the
palaces of Fine Arts, Agriculture, and Science, which are not.
Two pillars marked the entrance to the park itself. On top of
each pillar was a stone sculpture, one representing Commerce,
the other Industry, as if saying: We deliver. The central government, given to postures of a more spiritual nature, did not ap-
prove of this, and perhaps for that reason, too, did not contribute
more in the way of material aid to the effort. Both pillars can
still be seen.

"Why is it that Efrén, who is so unpolished, gets women
with no effort, while I, with all my cleverness, have to go to such
trouble?" Onofre asked himself. He never found a satisfactory
answer to this question. Unable to locate Efrén that morning,
though he made the rounds of their agreed meeting places, he
ended up walking down to the beach. A brigade of workmen
were raking the sand to efface the last traces of the encampment
that had been there over two years. A section of the beach now
housed several pavilions: the Marine Construction pavilion and
the Transatlantic Association pavilion, both maritime concerns,
and a pavilion to exhibit stud horses, whose neighing could be
heard between the crashing of the waves. There was a pier with
a luxury restaurant. The sun sparkled on the water, blinding
Onofre. Where were the women and children who used to live
here? he wondered. A spring breeze was blowing, heavy and
warm.

That night he returned to the boardinghouse. The lobby was deserted. The dining room, too.

Mariano the barber popped his head out. "What are you doing here? You frightened me."

"What happened, Mariano?" Onofre asked. "Where is everybody?"

The barber could hardly speak. He was extremely pale, as if he had dusted himself with flour.

"The Civil Guard came and took Señor Braulio, Señora Agata, and Delfina," he said. "They had to cart the three of them off on stretchers. Señora Agata, because she was in a bad way—at death's door, I'd say. Señor Braulio and his daughter, because they were bleeding and bleeding. It's dark, so you don't see it, but the hallway's filled with blood, from the pair of them, father and daughter. I don't know whether they took them to prison, to the hospital, or straight to the cemetery. A sickening sight, and I've seen a thing or two in my trade, believe me. What, you ask why they took them away? Blessed if I know. They didn't give me an explanation, as you can imagine. But I have heard rumors. The girl, that poor excuse for a scarecrow, belonged to a gang of thugs—you know, the ones they call anarchists. I'm not saying it's true, mind you, it's only what people say. And it seems she carried on with a fellow in the gang, a painter, and they nabbed him, too."

"And did they ask about me, Mariano?"

"Yes, now that you mention it, they did. They searched all the rooms, and yours more than any. They asked us what time you usually showed up. I said after dark. But Father Bizancio said you didn't live here any more, that you left the place days ago, and with his priest's gear and all that, they swallowed his lie and ignored the truth I told them. That's why they didn't leave a guard here."

Onofre made a quick exit. "It must have been Delfina who went to the police," he thought. To get her revenge on Sisinio

and himself, she had betrayed the entire organization. Now Sisinio was in prison; Pablo, too; even she was there. "But at the last
minute she chose to save me, even though I was really the cause
of all this upheaval." He would have to disappear from Barcelona, he concluded. In time the dust would settle; the anarchists
would be released, if they weren't executed; and he would resume his business, assemble the boy thieves again, and perhaps
even convince the anarchists that it was better to devote themselves to making money, that the revolution they dreamed of was
not practical.

But for now he had to make a run for it. First, however, he
would recover the money that was still in the boardinghouse, in
Father Bizancio's mattress. Going back was risky: Mariano probably had reported Onofre's appearance at the boardinghouse as
soon as he was out the door. But it was out of the question to
leave the money. Luckily Onofre knew how to go about it. He
found a ladder at the World's Fair and carried it to the boardinghouse. Though he had to cross half Barcelona with the ladder
on his shoulder, nobody took any notice, and since it was now
dark, he propped the ladder against the windowless back wall of
the building, as Sisinio had indicated, and went up onto the roof.
He knew where the trapdoor was, having used it before when
he greased the roof. The top floor was empty, its former occupants all in prison. If any police were keeping watch, they would
be downstairs, in the hall, expecting him to come in that way.

In the darkness Onofre went down a floor and pushed open
Father Bizancio's door. Hearing the old priest breathing in his
sleep, he slipped under the bed and waited. When the clock of
La Presentación's parish church struck three, the priest got up
and left the room. He would be gone only two minutes. Onofre,
feeling inside the mattress, discovered that the money had vanished. He felt again, groping in the straw. No, the money was no
longer there.

He heard Father Bizancio coming back from the bathroom.

His first impulse was to fly at the priest's throat and throttle him until he learned what had become of the money, but he checked himself. If the police were there and heard the noise, they would come up in no time, pistols drawn. There was nothing for it but to wait. Onofre had to spend an asphyxiating hour under the bed before the priest went back to the bathroom. Then he dragged his numbed body out, slipped into the corridor, and tiptoed up the stairs, onto the roof, and down the ladder to the street.

At daybreak Onofre saw Father Bizancio going to church. Making sure that no one was following the priest, he stepped out and accosted him.

"Onofre, my son!" exclaimed Father Bizancio. "I thought I'd never see you again." His eyes moistened with emotion. "You know what terrible things have been happening. Why, I was just now on my way to say Mass for poor Señora Agata, her need being greatest. Later on I will say Masses for Señor Braulio and Delfina."

"That's fine, Father, but tell me where my money is."

"What money, my son?"

Nothing indicated that the old man was lying. "Perhaps Delfina took the money and hid it elsewhere before she went to the police," thought Onofre. "Or else the police stumbled on it during their search. It's even possible that Father Bizancio found the money by chance and gave it to some charity without realizing what he was doing. After all, how could he have known that the money was mine? Ah, why didn't I spend it as I went along, like Efrén Castells?"

On his way to the World's Fair, to see if he could save at least part of the boys' loot, Onofre had to stop and wait for a colorful procession to pass: bulls were being led from the station to the ring, where they would meet their deaths at the hands of the acclaimed *toreros* of the day: Frascuelo, Guerrita, Lagartijo, Mazantini, Espartero, and Cara-Ancha. The beasts tossed their heads, butted at onlookers, and stopped to study with myopic stares the base of some streetlamp. As the bulls went by, an occasional joker would undo his neckerchief and parody a few *torero* passes.

At Citadel Park, Onofre went to the pavilion where they were keeping the timepieces and found it empty. "This is the end," he thought. On his way out, two men came up behind him and grabbed his arms. One of the men was extraordinarily handsome. Realizing that it was pointless to put up any resistance, Onofre let himself be led away.

Leaving the fairgrounds, he looked back over his shoulder. The outside walls of the pavilions had been finished overnight and sparkled in the sun. Through the swaying branches of trees, kiosks and statues, awnings and parasols, and the arabesque domes of stalls and booths could be seen. In the Plaza de Armas, opposite the former Arsenal, English engineers were testing the magic fountain. Even his kidnappers were momentarily impressed. The columns and arches of water changed in shape, in color, all done by electricity. "Life ought to be like that all the time," thought Onofre as he was led away, possibly to his death. "And Efrén? All the pesetas he cost me, and now that I need him, where is he?" He had no way of knowing that Efrén was following faithfully, at a distance, crouching in readiness.

"Into the carriage," they told him when they came to a berline. The lace curtains were drawn and the occupant inside, if there was any, could not be seen. Up on the coachman's seat was an elderly man with no uniform, smoking a pipe.

"I'm not getting in there," said Onofre.

One of the kidnappers opened the carriage door, and the other shoved him in. Only one man was sitting inside. He looked about fifty, but could have been younger; fat in the stomach and chin but narrow across the shoulders and cheekbones, he had a high, flat forehead topped by a thick mop of hair that was gray at the temples and cut evenly like a lawn. The man was carefully shaved from one earlobe to the other but sported a bushy twirledup mustache somewhat in the manner of the *maréchaux* of France. This was Don Humbert Figa i Morera, for whom Onofre was to work for many years.

In those days a monarch's retinue was numerous—for a variety of reasons, some practical, some symbolic. For instance, since the king was the counterpart of God on earth, it was not fitting for him to do anything for himself, not even lift a spoon to his lips. Also, the monarchs of Spain had never, from time immemorial, dismissed any person who served them, even if only momentarily, thus to any service rendered to the royal house was attached a lifetime tenure. Some monarchs, advanced in years, had gone off to war taking with them, besides seneschal, butler, and chamberlain, their aged wet nurses, dry nurses, and nurse-maids—for if the king stooped to say, "I no longer have need of this," that would imply the making of economies, and admit, moreover, that upon at least one occasion he had had need of something. Thus a maze, a throng formed around his person, making communication difficult between him and his generals in time of war, and between him and his ministers in time of peace.

H.R.H. Don Alfonso XIII (R.I.P.) was two and a half years old in 1888 when he arrived in Barcelona with his mother, Doña María Cristina, the queen regent, and his sisters and entourage. The city was paralyzed. The former residence of the governor of the Citadel and the building called El Arsenal were prepared to receive the royal family (those buildings offering an additional advantage in that, since they were already inside the fairgrounds, the royal family would be spared the bother of paying one peseta at the gate, or twenty-five pesetas for a season ticket), but the camerlengos and purveyors, huntsmen and equerries, houndmasters and taskmasters, ceremonial crossbowmen, pantrymen, chandlers, upholsterers, almsmen, ladies-in-waiting, stewardesses, and maids all had to be lodged, too.

The arrival of sovereigns, nobles, and dignitaries from other countries complicated matters further. There were anecdotes to suit all tastes, such as the case of the Saxon burgrave who had to share a bed for the night with "an artist newly arrived from Paris," as the Equestrian Circus poster put it. Then there was the con man who, passing himself off as the great mogul, wined and dined gratis in several inns and cafés.

People everywhere in Barcelona were hospitable to the visitors, even when it meant putting up with considerable trouble and inconvenience—for which they received no thanks, as is usually the case under such circumstances. Generally the visitors assumed a haughty air, fussed at the least thing, and remarked as they toured, "How disgusting, what a place, what inane people," etc. They believed that to show disdain was to show good breeding.

The World's Fair was inaugurated, as scheduled, on April 8. At three-thirty in the afternoon, H.R.H. the king and his retinue entered the Salón de Fiestas of the Palace of Fine Arts. The king took his place on the throne, resting his feet, which did not reach the ground, on a pile of cushions. At his side sat the princess of Asturias, Doña María de las Mercedes, and the infanta, Doña María Teresa. Beside the queen regent was the Duchess of Edinburgh. Then came, in this order, the Duke of Genoa, the Duke of Edinburgh, Prince Rupprecht of Bavaria, and Prince George of Wales. Behind them were the prime minister, Don Práxedes Mates Sagasta, and the ministers of war, development, and the navy, the royal gentlemen-in-waiting, such grandees of Spain as had accepted the invitation (flanked by their halberdiers, as was their privilege, and barefoot, if they chose to exercise that prerogative), local authorities in tailcoats, the diplomatic and consular corps, special envoys, generals, admirals, fleet commanders, the World's Fair board of directors, and innumerable public figures. Dotted here and there in the human mass around the venue were lackeys in short page-style trousers, charged with bearing the emblems of highborn visitors: the key, brass chain, coronet, whip, antler, talon, crossbow, or bell.

Five thousand people were present at this event. When the speeches were over, the tutors led out the royal children. The adults visited a few pavilions, beginning with the Austrian Pavilion, since H.R.H. the queen was Austrian by birth. In the French Pavilion a piece by Chopin was performed, and in the Governor's Palace refreshments—referred to as "lunch," in English—were served. When the Queen finished her "lunch," the last of those attending the inauguration were still filing into the Austrian Pavilion. At night there was a gala performance in the Liceo, at which the queen wore her coronet. The opera was *Lohengrin*. As late as the second act, some guests were still eating their "lunch."

All in all, the inaugural ceremony was solemn and well staged. The World's Fair site itself was in keeping with the distinction of those visiting it that day, though some buildings were not finished and some, long finished, were already in a state of disrepair. The press spoke of "enormous cracks" and "great confusion," but most people were pleased.

When viewed today, the exhibition centers, with their austere design, flowery carved-wood crowns, crepes, and canopies, have something of the burial chamber about them, but they conformed to what must have been the taste of the time, the conception then of elegance. Judgments should always be passed from the proper perspective. Seventy-eight warships had arrived in the port from different countries, complete with nineteen thousand men and 538 cannons. Whereas this might well be viewed as threatening nowadays, it was interpreted by the people of Barcelona as a gesture of courtesy and friendship. The Great War had not yet taken place, and weapons still had a decorative value. This sentiment is expressed by Melchor de Palau in his "Hymn on the Opening of the World's Fair," one line of which reads: "The dread cannon thunders but does not wound."

The World's Fair remained open until December 9, 1888. The closing was a simpler affair than the inauguration: a Te Deum in the cathedral and a short ceremony in the Palace of

Industry. It had lasted 245 days and had been visited by over two million people. Building costs totaled 5,624,657 pesetas and 56 centimos. Some of the buildings could be used for other purposes, but the debt incurred was enormous and weighed on the Barcelona City Council for many years thereafter. The memory of the days of splendor also lingered on, along with the notion that Barcelona, if it so wished, could again become a cosmopolitan city.

CHAPTER THREE

1

Not a great deal is known about Don Humbert Figa i Morera. He was born in Barcelona, and his parents had a modest dried-fruit-and-nuts shop in the Raval district. His schooling was provided by a group of missionary monks, whom political vicissitudes in remote lands had driven temporarily ashore in Barcelona. Then he studied law. He married late, at the age of thirty-two, and by forty was at the head of one of Barcelona's biggest legal practices. Its reputation was not, however, a good one, as we will now see.

Although by the middle of the nineteenth century no sane person disputed the equality of all before the law, things were quite different in practice. Citizens of quality, the upper crust, had the benefit of a degree of protection denied the rougher sort, who did not know their rights or, if they knew them, did not know how to exercise them—and it is doubtful whether the judiciary would have recognized those rights, anyway.

Not that the judges despised justice, but they applied it in their own way, expeditiously. They were not going to stand for any nonsense: one good look at the accused, and they knew what to make of him. If a gentleman of means and high birth committed a crime, they said, "He must have had some overpowering reason to behave as he did," and became very sympathetic. But if the author of the crime was a ruffian, they did not indulge in idle speculation about motives. Not only did his nature, passed on from father to son, incline him to mischief, they thought, but also such inclinations had not been checked by the dictates of religion, civic conscience, or formal education. In this they were in agreement with the sociologists. If the accused pleaded extenuating circumstances, they laughed. "The accused may extenuate to his heart's content. Off to prison with him." In prisons the attempts made to rehabilitate the prisoners yielded results that were often disappointing.

Faced with this state of affairs, Don Humbert Figa i Morera, who came from a humble background, adopted a different, more practical approach. "The problem for poor people that break the law," he said, "is that they lack a good lawyer to get them out of hot water." It was true: no lawyer worth the name would put his talents at the service of the less fortunate. Lawyers all wanted to serve men of position, with famous names. But since there were few of these, few lawyers earned a good living. "The poor," Don Humbert Figa i Morera said to himself, "are a vast reserve still untapped. The problem is how to tap it."

He began to frequent the destitute, to offer them his assistance. He had special cards printed that were easier to read than the ones with Gothic lettering current then. "If you get into trouble, remember me," he would say to the down-and-outs, handing them his card. Later on, when they did find themselves in trouble, a few of them remembered him and rooted out his card. "No harm in giving it a try," they thought. "If I end up in prison, as I probably will, I just won't pay him, that's all." The most hopeless cases were entrusted to him, and he took them on, treating his clients with every regard, never sneering or condescending in his manner, and worked with a will at every case.

At first the judges and prosecutors, believing that he was acting out of altruism, did their best to show him the error of his ways. "Do not waste your time, learned colleague," they would say. "These people have no good in them, they are made for crime, made for prison." He heard them out respectfully, but paid them no heed. He secretly agreed with what they were saying and was only interested in his fees.

He won most of his cases, against all the odds. No one was better versed than he in the ins and outs of procedure, and he always had a card up his sleeve. Though sputtering with indignation, the judges and magistrates had to admit that he was in the right, and prosecutors hurled their books and gowns to the floor with tears in their eyes. "Things cannot go on like this," they said. "We're being made to turn the law upside down." It was true: the law, abundant in dodges and loopholes, could be turned to the advantage of the dregs of society also—a possibility that had not been contemplated by its makers. A note of perplexity could be heard in the verdicts passed: "It seems we must dismiss the charges, and if we must, we do," etc. Nor could the criminals let off the hook get over their surprise. They would ask him in an awed voice, "Why do you help us?"—as if in the presence of a saint. "For money," he would reply, "for you to pay me my fees." With the unswerving sense of ethics that is so characteristic of them, the criminals paid him in cash, in full, and thus he grew rich.

One winter's night, he received an odd visit. His offices were on Calle San Pedro; besides himself, he had two clerks, a secretary, and a general assistant working there, and he was considering taking on more clerks. That night everyone had left except the assistant and the lawyer, who was putting the finishing touches to a case due to be heard the following morning. There was a knock on the porch door. "Curious," he thought, "at this time of night. Who could it be?" He told the assistant to go down and open up, but first to make sure that the callers, whoever they were, were men of good will. That was no easy order, since only sinister-looking types ever knocked at the door, but this time there was no problem: waiting in the street were three gentlemen of distinguished appearance, and one outlandish but not otherwise alarming character. The three gentlemen wore masks, which was not out of the ordinary in Barcelona at that time.

"Are you men of good will?" asked the assistant. The visitors said they were and entered, brushing aside the assistant with the pommels of their canes, which concealed stilettos. The three men in masks sat down around the long table in the office; the fourth character remained standing. Don Humbert had no trouble recognizing him despite all the years that had passed: it was one of the missionaries who had been his teachers. Now the missionary had come back, possibly to ask a favor, which Don Humbert could hardly refuse him. The missionary's vocation, as he learned later, had taken him to Ethiopia and the Sudan, where he made a number of converts, but finally he was converted himself to the paganism he had been combating, and returned to Barcelona as a missionary for the dervishes, preaching sorcery. In his right hand he held a cane topped with a human skull. Whenever the skull moved, a noise of pebbles could be heard.

"To what do I owe the honor of your visit?" Don Humbert asked the enigmatic party.

"We have been following your work with great interest," one of the masks replied. "Now we have come to make you a proposition. We are men of business, whose conduct is beyond reproach. That is the reason we need your help."

"If it is in my power . . ."

"You will see that it is. We, as I have said, are established people, and value greatly our reputation. And you, sir, have acquired a reputation among the scum of society. In short, we desire you to act as an intermediary on our behalf in the performance of a distasteful task. Expense, it need hardly be mentioned, is no obstacle."

"You are asking me to do something immoral," Don Humbert said.

At that point the apostate missionary intervened. Morality, he said, was of two kinds, individual and social. As regarded individual morality, there was nothing to worry about, since Don Humbert was not himself committing a reprehensible deed, but merely acting in his professional capacity. As for social morality, social morality meant social order, the smooth running of the cogs. "You, my son, have saved many a criminal from a richly deserved punishment. It is only just, then, that you now send others to the scaffold, thus restoring the balance." The masked men placed a great deal of money on the table.

Don Humbert accepted the assignment, and everything went like clockwork. Thereafter he was flooded with similar deals. Masked gentlemen—and not a few ladies—filed in and out of his offices every night, while the real criminals, having nothing to hide, came during normal hours, in broad daylight and un-masked.

"You wouldn't believe," he said to his wife, "how good business is."

He needed more and more staff: not only clerks and secre-taries, but also agents who could move freely in the underworld. He recruited these agents wherever he could, turning a blind eye to their past.

"I am told you are capable," he said to Onofre Bouvila in the carriage. "A smooth operator. You will work for me."

"What kind of work?" asked Onofre.

"Doing what I tell you," replied Don Humbert, "and not asking questions out of turn. The police are on to you. Without my protection you would be in prison now. This is your choice: you work for me, or you get twenty years."

Onofre worked for Don Humbert from 1888 to 1898, the year the last remaining Spanish colonies were lost.

First, he was put under the command of the handsome man who had kidnapped him in Citadel Park, one Odón Mostaza, originally from Zamora, twenty-two years old. They gave Onofre a knife, a truncheon, and a pair of knitted gloves. He was told not to use the truncheon without good cause, and the knife only as a last resort. In either case he was to put on the gloves first, so as not to leave fingerprints. "The main thing is that nobody should ever be able to identify you," Odón Mostaza told him, "because if they identify you, they may identify me, and if they identify me, they may identify the one who gives me my orders, and so on, like links in a chain, until they get to the boss, who is Don Humbert Figa i Morera."

In fact, everybody in Barcelona knew that Don Humbert had dealings with the underworld; it was an open secret. But since many prominent figures in the worlds of politics and commerce were involved in these goings-on, no one dared accuse him. Honest citizens kept their distance from Don Humbert, but in public treated him like a gentleman. Unaware of their true feelings, he believed he belonged to the city aristocracy and was a happy man. Odón Mostaza and the rest of the gang shared in this vanity. If they happened to be near Paseo de Gracia at midday, they would say to one another, "Let's go to Paseo de Gracia to watch Don Humbert pass by." Don Humbert appeared there every day without fail, mounted on a fine-looking Andalusian mare from Jerez. He would wave to other riders with his gloved hand, or greet the ladies, in their open carriages drawn by splendid teams, with his emerald-green velvet hat. Odón and the gang watched from a discreet distance so as not to cast a shadow on his prestige by betraying their association. "You should feel proud, boy," he said to Onofre, "to have the most elegant man in Barcelona for your boss—and the most powerful, too."

Most powerful was an exaggeration. Don Humbert Figa i Morera was a nobody. Even within his own field there was one more powerful than he: Don Alexandre Canals i Formiga. This gentleman was not seen mincing along Paseo de Gracia, even though he lived nearby; he had a three-story villa, built in the Mudejar style, on Calle Diputación, just a few yards from that renowned boulevard. His offices, in which he met his death, were in Calle Platería. His days were divided between his home and his offices, apart from an occasional visit to a merry-go-round set up not far from his house, where he took his little son, a slightly handicapped boy. Don Alexandre had had three other children, but they all died in the tragic outbreak of the plague in 1879.

At first Onofre was given only unimportant tasks, and he was not allowed to work on his own. He would go down to the port with Odón to supervise the unloading of some merchandise, or wait with him outside the door of some house, without knowing why, until somebody said, "All right, that'll do, you can go now." Then they had to make a full report to a character Odón called Margarito. Margarito's real name was Arnau Puncella. He had entered the service of Don Humbert many years before, one of the assistants the latter had employed in the early days of his practice, and had grown in his shadow, becoming one of his closest associates. By this time Margarito was in charge of all contacts with the criminal classes, all the shady operations. A short, slight man, he was none too healthy looking, with thick glasses, a jet-black toupee, and long fingernails that were less than immaculate. His clothes were shabby, with grease stains. He was married, and they said he had a lot of children, but no one knew how many, since he kept to himself and did not talk about his family. Shrewd, he soon noticed Onofre's extraordinary memory for dates, names, and numbers. ("In this line of business, brains are essential," he would tell his children, with whose education he took considerable trouble. "Just one error can mean catastrophe.") Then he began to see other qualities in the boy which frightened him.

Onofre was unaware that he had been singled out: he thought he was unobserved, not realizing that intelligence is just as difficult to conceal as the lack of it.

Odón Mostaza was known in every public haunt in and around Barcelona. Fun-loving and spendthrift as well as handsome, he was welcome everywhere he went. In Odón's company, Onofre, without meaning to, joined a circle of friends, something entirely new to him. He had moved to a boardinghouse slightly better than the one run by Señor Braulio and Señora Agata. There, since he had a regular income, he was treated like a prince. He would go out almost every night with Odón and his crowd, making the rounds of all the dives in Barcelona, where he found plenty of women willing to take his money in exchange for a moment of pleasure, a transaction he saw as mutually beneficial and convenient. From time to time he remembered Delfina. "How stupid I was," he would reflect. "All that effort and unnecessary trouble, and it's all so easy." He thought himself cured forever of the pangs of love.

When summer came, he went to the famous marquees, delighting in the chandeliers, carpets, garlands of paper flowers, the crowds, the perspiring bands, and the typical dances of those places, such as the candle waltz or the *ball de rams*. The marquees attracted a great many girls in full bloom, who came in groups, arm in arm, laughing at everything and anything; if someone spoke to one of them, they would all burst out laughing, and there would be no way to stop them. Of all those girls, the fish girls were the liveliest and most buxom, the maids the most innocent, and the dressmakers' assistants the most hard-bitten and dangerous.

Onofre and his friends went to La Barceloneta, too, to the bullring. Afterward they drank beer or red wine with lemonade in the bars there, discussing and arguing heatedly until the wee hours of the morning.

On one occasion a sudden whim took him to the World's

Fair, which was on everybody's lips just then. Barcelona was one big fiesta; property owners had been urged to fix up the façades of their buildings, carriage owners to clean and repaint their vehicles, and everyone to dress up their domestic staff. In the interests of foreign visitors, the City Council selected one hundred Municipal Guards, the most intelligent ones they could find, and made them learn French in a very short time. Now these guards wandered around the city like lost souls, muttering incomprehensible phrases, followed everywhere and harassed by children who imitated their guttural sounds and called them *gargalluts*.

Onofre went to the fair on his own and paid at the gate: entering the site like all the gentlefolk amused him. He let himself be swept along by the crowd, stopped for refreshments at the restaurant called the Castell dels Tres Dragons (it had taken over 170 men to build it, and he knew nearly all of them by their first names), then visited the Martorell Museum, the Montserrat Diorama, the Valencia Orgeat Works, the Turkish Café, the American Soda Water Stand, the Seville Pavilion, and so on. He had his picture taken (it has since been lost) and went into the Palace of Industry, where he viewed machinery made by Baldrich, Vilagrán, and Tapera, those three gentlemen from Bassora. The sight brought back unpleasant memories and stirred his blood. Suddenly he felt stifled and found the people around him unbearable; he left in a hurry, elbowing his way out. Once he was outside, the whole dazzling spectacle struck him as a cruel joke: he could not separate it from the hardships he had suffered there a few months before. He never went back to the World's Fair.

The nightlife of the old Barcelona, on the other hand, the Barcelona that had refused to let the World's Fair pomp alter its ways, carrying on as usual on the sidelines, excited in him the enthusiasm of a country boy. Whenever he could he went, alone or with his friends, to a place called L'Empori de la Patacada, a broken-down, evil-smelling establishment located in a basement on Calle del Huerto de la Bomba. By day it was forlorn and small; only after midnight did it come to life, with the help of a rough but devoted clientele. The place seemed to draw strength from somewhere, to grow in size: there was always room for another couple, and nobody ever went without a table. Two youths were stationed at the door with shotguns, necessary because the establishment was patronized not only by criminal types, who were well able to look after themselves, but also by dissolute youngsters of good family, and a few ladies, their faces veiled, accompanied by friends, admirers, or even by their husbands. They came for the thrill of it, seeking to alleviate the monotony of their lives. Later they would recount what they had seen, exaggerating everything. At L'Empori de la Patacada one could dance and, at certain set times, see *tableaux vivants*.

These were very popular in the eighteenth century, but by the end of the nineteenth had almost entirely disappeared. Motionless scenes enacted by live performers, they could be "contemporary" (Their Majesties the King and Queen of Rumania receiving the Ambassador of Spain; the Grand Duke Nicholas in lancer's uniform with his illustrious spouse, etc.), or "historical," also called "didactic" (the suicide of the Numantians, the death of the Spanish sailor Churruca at Trafalgar, etc.), or "Biblical" and "mythological." These latter were the most popular, since in nearly all of them the characters appeared naked.

For actors in the nineteenth century, naked meant wearing tight, flesh-colored leotards. This was not because people then were any more modest than they are now, but because what gave them pleasure was the human form; bare skin and body hair had a morbid rather than an erotic effect. In this respect customs had changed greatly. In the eighteenth century, as is well known, nudity was considered perfectly normal: people appeared naked in public without thinking twice about it or having their dignity suffer as a result; men and women took their baths with visitors present, changed in front of the servants, and urinated and defecated on public highways. The diaries and letters of the time contain abundant evidence of this. Thus one finds in the diary of the duchess of C——, *"Dîner chez les M——; Madame de G ——, comme d'habitude, préside la table à poil."* And a later entry reads: *"Bal chez le prince de V——; presque tout le monde nu sauf l'abbé K—— déguisé en papillon; on a beacoup rigolé."*

A four-piece band provided music for the dancing in L'Empori de la Patacada. The waltz had already won acceptance at all social levels; the *paso doble* and the schottische were limited to the lower classes; while the tango had yet to appear on the scene. At high-society soirées the rigaudon, the mazurka, the lancers, and the minuet were still being danced; the polka and the popular waltz known as the Java were all the rage in Europe, but not in Catalonia. Traditional dances such as the *sardana* and the *jota* were outlawed in establishments such as L'Empori de la Patacada.

Because of the heat of the summer months, business was best on autumn nights, when storms lashed the streets and the cold turned everyone's steps to some cozy spot. When spring came around again, the cafés with terraces and open-air dances would lure away a substantial portion of the customers.

Onofre was not able to enjoy fully what was offered in those quarters; nervous, ill at ease, he never entirely let himself go. Odón, who had taken a great liking to the boy and felt responsible for his well-being, was worried to see him always so stiff. "Come on, kid," he would say to him. "Why don't you go and have a good time? Hey, look at those women, aren't they enough to drive you crazy?" Onofre would answer with a smile, "Having a good time is too much like work." This would make Odón laugh. But Onofre was telling the truth. It would have taken an enormous effort for him to tear himself away from the memory of that horrible morning when a very odd character called upon his parents.

Uncle Tonet brought the man from Bassora in his trap. The visitor wore a threadbare frock coat, a dicky, spectacles, and a top hat, and carried a bulging briefcase. He was doing his best to avoid the puddles and mounds of dirty, thawing snow. A bird flapping on a branch frightened him to death. He introduced himself with much circumlocution, then hurried to the embers glowing in the fireplace to warm himself. The late-February sun was spilling through the open door and halfway across the room; its clear but cold light outlined every object with the precision of a freshly sharpened pencil.

The man began by saying that he was speaking on behalf of Messrs. Baldrich, Vilagrán, and Tapera. He himself was merely the clerical assistant to solicitors in Bassora, and he hoped they would not blame him personally for what he had been ordered to make known to them. The *americano* waved his hand impatiently, as if to say, "Get to the point."

The clerical assistant cleared his throat, and Onofre's mother said she had to feed the chickens. "The boy will come with me, so you will be left in peace," she added, looking her husband in the eye. "No," he said, "stay and hear what this gentleman has to say." The clerical assistant wrung his hands and coughed, as if the smoke from the embers had caught in his throat. In a low, almost inaudible voice he informed Onofre's father that his employers had decided to bring charges against him for fraud. "That is a very serious charge," the *americano* said. "Be so kind as to explain yourself."

The clerical assistant gave an embarrassed explanation. Joan Bouvila had told everybody in Bassora that he had come back from America a wealthy man; he had visited the city's industrialists and financiers in his outlandish clothes, leading them to believe that he was seeking a sound business in which to invest his fortune. Under this pretext he obtained advances, loans, gratuities. As time went by and the promised investments failed to materialize, Messrs. Baldrich, Vilagrán, and Tapera, their concern having paid out the most to the *americano*, initiated certain investigations. The investigations confirmed what everybody suspected: that Joan Bouvila had not a penny to his name. This was fraud and no doubt about it, said the clerk. Instantly he turned pale and added that the baldness of that statement did not reflect any moral judgment on his part. He was an instrument acting at the behest of others, no more.

Onofre's mother broke the silence that followed these words. "Joan," she said, "what is this man talking about?" The *americano* admitted, with some hemming and hawing, that everything the clerical assistant said was true. He had lied to everybody: in Cuba, where even half-wits became rich at the time, he had not managed to earn enough to live comfortably. The little he saved was cheated out of him by a fast Colombian woman. He was tricked by swindlers and confidence men. In the end he had to stoop to tasks beneath the dignity even of the black slaves. "There was no spittoon in Havana I did not polish, no boot I did not shine, no latrine I did not unclog, with tools or without." He saw down-and-out immigrants step ashore, and after just a few months they would be tossing coins into puddles in the street, for the amusement of seeing him fish them out, plunging his arm in up to the elbow. He ate banana skins, fishbones, rotten vegetables, and other things he preferred not to mention in the present company. Finally he said to himself, "That's enough, Joan, you've had enough."

"I obtained a little money," the *americano* went on, "by ignominious means: arranging pleasures for English sailors, pleasures of the most degrading sort. With that sum, I bought the suit I'm wearing, a monkey, and a ticket back on a tramp steamer."

Shortly before leaving, he made the rounds borrowing one last time, then went aboard one night in the middle of a downpour, so as not to be seen by any of his creditors. "That was how I left the promised land, which for me was a land of bondage, degradation, and shame." Afterward he lived by swindling, always knowing that sooner or later the truth would come out. But this confession had taken a weight off his mind. He was glad to put an end to the web of lies.

But the lies were made not out of meanness or greed, they

were made out of vanity. The truth was that he had lied for his son, wanting him to have some glimpse of what life could have been like had the boy had a father other than the useless one God gave him.

In the end the lawsuit came to nothing. Concluding that it was not possible to recover their money summarily, Baldrich, Vilagrán, and Tapera withdrew the charges. In exchange they forced the *americano* to work for them, deducting a percentage from his wages to pay off the debt.

Now Onofre could not put this out of his mind, though he drank without moderation and was a regular client in several brothels. He also spent a lot of money on fancy clothes, but he never got into debt, and he avoided gambling like the plague.

He had stopped growing. Even if he would not be a tall man, his chest and shoulders had developed well; he was stocky in build, robust, and not disagreeable in appearance. Although reserved, he was amiable enough, and frank in his dealings with others. The ruffians, prostitutes, pimps, drug pushers, policemen, and informers thought highly of him, and most of them went to considerable lengths to win his friendship. They all instinctively recognized his innate qualities as a leader.

Odón Mostaza himself, Onofre's boss, fell under his influence, and left all the decisions to him, even the accounting, when necessary, with Margarito. This confirmed the latter's suspicions. "That boy is going places," he said to himself. "He's been with us only a year and already he's leading his pack. If I don't watch my step, he'll crush me. I should eliminate him, but I can't think how. He's too small a fish now—he'd slip through my fingers— but if I wait too long, it may be too late."

Margarito tried to win the young man's confidence. He praised the suits Onofre had had made, for like every person devoid of dress sense, Onofre was acutely aware of elegance in those around him. He failed to notice that his colleague was a walking ragbag and genuinely believed that they shared a taste for stylish clothes; he even asked Margarito's advice where to buy ties, boots, etc.

He became a dandy; around his boardinghouse he would always be draped in a printed kimono that went below his ankles.

Sometimes a vague anxiety weighed him down. On warm, sticky summer nights, when he could not sleep, he would throw on the printed kimono and go out onto the balcony to smoke a cigarette. "What's the matter with me?" he wondered. "Why am I so restless?" Then the memory of his father would come back to him.

He believed he hated his father for having betrayed his hopes, for not having lived up to the expectations of his fantasies, expectations to which he was convinced he had a right. He believed he had fled from home for that reason. "It was he who forced me to come here, he who is really responsible for whatever trouble I get into here." Yet the admiration he had always felt for his father was still there. As if his father was really not a failure at all but, rather, the victim of a vast plot that had cheated him of his due success and fortune—which now gave Onofre the right to seek compensation, to take without qualms what was his by right.

But these disjointed, angry thoughts were not in harmony with the things around him now. His poverty was a thing of the past; he had left the sordid world of that first boardinghouse, and the memory of Delfina was fading with the passing months. He had friends, he was doing well for himself, and when he managed to forget his resentment he felt full of life, almost happy.

On those summer nights when he went out onto the balcony, he heard familiar noises from the street: the clinking of plates, soup bowls, glasses; laughter, shouts, quarrels; the chirping of goldfinches and canaries in their cages; a far-off piano, the warbling of a would-be soprano; the yapping of a persistent dog; the diatribes of drunkards wrapped around lampposts, blind beggars pleading for a penny for the love of God. "I could spend the whole night on this balcony," he thought, "spend the whole summer here, lulled by the sounds of the city."

But discontent seized him again. The flattery of the riffraff was not enough to efface the injury done him, the humiliation whose memory followed him everywhere, the stigma that he felt was stamped on his brow. "I must rise higher," he said to himself. "I can't stay where I am. If I do, my fate will be sealed— I'll end up just another thug." Though he loved the easy life of a gangster, his reason told him that these people on the fringe of society were really living on borrowed time, tolerated for the moment because they had their uses, or because it seemed too expensive to eradicate them. But they thought they could ride roughshod over everybody, just because they carried knives in their belts, or because some women pretended to melt under their gazes.

Onofre lacked the strength of will, however, to abandon that merry fellowship of swashbucklers and brazen ladies. He felt at ease in that world, and would have gone on in this way for years and years, oblivious to the world beyond, ending up, like many others, knifed, imprisoned, or sent to the gallows, had Margarito not crossed his path. Eventually Onofre was forced to change as a simple matter of survival.

2

During those years the unseen strings controlling Barcelona's political life were held by Don Alexandre Canals i Formiga. A stern, undemonstrative man with a broad forehead and a pointed black beard, he was always meticulously groomed. Every morning a barber, a manicurist, and a masseuse came to his office, which he rarely left. These were the only pleasures he allowed himself. The rest of his workday, which went on well into the night, was devoted to making grave decisions and taking measures of the greatest import for the community at large: he rigged elections, bribed officials, and made and destroyed political careers. Completely unhampered by scruples and devoting all his energy to these affairs, he had accumulated limitless power, but refrained from using it—he hoarded it as a miser hoards coins. Men of influence feared and respected him, and turned to him unhesitatingly. It was said of him that he was the only man who would be able to control the trade-union unrest that the far-sighted saw gathering on the horizon.

If obtaining his ends involved resorting to violence, he did not shrink from it. For that purpose he had at his disposal a group of thugs and gunmen captained by one Joan Sicart, a man with a turbulent past who was from Barcelona but had been born and bred in Cuba, where his parents had gone, like Onofre's father, to seek their fortune. Fevers claimed both their lives when Joan was still very little; he was left utterly at the mercy of fate. Drawn to both violence and discipline, he wanted to become a soldier, but could not; he was refused admission to the academy on account of a mild chest complaint. He returned to Spain, lived for a while in Cadiz, was put behind bars on a number of occasions, and ended up in Barcelona at the head of Don Alexandre's cohorts, whom he ruled with an iron hand. He was bony, with pronounced features and small sunken eyes, giving him an Oriental look. Surprisingly, he had straw-colored hair.

It was inevitable that the activities of this fearsome organization and those of Don Humbert Figa i Morera should occasionally come into collision. There had already been a few brushes, but they were smoothed over with no great difficulty. Both Don Humbert and Margarito, his deputy, were moderate men able to make compromises. They even tried to negotiate with Don Alexandre with a view toward a formal treaty, but the latter, knowing himself to be the more powerful, did not wish to consider such a proposal. The disparity was obvious. Besides being stronger in numbers, Don Alexandre's men were much better organized: they could form squadrons like militia, and were well versed in breaking up strikes and disrupting meetings. Don Humbert's men, on the other hand, were a pack of hooligans good only for brawling in taverns. But the city, small and poor, could not support both groups—and growing groups at that. Sooner or later there would be a showdown.

The showdown occurred one Friday evening in March. The sun was setting, the sky was clear, and the first signs of spring were visible in the trees out in the square. Don Humbert pushed the curtains aside with the edge of his hand and looked out on the square, resting his forehead on the windowpane. "I do not know if my course of action is the correct one," he thought. "Time flies and nothing changes, and I feel sad without knowing why." His mind wandered to the World's Fair, then to Onofre Bouvila, and the two images were linked: the fair and the country boy trying so hard to cut a path for himself. By now the fair had closed its doors: of that colossal effort almost nothing was left— a few buildings too big to be of any practical use, a few statues, and a mountain of debt that the City Council could not think how to cancel. "Society rests on these four pillars," he thought: "ignorance, negligence, injustice, and folly."

The evening before, Margarito had paid Don Humbert a visit, and what he had had to say had upset him greatly: things could no longer continue in the old way.

"Violent acts are called for," Margarito told him, "if we are not to resign ourselves to extermination."

"We all knew it would come to this, one day or another, but I did not think it would be so soon," Don Humbert replied. The plan seemed pure madness to him; he saw no chance of winning. "Whatever made you think up such a wild scheme?"

It was not a question of winning, Margarito said, but of reasserting themselves. The idea was to strike first, and then re-open the negotiations right away. "Let them see that we are not cripples, that we will not be frightened off. That is the language Don Alexandre understands, not the voice of reason. We will lose a few men, that is unavoidable."

"And ourselves—nothing will happen to us?" Don Humbert asked.

"There is nothing to fear on that score," his deputy replied. "I have thought everything through, planned the whole operation with the utmost care, to the last detail. Besides, I've been watching the boy for quite some time. He has what it takes. It's a pity," he added, "that we must sacrifice him."

Margarito was a kindhearted man, but envy and fear had him in their grip. He summoned Onofre to his office and said that a very important job was being entrusted to him. Then Don Humbert entered through a tall, narrow double door. "Don Arnau Puncella tells me that you have what it takes," he said to Onofre. They carefully spelled out the plan. Onofre listened, openmouthed. "He suspects nothing," thought Margarito, watching him.

On his own again, Onofre mulled the matter over for several hours, then went to find Odón. He told the ruffian, "Listen, this is what we are going to do." He had decided to discard the plan outlined to him in Margarito's office and had drawn up a plan of his own. "The obedience has gone on long enough," he said to himself. He had known of the existence of Don Alexandre Canals i Formiga, and of Joan Sicart and his formidable army of thugs, for a long time: Odón had told him all about them. Onofre had even considered the possibility of offering his services to Sicart. Though not disloyal by nature, he knew where the real power lay and was not one to support lost causes. He knew that the entire organization revolved around Sicart. On this fact he based his plan.

"Our inferiority," he told Odón, "is so obvious that nobody will take us seriously—we have that advantage over them. We can add to that our speed and our boldness." He did not add "and our brutality," but he thought it. Perhaps, if the opposing forces had been more evenly matched, he would not have had to act with such brutality.

The war began that very night. Some of Sicart's men frequented a wine bar on Calle del Arco de San Silvestre, near the

Plaza de Santa Catalina. A group of toughs led by Odón went there, acting as if they were looking for a fight. This was not out of the ordinary, and nobody took any notice. Sicart's men smiled. "There are more of us and we are better trained," they seemed to be saying. The toughs drew knives, stabbed the men nearest them, and ran from the bar before the others could react. A horse-drawn carriage was waiting for them in the Plaza de Santa Catalina, and they made their getaway in it.

The news spread rapidly through the underworld. In less than two hours came the reprisal: twelve men armed with shotguns entered L'Empori de la Patacada and opened fire, interrupting a *tableau vivant* entitled "The Sultan's Slave Girl." The balance was two dead and five wounded, but neither Onofre Bouvila nor Odón Mostaza was among the casualties. The gunmen left the establishment; outside, in the dark, deserted street, they realized their mistake, but it was too late. Two closed carriages immediately came into view, bearing down on them at full gallop. The twelve attempted to flee, but were caught in a crossfire from the two wagons, with those inside shooting through the windows with American six-shooters. Onofre's men could have finished off all twelve, but contented themselves with a couple of bursts and hit seven; one died instantly, two others a few days later.

Joan Sicart was nonplussed. "I don't understand. What do they hope to accomplish? How far will they go? What's their motive, what are they after?" he wondered.

He was told that a woman wanted to see him. She did not wish to reveal her identity, but claimed to have the solution he was vainly seeking. Sicart had her shown into his office. He had never seen her before, but, not insensible to feminine charms, greeted her politely. "Onofre Bouvila sent me," was the first thing she said. Sicart said that he did not know who Onofre Bouvila was. The woman went on, ignoring that reply. "He wants to see you," she said bluntly. "He is worried, too, and does not understand what all this killing is about." She spoke the way an ambassador might to one head of state on behalf of another head of state. "If you wish to put an end to this absurd situation, go and see him, or receive him here, on your own ground. He will not refuse to come if you give him sufficient guarantees." Sicart shrugged. "Tell him to come if he wants, but alone and unarmed." "Have I your word that he will emerge safe and sound?" the woman asked. Through the veil covering her face, the woman's eyes showed anxiety. "His lover or his mother," Sicart thought. The uneasiness with which his power filled the beautiful woman made him smile arrogantly. "You have nothing to fear," he said. They agreed on a time for the meeting.

Onofre appeared punctually. When he saw him, Sicart grimaced. "Now I know who you are. You're Odón Mostaza's sidekick. I've heard about you. What did you come to sell me?" This, in a supercilious tone, but Onofre did not take offense. "I have no need of new recruits, spies, or traitors," Sicart added with a sneer. Finally Onofre's silence exasperated him and he raised his voice: "What do you want? What are you here for?" Out in the hall his men, hearing him shout, did not know whether they should step in or stay out of it. "If he needs us, he'll let us know," they concluded.

"If you don't want to hear what I have to say, why did you ask me to come?" Onofre said at last, when Sicart had vented his anger. "I am on enemy ground here."

Sicart had to concede that. It irked him to have to deal with a whippersnapper on equal terms, yet he could not help being impressed by the composure of the little brat. In a moment his contempt turned into respect. "Very well, out with it," he said.

Onofre realized that he had won the first round. "He's crumbling," he thought. Out loud he said that the warfare that had just broken out was nonsensical; it had to be based on some mistake; nobody knew how it had begun, but now it was a fact and could snowball and bury them all. "Don't you think we should put an end to this undesirable situation?"

"Just a minute," exclaimed Sicart. "It wasn't us that started it, it was you people."

"What does that matter at this stage?" said Onofre. "The main thing is to halt the chain of reprisals." Then he lowered his voice and said confidentially, "This war is not in our interests— what could we hope to gain from it? There are fewer of us, and our resources are not equal to yours. You could eat us for breakfast. All the advantages are on your side. Believe me, there are no secret aims behind my visit. I came only to make peace."

Sicart didn't trust Onofre, but he wanted to believe in his sincerity: he, too, found the senseless war repugnant. His men were being gunned down, and the city was tense. It was bad for business.

Nothing was settled in that meeting, but they agreed to get together again. Convinced by Onofre that all the winning cards were in his hand, Sicart was unaware that he was walking into a trap, digging his own grave. The shooting would have continued that night, except that it rained hard from sunset till after midnight. Only two small groups ran into each other in a dark side street, and fired away through the rain with the pistols and musketoons they now always carried on them. The flashes from their guns lit up the sheets of water pouring from the rooftops. They went on firing, their feet sunk deep in the mud, until they ran out of ammunition. Because of the downpour, neither side had losses to report.

There were two other incidents. A sixteen-year-old boy belonging to Don Humbert's gang died when he fell off a wall he had climbed to escape from real or imagined pursuers. That same terrible night, somebody threw a dead mastiff in the window of a brothel frequented by Odón Mostaza, Onofre, and company. Nobody understood the significance of the macabre present, but that night they stayed away from the brothel. The prostitutes didn't sleep, fearing an attack. At three in the morning they said the rosary. It was common knowledge in the city that war was being waged, but the press was too afraid to report these events.

The following day, the mysterious woman paid a second visit to Joan Sicart; she told him that Onofre Bouvila wanted to see him again. But prudence and his personal safety, things being as they were, advised against his coming there. "It isn't that he mistrusts you, it's your men; he fears that your control over them might not be absolute. He fears to put his head in the lion's mouth. He says that you should pick a neutral spot. He will go alone; you can bring with you whomever you please by way of an escort."

Sicart arranged a meeting in the cathedral cloister. His men surrounded the cathedral and took up positions in every side chapel; the Right Reverend Bishop judiciously chose to ignore the presence of armed men in that holy place. Sicart had, moreover, kept tabs on all Don Humbert's gang; thanks to this, he knew Onofre was coming to meet him alone. He had to admire the fellow's boldness.

"There is still time to make peace," said Onofre. He spoke slowly and quietly, as if affected by the solemnity of their meeting place. After the rain of the previous night the rosebushes in the cloister had bloomed, and the recently washed stone paving shone like alabaster. "Tomorrow may be too late. The authorities cannot remain idle much longer, faced with a situation like this. Sooner or later they will be forced to intervene, perhaps to declare a state of emergency and have the army occupy the city. That would be the end of us. Your boss and mine would emerge unscathed, but you and I are food for the gallows. We'll end up in the ditches of Montjuich, as an example. With the trade-union problem that's blowing up, they won't let slip by a chance like this to show they mean business. You know I'm right. And your own boss might even have a hand in it."

Sicart's distrust was growing all the while, but he could not shut out Onofre's arguments, which weakened his will.

"I have no reason to suspect Don Alexandre Canals i Formiga," he replied haughtily.

"You're the best judge of that," said Onofre. "For myself, I trust nobody. I wouldn't stake my life on either of them."

While he sowed the seeds of doubt in Sicart's mind, the mysterious woman was wangling her way into the presence of Don Alexandre himself. She spun a confused yarn, with sentimental threads attached. Don Alexandre swallowed the bait and had the woman shown in. Before she entered, he scented himself with an atomizer he kept beside his revolver in his desk drawer. She would not unveil her face. Without preamble she said that Joan Sicart was preparing to betray him. "He will go over to the enemy, and at the crucial moment you will be left defenseless," she said with a faltering voice. He laughed. "What you are saying is simply beyond the bounds of possibility, madam. How did you come to imagine such a thing?" "I am afraid for you," she admitted tearfully. "If anything were to happen to you . . ." Flattered, he tried to calm her. "There is no cause for concern," he said, and offered her a glass of liqueur, at which she sipped nervously. Then she added, returning to the subject that alarmed her, that Sicart had already met twice with the enemy, once in his own headquarters and the second time in the cathedral cloister. "Investigate for yourself, and you will see that I am telling the truth. If Humbert Figa i Morera's men were not counting on Sicart's complicity, why would they, hopelessly outnumbered, start a war? I tell you, Sicart is in cahoots with Humbert Figa i Morera."

Don Alexandre did not wish to enter into a discussion of such gravity with an unknown lady. "Leave now, please. I have important business to attend to." But when she was gone, he sent someone to the bishopric, to confirm Sicart's alleged visit to the cathedral. "I do not believe a word this deranged woman has told me," he said to himself, "but it is always a good idea to take precautions, especially in times like these."

The mysterious woman's visit actually made a deeper impression on him than he would have cared to admit. "Who would have guessed that I, with the monastic life I lead, should be on the mind of such an attractive woman, so that she secretly worries over my safety?" he mused. "Dear, dear, dear, there is a distinct whiff of lust in this. Be that as it may, I cannot disregard the information she has brought me. An obvious exaggeration, or a mistake—but what if it is not?"

Word came back from the bishopric confirming Joan Sicart's presence in the cathedral cloister. Don Alexandre summoned him and tried to get the truth out of him by subterfuge. When Sicart perceived this subterfuge, the suspicions Onofre had planted in his mind were reinforced. But he pretended to notice nothing amiss in his boss's behavior, so as not to give himself away. "Maybe he wants to have me replaced but doesn't know how to go about it," he thought. Sicart had a deputy named Boix, a none-too-bright fellow with animal instincts, who had been eyeing Sicart's position with envy for some time. Maybe Don Alexandre had Boix in mind; maybe Boix had reached a secret agreement with Don Alexandre.

During the course of the conversation, both parties observed the strain behind their apparent camaraderie. This did not prevent the two from agreeing to launch a frontal attack on Don Humbert's men. Sicart took leave of his boss with the promise to wipe them out.

Alone again, he wondered: "Perhaps it's all part of the plan. While he has an enemy to deal with, even if it's only an insignificant enemy like Don Humbert, he will still need me. But if I dispose of his rival's gang, what would stop him from getting rid of me then? No," he said to himself, "I must come to some agreement with Onofre Bouvila. Peace is as much in my interest as in his, and he seems a reasonable man. I'll see him, and between us we'll get things back to normal."

In his office Don Alexandre collapsed into his leather armchair, his arms flopping. He was on the verge of tears. "My most faithful servant is deserting me. What will become of me?" He saw his own life at risk, but was more worried about what might happen to his son. This son, twelve years old, had been born with a malformation of the spine and had difficulty moving. As a little boy he was unable to take part in any games or mischief-making; on the other hand, he was interested in his studies and showed a remarkable aptitude for arithmetic. He was a sad child, with no friends. Since the couple's other children had died in the 1879 epidemic, Don Alexandre felt for this handicapped boy a limitless affection—unlike his wife, who after the tragedy harbored an understandable but unjustified resentment against the survivors.

Now Don Alexandre was thinking, "If these scoundrels are planning something big, they might get it into their heads to make an attempt on my son's life. They know that would be a mortal blow to me. Yes, that's what they'll do if I don't move first." The following day his son, Nicolau Canals i Rataplán, in the company of his mother, a governess, and a maid, set off for France, where his father had friends and money set aside.

When he heard of the departure of his boss's family, Sicart was convinced that he had been betrayed. He sent this message to Onofre Bouvila: "Joan Sicart wishes to see you urgently." "This time," Onofre answered, "it's you and me alone." "As you please; name the place." Onofre pretended to give the matter some thought for a moment or two, although really he had it all worked out. "In the Church of San Severo, half an hour before seven o'clock Mass." "The church will be shut then," said Sicart. "I'll open it." The day was spent in this exchange of messages. There was no fighting, but the streets of Barcelona were empty; the people would not risk leaving their homes if they could avoid it.

Before the sun came up, Sicart's men had taken positions in

the adjoining streets, under the arcades, in an oil warehouse next to the church, and in the ruins of an abandoned palace. They expected to see Onofre arrive, but he had beaten them to it: he spent the night in the church. It was he who opened the doors for them at the agreed time. Three of Sicart's followers rushed inside, brandishing their weapons, in case Onofre had prepared an ambush for their boss. But they saw only Onofre by the door, unarmed and calm, and a chaplain, quaking with fear, huddled in front of the altar. Though he feared for his life, he feared a desecration even more. The three gangsters were disappointed. "As you can see, these precautions were hardly necessary," Onofre said gently. They did not see the beads of sweat on his brow; they took the chaplain and dragged him out onto the street, before Sicart. "The coast is clear," they told him, "but we brought this chaplain, so he can confirm it." Sicart turned to the chaplain.

"Do you know who I am?" he asked.

"Yes, sir," the chaplain replied in a whisper.

"Then you know what will happen to you if you lie to me?"

"Yes, sir."

"Tell me the truth: who is in that church?"

"Only the boy."

"Do you swear to God it's true?"

"I swear to God and all the saints."

"What about Odón Mostaza?"

"He is waiting with the rest of the gang in the Plaza del Rey."

"Why in the Plaza del Rey?"

"Onofre Bouvila told them to wait there."

"All right," said Sicart, removing his gaze from the chaplain.

Sicart had stayed up all night thinking, and that had not done him any good. Now he found himself faced with a critical choice. On the one hand, he wanted to reach an agreement with Onofre Bouvila and maintain the status quo; on the other, his character balked at negotiating: he was a warrior, and the chance of achieving victory over the enemy blinded his reason. "What's to stop me from sending my men to the Plaza del Rey and having them wipe out Odón Mostaza and his crew, every last one of them? I could take care of Onofre Bouvila myself, that little pup waiting in there. In a couple of minutes we'd have cleared the city of our enemies, and Barcelona would be ours for the taking." But other ideas came and challenged these, and he was paralyzed.

His deputy urged him to do something: "Come on, let's have some action, what are you waiting for?" It was Boix, whose loyalty he doubted. Now, however, it all seemed so obvious that all doubts were dispelled, like the scenes of a nightmare when one awakens.

"As soon as you see me go into the church, leave three men at the door, take the rest, and go to the Plaza del Rey," he told Boix. "Odón Mostaza's men are there. Kill them all, every single one of them. Get this clear: there must be no survivors. I'll join you shortly."

3

The sun had already risen when Joan Sicart went into the Church of San Severo, a baroque church of average size. "It'll be no trouble disposing of him," he thought as he entered. "That way, we'll settle this dangerous and stupid situation once and for all. As soon as he comes within range, I'll shoot him. True, I did guarantee his safety, and so far he's kept his word. But since when did I start worrying about that honor business? I've been a scoundrel all my life, and now, suddenly, I get scruples—bah!"

In the dark, he could not make out anything for a moment or two. Onofre's voice came from the altar. "I'm over here, Sicart. You have nothing to fear."

A shiver ran down Sicart's back. "It's as if I was going to kill my own son," he thought. Once he got used to the darkness, he began to move forward between the two rows of benches, his left hand in his trouser pocket grasping the weapon: a small pistol, of the kind that fired one shot and could be used only at close range. These pistols, manufactured in Czechoslovakia, were almost unknown at that time in Spain. Sicart assumed Onofre would not know of the existence of such a pistol, and would thus not guess that he was carrying one in his pocket.

A pistol identical to the one Sicart was carrying, but made of silver studded with diamonds and sapphires, had been given as a present by the Emperor Franz Joseph to his spouse, the Empress Isabelle. To avoid hurting her feelings, since one does not offer weapons to a lady, especially if she is of high birth, the gunsmiths were instructed to make the pistol in the shape of a key. "Nobody need see it," said the emperor. "Keep it in your bag just in case. There are too many assassination attempts nowadays, and I fear for you and the boys." She did not reply to his expression of concern: she did not love her husband, and always treated him with disdain, even at official ceremonies and receptions, showing him all the coldness she could muster—and she could muster a great deal. Even so, she was carrying the pistol in her bag that fateful morning of September 10, 1898, when, as she was about to embark on a steamer at the Mont Blanc quay in Geneva, Luigi Lucheni assassinated her. He had been waiting for her for two days outside her hotel, but until then their paths had not crossed. Not having the money to purchase a dagger (they cost twelve Swiss francs), he had fashioned a homemade one out of brass. The day before, the empress had gone to visit the Baroness de Rothschild, on whose property strutted exotic birds and porcupines brought over for her from Java.

The Empress Isabelle was sixty-one when she died, but had kept her slim figure and her beautiful face; she was the embodiment of all that was left of elegance and dignity in Europe. She composed elegiac poetry. Her son had killed himself; her brother-in-law, the Emperor Maximilian of Mexico, had been made to face a firing squad; her sister had died in a fire in Paris; her cousin, King Louis II of Bavaria, had spent the last years of his life vegetating in a lunatic asylum. Luigi Lucheni, the man who killed her, was to commit suicide two years later in Geneva, where he was imprisoned for life. He was born in Paris but brought up in Parma. If Empress Sissi, as her subjects were wont to call her, had made use of the pistol the emperor had given her, she could have escaped death, beating her slayer to it. Before driving home the lethal blade, Lucheni wasted several seconds: because the empress and her companion, Countess Szarary, were carrying parasols to keep the sun off their faces, he had to peer under each parasol; dazzled as he was, he could easily have made a mistake that would have turned him into a laughingstock of history. Squinting, he murmured as he went along—"*Scusate, signora.*" But the empress probably forgot that she had a pistol in her bag, or remembered but chose to forget: she was, as she herself said, tired of life. "Life weighs so heavily on me," she had written to her daughter shortly before, "that I often feel a physical pain, and I think I should prefer to be dead."

The other hand, the one Sicart did not need to clutch the pistol, was held out to Onofre, as if in greeting. But Onofre, not needing to look to see what Sicart was doing with the hidden hand, threw up his arms, dropped to his knees, and cried "Sicart, for God's sake, don't kill me, I'm too young to die."

Sicart hesitated for a second, the last second of his life. A man emerged from the darkness, jumped on him, and wrung his neck. Blood streamed out of his mouth and nose. It happened so quickly that Sicart had not even time to draw the pistol from his pocket, let alone use it, like the empress herself years later. The man who killed him was Efrén Castells, the giant from Calella, whom Onofre had been keeping out of sight all those months, nobody knowing of his existence, ready to bring him into play at his hour of greatest need. Now Sicart's lifeless body lay before the altar: a great sacrilege, but the deed was done. Onofre and

Efrén walked up the central nave, shut the doors and bolted them. The men Sicart had left on guard out in the street, suspecting that something nasty was happening to their boss, tried to enter the church but failed.

Meanwhile, the rest of Sicart's men had gone off to the Plaza del Rey. The three men caught up with Boix and told him what had happened. "The church door is bolted and barred, and there's no sign of Sicart," they said. Boix paid little attention to this information—and the idea of Sicart falling into a deadly trap was not altogether disagreeable to him. Blinded by his ambition, he led the whole band straight into the square, in a body, without sending scouts ahead or taking any other precaution, a rash move of which Sicart would never have been guilty had he been in charge. Boix himself realized, too late, his mistake: the square was empty, Odón's men had vanished. Boix's men stopped and gave him a questioning look. "What are we doing here?" they seemed to be asking. He was at a loss. Then Odón's men, who had split up and were perched on the rooftops, opened fire and raked the men below. A battle ensued, lasting nearly two hours. Boix's side, despite its superiority in numbers, never had the upper hand. The very discipline of the group was its undoing: with Sicart gone and Boix—who anyway was one of the first to fall— discredited in the eyes of his men, nobody knew what action to take. Mostaza's band of ruffians, on the other hand, was in its element in the confusion: this was what his men were used to. Finally Boix's men fled in disorder, throwing down their weapons. Odón let them get away, unable to regroup his forces and set off in pursuit.

News of this embarrassing defeat, which had dealt a fearful blow to his empire, had yet to reach Don Alexandre. He was in excellent spirits: the masseuse had just left, and his valet was helping him on with his tie; he knew his son was safe in Paris, and he had rid himself of his wife, with whom he did not get along very well. The sun was streaming into his office through the window when he was informed of another visit from the mysterious woman. He kept her waiting only as long as it took him to perfume his beard. This time he made so bold as to put his arm around her waist when he offered her a seat on the cherry-colored velvet sofa.

The woman put up an absentminded resistance to this liberty. Her eyes were glued on the window. She was evasive, incoherent in her conversation. After a while, by which time he had snuggled up very close to her, she saw a light flashing on a nearby rooftop. By means of a hand mirror, Onofre and Efrén were signaling to her. "It's all over," they were saying. "Act now." For greater freedom of movement she removed her veil and pulled off her hat and wig. Don Alexandre's mouth dropped open. She drew a dagger from her false breasts and shut her eyes momentarily. "May God forgive me for what I am about to do," Don Alexandre heard her mutter before he fell dead on the sofa. As he died he found time to think of his son: "A good thing I put him out of harm's way." For himself he could spare only a sarcastic reflection: "And I thought I'd made a conquest!"

The false woman was Señor Braulio, Onofre's ex-landlord, whom Onofre had gone to find in La Carbonera specifically for this job. Señor Braulio was always there, trying to drown his troubles and his loneliness with constant recourse to drugs and letting himself be beaten.

After his second arrest, this time as a suspected member of an anarchist cell after Delfina made her statement, he was released, having little trouble proving his innocence this time, satisfying the police and examining magistrate that his inclinations were of a different nature. Upon his release he made an attempt to take charge of the boardinghouse once more, but the scene he found there was one of desolation. His wife had died in the hospital, and Delfina and her accomplices were about to be tried: the charges they faced were grave indeed, entailing life sentences if not the maximum penalty. "I will never see my daughter again," the landlord thought.

During his absence nobody had tried to keep the boarding-house in a decent state: there was dust everywhere, and the remains of meals were decomposing in the kitchen. He started to put the house in order, but his will failed him. With the help of Father Bizancio and the barber, he had advertisements printed in the newspapers and soon found a buyer for the business. That money he used to immerse himself in La Carbonera, going from bad to worse until he began to feel on his emaciated cheeks the breath of death. Death was what he had been seeking there, but when the moment came, fear took hold of him again.

One night, as he was leaving some dive, he ran straight into Onofre Bouvila. At his wits' end, he threw himself in Onofre's arms. "Help me," he begged. "Don't leave me to die here." Onofre said to him, "Come with me, Señor Braulio. Enough is enough."

From then on Señor Braulio did as he was told, never stopping to wonder if it was right or wrong. Now he unburdened himself of his disguise and hid it behind the sofa on which lay the man he had just murdered. He went to the window in his underclothes and with the little mirror of his powder puff signaled to Onofre and Efrén on the roof that the deed was done.

Telling Señor Braulio what he had to do, Onofre had insisted that he lock the office door and not open it to anyone until Onofre himself arrived. Now it dawned on Señor Braulio that in the heat of the moment he had forgotten the door. He heard hurried steps and shouts in the corridor outside—Don Alexandre's men coming to the aid of their boss. Somebody tried to enter and Señor Braulio nearly fainted, but nothing happened: Don Alexandre himself had locked the door, to make sure that the woman he hoped to seduce would not be able to escape. Thus he had unwittingly saved the life of his murderer. "Men! They're all the same," thought Señor Braulio when he realized that the door was locked. "Filthy beasts!"

Being forced to sit so long with the body of his victim played havoc with Señor Braulio's nerves. Onofre and Efrén found him on the point of suicide. Preparing to throw himself out the window, he had tied a heavy bronze base to his neck lest the drop prove insufficient to cause death, as he explained. Onofre and Efrén took all the papers they found in Don Alexandre's office.

"With this, we'll have half the city dancing to any tune we care to call," said Efrén. "That's Barcelona just about sewn up."

The same afternoon, Onofre and Efrén presented themselves in Margarito's office and said, "Mission accomplished." They showed him Don Alexandre's documents. Glancing through them, he whistled appreciatively. "That's Barcelona just about sewn up," he said. Hearing his own expression repeated, Efrén laughed out loud. Margarito, pretending only now to notice the giant, asked Onofre who he was. Onofre replied, "He is Efrén Castells, my friend and right-hand man. It was he who killed Joan Sicart." Hearing this, Margarito began to tremble, for he realized that his time was up. "If they don't mind my knowing that, it's because they're going to kill me," he thought. At that very instant, Efrén lifted Margarito out of his armchair and carried him in mid-air as effortlessly as if Margarito were a babe and not a full-grown man.

"What kind of a joke is this?" he shouted, kicking helplessly. But he knew it was no joke. Then he asked in a high-pitched, almost inaudible whine, "Where are you taking me?"

"Where you deserve to go," Onofre said. "You contrived all this to bring about my downfall. You wanted me to be killed by Sicart's men, and I always return a favor."

He opened the door to the balcony, and the giant from Calella tossed Margarito over the railing. It was on that same balcony that Don Humbert had been meditating on the meaning of life a few days before. Now the door of his office was opened wide, and in walked Onofre and Efrén. They came to report the success of the operation, they told him. Don Alexandre's gang had been broken up; his deputies, Sicart and Boix, were dead, and Don Alexandre was dead, too; all his papers were now in

Onofre's possession. Their losses were low: a total of four dead and half a dozen wounded. To this total had to be added, unfortunately, Arnau Puncella, alias Margarito, who had just suffered an inexplicable accident.

Don Humbert did not know what to say; he was appalled by so much bloodshed. Also, having just heard the heart-rending scream of Margarito, he realized that from now on things were going to be very different. "Well," he thought, sighing inwardly, "there's nothing to be done about it, and I'll just have to get used to the idea. The main thing, at the moment, is to come out of this meeting alive." He asked for a few additional points of information, more to gain time than anything else.

Onofre filled him in succinctly on the facts, though he knew Don Humbert was not listening. Onofre, with his show of deference, indicated that he was willing to go on working for him. Odón Mostaza and his men admired and loved Don Humbert and would never let themselves be dragged into betraying him, not even by Onofre Bouvila. Onofre, fully aware of this, was not thinking of trying anything along those lines.

Don Humbert eventually saw that, and they had a long talk. "The whole city belongs to me, but I am not up to taking on so much power," Don Humbert thought, "especially now that I have just lost my closest collaborator, whose body is still sprawled beneath my window. What am I to do?" Onofre took it upon himself to answer these unvoiced doubts: he had thought everything out. Without haughtiness, but with an assurance far beyond his years and rank, which Don Humbert had no chioce but to endure as best he could, he said it was necessary to take over Don Alexandre's organization, "but not by merging it with our own." He said "our own" with calculated insolence. Don Humbert had the urge to thrash him with the pizzle whip he always had at hand, but was dissuaded from doing so by the menacing presence of Efrén Castells. "Besides, what the boy is saying makes sense," he thought. "It is true that one shouldn't mix things together. I

159

am me, and Canals—may God have mercy on his soul—was Canals."

The crux of the matter now, with Margarito dead, was whom to put at the head of Canals's affairs. Onofre said he had the very man for the job. Don Humbert grew uneasy. "Surely not Odón Mostaza or this thug you have here?" Onofre did not take offense. "No, of course not. Every man to his own place. The person I am talking about has a talent for these things, and his loyalty is absolute. As it happens, he is waiting outside your door. With your permission, I would like you to meet him." Permission granted, he showed Señor Braulio into the office.

The fact that he had murdered a human being with his own hands unhinged Señor Braulio to such an extent that he could not think straight. The two facets of his personality blurred together: one minute he would be speaking with the manly composure of the landlord, the next he would be off on a wild tangent.

"I am a person of extremes," he confided to Don Humbert when they were introduced. "Whenever I go off men, I get depressed, I think of suicide. Fortunately, it didn't come to that. Ah, but you should have seen me with the dagger between my breasts and blood all over me."

Don Humbert smiled politely, scratching his neck, at a loss. What was a loony like this doing mixed up in affairs of such importance?

4

By summer, the dust had settled: the shoot-outs and running battles of a few months before were forgotten. Although at first there was much protesting, people gradually came to accept Señor Braulio in Don Alexandre's place. Señor Braulio was a model of tact and conservative in his approach; he never overstepped his authority, and he kept the accounts scrupulously.

Onofre forbade him to go back to his old ways. "There's to be no more gadding about in La Carbonera," he said. "We're respectable folk now. If you need to let off steam or go on a binge, get your wallet out and fix it up at home. We're earning plenty now, you know, and that's what money is for. But once you set foot in the street, you become an upright citizen again."

Señor Braulio moved into a second-floor apartment on Ronda de San Pablo, with his offices below. Some nights, the neighbors could hear singing coming from his apartment, and the sound of scuffling and furniture being broken. Then he would attend meetings with the leading lights of Barcelona, sporting a bandage on his forehead, a black eye, etc.

The only thing that preyed upon his mind was that his daughter was still in prison. He had the power now to have her released—obtaining that kind of favor was in fact his specialty—but Onofre said no. "We cannot yet afford to do that kind of thing. A move like that would get people talking and stir up the past. We'll deal with Delfina later on, when our position is more secure." The poor ex-hotelier adored his daughter, but obeyed Onofre. Secretly he sent food and preserves to her cell, not to mention bed linen and top-quality clothes. Delfina tore the clothes to shreds with her teeth and sent them back without a word of thanks.

Odón Mostaza was now working with Señor Braulio, taking over the role of Joan Sicart. Though he had neither the latter's leadership qualities nor his talents, he won the affection of his men. And since Odón was an enormously attractive man, Señor Braulio was delighted with his new colleague. Onofre assumed Odón's former duties, as well as those of Margarito.

Don Humbert gave his blessing to all these arrangements. His life was paradise on earth: he found himself at the head of the underworld of Barcelona, never having dreamed of rising to such heights. He was a man of contradictions, a curious blend of shrewdness and inanity, of duplicity and innocence. Extremely vain, he loved to be seen. However pressing the affairs awaiting his attention, he never missed a day without riding his famous dapple-gray mare down Paseo de Gracia at midday dressed to the nines.

This Andalusian mare, for which he had paid a fortune, was well trained; it trotted from Calle Caspe to Calle Valencia, prancing among the tilburies. The display did not always go off well: the mare was weak in the legs and sometimes fell, dumping her rider in the dust. Both would swiftly spring to their feet, the mare neighing and he brushing off pieces of horse manure still clinging to his frock coat. An urchin would dart out, dodging between the carriage wheels and the horses' legs, to pick up the top hat and riding whip and hand them to Don Humbert when he had regained his seat in the saddle. Unruffled, Don Humbert would toss a glinting coin in the midday sun as a tip, thus transforming the accident into a ceremony of vassalage.

That was how the bourgeoisie saw it; entirely lacking a sense of humor, they would pay him the homage of their finest smiles. "That," they said, "is the mark of a true gentleman." He, fool that he was, thought they admired him, but they admired only his money. The man they considered a climber and an upstart. Of this he was ignorant.

His wife, who regarded herself as the personification of beauty, intelligence, and distinction, found nothing quite good enough for her, and was of the opinion that she had married below her station. She treated Don Humbert like an unwanted dog, and the servants by and large followed her example. He submitted to these vexations without complaint; nobody had ever seen him annoyed, and he seemed to live in a world apart. Accustomed to being ignored, he would wander about the house making inarticulate sounds, not in the hope of being noticed but simply for the pleasure of hearing his own voice. Or sometimes he would say nothing but think he had. This total breakdown in communication did not bother him. All his energy went into his work, his self-esteem was satisfied by his limited social success, and his need to love was wholly fulfilled by his daughter, whom he idolized.

The notion of a summer vacation then differed greatly from our present-day notion. Only privileged families, following the practice of the royal family, changed their residence in favor of a more elevated and less humid location when the heat came. Not wishing to move far from Barcelona, they spent the summer in Sarriá, Pedralbes, or La Bonanova, all of which have now been absorbed by the city. The remainder of Barcelona's citizens sought relief from the heat in fans and pitchers of cool water. Bathing in the sea was beginning to become popular among the Frenchified youth, to the outrage of their elders. Since almost nobody knew how to swim, drownings were frequent. Then priests in their sermons would take these sorry statistics as proof of God's wrath.

Don Humbert appeared too late on the scene to acquire a summer residence in a well-established neighborhood, so he had to build his own on an estate north of the city known as La Budallera. There he bought an uneven site covered with pine trees, chestnut trees, and magnolias, and had an unpretentious house built. As is often the case with lawyers, no precautions were taken over the purchase of the land. Now he found himself obliged to spend time, energy, and money to settle predial disputes going back several centuries. The fact was, he had been at the receiving end of a piece of fast dealing: the site, murky, damp, and infested with mosquitos, was held in such low esteem that all he had for neighbors were a few hermits who lived in unhealthy caves, fed on roots and tree bark, wandered over the hillside with their private parts in full view, and had lost over the years their faculties of speech and reason.

"Only an imbecile like you would have bought a plot in such a refuse dump," his wife reproached him daily. Some days she would repeat this remark several times. She wanted to go bathing in Ocata or Montgat, mixing with the most chic set of the young bourgeoisie. But her husband, for once, put his foot down.

"Neither you nor our little girl can swim," he said, "and some current might pull you out to sea. I've been told, too, that there are octopuses and lampreys at the bottom that bite and maul bathers as their family and friends look on horrified."

"That is because they bathe naked," she answered. "Exposing their flesh, they arouse the fauna, who can distinguish between the human and the animal only by the clothing of the former." Her mouth twisted in a sneer as she said this, as if she took pleasure in the misfortune of those who did not know how to dress properly. As for herself—still wearing crinoline in the teeth of fashion, dragging a bordered train a good two yards long behind her, and profusely decked with jewels, whatever the hour— she was sure no animal would dare sink a tooth in her.

It was to this summer residence that Onofre Bouvila went to pay Don Humbert a visit in the summer of 1891.

He went up the hill at full gallop and found himself lost in the woods. His horse was covered with lather and panted in short, irregular gasps. "It'll die under me and leave me stranded," Onofre thought. "It's ironic that I of all people should get lost in the woods. I've become a city slicker."

Eventually he spotted a house surrounded by a luxuriant garden and a low, dark stone wall. A column of smoke was rising from the chimney. He dismounted and drew nearer on foot, leading the horse by the reins, heading for the wall to see if there was anyone he could approach for information.

The garden was deserted: birds chirped, flies and wasps buzzed, and butterflies fluttered. Through the trees he saw a girl go by. She was wearing a white organdy short-sleeved dress with lace festoonery, adorned with scarlet velvet braiding. Two curly locks of copper-colored hair had escaped from under a crimped hair net, also white, which was bordered with tiny flowers. The hair net and the curls permitted only fragmentary glimpses of her face: the arch of the nose, an oval chin, a glowing cheek, a gently curving forehead, etc.

Onofre was rooted to the spot; when he recovered, the vision had vanished. "Who could that have been?" he wondered. "She did not look like a country girl, but out alone like that in the country, with no company—how mysterious!" While he was occupied with these thoughts, a boy appeared. Onofre waved him over and asked if this was the place he was looking for. Since it was indeed the place, he handed the reins of his horse to the boy and had himself announced.

Don Humbert had strictly forbidden his men to come to his summer residence: he did not want to be disturbed there on any account, nor did he want his family to be involved in his affairs. Onofre disregarded this order, wanting to see just how far Don Humbert was prepared to tolerate his disobedience.

A maid showed him up to a hexagonal room on the second floor. Several doors opened onto this room. Since the only source of light was an opaque skylight, the room was dim and gave a pleasant impression of coolness. The nacreous stucco of the fireplace glimmered, and on the mantelpiece was a tall gilt-framed mirror, a bronze candelabrum, and an Empire-style clock enclosed in a glass dome. The only furnishings in the room were a corner table of painted wood with an alabaster Venus, a Moorish-style pedestal table, and a pile of satin cushions. Onofre was lost in admiration. "What elegance," he thought.

A noise behind him made him spin around, his hand automatically reaching in his trouser pocket, where he now kept the pistol he had taken from Joan Sicart months before. One of the doors had opened without warning, and there was the same girl he had glimpsed earlier in the garden; she had taken off her hair net and was holding a black prayer book. The unexpected presence of a stranger in the room made her stop in her tracks in the doorway. He opened his mouth to speak, but nothing came out. She, perhaps less shy, shut her book, curtsied gracefully, her knee touching the ground, and murmured something Onofre did not catch.

"I beg your pardon?" he managed to get out. His stare made her lower her eyes to the arabesques of the floor tiling.

"The peace of the Lord be with thee," she said finally in a tiny whisper.

"Oh," exclaimed Onofre, "and with thee."

"I did not know there was anybody in the room," she said, blushing. "The maid did not tell me . . ."

"Not at all, not at all," he interrupted her hastily. "On the contrary, it is I who should apologize, if I frightened you . . ."

Before he could finish his sentence, she left, closing the door behind her. On his own again, he paced up and down. "Fool, idiot, imbecile," he said to himself out loud, not caring if he was overheard. "Why did you let her leave? Now God only knows if you'll get another chance to see her." Never until that moment— and he had found himself in much tighter situations—had he hesitated; he had always been quick to seize an opportunity. "If I wasn't, I wouldn't be here now to tell the tale." He groaned, dropping to his knees on the soft cushions on the floor. "And I thought I was safe forever from these storms. . . . She's just a child. If I spoke to her of love, she would only be frightened, or, worse still, laugh at me. After all, what am I? A mule, a hired gun, a thug."

He was struggling to tear from his heart the arrow that chance had embedded there, fighting the tide that was sweeping over him. But his efforts were as futile as dikes of sand built to hold back the sea. In his fury he seized the alabaster Venus and hurled it with all his might into the mirror on the mantelpiece. First to hit the ground was the figurine, which burst into tiny pieces; the glass of the mirror, cracking, held for a split second— just long enough to reflect the girl's distorted face—before crashing down in several pieces that smashed to smithereens and scattered throughout the room. All that was left in the frame was quicksilver and mortar. He heard another noise behind him, a stifled cry this time. She had returned and was staring, aghast, at the mirror, which no longer reflected anything, as if the room and its occupants had ceased to exist. In this, she grasped what he had wanted to tell her; in his vandalism she saw meaning. She let him press her tightly to his chest and felt the impassioned young man's furious heartbeat.

"No one ever kissed me before," she said with what breath she had left.

"Nor will anyone as long as I live," said Onofre, "unless he wants his brains blown out." He kissed her mouth again and added, "And yours."

She let her head sink, her shoulders, and her copper-colored hair fell loose below her waist. Her arms, too, hung limp at her sides, until her fingers brushed the cool floor. Her knees bent, and she was supported only by Onofre's arm around her body. From her half-open lips came a long sigh and the word "Yes": thus in an instant did she commit herself and her future.

Onofre looked up and blinked: there was somebody else in the room. It was Don Humbert, who had just come in with two other gentlemen.

One of these gentlemen was Cosme Valbuena, an architect. Don Humbert, who was bored to death, had decided to build an extension to the house, taking advantage of a structure already attached to it, a former henhouse and dovecote. Carrying out the work, however, meant encroaching on the adjoining plot. This appropriation of a couple of feet of land had given rise to a lawsuit with the owner of the neighboring property, who was, as it happened, a friend and an occasional business partner of Don Humbert. The latter, too busy with weightier matters to waste time over such trifling disputes, had sent to Barcelona for the services of a young but highly respected lawyer, a specialist in boundary disputes.

These three men had spent the entire day going over the

house, the garden, and the surrounding fields. The lawyer took measurements with a piece of string and made architectural proposals, which the architect did not dignify with a response. But the architect in turn suggested legal steps to Don Humbert to help him win the case he had on his hands. They argued, got worked up, and generally had a wonderful time. Then they sat around the table and ate with enormous appetites.

Don Humbert's wife made no protest over the presence of these parasites, since she saw her daughter rapidly approaching the eligible age, and both the lawyer and the architect were bachelors with bright prospects. At the very least, both had access to their respective professional circles, "which is more than that useless lump of a husband of mine can say," she thought. Don Humbert laughed at her reasonings. "My dear, the things you get into your head: the girl has just turned ten."

But now he did not know what to think. He was not so stupid, however, as to be unable to grasp the significance of his daughter's languidity, or of his subordinate's fierce and thirsting gaze. Nor so stupid as not to realize that the best policy was to pretend to have seen nothing.

'Well, well," was all he said, "I see you two have introduced yourselves and are getting along like a house on fire."

It took them a while to disentangle and compose themselves, both extremely embarrassed. Onofre, who only minutes before had despised Don Humbert, saw in him now the father of the woman he loved, and was prepared to show him every mark of respect. His attitude of defiance changed immediately into one of deference. The lawyer and the architect poked around the room, assessing the extent of the damage.

"The most important thing," said the lawyer, "is that nobody gets hurt on the broken glass."

Onofre returned to Barcelona with the sun at his back. From the underbrush came the noise of crickets, and the sky was filled with stars. "What will become of me now?" he wondered, his eyes fixed on that celestial map. He knew that as long as she returned his love, he could not betray Don Humbert Figa i Morera.

Before the summer drew to a close, the architect and the lawyer both asked for the hand of Don Humbert's daughter. Their rivalry gave her the chance to play for time, but finally she refused point-blank to be married to either one. Her refusals were sometimes apologetic, and sometimes involved fits of rage. Being a delicate creature, she hurt herself when banging her head against the wall or laying into the furniture with her fists, and wore bandages a good deal of the time. This resistance, with the veiled threat that her fits might grow more serious if she did not get her way, had the desired effect on her father, who immediately gave in.

Her mother, however, suspected that her resistance was motivated not so much by dislike of the suitors as by another, more powerful cause. She recalled the incident of the broken mirror and alabaster figurine, and the fact that this double mishap coincided with the unprecedented visit of one of her husband's subordinates to their Budallera estate, and drew her own conclusions. When she interrogated Don Humbert, he admitted that he had indeed chanced upon a scene which "might lead one to suppose that the girl was in some way inclined toward the boy."

"And this boy, who is he?" his wife demanded. Don Humbert gave a garbled explanation, to which she paid no attention. What interested her was not so much what her husband was telling her as what he was trying not to tell her. From his stammering she deduced that Onofre Bouvila was the least suitable suitor of all. "Very well," she said to herself, "we'll do without the lawyer and the architect, but we'll put the girl where that boor can't get at her. There will be time enough to find her a husband when she's forgotten him. She is young yet and can afford to let a few chances slip by." At his wife's behest, Don Humbert had their daughter sent to a boarding school.

The girl put up no fight over this: there she was free from

further courtships. "All in all, it's the best thing that could happen to us," she decided. When he got over his initial indignation, Onofre saw it that way, too. "One day she'll be mine," he thought. "For the moment, however, patience is called for."

Hundreds of letters from him reached her in the boarding school by the most devious paths. There was merit in this: since he barely knew how to write his own name before, it could be said that he learned to write fluently in those love letters. Greater intervals separated her answers, for she had to dodge the nuns' censorship. "Above all else," she said in one letter, "I give thanks unto God through Jesus Christ, since God, for whom my spirit doth profess the profoundest veneration, is witness to the constancy of my remembrance of you, and I beseech Him ever in my prayers, if it be His will, to appoint some day favorable to our being reunited, for my soul doth desire to see you." Such language, modeled on Saint Paul, was odd coming from an enamored adolescent; it could be explained by her fear of the letters' falling into the hands of the nuns or her parents, or by genuine devotion on her part. Later on, as a married woman, she always seemed very devout. Those who knew her and had dealings with her in her mature years gave contradictory accounts of her; "serene" and "distracted" were the terms most commonly applied to her. Some were of the opinion that she sought solace in religion because she was so unhappy all her life on account of Onofre Bouvila.

Meanwhile, Barcelona, burdened with more fears than hopes, was making ready to cross the line that separated the last century from this one. "In my opinion, what we have achieved with so much effort will turn out to be no more than a nine days' wonder," said upright citizens from the somber hush of their clubs, circles, and salons. The recession would not go away. Shops selling luxury goods along Calle Fernando were closing their doors one after another; in their place, big department stores opened in the Ramblas and on Paseo de Gracia—a novelty greeted with reserve by the people of Barcelona. "The department stores: Aladdin's Lamp or Ali Baba's Cave?" was the headline given to a report by one newspaper.

The government's economic policy did not help matters. Turning a deaf ear to the arguments and pleas of the Catalans who came to Madrid for this purpose, and of a few Castilians farsighted or well paid enough to side with them, the government annulled all protectionist measures sheltering domestic industries. With no customs barriers to face, foreign products that were better, cheaper, and easier to use than their homespun counterparts finally killed off a market that had been in poor shape to begin with. Factories closed, and the massive layoffs that resulted added to the misery of the working classes.

On top of all that were the wars in Cuba and Melilla. Every week hundreds of youngsters, many of them little more than children, were packed off to America or Africa. On quaysides and railroad platforms there were heart-rending scenes. The Civil Guard were often obliged to charge groups of mothers trying to stop the transportation of the troops by hanging on to the ships' mooring ropes or blocking the path of the locomotives. Of the hundreds and thousands of young people sent to the front lines, few returned, and those that did returned maimed or seriously ill.

These events added fuel to the fire—as if fuel were needed—of popular unrest. The workers' associations that had so preoccupied the late Don Alexandre were gathering momentum again, especially the anarchist ones. Among the anarchists were supporters of Foscarini, followers of de Weerd, and champions of leaders who had appeared more recently on the scene. Occasionally these groups joined forces to call and carry out general strikes, but the strikes did not live up to expectations. Frustrated by so many failures, by so much useless striving, some turned to more direct action.

And so began the black decades of the terror. No public event, parade, procession, or entertainment was entirely free from the menace of a bomb. Deafened, blinded by the smoke, the survivors would search the rubble for the bodies of family or friends; others fled in all directions, wild-eyed and bloodstained, not stopping to see if they were injured or not. Wherever the well-to-do congregated, a bomb would give vent to rage and desperation.

Whenever such an event occurred, Onofre remembered Pablo and the anarchist ideas he had preached, ideas that Onofre himself had reluctantly helped to propagate. Sometimes he wondered if it was Pablo who planted the bomb for Martínez Campos, or the bomb in the Liceo, whose tragic echoes, though faint, can still be heard today on gala nights in the boxes and galleries of the celebrated opera house. But he kept such reflections to himself: given his present position and romantic ties, he preferred not to divulge his former association with the anarchists. Indeed, he told his sweetheart and all his professional acquaintances that in reality he was a young man of good family obliged by adverse fortune to perform tasks of a dubious nature, such as those he carried out on Don Humbert's behalf. By then nobody remembered his role in the violent days that put an end to the empire and the life of Don Alexandre. At every opportunity, Onofre repudiated violence, advocated the severest measures against anarchists (whom he unflinchingly called "rabid dogs"), and praised the government's bloodthirsty measures to restore order.

This posture was well received among those members of the upper bourgeoisie with whom Onofre came into contact. Seeing their patrimony as well as their very lives threatened, they called a truce in their age-old quarrel with Madrid. However damaging the government's attitude might have been with regard to Catalonia's commercial interests, far worse would be the consequences of being deprived of its armed protection in this struggle. In private, they bemoaned having to renounce their old hostility. "It is a sorry state of affairs," they sighed, "when we have to go running to some decked-up general when Catalonia has given the Spanish army its fiercest lions." This was an allusion to General Prim, hero of Mexico and Morocco, and General Weyler, who at that time was keeping the Cuban rebels in check. What most worried the fainthearted was the prospect that the Catalan nationalists, who were growing in strength, might win some election, and that that might infuriate those powers in Madrid to whose benevolence they felt they owed their lives.

So the business dealings arranged by Señor Braulio flourished. Onofre secretly rubbed his hands with delight. Years later he would say, "I always thought that at the root of Spain's problems lay the fact that all the money was in the hands of boors and cowards." The government, for its part, sat back and reaped the fruits of the situation, dragging its heels when it came to tackling Catalonia's internal problems, as if Catalonia were just another colony. It dispatched military troglodytes who knew only the language of the bayonet and whose idea of imposing peace was putting half of mankind to the slaughter.

"These are splendid times," Onofre thought, "for the man who is imaginative, rich, and bold. I have no problem with the first and the last, but how do I obtain the money? Yet I must obtain it somewhere, for one gets a chance like this only once in a lifetime, if at all."

Having a sweetheart only quickened his ambition, and not seeing her left his energies intact. He no longer went out on the town with Odón Mostaza and his crew, preferring not to be seen in public with ruffians. The few little pleasures he allowed himself were arranged through Señor Braulio and Efrén.

At around that time, the newspapers reported that the comet Sargon, having a diameter of approximately fifty thousand kilometers, was heading for the earth; there were the usual prophets announcing the end of the world, to which the current social unrest and gloom were only a prelude. There was concern, but in the end nothing came of it.

CHAPTER FOUR

1

The traveler coming to Barcelona for the first time soon notices where the old city ends and the new begins. The old, crooked streets suddenly run straight; they become broader, the pavements more generous, the buildings more imposing, and stout banana trees provide welcome shade. The traveler is occasionally bewildered by the change, believing himself whisked off to some other city by magic. Consciously or unconsciously, the people of Barcelona reinforce this impression: on passing from one sector to the other, they change in appearance, attitude, and attire. It was not always thus; the transition has its explanation, its history, its legend.

Over the centuries, the capture or the sacking of Barcelona was never halted by the city walls. The city's growth, however, was. While within the walls the population density went on rising, making life intolerable, without lay open fields and wasteland. In the evenings or on public holidays, people in neighboring villages would go up on the hilltops (today known as Putxet,

Gracia, San José de la Montaña, etc.) and look down, sometimes with brass telescopes, on the citizens of Barcelona milling busily to and fro, orderly and punctilious, greeting one another, disappearing from sight in the maze of back streets, only to meet again later with more handshaking, further inquiries as to their respective healths and fortunes, and another round of leavetakings. The villagers enjoyed the spectacle. Occasionally a simple rustic would attempt to score a hit on a city dweller with a stone, though this was impossible, given the distance, not to mention the walls.

The overcrowding was ruinous to public health: any illness soon turned into an epidemic, and those stricken could not be quarantined. The city gates closed to contain the plague, and the villagers outside formed vigilante groups—cudgeling fugitives back into the city—and trebled the price of foodstuffs.

It was also ruinous to public morals. "Taking lodgings in a hostelry of whose excellence I had had glowing report," writes a traveler in his chronicle, "I discovered I was to share a room of no more than six square meters with as many persons, that is to say five persons and myself. It transpired that two of the company were newlyweds on their honeymoon, and no sooner had they retired to bed, the room being in darkness by then, than they began to disturb our slumber with a profusion of grunts, screams, and sniggers. And all this at an exorbitant price—and one was expected to be grateful to boot!" More concisely, the Reverend Father Campuzano writes: "Rare is the citizen of Barcelona who before reaching the age of reason has not graphically ascertained for himself the manner of his begetting." There were frequent epidemics of a venereal nature, much rape and seduction, and in some cases, such as that of Jacinto (or Jacinta) Peus, psychological disorders: "Consequent upon my seeing with such frequency my parents and my brothers and my sisters and my uncles and my aunts and my grandfathers and my grandmothers and my cousins and the domestic staff all stark naked, in the end

I could no longer tell which were men and which women, nor to which gender I should assign my own person."

The housing shortage was acute in the extreme; the astronomical price of accommodations consumed the greater part of family incomes. Of some use in this context are a few easily grasped statistics. In the middle of the nineteenth century the surface area of Barcelona was 427 hectares. In the same period Paris covered 7,802 hectares, Berlin 6,310, and London 31,685. Even an apparently small city like Florence occupied 4,226 hectares—i.e., ten times the area occupied by Barcelona. The population density per hectare is also revealing: 291 in Paris, 189 in Berlin, 128 in London, 700 in Barcelona.

Why were the city walls not demolished? Because the government would not give permission: on strategic pretexts that did not stand up to analysis, it kept the city in a state of suffocation, kept it from growing in size or power. The kings, queens, and regents who in turn occupied the Spanish throne claimed that they had more pressing problems to deal with. The government was at best indifferent, at worst sarcastic: "If they need more land, let them burn down more convents"—an allusion to the convents burned by mobs in the outbreaks of civil disorder that occurred during those turbulent decades, and to the fact that those sites were later used for community purposes: as public squares, markets, etc.

Finally the walls were taken down. "It looks as if we'll be able to breathe at last," said the people of Barcelona. But the reality had not changed: with walls or without them, the city remained just as cramped. People lived out their lives in tiny squalid rooms, in evil-smelling and indecent promiscuity; they lived on top of one another, with their domestic animals thrown in. With the city walls gone, the valley that swept out to the foothills of the Sierra de Collcerola was in full view all day, so that the overcrowding became even more glaring. "Damnation," the citizens would say, "all that empty land, and here are we stuck like rats in holes. Is it fair that we should be worse off than those lettuces?" In this frame of mind, the city folk turned to the mayor.

The mayor of Barcelona was not the same one that years later was to carry out the World's Fair project. A short, potbellied man, he was very religious: he heard Holy Mass and went to Communion every day. In those moments of seclusion, he did his best not to let his thoughts turn to municipal problems, wishing to devote his full attention to the miracle of transubstantiation. But the urban-development problem, the bane of his life at the time, would nonetheless distract him. "Something has to be done," he would say to himeself, "but what?" He had studied the expansion of other European cities—Paris, London, Vienna, Rome, Saint Petersburg. The schemes were good, but costly. And none took into account the peculiarities of Barcelona. When someone discussed the pros and cons of the Paris model, the mayor would always reply that it was a good model "but does not take into account the peculiarities of Barcelona." He would say the same of the Vienna model, and so on. Barcelona, he was convinced, had to have its own plan, repudiating imitation.

One day, receiving Holy Communion, he had a vision. He was sitting in the mayor's chair in his office, and in came a macer to announce a visit. The mayor wondered whether the visitor was a committee member or some delegate. The macer, interrupting the mayor's surmises, said, "It is a gentleman from Olot." Without further ado, the visitor entered. The mayor was amazed: the man was enveloped in a halo, radiating light all around; his skin was silvery, as if coated with silver paint, and his hair, down to his shoulders, consisted of silver strands. His tunic also had a silvery sheen, as if all his person were made of some supernatural alloy. The mayor did not dream of asking for an explanation of all this, but merely asked to what he owed the honor. "We have observed," said the visitor, "that for some time now your mind has been wandering when you receive the Sacred Host." "It is my attention, not my devotion, that is flagging," the mayor apologized. "It's this urban-development business—it's driving me to distraction. I don't know what to do." "Tomorrow at cockcrow," said the visitor, "wait at the Western Gate. There you shall see the chosen one come, but do not tell him that I appeared to you." The mayor woke with a start: he was in the church, on his prie-dieu, with the consecrated Host still on his tongue. He had dreamed the whole thing in a twinkling.

The following day, at the appointed time, the mayor was at the spot where, as chance would have it, the Arco de Triunfo was to be built as the entrance to the World's Fair. People, animals, and carts were already on the move. To avoid being recognized, the mayor wore a simple cape and a wide-brimmed hat; he carried some white goat's cheese in an earthenware bowl, and every now and then gave it a sprinkling of oil and thyme, as he had seen done as a child in the farmhouse where his grandparents lived. Thus the day went by. The people on the street commented on the agitation in the city over the mayor's disappearance: he had failed to show up in the church where he invariably heard Mass. Not a penny was missing from the public coffers, the passers-by said; they all agreed that this was the strangest aspect of the whole business.

In the evening, as the sun turned into a red circle, enormous in circumference, the mayor saw a strange being approach. From a childhood scalding, the left side of the man's face was smooth and beardless; the other side, however, was deeply wrinkled and bore half a mustache and half a beard of noteworthy length, since he had just completed or was about to undertake on foot a pilgrimage to Santiago de Compostela. He was called, he said, Abraham Schlagobers, which in German means whipped cream; he said he was not a Jew, despite his name, but of a longstanding Christian family, that he was on a pilgrimage to keep a vow he had made, the motive for which he would not disclose, and that he was a builder. The mayor immediately took him to the town hall, showed him the maps of Barcelona and its environs, and put at his disposal everything necessary for him to design a city. "This will be," Abraham Schlagobers told him, "the City of God that Saint John speaks of, the new Jerusalem." Since Jerusalem was pulled down and could nevermore rise again, the Lord having said that no stone would be left upon a stone, another city was destined to act as its substitute, as the center of Christendom. Barcelona was on the same latitude as Jerusalem, and was a Mediterranean city—everything converged to make it the chosen city. Together they recited the words of the revelation:

> *And I saw the holy city, new Jerusalem, coming down out of heaven from God, prepared as a bride adorned for her husband; and I heard a great voice from the throne saying, Behold, the dwelling of God is with men. He will dwell with them, and they shall be his people, and God himself will be with them; he will wipe away every tear from their eyes, and death shall be no more, neither shall there be mourning nor crying nor pain any more.*

The project was finished in less than six months, after which Abraham Schlagobers disappeared without a trace. It has been suggested that this person never really existed, that it was the mayor himself who drew up the plans. It has also been suggested that the man did exist but that the name he gave was not his real name, and that he was neither a pilgrim nor a builder but simply an adventurer who took advantage of the unorthodox ways of the mayor, astutely putting down on paper his protector's visions while living at municipal expense for the duration—a not implausible theory. When the plans were completed, the mayor found them to his satisfaction and submitted them to the plenum for its approval.

These plans no longer exist: they were either deliberately destroyed or else are buried irretrievably beneath a mountain of archives. All that has come down to us are partial sketches, and none too reliable at that, fragments of self-justifying memory. The units of measurement used were the fathom and the parasang, the cubit and the stadium, which no doubt would have greatly confused the builders had work ever begun. From what is now known as the Tibidabo down to the sea, a navigable canal was to flow, and from the left and right of it would spring twelve narrower, shallower canals (one for each of the twelve tribes of Israel), which in turn were to flow into as many artificial lakes, around which were to be organized the districts—semireligious, semisecular units each administered by a deputy mayor and a Levite. There is no mention of where the water for the canals and its effluents was to come from, although there are veiled allusions to wells situated in what today are Vallvidrera, La Floresta, San Cugat and Las Planas. In the center of the old city (which according to the plans was to be leveled, except for the cathedrals Santa María del Mar, El Pino, and San Pedro de las Puellas), five bridges would cross the canal, representing the five theological virtues. The town hall, the City Council chamber, and the government house were to be replaced by three basilicas corresponding to the three faculties of the soul. There was a temperance market, a fear-of-God market, etc. Other aspects of the project remain unknown; we shall never know what they were like.

The plenum was flabbergasted. It finally chose to give the project the unanimous and unreserved support of the municipality. The council, however, pointed out the need to observe the regulations in force at the time: the project as passed by the plenum had to be submitted for approval to the minister for internal affairs, who had jurisdiction over all the town halls in Spain. The mayor flew into a temper. "Must even the will of God first go through Madrid?" he stormed. "It is the law," sighed all the councillors, privately relieved. They made a show of solidarity with the mayor's fury, but in truth were passing the buck to

Madrid. "Whenever they can, they dump on us," they thought. "For a change, let them do us a big favor and turn this down."

Madrid replied that the Right Honorable Minister for Internal Affairs acknowledged receipt of the so-called Enlargement Plan for the City of Barcelona, but that he could not take it into consideration because the manner of its presentation did not conform with the procedure detailed in the appropriate legislation. Indeed, the law required that three alternative projects be submitted, the minister to choose among them.

The mayor hit the ceiling. Everyone strove to calm him down. "Let us invite tenders, and send our project along with two others to Madrid. The minister cannot fail to select ours—he cannot help perceiving that it is clearly the best," they told him. The mayor believed his project had been inspired by God and that there was not, nor could there ever be, one better than it, so he let the competition be announced, and impatiently waited for the projects to be submitted, judged, and the winners declared; he even agreed to have his project submitted along with all the rest, in the conviction that it would be declared a winner, as proved to be the case. As a result, the mayor's project, which until then had been seen by only a few, went from hand to hand, from mouth to mouth, and became the talk in all the city's enlightened coteries. At last the three winning projects were sent to Madrid. There the minister stalled as long as he could, offering no explanations. The mayor was hopping from foot to foot. "Any news from Madrid?" he would ask at midnight, waking with a start. His valet would have to go into his bedroom and calm him, for he had no wife.

The minister's answer, when finally it came, was shattering: none of the three projects was acceptable. On the other hand, he approved with his signature a fourth project, a project that had not been entered for the competition or that possibly had been but was rejected by the jury. It was later to be called "the Cerdá scheme."

"I am of the persuasion," the mayor wrote the minister, "that the honorable gentleman wished to have a little jest at our expense, pretending to give his approval to a scheme that not only was not included in the recent dispatch to Your Honor, but that also has met from the outset with the disfavor of all the citizenry of Barcelona." This time the minister's reply came like lightning. "The citizenry of Barcelona, my friend, will show itself duly grateful for small mercies if the Cerdá scheme one day sees the light of day in the manner approved by me," he wrote to the mayor. "As for you, my worthy mayor, allow me to remind you that your duties do not extend to determining when a minister is or is not having a joke. Kindly restrict yourself to carrying out my instructions faithfully, and do not oblige me to remind you upon whom your post in the last instance depends," etc., etc.

The mayor summoned another plenum. "Our ears," he said, "have received a good boxing, and a richly deserved one. Why did we turn to Madrid instead of acting on our own, as our condition permits and our honor demands? Now, thanks to our cowardice, Barcelona stands offended. Let this be a lesson to us all." There was a burst of applause. The mayor commanded silence and spoke again. His voice resounded in the Salón de Ciento. "Now we must make our reply," he said. "The measure I am about to propose may seem drastic, but I beg you not to judge the matter hastily. Think it over, and you will see we have no other way out. What I propose is this: that since Madrid will not hear us, but with arrogance and disdain seeks to impose its will, each one of us, representatives as we are of the people of Barcelona, should challenge the civil servant of the ministry who corresponds to his own rank, and slay that person in a duel or die defending our rights and dignity, just as I—here, now—publicly hurl my gauntlet to the floor of this historic chamber and challenge the Right Honorable Minister for Internal Affairs to a duel. Let him and his accursed bureaucrats know once and for all that when a Catalan is denied justice in a government office, he will seek it on the field of honor."

And he hurled his gauntlet to the floor—a gray kid glove he had purchased the day before at Comella's, and over which he had carried out an all-night vigil before the altar to Saint Lucia. The assembly cheered him loudly, paying him tribute with an unending ovation; those who had gloves with them followed suit; those who had not, hurled down hats, dickies, and even shoes. The poor mayor was moved to tears—unaware that the same men who at that moment so warmly endorsed his proposal had not the slightest intention of carrying it out, that some had in fact already sent letters to Madrid expressing their support for the minister, deploring the mayor's attitude, and voicing doubts as to the latter's mental health.

Knowing nothing of this, the mayor sent a letter of challenge to Madrid, which the minister returned torn to pieces in a wax-sealed envelope on the back of which he had written in his own hand: "Take your buffoonery somewhere else." The councillors suggested to the mayor that he should not persevere, that there was nothing more to be done, that he should take a vacation. It finally dawned on him that they had left him out on a limb.

He resigned the mayoralty, took up residence in Madrid, and tried to interest the Parliament in his idea. A few members feigned interest for reasons of political expediency: some thought thereby to win the good will of the Catalans, others expected compensation of a financial nature for their intercession. When they realized that the ex-mayor was simply a crackpot representing nobody but himself, they indignantly dropped him and his schemes. He resorted to bribing the more venal officials, throwing away his personal fortune in this—and it had been a sizable one.

Three years later, ruined and heartbroken, he returned to Barcelona, ascended Montjuich, and looked down on the plain below. From there he could see the new streets, the trenches where the trains would run, the drains and the aqueducts. "How can it be," he asked himself, "that a mere bureaucrat can foil

God's express will?" So great was his despair that he threw himself off the cliff. His soul went straight to hell, where it was explained to him that the visitor of his dream had really been Satan himself. "Ah, dread dissembler," exclaimed the ex-mayor, seized with remorse at having been so foolish, "you took me in, telling me you were an angel." "I never said that," returned Satan. "We devils may adopt whatever shape best suits our purpose while tempting mortals, but not the shape of a saint or an angel, and certainly not that of Our Lord God or His Holy Mother. Therefore I said I was a 'gentleman from Olot,' which is the nearest thing I know to a celestial body. The rest was supplied by your vanity and your blindness, whose terrible consequences will be suffered by Barcelona and yourself for all eternity." And with that he roared with sonorous and chilling laughter.

The passing years were to prove, as is their way, that of all the characters in this legend—always excepting the devil, as ever a law unto himself—only the mayor was in the right. The plans forced through by the ministry, for all their good points, were excessively functional, suffering from an exaggerated rationalism: no provision was made for open spaces necessary for public events; for monuments to symbolize the great deeds and qualities which all peoples are inclined to attribute, rightly or wrongly, to themselves; for gardens and wooded parks to incite people to romance and crime; or for statued avenues, bridges, or viaducts. Instead, the new city was an unbroken grid that disconcerted strangers and local people alike, designed solely to facilitate vehicular traffic and the more prosaic of life's functions. Had the initial conception been realized, the city would at least have been pleasing to the eye, comfortable, and healthy; built as it was built, it lacked even those virtues.

The people of Barcelona did not object to the scheme as forcefully as the visionary ex-mayor prophesied, but neither did they make it their own. It did not captivate their imagination or touch any ancestral chord. They proved reluctant to buy, build, and occupy the space that for centuries they had claimed and longed for; they peopled it little by little, impelled by demographic pressure, not by desire.

Given the general indifference, and with the connivance of those who might perhaps have been able to prevent it (the same set that had sent letters to the minister behind the deranged ex-mayor's back in order to protect their sinecures), speculators ended up in control of the land, distorted the original plans, and turned the area into a noisy, pestilent conurbation as cramped as the old Barcelona that the plans had been intended to supersede. Through a lack of ideological commitment (such as that of the ill-starred ex-mayor), Barcelona was left with no center (except possibly the Paseo de Gracia, bourgeois and pretentious, but efficient even today for strictly commercial purposes) to accommodate public celebrations, meetings, coronations, and lynchings. The successive expansions of the city took place haphazardly, the only aim being to create space to put the people who would not fit in the sectors already built, and to make as much money as possible in the process. The deterioration of all that was old became the only indication of progress.

2

Uncle Tonet had aged, and farsightedness increasingly impaired his vision, but he went on driving his trap every day, or nearly every day, from Sant Climent to Bassora and from Bassora to Sant Climent. One day, in her eighteenth year, his mare was found dead in the stable. She had never been known to fold her legs under her to rest; now she lay on her back with her legs sticking straight up, as if trotting on the South Pole.

Uncle Tonet bought himself another mare instead of retiring, as he ought to have done. The new mare did not know the road: a mare, however smart, takes several years to learn a road as long and as complicated as that one. What with the mare's blundering and the driver's poor sight, they got lost many times, and once seriously. Night overtook them, and Uncle Tonet had not the faintest notion where they were. In previous years he could have consulted the stars, but now he lived in an ever-deepening mist. Wolves howled, and the mare, unnerved, could only be persuaded to continue by the generous use of the whip.

Finally they caught sight of bonfires and went in that direction. Uncle Tonet took these for shepherds' fires, even though the rocky terrain was not fit for grazing of any kind. In fact, it was a brigands' camp, that of Cornet and his band. These brigands were survivors from the last of the Carlist civil wars; instead of laying down their arms and trusting in an amnesty, they chose to take to the mountains. "If we give ourselves up, we'll be put to the sword," said Cornet to his men, whose devotion he had managed to win over the years of that bloody campaign. "Let us become brigands. Since we're marked for death in any case, why not risk our lives over trifles?" Convinced by this argument, his men displayed a singular recklessness. They gave the slip to all the armed contingents sent out after them and became famous in the region as romantic daredevils. The farmers and shepherds tolerated them. Though they did not protect them — tired by then of the centuries of constant skirmishes on their doorstep — neither did they give them away or shoot them down when they had the chance. The brigands, expecting to live fast and die with their boots on, ended up growing old in the mountains, forgotten by the authorities.

When Uncle Tonet stumbled across their camp, he found a group of old men so weak, they could scarcely lift their blunderbusses to their shoulders. "I thought you folks had disappeared years ago," he said to them, "that you were just a legend." They gave him supper and let him spend the night with them. They said little, unaccustomed to strangers, and because among themselves they had long ago run out of things to talk about. They knew Uncle Tonet by sight, having watched from a distance the comings and goings of the trap hundreds of times, but they never waylaid it, for they knew he was bringing things the country people badly needed.

The following morning they pointed him in the right direction and gave him a hunk of bread and a generous length of Catalan sausage. Before he set off, they took him to the little cemetery where lay the mortal remains of the brigands who had died of illness in the mountains: the dead were almost as numerous as the survivors. They kept wild flowers on the tombs and a great show of crosses, for they were all unshakable in their faith.

This encounter occurred some time ago. By now the mare was nearly familiar with the route, and Uncle Tonet was nearly blind.

"But your voice," he said as he finished telling this tale to the traveler who had hired his services in Bassora that afternoon, "is not altogether unfamiliar to me." When the traveler remained silent, Uncle Tonet guffawed. "Why, of course! You are Onofre Bouvila! Don't deny it." Onofre neither denied nor confirmed it, and Uncle Tonet laughed heartily. "It has to be. The voice was familiar enough, but this angry silence settles it: you're like that madman of a father of yours, whom I knew well. When he went off to Cuba, I took him in this very trap to Bassora. He can't have been much older then than you are now, but already he was putting on those same haughty airs, as if we all had cow manure on our boots, and in our boots, too. When he returned from Cuba, I brought him back home. Everybody was gathered in front of the church—I can see it now, despite these useless eyes. Your father was sitting right there, where you are now, bolt upright. He was wearing a white drill suit and a straw hat, one of them they call a Panama, like the country. Never said a word all the way. He was letting on that he was rich, but he didn't have a cent. Instead of money, do you know what he brought back?"

"A monkey," answered Onofre.

"A sick monkey—yes, sir—I see you have a good memory,"

said Uncle Tonet, lashing at the mare, which had stopped to munch some weeds at the side of the road. "Don't start eating now, Persa, at this hour, you know it doesn't agree with you." He cracked the whip in the air. "Persa," he explained, "is her name. She already had it when I bought her. Now, what were we talking about? Yes, your father's stupidity: a cretin, if you want my opinion. Ouch! You wouldn't hit an old man that's nearly blind, would you? Well, it's plain enough you would. All right, I'll watch my tongue, but that won't change the way I think. You people are all like that: you only want to hear what you want to hear, even when you know that that's not what people are thinking. Stupidity, I call it. But it doesn't bother me, doesn't surprise me: I sized up human vanity years ago. I've met a lot of people in my time, and I've had time to think. Whenever I make this trip without a passenger, I use the time to think. And I figured out I'm not going to change them, however hard I try. And even if I could change them, I'm not sure I'd want to. There are folks as have garlic soup for eyeballs. They open their eyes and all they see is garlic soup."

The coachman rambled on like that, with the incoherence that in old people and simpletons sometimes passes for wisdom. Onofre was not listening; he was gazing at the rough road he had traveled going the other way eight years ago.

He had set out one spring morning, as the sun was just appearing. The day before, he had announced to his parents his intention of going to Bassora. He would call on Messrs. Baldrich, Vilagrán, and Tapera, he told them; they would most certainly give him a job in one of their firms, and that way he could help pay off the debt contracted by his father. His father disapproved: he was entirely responsible for the tight situation they were in and would not allow his son to sacrifice himself. . . . Onofre cut him short; his father, who had lost all authority, fell silent. The boy told his mother he would stay in Bassora for as long it took to accumulate the money they needed. "It'll be a few months, a year at most. I'll write," he promised. "I'll keep you up to date on what's happening through Uncle Tonet."

But in fact he had decided to go to Barcelona and never come back. At the time he thought he would never see his parents again, never again set foot in the house in which he was born and had lived until that day. When he climbed onto the trap, his father handed up the bundle containing his personal belongings. Onofre placed this bundle carefully on the floor of the carriage. His mother had wrapped his scarf around his neck. Since nobody spoke, Uncle Tonet stepped up to the coachman's seat and said, "If you're ready, we'll be off." Onofre nodded, lest his voice sound strange and betray what he was feeling. Uncle Tonet cracked his whip and the mare moved off, sinking its hoofs into the mud. "It'll be a rough trip," Uncle Tonet said. His father waved his Panama hat, and his mother said something Onofre did not catch. Then he turned to look at the road ahead, and did not see his parents receding behind him.

The trap passed the river path, the enchanted-grotto path, the bird-hunting path, the fishing path (not the same as the river path), and the autumn mushroom-picking path; it had never occurred to him that there were so many paths. When the valley disappeared under the morning mist, he could still see the church tower. Flocks of sheep were up ahead. Shepherds greeted him, raising their crooks and laughing. Their chins were muffled in their scarves, and they were wearing caps and sheepskin coats. These shepherds had known him from the day he was born. "I will never again meet anyone who knows me that way," Onofre thought.

Then they came to abandoned farmhouses. The cold and the rain had made the doors and shutters come loose from their hinges, revealing the interiors of those empty houses full of dead leaves; birds flew out of some of them. These were the homes of those who had gone to Bassora to seek jobs in the factories there; they had let the fire in the hearth go out, as they put it.

189

Now eight years had passed, and Onofre had done many things in those years; had met many people, many of them odd, most of them bad; and he had killed some of them without really knowing why. Though with some he had formed alliances. Now the trees, the color of the sky through the foliage, the murmur of the wind in the woods, and the country smells all seemed familiar to him. He had the impression he had never left this valley, that he had dreamed all the rest. Even Don Humbert's daughter, for whom he felt such a fierce love, seemed to him now a fleeting vision, a flash in his imagination. He had to make an effort to remember her features. Those features merged in his mind with others: the hapless Delfina, who was still in prison after all this time, or the young girl he had met the week before. Barely half a dozen words had passed between him and this girl, who was part of a troupe of puppeteers whose performance he had seen by pure chance. She struck his fancy because, though not ugly, she had a doggy face. She was so young, he had been obliged to negotiate with her parents, handing over the money to them in advance. This had obviated the need for conversation with the girl later. All he said to her were a few kinds words of parting in the morning; he also gave her a magnificent tip. He had already acquired the habit of giving disproportionate tips whenever he sensed good will on the part of those in his service; in this particular instance he had been well satisfied. The girl took the money absentmindedly, being too young to realize how generous it was, as if both the remuneration and the manner of its obtaining had nothing to do with her. She merely looked at him in a strange way, which he now remembered with an uncomfortable feeling.

"What am I complaining about?" Uncle Tonet was saying just then. "Am I complaining about this mist around us? No, sir, I am not. About our climate? I am not, sir. About the soil in these parts? No, sir, I am not complaining about the soil in these parts, either. Then what am I complaining about? Human stupidity. Of which, as we were saying, your father is a prime example. Why am I harping this way about him? Could it be envy? Yes, sir: I am harping about him out of pure envy."

It was night when they drew up at the church door. The coachman asked if his parents had been sent word of his visit. "No," said Onofre. "Ah, you wanted to give them a surprise," said Uncle Tonet. "No," replied Onofre, "I didn't tell them, that's all." "Remember me to them," Uncle Tonet said. "I haven't seen them for years, even though your father and I were good friends at one time. I took him to Cuba when he got the crazy notion to go and emigrate, did I tell you that?" In the square, Onofre left the coachman groping his way to the bar and headed for his house.

His mother was at the door: she was the first to see him coming. She had just stepped outside to take a look at the night, something she had not done for the last few years. When Onofre disappeared, she had got into the habit of standing at the front door at sunset, since that was the time the trap arrived—when it arrived. Then, without saying anything about it to her husband, she stopped going to the door: she realized that Onofre would never come back. "I'll put supper on," she said when she saw him coming. "And my father?" he asked. She indicated that he was inside.

On first impression Onofre found his father much aged. The *americano* was still wearing his drill jacket, now frayed and threadbare, yellowed from all the washings and misshapen by innumerable darnings and patches. When he lifted his face from the table he had been staring at, his eyes filled with tears. His expression did not change, however, as if nothing unexpected had come in through the door. He waited for his son to break the silence, since it was plain he had come for a reason, but when Onofre said nothing, he thought he would help out with some remark: "How was your trip?" Onofre answered, "Fine." Silence fell again under the watchful gaze of the mother. "You're very well dressed," said the *americano*. "I'm not giving you any money," Onofre said sharply. His father went pale. "I had no intention of asking you for money, boy," he muttered between clenched teeth. "It was just for the sake of saying something." "Then say nothing," said Onofre dryly. The *americano* realized that in his son's eyes he had become a contemptible figure. He sprang lightly to his feet and said, "I'll see if I can find some eggs in the yard." He went out, taking a low stool with him, not saying why he needed a stool in the yard.

When Onofre was left alone with his mother, he looked over the house. He had known before he came that it would look smaller than he remembered it, but he was surprised to see it so poor and rickety. There was his bed, alongside his parents', still made and seeming to have been used the night before. His mother answered his unspoken question. "When you went away, we felt lonely," she said apologetically. Onofre dropped onto a chair, tired from the jolting he had got in the trap. "So I have a brother." His mother lowered her eyes. "If we'd known where to write to you . . ." she said finally, evasively. "Where is he, then?" asked Onofre. His tone suggested, "Let's get this farce over with." His mother said he'd soon be back.

"He's a great help," she added after a while. "You know how farm work is. Your father's hopeless at it: he was never good at farming, even as a young man. I suppose that's why he went to Cuba. He's suffered a lot," she went on, as if talking to herself. "He thinks it's all his fault that you left home. When the months went by and there was no sign of you, he made a few inquiries. He was told you weren't in Bassora, but probably in Barcelona. He went there to look for you. He was in Barcelona for nearly a month, asking everywhere about you. In the end he had to come back. I felt sorry for him. Then we had the child— you'll see him any minute now. He isn't like you: he's quiet, too, but he hasn't got your character. In that he takes more after his father."

"What does he do now?"

"Things could have worked out worse," she said. She knew he was referring to his father. "Those gentlemen from Bassora that nearly had him put in prison, do you remember? They gave him a job so he could earn his living. I think that was good of them, when all's said and done. They gave him a briefcase and sent him to the villages and farms selling insurance—some new thing. Since his story has been all around these parts from mouth to mouth, he's known everywhere he goes. People go up to him when they see him in his white suit. Some make fun of him, but he sells a policy now and then. What with that and the land and the hens, we don't do so badly." She went over to the door and peered out into the darkness. The mist was gone, and bats could be seen darting in the moonlight. "What worries me now is his health. He's getting on, and this job doesn't suit him. He has to trudge for miles in the cold and the heat, he gets tired out, he drinks too much and doesn't eat properly or enough. And the worst of it is that one day—it must be four or five years ago— he lost his hat: a gust of wind carried it into a wheat field. He searched and searched for it, until nightfall. I've tried to persuade him to buy a cap for himself, but he won't hear of it. . . . Ah, here he comes."

"I went to see if they'd give me a few onions and some mint," said the *americano* as he came in. There was no sign of the stool.

"I was telling Onofre about you and your hat," she said.

He put what he had brought on the table and sat down, pleased to have something to talk about. "An irreparable loss," he said. "You can't get anything like that around here: not in Bassora and not in Barcelona. A genuine Panama."

"I told him about Joan, too," said the mother.

The *americano* went as red as a beet. "Do you remember," he said, "when you and I went to Bassora to have the monkey stuffed? You'd never been to a city before, and you found every- thing. . ."

Onofre was eyeing the boy who stood in the doorway, not

daring to come in. It was Onofre who said, "Come over to the light so I can have a look at you. What's your name?"

"Joan Bouvila i Mont, at your service, sir," said the boy.

"Don't sir me. I'm your brother, Onofre. But you knew that, didn't you?" The child nodded. "Don't ever lie to me," Onofre said to him.

"Sit at the table, all of you," said the mother. "Let's have some supper. Onofre, say grace, will you?"

All four ate in silence. When they finished, Onofre said, "Don't start thinking I've come to stay." Nobody answered: nobody had in fact thought that. One look at him was enough to see that that could never be. "I've come to have you sign some documents for me," he said to his father, took a document out of his jacket pocket, and left it folded on the table. The *americano* put out his hand but did not take the document: he stopped halfway and lowered his eyes. "It's a mortgage on this house and lands," said Onofre. "I need money to invest, and this is the only way I can get it. Don't worry. You can go on living in the house and working the land. They won't turn you out unless things don't work out for me, but that won't happen."

"Your father will sign it, won't you, Joan?" said the mother.

The father signed the contract Onofre put before him without even reading it. Then he got up and left the room. Onofre looked at his mother. When she nodded to him, he went out into the fields to find the *americano*. Eventually he found him sitting under a fig tree, on a three-legged stool of the type used for milking. It was the stool his father had taken out before. Without saying anything, Onofre leaned against the trunk of the fig tree; from there he could see the *americano*'s back and neck, the sunken shoulders. His father began to speak with no prompting.

"All my life I thought that everything we see here," he said, pointing vaguely to the horizon, but really indicating everything that was lit by the moon, "was always like this, just as we see it now, and that it was the result of natural cycles, seasonal changes that came regularly, year in, year out. But finally I realize how wrong I was: that every inch of these fields and woods has been worked at with shovel and spade, hour after hour, month after month; that my parents, grandparents, great-grandparents, and ancestors before them all fought with nature so that we now can live here. Nature is not wise as they say she is, she is stupid and cruel.

"Over the generations people have been changing nature: the course of rivers, the location of mountains; they've domesticated animals and changed the ways of trees, cereals, plants in general. What was destructive they made productive. The result of these generations of effort is what we have here in front of us. And I could never see it before: I thought cities were the important thing and that the land was nothing, but now I think it's more the other way around.

"The problem is, work on the land is slow; it has to be done little by little, each job in its place, exactly at its appointed time, not a day too soon, not a day too late, and so it looks as if no great change has taken place. This is not the case in a city. We see at once a city's size and height, the infinite number of bricks needed to build it up from the ground—but we're wrong, because any city can be built from start to finish in a few years.

"That's why country folk are different: quieter and readier to accept things as they are. If I'd understood this before, perhaps my life would have gone a different route, but that was not to be: either you have sense the moment you're born, or you learn everything the hard way, through years of misery and mistakes."

"It'll be all right, Father," said Onofre. "Everything will turn out as I say."

"Don't think I'm worried about the mortgage, son," replied the *americano*. "I'd actually never realized these lands could be mortgaged until today. Had I known, I would have mortgaged them myself years ago to get started in some business, and they wouldn't be ours now. But it'll be different with you, I'm sure."

"It can't go wrong."

"Don't give it another thought. You'd better go to bed," said the *americano*. "You have a long journey ahead of you tomorrow."

The following day Onofre set out for Barcelona. On the way through Bassora, he had the contract signed and sealed by a notary. He had spent the night in his old bed: little Joan slept with his parents. As Onofre left, easier in his mind, he viewed the countryside. "Eight years ago," he said to himself, "I thought I was seeing these fields for the last time; but now I know I'll never get away from them completely. Well, if I'm to see them often, I might as well profit from them." That was, at the moment, his entire philosophy: buying and selling, buying and selling.

3

The growth of Barcelona's "Ensanche," the "enlargement" plan the Ministry for Internal Affairs in Madrid seemingly pulled out of a hat one fine day, followed a more-or-less logical pattern at the outset. The valley was divided into lots, and the first lots to be developed were those enjoying a natural water supply, situated near a stream, an irrigation canal, or a riverbank—one example of the latter being present-day Bruch Street, which until quite recently was navigable as far as its intersection with Aragón Street. Likewise favored were areas by wells, underground waterways, or quarries. Such proximity meant lower building costs. An area was also desirable if a streetcar line went out that way, or if the railroad passed through it, and so on.

Wherever buildings began to appear in response to these factors, the price of the lots rose sharply, for there is no people in the Western world more gregarious than the Catalans: where one Catalan goes to live, the others want to go, too. "Anywhere at all," was the motto, "but all together." Thus property speculation followed this pattern: a man would buy as many lots as he could in an area he considered promising, then have a block or two built, then wait until all the houses were sold and occupied, then put the rest of the lots up for sale at a price far above what he originally paid. The new owners of those lots, wanting to turn a profit themselves, would divide each lot in half, build on one half, and sell the other for the price they had paid for the whole lot. Naturally, the buyer of the other half followed the same procedure, dividing it in half . . . and so it went. Consequently, the first block built in a given area would be of a respectable size, the next one smaller, and so on, until the last buildings to go up would be so narrow that only one apartment could be fitted on each floor. They were extremely rickety, made of the cheapest materials, dingy, and lacking in ventilation, comforts, and services.

These hovels, which can still be seen today, cost twenty-five, thirty, even thirty-five times what was originally paid for the spacious, sunny, and salubrious dwellings built at the start of the process. As someone put it, "The smaller and smellier the house, the more expensive." But that was not the case. In reality, the owners of these favored properties, these "first-round dwellings," as they were sometimes called, sold them as soon as the circle was closed, at a price forty, forty-five, or even fifty times that of the most expensive (i.e., the smallest and worst) properties. Once all the first-round dwellings were sold, the second-round dwellings went up for sale, those built on half-lots: then the next rounds, until all changed hands. And then sometimes a third wave of sales would begin forthwith, or even a fourth. When there were buyers, there were sellers, and vice versa.

To understand this phenomenon, this fever, one must remember that the people of Barcelona were an eminently mercantile breed, and that for centuries they had been used to living all crammed together like lice. They didn't give a damn about their homes as such, about creature comforts, but the prospect of making a quick profit captivated them like the song of a mermaid. This reckless speculation was not the exclusive preserve of well-off gentlemen with surplus cash; many less fortunate people also risked what they had in an attempt to get rich.

The affluent bought and sold lots, buildings, and apartments (as well as purchase and repurchase options, leases and emphyteuses, and rights to transfer, exchange, and pawn), but they all lived in rented quarters, since at that time any man who "sat on his own capital" was considered a fool. "Somebody else can tie up his money," they would say. "I'll pay by the month and put my money to work."

The less-than-affluent, on the other hand, often ended up in dire straits, obliged to sell their homes at the most inconvenient moment. They would take to the streets with family, servants, possessions, and all, and go from door to door looking for a place to spend the night, or somewhere to leave a sick relative or an infant. It would bring tears to one's eyes seeing them wander the streets of Barcelona on a winter night or in the rain, their furniture piled on handcarts, their children frozen stiff, and them still muttering under their breath: "Invested, so much, gained, so much, to be reinvested, so much," etc. Those more sensible tried to avoid selling when it did not suit them for personal reasons, preferring to let the chance go by and preserve instead the family's health and dignity. But they were not permitted to do so, for that would have broken the speculative cycle to which the whole city was tied. As a result, there were families who within a year moved seven or eight times.

It should not be assumed from this that every speculator grew rich. As with any investment, there were losers. For the business to be successful, the first building to go up in the area had to be sold—and well sold—and above all its new owners or occupants had to lend a certain touch of distinction to the area, making it desirable by their presence. There were families who could make or break a district, such as the family that went by the name of Gatúnez, originally from the La Mancha region. It was never quite clear what this family, fairly large, did or did not do, but what *was* clear was that shortly after they moved in, the demand for the adjacent dwellings fell. Since the owners of these properties could not prevent the sale to the Gatúnez family, they had no choice but to resort to the unpleasant expedient of paying the Gatúnezes to go away, or purchasing the house from them at whatever price they cared to name. The opposite would happen with certain aged couples with foreign surnames, especially retired consuls of some world power. Or it could happen that a factor that led to the growth of a district would suddenly disappear: a stream could dry up, or the railroad company, after announcing its plans for a branch line out to such-and-such a place, could change its mind, leaving that place, already developed, in sorry isolation.

In this way fortunes were lost. Since not all these factors were due to chance, it was vital to have quick access to reliable information. As for the role that chance played, nothing could be done about that—though occasionally a would-be buyer, blinded by greed, would try to delve into nature's secrets, usually ending up in the clutches of phony water-diviners and other unscrupulous characters, who would take him for a ride. There were swindlers on the scene, too, claiming to have a friend or relative in a utility company or some local government office; they received extraordinary sums for their tall stories.

It was into this murky minefield of a market that Onofre Bouvila cautiously moved, in the month of September 1897.

With the money from the mortgaging of his family's land he could buy only a medium-sized lot in a place that seemed to offer no prospect of development. As soon as it was in his hands, he put it up for sale.

"No one will buy that godforsaken hole off you," Don Humbert told Onofre. Onofre was given a great deal of advice, but heeded none of it. "We shall see," was his answer. Six weeks went by, and only one purchaser showed up, offering the same amount that Onofre had paid for the site. Onofre gave him a black look.

"Sir," he said to the man "you are making a little joke at my expense. The lot is currently worth four times that, and the price is going up daily. If you have no serious offer to make, I would ask you not to waste any more of my time."

Taken aback by such aplomb, the man raised his offer a little. Onofre lost his temper: he had Efrén Castells chuck the man out into the street. The prospective purchaser went away wondering if what Onofre had told him was perhaps true. "Maybe it *is* worth that much," he thought, "insignificant though it looks." He made discreet inquiries, and soon heard a rumor that had him tossing and turning in his bed: that the confectioner's establishment Herederos de Ramón Morfem Ltd. had acquired the lot adjoining the one Onofre was putting up for sale and, furthermore, that Herederos de Ramón Morfem Ltd. would be moving its main branch to that very spot within a year. "By God," he said to himself, "that rascal knows all about it, and that's why he won't sell at the price I'm offering. But if my information is correct, the lot will soon be worth not four but twenty times what it's worth today." If the rumor was true, that meant, of course, the entire city was at last moving outward, for in late-nineteenth-century Barcelona nothing had the distinction and respectability of a high-class confectioner's.

Being served there was no easy matter; having one's name added to the list of clients could take a lifetime of persistence, a substantial financial outlay, and good contacts. Even then, even if one belonged to this select circle, a good *tortell* had to be ordered a week in advance; a tray of assorted cakes, a month in advance; a *coca* for Saint John's Day, three months or more; and a Christmas *turrón* no later than January 12. Although no high-class confectioner's had tables and chairs, and none served hot chocolate, tea, or cold drinks, they all had spacious and elegant foyers, generally Pomeian in style. There, on Sunday mornings after Mass, the high society of each district would meet and converse a while, preparing themselves for the family dinner, which would generally last four to six hours.

"If Herederos de Ramón Morfem moves from Calle del Carmen," the purchaser was saying to himself, "that whole district will go down the drain, and the Pla de la Boquería will not be what it is today: the nerve center of Barcelona. On the other hand, if the rumor is not true, the lot will be worth nothing. . . . And worst of all," he groaned, "I can do nothing to have the rumor confirmed or denied, because if the news spreads, then goodbye to the purchase. What a predicament!"

In the end his greed overcame his better judgment and he went through with the purchase at the price Onofre was asking. No sooner was the transaction completed than he hurried to the confectioner's on Calle del Carmen and asked to see the owners. They gave him a most polite welcome. Both heirs of the legendary Ramón Morfem, Don César and Don Pompeyo, arched their flour-whitened eyebrows when they heard the unfortunate purchaser's question. "Move our store? Never in the world. This rumor you have heard, sir, is untrue," they told him. "We have never had any intention of moving, and certainly not to that area you speak of—there is nowhere in the Ensanche more ugly, more incommodious, and less suitable for a confectioner's. Why, Papa would turn in his grave," they concluded.

After that, the purchaser went back to Onofre and demanded to have the sale revoked. His hair was all mussed and he dribbled at the mouth. "You spread that rumor," he told Onofre. "You owe me reparation." Onofre allowed him to let off steam and then had him shown to the door. And that was the end of that, because there was no way it could be proved that Onofre had started the rumor, even though everybody took it for granted that he had. The Herederos de Ramón Morfem case became famous, and the expression "to go the way of that Herederos de

Ramón Morfem fellow" enjoyed a brief popularity, being applied to those who, thinking themselves very crafty indeed, paid a high price for what was worth very little.

"Go carefully, now," Don Humbert advised Onofre. "If you get a bad name, no one will want to do business with you."

"That remains to be seen."

With his profit from this first sale he bought more lots in another place. "Let's see what he'll do now," said the experts in that kind of business. After a few weeks, seeing that he was doing nothing at all, they lost interest in him. "He's probably going straight this time," they said among themselves. The lots were far from the city center—at what is now the corner of Rosellón and Gerona streets. "Who would want to live there?" people said. One day, several carts appeared; sunlight gleaming on lengths of metal could be seen by the masons working on the towers of the Sagrada Familia not far from there. These were streetcar rails. A team of laborers began digging trenches in the stony ground of Calle Rosellón. On that same corner another, smaller team was busy constructing a barrel-vaulted rectangular pavilion: a pen for mule teams, since streetcars in those days were not powered by electricity.

"This time it's for real," people said. "This area is going places without a doubt." Within three or four days Onofre was relieved of all his lots for the price he chose to name. "This time," Don Humbert told him, "you've had better luck than you deserve, you rascal." Onofre made no reply, but chuckled to himself: a few days later, the same workmen who began laying the rails pulled them up, loaded them back on the carts, and took them away.

This time mercantile and financial circles had to admit that the maneuver showed ingenuity. They replied to the tears of the purchasers with scorn. "You should have asked the streetcar company if the work was real," they told them. "And what was there to suggest that it wasn't real?" the purchasers replied. "We saw the tracks and the mule pen and we thought . . ." "Well, you shouldn't have thought," was the answer they got. "Now, in return for a small fortune, you own a scrap of land not good enough for a garbage dump, and a half-built pen that you'll have to have knocked down at your own expense."

This operation, which everyone referred to as "the streetcar swindle" to distinguish it from the "Herederos de Ramón Morfem swindle," was followed by many more. Although everybody was wise to him, Onofre always managed to sell his lots quickly and at a huge profit. Each time, he came up with a way of creating great expectations in the mind of his buyer, but nothing ever came of those expectations: they were mirages of his own conjuring.

In two years Onofre was rich. But as a result, irreparable harm was done to the city, since the victims of his sharp dealing were left with worthless land for which they had paid large sums, and with which they were now obliged to do something. In the normal course of events these lots would have been set aside for cheap housing, to be occupied by poor immigrants. But because their initial value had been so high, they were used for luxury dwellings. These "luxury" dwellings had no running water, or so little that water only came from a tap when all the others in the building were turned off; some were built on odd-shaped lots, resulting in apartments full of corridors and box rooms, like rabbit burrows. To recoup some part of the capital they had lost, the owners skimped on the building materials: the cement was so generously mixed with sand and even salt that not a few buildings collapsed within months of their completion.

Great care was taken, however, with the façades. With stucco, plaster, and ceramics, dragonflies and cauliflowers were fashioned, from the seventh floor down to the street. Grotesque caryatids were embedded on balconies; sphinxes and dragons peered out from galleries and sun roofs. Mythological figures peopled the city; by the greenish light of the streetlamps at night they were positively unnerving. Beside doorways slim, effeminate angels covered their faces with their wings, sentries more appropriate for a mausoleum than a private home; and stout, mannish women stood in full battle dress, mimicking the Valkyries. All the rage at the time, these were painted with loud colors.

So the city grew with feverish haste. Every day thousands of tons of earth were moved by unbroken strings of carts and dumped behind Montjuich or into the sea. Mixed in with this earth were the remains of more ancient cities, Roman, Phoenician, and the skeletons of citizens of Barcelona from other epochs and less turbulent times.

4

By the summer of 1899 Onofre was twenty-six years old and the owner of a sizable fortune, but cracks were appearing in his empire. The election rigging controlled through Señor Braulio was not paying off, or would pay off only after much trouble and effort. The mood of the country had changed after the disastrous loss of the last remaining Spanish colonies in 1898; other, younger politicians were hoisting the banner of reform, appealing to the people and hoping to breathe new life into the old social structure. Onofre saw that for the time being it would be unwise to take them on; instead, he disassociated himself from the past and pretended to side with the winds of change, to take the new ideals to heart.

To this end, he sent Señor Braulio into retirement, since Señor Braulio had become a symbol of corruption. But this also meant separating him from Odón Mostaza, with whom he had fallen hopelessly in love. Señor Braulio burst into tears and at once began thinking of a way to kill himself, only shelving that project because he feared for the safety of the man he loved.

Odón was not bright; adapting to their new life had been beyond him. He was still a ruffian, ready to reach for his gun over nothing at all. Women still fell all over him, and on several occasions persons in positions of authority had to be approached to have scandals hushed up; there were corpses to be disposed of, and policemen to be paid off. Onofre warned him about this several times. "Things can't go on like this, Odón," he told him. "We're businessmen now." The ruffian swore to mend his ways, but he soon backslid. He greased his hair and dressed garishly. Though he ate and drank to excess, he never put on weight. Sometimes he won at the gaming table, and would then buy drinks all around—his sprees on such occasions were legendary. Other times he lost everything he had and more, running up large debts, and would have to turn to Señor Braulio for help. Señor Braulio would admonish but could not refuse him, and then covered up for him. Now he feared that without his protection the full weight of Onofre's wrath would fall on Odón.

This time Onofre went to the Budallera estate in a closed carriage, despite the heat. He wore a double-breasted, black wool suit made for him by a renowned tailor who worked from an apartment on the Gran Via between Calle Muntaner and Calle Casanova; Onofre went for fittings all that summer. Now he was wearing the suit for the first time, with a gardenia in his lapel. He felt ridiculous, but he was going to ask for the hand of the daughter of Don Humbert Figa i Morera. He had bought a ring from a jeweler's on the Ramblas.

Onofre had seen her only a few times, when she left the boarding school to spend the summer with her parents in the Budallera house. Since he was not admitted there, he had been obliged to meet with her out in the country when she was on some excursion, and then always in the company of many people and only for a few moments. She related the trivia of her life at the boarding school. Accustomed as he was to the foul-mouthed talk of prostitutes, he took this for the language of true love. He himself was at a loss for what to say. He tried to interest her in his real-estate investments, but soon saw she could not follow all that. They would part with a sense of relief and promises of fidelity. Their correspondence had not flagged all those years.

Now he was rich and she had left the boarding school for good: her debut in society would be that very autumn. The chances that Barcelona society would accept Don Humbert's daughter were slim, but there was always the possibility that an eligible young man would fall for her charms, overcome the opposition of his family, and marry her, thus legitimizing her position—and, indirectly, that of her parents into the bargain. Onofre wanted to avert that danger by getting in first with his request for her hand. He was thoroughly convinced that her beauty would triumph in the salons.

"If my girl sets foot in the Liceo, it's goodbye to her," he confided to Efrén Castells. The giant from Calella had changed over those years: he had stopped drifting easily from woman to woman and married a young little seamstress, very sweet in manner but very firm in character. They had two children, and he had become domesticated and responsible. Although he would carry out any order from Onofre without hesitation, he now preferred the activities that were legal. Following in Onofre's footsteps, he had pulled off a few deals, had not spent the proceeds but reinvested them, and was by now comfortably off.

"Talk to Don Humbert," he said to Onofre. "He owes you a lot. He will listen to you, and if he is an honorable man—and I think he is—he will recognize that his daughter's hand should be yours before anyone else's."

Onofre was shown to a little room and asked if he would be kind enough to wait. "My master is in a meeting," said the butler, who did not know Onofre. It was stifling in the little room. "It's as hot here as it is in Barcelona," he thought, "and my throat is awfully dry. They could at least have offered me a drink. Why are they so inconsiderate, today of all days?"

After what seemed a long time to him, he left the room and went down a corridor with whitewashed walls. As he passed a closed door, he heard voices, recognized Don Humbert's among them, and stopped to listen. His interest aroused by what he was hearing, he opened the door abruptly and entered what turned out to be Don Humbert's study.

Don Humbert was with two other gentlemen. One was a North American named Garnett—a fat, perspiring man, who was a traitor to his country, having served Spanish interests in the Philippines during the recent Spanish-American conflict there, until its outcome forced him to make himself scarce for a while. The other was a puny man from Castile with a tan and a graying mustache, whom the others called simply Osorio. Both he and Garnett were wearing striped cotton suits, white shirts with celluloid collars open at the neck in the colonial style, and esparto rope-soled shoes. Resting on their knees were their hats, a pair of Panamas, which instantly reminded Onofre of his father: he still had not raised the mortgage weighing on the family land. Onofre's sudden entrance brought the conversation to a halt. All eyes converged on him. The black suit, the gardenia on his lapel, and the jeweler's bright package were out of place in the study. Don Humbert introduced him to the others.

Garnett went on with his story, telling how on the eve of the naval battle fought in the month of May the year before, in the Philippines, he arranged to meet Admiral Dewey, the commander of the enemy fleet, to make him an offer from the Spanish government: 150,000 pesetas if he allowed the Spanish ships to sink the American ones. This meeting took place in the then-British colony of Singapore. At first Admiral Dewey thought he was mad. "Are you aware," he said, "that your Spanish warships are so inferior that ours can send them to the bottom of the sea without even coming within range of your guns?" Garnett nodded: "You know that and I know that, but our military experts have assured His Majesty's government that the opposite is true.

If the Spanish Navy is sunk now, imagine the disappointment in Spain." "There is nothing I can do about that," Dewey replied.

"So that was how we lost our last colonies," said Don Humbert when the American finished his story. "And now the ports are crawling with repatriated soldiers."

Ships were indeed arriving daily with survivors from the wars in Cuba and the Philippines. The soldiers had fought for years in putrid jungles and, although young, they looked like old men. Nearly all had malaria. Their families would not take them in for fear of contagion, nor could they find jobs or any other means of subsisting. There were so many of them that even to beg in the streets they had to line up and wait their turn. People gave them nothing. "You let the honor of the fatherland be trampled underfoot, and now you expect sympathy," they sneered. Many soldiers simply wasted away, dying of starvation on street corners, their spirits broken. Now investment in the ex-colonies had to go through middlemen like Garnett, who was a United States citizen. The man called Osorio turned out to be General Osorio y Clemente himself, ex-governor of Luzon and one of the most important landowners of the archipelago. Don Humbert was trying to reconcile their differences so they could do business.

When they left and the lawyer and Onofre were alone, Onofre awkwardly broached the purpose of his visit. Don Humbert was embarrassed, too. He had spoken to Onofre about the matter before and although not committing himself in so many words, had nevertheless given the young man to understand that he already considered him his son-in-law. Now he seemed to be groping for some gentle way to go back on that.

"It's my wife," he finally confessed. "Nothing in heaven or earth will make her yield. I've gone hoarse trying to convince her, but she's like that over this kind of thing, and in these affairs, as you'll discover for yourself when you have children, the woman is the boss. I don't know what to tell you, except to resign yourself and look elsewhere. Believe me, I'm truly sorry."

"And she?" asked Onofre. "What does she have to say about this?"

"Who? Margarita?" said Don Humbert. "Bah, she'll do whatever her mother says, however badly she takes it at first. Women suffer a lot over love, but they never put their future in jeopardy. I hope you understand that."

Without replying, Onofre picked up the jeweler's package and left the house, slamming every door on his way out. "You'll come looking for me yet," he muttered through clenched teeth. "You'll come on your knees begging me to forgive you, but I won't forgive you. The most battered old whore out in La Carbonera is worth a thousand of you."

But as his carriage bumped its way over the stones, his anger left him, and he arrived back in Barcelona in a state of utter dejection. He locked himself in his house and refused to see anybody for a fortnight. A maid he had taken on three years before, and to whom he paid an exorbitant wage to guarantee her loyalty, looked after him. He finally agreed to let Efrén Castells in. Efrén, worried about his partner, whom he had never seen in such a state, had been making inquiries, the results of which he now wished to divulge to Onofre.

There was nothing stupid about Don Humbert's wife: she knew full well that no young man of good family would be fool enough to marry Margarita. But neither was she willing to hand her daughter over to a pariah like Onofre Bouvila without a fight. Turning the problem over in her mind day and night, she finally came up with the ideal candidate for her daughter's hand: Nicolau Canals i Rataplán, the son of the same Don Alexandre Canals i Formiga whom Señor Braulio stabbed to death eight years ago on Onofre's orders. Since then, Nicolau and his mother had lived in Paris. Don Alexandre, like many other Catalan capitalists of his time, had "put his money to work" in French companies; his shares, which amounted to a small fortune, were to pass in their entirety to Nicolau as soon as the boy came of age. In the interim Nicolau's mother administered that wealth prudently, and had actually added to it through a few judicious and well-timed transactions. Mother and son moved into a spacious, comfortable, but discreet house on Rue de Rivoli, where they lived a sequestered existence.

Now eighteen or nineteen years old, he was a melancholy boy, still brooding, despite the intervening years, over the death of his father, whose memory he venerated. On the other hand, he did not get on well with his mother, though neither of them was to blame for this. The death of her two oldest children was a blow from which she never recovered; irrationally she blamed her husband for what happened, and lost any affection she might have felt for him. Her only surviving son was included in this estrangement. This was unjust, and she knew it, but could not help it. To make matters worse, Nicolau's physical flaw, a medullary defect that had resulted in his growing up slightly deformed, seemed to her a constant reproach for her lack of love. From the time he was an infant, she avoided looking at him, entrusting him to the care of a long string of wet nurses, nannies, and governesses. Now circumstances obliged her to live in seclusion, her only companion being the boy she had never loved and on whom, furthermore, she now depended legally and financially, since everything, even the bread they ate, was his by law. He, aware of the discomfort his presence caused her, and having no illusions about her affection for him, kept out of her sight. His physical deformity also prevented him from making friends with those his own age, so he lived in complete solitude. All he had in the world was Paris.

When he and his mother had arrived, fleeing Barcelona, Paris seemed a hostile city to him, its inhabitants little more than savages. But gradually he came to love the city, and loved it with a passion. Now it was the sum total of his bliss—walking the streets, sitting in the squares, strolling through the various parks, he observed the people, the light, the houses, the river. Sometimes, on one of these walks, he would suddenly stop, overcome with an emotion so intense, he was unable to hold back the tears. If it was raining, he could close his umbrella and let himself be drenched to the skin. His anonymous, hunched-up form, shaking with sobs and soaked, would rend the hearts of passers-by, who did not know that his tears were tears of joy. But sometimes fear would assail him. "What will become of me," he would think, "if for some reason we have to leave Paris?" The knowledge that Paris was not really his home filled him with anxiety. Little did he know how well grounded was his fear.

Don Humbert's wife wrote a long and disjointed letter to Don Alexandre's widow. After many circumlocutions, she got to the point. "Pray forgive, dear friend, my boldness in approaching you with such disregard for protocol, but I am convinced your mother's heart will at once appreciate my position." Then she unfolded her scheme—to have her daughter, Margarita Figa i Clarença, married to Nicolau Canals i Rataplán. Both were only children, she pointed out, and therefore sole heirs to their respective family fortunes. Both, she hinted, were excluded from Barcelona high society. And could Nicolau hope to fare better in Paris, where he would always be a foreigner and consequently never fully accepted? "With this union," she went on, "the long-standing commonality of interests which has bound our two families would find its highest expression." She concluded by saying that "although Margarita and Nicolau have not yet had the opportunity of meeting, I have no doubt but that they, both being young, intelligent, well endowed by nature, and of good character, will swiftly profess for each other that mutual respect and affection upon which is built all genuine conjugal felicity."

She found out, heaven knows how, the address of Don Alexandre's widow and sent her this letter. Then she told her husband what she had done, showing him a copy of the letter. Don Humbert could not believe his eyes.

"How . . . how could you have . . . ?" he finally managed to say. "Offer our daughter like a piece of merchandise . . . Words fail me. . . . The audacity of it! And to the son of my former rival, of whose death some even suggest that I am not entirely blameless. What mortification! And what possessed you to say that that lad was 'well endowed by nature'? Don't you know the poor soul is a cripple? I am ready to die of embarrassment."

"Now, don't upset yourself, Humbert," his wife said, unruffled. She realized the folly of her action, but trusted to her star.

Meanwhile, Don Alexandre's widow received the letter and read it pensively in the dim light of her home on Rue de Rivoli. "There's a cool customer," she thought. "That beggar woman doesn't know the meaning of the word 'shame.'" Under normal circumstances she would have torn the letter to pieces. She was nearly forty, and from her bitter life, a life that was a string of frustrated hopes, little remained of her former beauty. "*Une vie manquée,*" she murmured. She left the letter on the coffee table and wearily fanned herself with an ostrich feather, her bracelet tinkling. From the street came the continual noise of carriages passing by.

"*Anaïs, sois gentille: ferme les volets et apporte-moi mon châle en soie brodée,*" she said to the maid, a Negress from Martinique who wore a yellow kerchief on her head.

A year earlier, the widow met a poet of obscure origins called Casimir. Only twenty-two years old, Casimir took her to the literary coteries of Montparnasse, where the bohemians read poetry and drank absinthe. Together they went to the funeral of Stéphane Mallarmé. But she was too conscious of the differences in their age and condition to marry him. He would send her flowers stolen from cemeteries, and fiery love sonnets. In the eyes of the world the situation was indelicate and lay her open to malicious talk. "But why should I care?" she thought. "I have been unhappy all my life, and now that fortune has left this gift on my doorstep, am I to reject it for fear of gossip? Besides, this isn't Barcelona, this is Paris."

Still, she was inhibited by her son's presence: he was the one obstacle to her happiness. Had she explained the situation to him, he would have understood, he would have supported his mother, pleased to be able to show her an adult solidarity. But the years of distance had closed the channels of communication. With pangs of guilt she considered ways to rid herself of him, the irksome witness.

Now she gave thought to the letter she had just received. The idea was tempting, but everything urged her to reject it: behind this matrimonial proposition she suspected some dark design. "Who could want my Nicolau," she told herself, "as a son-in-law? He is a nobody, deformed, doltish. What can they see in him apart from money? It must be the money. In which case, Nicolau's life would be in danger. If that villain had my husband killed, may he rest in peace, why should he not now plot the death of his heir, too? This might be one of those assassination vendettas that have been going on in Istanbul for centuries."

She had met in a salon the ambassador of Abdul-Hamid the Accursed, that decrepit sultan who presided over the last gasps of the dying Ottoman Empire. The ambassador, a follower of Enver Bey and consequently a "Young Turk" sympathizer, took every opportunity to discredit the state he was supposed to be representing and from which he received his salary. Believing himself to be an idealist, he was in fact a living example of the very moral decadence he and his coreligionists were seeking to remedy.

A shiver made her draw more tightly the embroidered silk shawl the maid had draped around her shoulders. She pulled the cord beside her; when Anaïs appeared, she asked if her son was in. *"Oui, madame,"* came the answer. *"Alors, dis-lui que je veux lui parler. Vas vite,"* she said.

She wanted to be gentle with him, to treat him as an equal, but her face fell when she saw him enter the drawing room. "What's this?" she said, displeasure in her voice. "This time of day and already in your *robe de chambre?*" Nicolau garbled an apology: he didn't intend to go out, he had decided to spend the evening reading, but if she had something else in mind . . . "No, it's all right," she said. "Run along now. I have a terrible headache. I do not wish to be disturbed until the morning."

She locked herself in the study and wrote and tore up rough drafts of letters well into the night. Finally she hit on a tone she thought suitable. "Your letter, dear friend, made me feel at once flattered and disconcerted, as you will readily understand," she wrote. "I have always felt that in matters matrimonial the decision should rest with those directly concerned, and not with us, their mothers, however well meaning we may be," etc.

Don Humbert's wife, reading this letter, realized that she had won the day: the letter, though evasive, established a common language, and opened the door for dialogue and negotiation. She showed it to her husband with pride.

"Here it says that the marriage is impossible," was all he could find to say.

"Humbert, don't be a ninny," she retorted. "The mere fact she replied at all means a yes, even though she wrote to say no."

Nicolau's mother presented him with the whole affair as a *fait accompli*. Caught off guard, not having seen the storm clouds gather, he put up feeble resistance.

"Tut tut," she interrupted, tapping her heel impatiently on the parquet floor. "What do you know of life? I, on the other hand, have a great deal of experience, I have suffered, I am your mother, and I know what's best for you." Then she said with great conviction, "Going to Barcelona and marrying that girl is best for you. There is no reason you should not be happy there."

"But what do you know about those people, Mama?" he stammered. "They are the ones who had Papa killed."

"Gossip," she snapped. "Anyway, it was not the girl that did it. She can't have been more than a baby at the time. Besides, what's done is done. A lot of water has gone under the bridge since then. Let us not be ruled by the past. Well, what do you say?"

Nicolau walked the streets for hours, then returned to the apartment in the evening and went straight in to see his mother. "I do not want to get married, Mama. Not with that girl, whose good qualities I have no reason to doubt, or with any other. What I want is to stay here with you. Here, in Paris, we are happy, are we not, Mama?"

She did not have the courage to say that she was not happy and that he was to blame. "That has nothing to do with what we were speaking about earlier," was her reply. "You are too old to be clinging to your mother's apron strings."

Seeing a glimmer of the truth, he opened his arms in a gesture of acquiescence. "If living with me is what is upsetting you," he said, "I can go and live in an attic in Montparnasse."

After a long struggle they reached an agreement: Nicolau would make the trip to Barcelona, meet Margarita Figa i Clarença, and then and only then, being in full possession of the facts, make a decision. He still had the option of returning to Paris. This amounted to a capitulation on her part, but she did not feel strong enough to push him further. And she found, also, that she was close to her son after all. Though eager to be rid of him, the imminence of his departure now filled her with sadness, and dark forebodings assailed her.

Meanwhile, all these events had reached the ears of Onofre Bouvila, who, in his voluntary seclusion, was scheming to change a situation that was so unfavorable to his interests.

5

Onofre's first step was to have two men located and tailed: Osorio, the Luzon landowner, and Garnett, Osorio's American agent in the Philippines, the men he had met by chance at the Budallera estate that fateful afternoon when he went to ask for the hand of Margarita. He soon learned that the American was staying at the Hotel Columbus (situated at that time in the Plaza de Cataluña, beside Paseo de Gracia), that he always ate in the hotel, and that he ventured out only in a closed carriage he hired twice a week, on Tuesdays and Thursdays, to take him to the door of an opium den in Vallcarca. There he would spend the night. In the morning the same carriage would pick him up at the den and take him back to the hotel.

This celebrated opium den, the last of the many known to have existed in Barcelona, was patronized by high-society gentlemen and not a few ladies, but dressmakers' assistants and other girls serving apprenticeships also went there. It was not generally known then that opium and its derivatives were addictive; its consumption was neither illegal nor carried any social stigma. Many of the girls, to obtain with the required frequency a pleasure that their modest means did not otherwise permit, resorted to prostitution. Thus many of those running opium dens also ran brothels in which underage prostitutes were commonly found.

Garnett passed the rest of his time in his hotel suite reading the adventures of Sherlock Holmes, unknown at the time in Spain but already enjoying considerable popularity in England and in the United States, whence he had copies sent by American Express.

As for Osorio, he had rented an apartment on Calle Escudellers, considered a good area then, where he lived with a Filipino servant by way of domestic staff and a Pomeranian by way of company. He heard Mass every day in the Church of San Justo y Pastor. In the afternoons he would go to a bullfight enthusiasts' club, whose members were for the most part retired military men like himself, top civil servants posted in Barcelona, or high-ranking police officers. Apart from discussing the latest *corridas*, they would play cards.

Onofre decided to approach Garnett and went to see him in his hotel. He got straight to the point. "Osorio is finished," he said. "He is old and the tropics are relentless with old men. If something unfortunate were to befall him, you could arrange things so that Osorio's properties, now held under your name, instead of going to his heirs, could go, for instance, to me."

The North American narrowed his eyes. He was sipping at a mixture of lemonade, rum, and seltzer. "From the legal point of view," he said finally, "the situation is more complicated than it seems."

"I know," said Onofre, showing him a batch of handwritten papers. "I obtained copies of the contracts you signed in the presence of the lawyer Figa i Morera."

"Yes, of course," said Garnett, glancing through the contracts, "Don Humbert's cooperation would be necessary."

"I can see to that," said Onofre.

"And Osorio, who will see to him?" asked Garnett.

"Leave that to me," said Onofre.

The American said he would prefer not to go on discussing the matter. "Come and see me in three or four days. I have to think it over."

When the time was up, they met again. Now the American voiced his scruples: "If something—how did you put it? something unfortunate, that's it—were to befall him, might I not be easily linked to that misfortune?"

Onofre smiled. "Had you not raised that objection," he said, "I would have annulled our agreement myself. Now I can see that you are a careful man who weighs everything. I will tell you my plans."

When he finished speaking, the American declared himself satisfied. "Now," he said, "let's discuss percentages." They reached agreement on that point, too.

"Naturally," said Onofre as he was taking his leave, "there is not and never will be any written record of what we have discussed here."

"I have had dealings with people like you before," Garnett said, "and I know a handshake is enough."

The two men shook hands.

"As for silence . . ." said Onofre.

"I won't say a word to anybody," said Garnett.

Meanwhile, Efrén Castells, the better to serve Onofre, had gone back to exercising his talents as a Casanova behind his wife's back and managed to win over a maid employed in Don Humbert's household. Through her they knew all that was going on there and could keep a close watch on the devious path leading to the wedding of the daughter to Nicolau Canals i Rataplán.

As Don Humbert had predicted, the mother's will prevailed over the daughter's heart. Margarita made some attempt at rebellion, but could do little against the machinations of her mother. The mother, instead of coming straight out with a proposal as her counterpart in Paris had done with her son, wrung concessions from the girl one by one. She had the advantage: she knew of Margarita's involvement with Onofre, but Margarita, unaware of this, did not dare use that as an argument to justify her aversion to her mother's schemes. Unable to argue convincingly, she had to yield. Thus she agreed to an exhange of letters between her parents and Don Alexandre's widow, which gradually turned into a series of matrimonial capitulations. Then, already committed in ink, she was forced to accept the arrangements for the official engagement. Step by step she was being tied up.

"Don't start making a fuss now," her mother would say whenever Margarita showed signs of resistance. "This doesn't bind us to anything, and courtesy demands we do it."

"Oh, Mama, that's what you said the last time, and the time before that and the time before that. And without doing anything at all, as you say, here I am nearly at the altar."

"Nonsense, my dear," the mother answered. "Anyone listening to you would think we were still in the Middle Ages. You have the last word; nobody is going to make you do anything against your will. But I see no reason why we should now turn our backs on all the trouble that charming lady has gone to over us—and her son, so intelligent, honorable, and rich."

"And hunchbacked."

"Don't say that until you've seen him. You know how people like to exaggerate defects in others. Besides, bear in mind that physical attractions soon prove wearisome. But the beauty of the soul—I don't know—I suppose it gives more and more pleasure every day, and don't make me go on talking like this, because all this arguing is wearing me out!" She rang a little bell to summon the maid, and asked for a basin with water and vinegar and some linen cloths to soothe her forehead and temples. "Between all of you you'll be the death of me. Such ingratitude, Lord God!"

At which point Margarita would be at a loss for words.

Efrén passed on news of these disputes to Onofre.

"All right," Onofre said finally, "time to take action."

When the appointed night came, the iron gate was unlocked—the maid had bribed the porter, the gardener, and the gamekeeper—and the dogs were muzzled. Efrén, carrying a ladder five meters long, had to stop frequently to stifle his laughter with his handkerchief. "What the hell's got into you?" asked Onofre. The giant from Calella replied that this situation reminded him of old times: "When you and I stole watches from the World's Fair warehouses, remember?" "That's over and done with," Onofre said. Eleven years had gone by since then, and here Efrén was back playing the clown. The dogs, roused by their voices, began to bark. Don Humbert appeared on a second-floor balcony, wrapped in a silk dressing gown. "What's going on down there?" he called out. The porter emerged from his lodge and took off his cap. "Nothing at all, sir. The dogs must have seen an owl." When Don Humbert went in again, Onofre and Efrén continued on their way. "Well, it seems like yesterday to me," said the giant.

The maid was waiting for them by the wall of the house: her apron and coif stood out against the ivy. She pointed up at the window and rested her cheek on her two hands to mime a person sleeping. Efrén put the ladder against the wall and tested it. "You two wait here," said Onofre. "Don't move until I come down." The giant from Calella steadied the ladder while Onofre climbed up. He had lost some agility over the years and didn't look down for fear of getting dizzy. "Damn!" he thought. "It seems like yesterday to me, too."

There was a blow on his hip: the butt of his revolver had hit a rung of the ladder. He took it from his pocket and whistled. When he saw Efrén look up, he dropped the revolver, which the giant deftly caught. Then he went on up to the window. It was shut; neither the heat nor any considerations of health as propagated by the press at the time had sufficed to persuade Margarita to sleep with the window open. He had to knock several times before her drowsy, bewildered face appeared at the window.

"Onofre!" she exlaimed. "You! What is the meaning of this?" Onofre waved his hand impatiently. "Open the window and let me in," he said. "I must talk to you." The giant and the maid told them to be quiet from below. "Keep your voices down," they said. "You'll wake the whole neighborhood."

Margarita opened the window an inch. Her loose hair fell over her shoulders, its copper tones contrasting with the whiteness of her throat. The heat and her sleeping had flattened the curls on her forehead—Onofre couldn't remember ever having seen her look so beautiful.

"Let me in," he said, desire in his voice. She blinked. "I can't," she said in a whisper. Onofre felt his blood pound as it had done that afternoon when he broke the mirror and the little alabaster statue. "Is it true you're marrying a hunchback?" he asked in a tone that frightened her: for the first time the magnitude of what her mother intended dawned on her. "My God," she murmured, "what can I do? I don't know how I can avoid it." Onofre smiled. "Leave that to me. Just tell me if you love me." She clasped her hands together and raised them above her head, as if imploring the heavens; she shut her eyes and threw back her head, as she had done years before when he took her in his arms for the first time. "Yes, oh, yes!" she said in a hoarse voice that seemed to come from deep in her breast. "Yes, my love, my life, my beloved man."

Onofre let go of the ladder and thrust his arms through the narrow gap in the window; his fingers tore open her nightgown, baring her white shoulders. This made him lose his balance. She perceived the danger and took him by the arms, pulling him toward her: with a force born of desperation, she pulled him completely inside. To their astonishment they found themselves in her bedroom and in each other's arms. Feeling his breath on her bare shoulders, she succumbed, swooning, but with no regrets.

While they consummated their long-repressed love until dawn, the train bringing Nicolau Canals i Rataplán to Barcelona was drawing in at Port Bou, on the frontier. There all the travelers were obliged to get off and change trains, since the gauges of the railroad tracks in France and Spain were not the same. He asked how long it would be before they could set off again, and was told half an hour or more. He decided to walk along the platform, stretching his legs and shaking off the stiffness in his limbs. From Paris to the border he had had to share his compartment with a fellow who first claimed to be a businessman and then a consular agent, and who got on his nerves with his talk and afterward with his snoring. "In any case," Nicolau said, resigning himself, "I would not be able to sleep." Wandering from the station, he came out on an embankment from which he could see the Mediterranean under the merciless, all-revealing light of dawn.

He was setting foot in Catalonia after a long absence, and he felt a stranger. His only clear memory from Barcelona was of his father, of the afternoons when his father would leave the office and take him for a spin on the merry-go-round decorated with little paper lanterns and worked by an old horse: a small grimy contraption that was the prettiest thing in the world to him then. And now, too. As Nicolau contemplated the clean, precise dawn, the thought came to him that his end was not far off, that he would never again see the foggy, rainy Paris he had grown to love so much. He shuddered, then shrugged: given to hypochondria, he was used to such sudden attacks of gloom and had learned not to take them seriously. When the train set off again, the sun was already high in the sky.

Efrén, worried, looked up at the window. "Soon the household will be stirring. We'll be caught in the most compromising situation imaginable, and what'll we do then?" he was thinking. Spending the night on watch in the garden, beside the maid, he had not been able to restrain himself: "It's the scent of the jasmines and the smoothness of your skin." Now the maid, still naked, was crying behind the bushes: she was so upset, she did not even try to put on her uniform again.

Her tears were not entirely unjustified, as it turned out: as a result of this indiscretion she became pregnant and lost her job. She went to find Efrén and asked for help. Efrén, afraid that his wife would hear of this, consulted Onofre. "Pay her what she asks and tell her to keep quiet," was his recommendation, and that was what was done. In due course a boy was born. Years later that boy, who inherited his father's size and physique, became a player in the Barcelona Football Club alongside Zamora, Samitier, and Alcántara; the club had been founded the very year of his conception.

Efrén tried to return to its owner the pistol tossed from the ladder, but Onofre spurned it. "From now on," he said, "I am not carrying weapons. Others can carry them for me."

Nicolau took a bright, spacious room in the Gran Hotel de Aragón. He had his breakfast on the balcony, with the colorful bustle of the Ramblas at his feet; there he could breathe the scents from the flower stalls and hear the varied songs from the bird stalls, and this restored his good spirits. "I'll spend a few pleasant days here and then return to Paris," he thought. "A short change always does one good. When I go back, I'll be all the happier to see Paris again, and after my absence Mama is more likely to welcome me with affection." The doom he felt at the Port Bou station was now dismissed as the product of his insomnia.

In his thoughts about his mother Nicolau was not far off the mark: she now regretted having let him go away. Shortly after his departure she had gone to meet Casimir and had taken him home with her to Rue de Rivoli. "You'll be just fine here," she told him. "I'll look after you and you can devote yourself to your writing." At midnight she woke with a start and saw that he was not at her side. She tossed a peignoir over her nightgown and left her bedroom to look for him. She found him in the little drawing room, standing at the window: he seemed to be gazing spellbound at the stars. *"Qu'avez-vous, mon cher ami?"* she asked. Since Casimir made no reply, she stood next to him and gently took his hand in hers. The hand was burning. She realized that in a short space of time she had lost both her son and her lover.

The following day she wrote to Nicolau. "Come back to Paris," she said. "This is all a mistake, pure folly. You ought to know, too, Nicolau, my son," she added, "that for some time now I have had a lover called Casimir. I did not dare tell you about him, afraid that you would not understand. I wished to force you into a marriage as repugnant to you as it is to me—out of self-ishness, wanting to enjoy my freedom in your absence. Now Casimir is dying of consumption, and soon I will be all alone. The years are not easy to bear, and I need you at my side." This letter, which under other circumstances would have delighted Nicolau, arrived too late.

Don Humbert's family had returned to their estate in Budallera when Nicolau wrote to them to announce his arrival in Barcelona. He sent a note to Don Humbert's wife presenting himself as her humble servant. The note came with a bouquet of flowers.

"There's no denying he's a gentleman," she said. The following day they had an invitation sent to Nicolau to join them in Don Humbert's box during the intermission, where refreshments would be served. It was a while before he guessed that the invitation referred to the Liceo Opera House; they had taken it for granted that he would be attending the opening-night performance there. Nicolau sent one of the hotel boys out to buy a ticket for the stalls and asked to have his dress coat ironed without delay. Because of his shape, making that coat had been no easy task, and now, however much they ironed it for him, he still looked like a ragman.

Arriving at the Liceo, he found the entrance blocked by a three-deep cordon of policemen. He wondered whether there had been another bombing like the one perpetrated five years before in that same theater by Santiago Salvador, an incident he had heard a lot about from the Catalans who from time to time called at their house on Rue de Rivoli when visiting Paris. Actually, the cordon was because of a royal visit; Prince Nicholas I of Montenegro had deigned to grace with his presence this opening night, which marked the climax of Barcelona's Fiestas de la Merced. Nicolau finally managed to make his way to his seat as the gaslights began to dim.

That night was the Liceo's premiere of *Otello*, by Verdi. In Paris Nicolau had become an enthusiastic follower of Debussy, considering him the greatest musician after Beethoven; he had attended the first performances of all his works except *Pelléas et Mélisande*, from which he had been kept by an untimely bout of influenza. On that occasion he would not rest until his mother, despite the cold weather they were having, went out into the streets to buy a copy of the score for him, which he took comfort in reading during his convalescence.

Now Verdi's music struck him as raucous and grandiloquent. "I shouldn't have come," he thought. When the lights were turned up, he went to fulfill the social obligation to which the invitation had committed him. Ignorant of the social life of Barcelona, he had to ask in the corridors for the location of the

Figa i Morera family box. As he drew near it, he was overcome by anger and shame. "What the devil am I doing here, having refreshments with my father's murderers?" he asked himself. He hoped the box would be crowded and his presence scarcely noticed. But in the box there was only Don Humbert, his wife, Margarita, and a servant in a long coat and trousers tied below the knee, who held a tray of sponge cakes and *petits-fours*. Nicolau did not know that Don Humbert sent out many invitations but received only replies with excuses for not accepting. So they were alone. Nicolau clumsily uttered the formalities customary on such occasions.

"Since you come from Paris, all this must of course seem so very provincial to you," said Don Humbert's wife, taking the tray from the servant and offering him a cake herself.

"No, madam, not at all. Quite the contrary," he replied, grateful for the simplicity of his hostess.

The waiter served champagne, and they drank to a happy stay in Barcelona for young Nicolau. "A stay that will, we trust, be as happy as it will be long," said Don Humbert's wife, slyly narrowing her eyes.

"He is a parvenu," Nicolau thought, "she a puffed-up fish-wife, and the daughter a cocotte being sold off by her parents to the highest bidder." The gong sounded to announce the resumption of the performance; he began to take his leave, but Don Humbert seized his arm.

"I won't hear of it," he told him. "Stay with us. As you can see, there is room to spare, and you will be a hundred times more comfortable here than in the stalls. Come, come, no objections, the matter is settled."

Nicolau had no choice but to accept, and sat in a chair behind Margarita. When the chandeliers and candelabra went out and the curtain lifted, he could see, outlined against the footlights, the curve of her shoulders emerging from her evening dress. Her hair was gathered in a bun and held in place by a diadem of small but perfect pearls; this exposed the back of her neck. He stared at her back and shoulders, and the music and the champagne produced an agreeable lethargy in him.

Later that evening, he took out onto his hotel balcony the table and little wicker armchair he had used at breakfast, gathered his writing materials, lit the oil lamp, and breathed deeply the warm air coming up from the Ramblas that early-autumn night. "Tonight," he wrote, "as we listened to Verdi's *Otello* from your esteemed parents' box, I was tempted to kiss your shoulder. That would have been, I know, completely unacceptable, and so I restrained myself. To win your love, no doubt, I would have to be a different man, a man capable of following an impulse instead of being frightened off by it, instead of cowardly confessing his guilt by letter. But now I will confess the entire truth: to this matrimonial link that has been forged, and forged without, I am sure, your consent, I gave mine only with the greatest reluctance, never dreaming that this night, as we listened to Verdi's *Otello*, I would fall in love with you."

He stopped, put down the pen, thought for a moment, then got up, took the lamp, and went to the mirror in his bedroom. He was still wearing his dress coat. "Look at you," he muttered at the image in the mirror. "You look like you just peed in your pants. . . ." He went back to the balcony and took up his pen again. "Now I know," he went on, "that I will never go back to Paris."

By the time he finished putting on paper the ideas and feelings that were rushing into his head, the letter covered several pages. Dawn was breaking, and he had to put on his bathrobe to protect himself from the chill and the dew. It was a quarter to eight, and people were already out and about in the Ramblas, when he folded the letter without rereading it and put it into an envelope.

A chambermaid came in with his breakfast. "Do you wish to eat on the terrace, sir?" she asked.

226

"No, don't go to any trouble," he said. "You may leave it inside. Would you please have this letter sent to the address on the envelope and make sure it is delivered by hand to the person indicated?"

"There is a letter for you, too, sir," she said, pointing to the tray.

He picked it up, thinking it was from his mother, but a glance told him it was from Margarita. "You may go," he said to the chambermaid. "And the letter, sir?" "I'll bring it down to the *comptoir* myself later on," he said. Margarita's was a long letter, too. "She couldn't sleep last night, either," he thought.

She began by apologizing for her audacity in writing to him. She confessed to having harbored certain doubts regarding his person and the honesty of his intentions, but that night, in their box at the Liceo, he had struck her as a "polite, sensitive, and kindhearted man." That was why she now made so bold as to appeal to him. "For years I have been in love with a man and he with me," said the letter. "He is of humble origin, but I have secretly surrendered to him not only my heart but also something that modesty forbids me to mention." The union to which her mother, "moved, no doubt, by the highest intentions," had led them both was therefore a great embarrassment to her. "If you will not help me in this plight, my whole life is finished, for I cannot struggle unaided against destiny. I am not strong enough," she concluded.

Nicolau tore up the letter he had spent all night writing and wrote another, shorter one. He thanked her for her honesty and begged her to consider him, for that moment, "a loyal and disinterested friend. I cannot allow you to address me in pleading tones of which I am unworthy," he added. "Let me, rather, plead with you to abandon this attitude of fatalistic resignation. Each of us has the sacred duty to be happy, even if that means taking things into our own hands."

When he reread his letter, he found it presumptuous and

insincere. His other attempts were no better. He freshened up, put on a suit, and went down to the hotel foyer. "Kindly have a box of chocolates and my visiting card sent to this address, would you?" he said to the man at the reception desk. He scribbled a few polite formalities, thanking the Figa i Morera family for the kindness they had bestowed upon him the previous night in their box at the Liceo, then sent for a hackney carriage and was taken to the San Gervasio cemetery.

The cemetery was a distance from the city, and the air was hot and humid when he arrived, at midmorning. There he had to ask which was his father's tomb. When his father died, they had not attended the funeral, for reasons of safety, remaining instead in Paris, where they had already spent several days. "I do not even know who arranged the funeral," Nicolau thought. Perhaps the murderers themselves. He tipped the gravedigger who showed him the way. With no attempt at discretion, the man was eating a greasy sandwich. Nicolau had not touched his breakfast and felt a pang of hunger; it crossed his mind to offer to buy the sandwich from the gravedigger, who was clearly relishing every mouthful. Then he felt shame at having entertained such a thought, and here of all places, before the tomb of his father, which he was visiting for the first time. "Forgive me, Papa, but I cannot help it," he murmured in front of the mausoleum on whose door was written in bronze letters: THE CANALS FAMILY. "I am desperately in love," he added with a lump in his throat. The gravedigger was still there beside him. "How many can fit in there?" Nicolau asked, pointing to the mausoleum.

"As many as necessary," was the answer, which for some reason Nicolau found reassuring.

"Take care to have plenty of flowers put here," he said to the gravedigger. "I will visit from time to time." He walked back to the carriage; it had not rained for two weeks, and his shoes sank into the sun-bleached dust.

At the hotel, he was handed another letter, this time from

his mother: it was the letter telling him of Casimir's existence and consumption, and containing her plea for him to come back to Paris. "Circumstances are such that I must for the time being postpone indefinitely my return," he replied that same day. He expressed his fervent hope for the speedy and total recovery of Casimir, with whom he had not yet had the opportunity of becoming acquainted. "I trust soon to be able to make good this deficiency, and meanwhile urge that no trouble or expense be spared in ministering to his illness. All my assets, Mama, which are yours, too, are at your disposal. But for the present do not expect me in Paris: I shall soon be twenty and it is time I started leading an independent life."

That afternoon, in his hotel, he received a visit from Don Humbert. "I have come to see you, my dear friend, both as a lawyer and a father," he said without preamble. "If your intentions regarding my daughter are honorable, as I have every reason to believe they are, we must discuss certain points—your situation and your means, I mean."

Nicolau raised his eyebrows, thinking, "This riffraff no doubt noticed the effect their daughter had on me, and now wants to raise the price of the merchandise." He would have shown his contempt, but knew that would mean losing her forever. "It is only with the complicity of these base and grasping parents that I can hope," he thought. Yet he did not want that, either. The same weakness of character that prevented him from renouncing this impossible love and leaving at once for Paris also prevented him from making her his own through means he considered reprehensible. "If I loved her the way she deserves to be loved, I wouldn't think twice about selling my soul to the devil," he thought. Numbed by his dilemma, he played for time, feigning an innocence that would have come naturally to him only a day before.

"I thought my mother and your gracious wife had reached some agreement on those points," Nicolau said. "In any event, I cannot broach such matters until I have paid a visit to my bankers in Barcelona." Don Humbert backtracked hurriedly: he had in fact come to the hotel merely to say hello, since he happened to be in that part of town. He wanted to thank Nicolau in person for the chocolates he had so thoughtfully sent and to make sure he was wanting for nothing.

As they spoke, Onofre Bouvila, who was *au fait* with all his rival's moves, was getting ready to put his plans into operation. Two days before, he had received a coded message from Garnett, the American agent of the ex-governor of Luzon. The message was: "All set. Awaiting instructions."

Onofre rang a handbell, and a secretary came in. "Did you ring, sir?" he asked.

"Yes," said Onofre. "I want Odón Mostaza found and brought here."

The following morning, Nicolau was awakened by a noise; he didn't need to be told it was shooting. Then he heard hurried steps and shouts. The commotion lasted only a few seconds. He leaped out of bed, threw his bathrobe over his shoulders, and imprudently went out on the balcony.

A man on the next balcony told him what had happened. "The anarchists killed a policeman. Now they're taking the body away on a stretcher."

Nicolau rushed downstairs and went out into the street, but all he saw was a group of onlookers huddled around a pool of blood. With everybody talking at once, he could form no clear picture of the incident. But it made a deep impression on him.

From then on, he felt part of the life of the city. That afternoon he went to a tailor called Tenebrós on Calle Ancha and ordered several suits; in the Roberto Mas outfitter's on Calle Llibretería he bought several dozen shirts and other garments. He was getting himself a wardrobe for winter in the city.

When he returned to his hotel, he found an invitation waiting for him: the Figa i Morera family requested the honor of his company at dinner the following Saturday at their home—now on Calle Caspe. "I shouldn't go," he told himself. "This is my last chance to steer clear of this seedy business." But he remembered her shoulders and replied without further hesitation that he would gladly attend. He sent as a present a goldfinch in a gilt cage—a rare and much-prized species, he was assured. The bird came from Japan and sang with sweet nostalgia.

Around this time, Osorio, ex-governor of Luzon, received a parcel containing a dead turtle whose shell had been painted crimson. The ex-governor's Filipino servant paled when he saw it. Osorio put on a show of indifference in front of the servant, but that afternoon he went to have a word with Inspector Marqués, one of the police officers who frequented his bullfighting enthusiasts' club. "Among Malayan tribes this means vengeance," Osorio told him.

"Perhaps someone has bad memories of your rule over there," said the police officer.

"Piffle, my friend, piffle," the ex-governor replied. "My conduct was above reproach. It is true that in the course of my duties I made an occasional enemy, but I assure you that none of those individuals has the means to pay for the voyage to Barcelona."

"But we cannot take action," said Inspector Marqués, "merely because you received a turtle in the mail."

A few days later the ex-governor received a second parcel, this one containing a plucked chicken with a black ribbon tied around its neck.

"The sign of the pinion," exclaimed the ex-governor's servant. "We are done for, General. Resistance is useless."

"I had a word with my superiors about this turtle business," said Inspector Marqués. "Indeed, they were not inclined to take it seriously. But now, with this chicken, I don't know. . . ."

"My friend," the ex-governor broke in, "the first time I did not attach too much importance to what I considered a joke in

231

poor taste, but with this chicken, believe me, my life is in danger."

When the inspector came with his superiors' reply, he found the ex-governor a nervous wreck. "You look as if you've just had a visit from all the devils in hell," Marqués commented.

"This is no time for humor," the ex-governor replied. That morning he had received the third and last parcel: a dead pig in an aubergine satin tunic. The parcel was so heavy, it had to be carried in a handcart to his house on Calle Escudellers. And for this he had to pay a special fee, which he protested: postage should cover transport to the addressee, he argued. Yes, but not the use of a handcart, they said. When he saw the pig, he lost all appetite for further disputation, paid the fee, bolted all the doors and windows, took a regulation pistol from a trunk, loaded it, and put it in his belt in the colonial fashion. Then he clapped his servant, who had wet his pants, on the back. "Be brave," he told him.

The ex-governor, too, was frightened. Experience had taught him that the Malayans were a kindhearted, cheerful, and unusually generous people, but they also could be violent and cruel. During his tenure as governor it had fallen to him to preside over certain ceremonies that the metropolitan government, not wishing to alienate local chieftains, had decided to tolerate. There he had seen acts of cannibalism. Now he recalled the savages in their war paint letting out belches after their vile repast. In his imagination he saw them behind every banana tree along the Ramblas, in every doorway of the elegant houses on Calle Escudellers, with fearsome krises between their teeth.

Inspector Marqués promised to inform his superiors of all this, but dared not tell the ex-governor that his superiors paid no attention to him, for he had let the other members of the bullfighting club believe that he wielded much greater influence on the force than was actually the case.

Nicolau could not eat or sleep, and medicines were useless for the dull pain he suffered. When Saturday came, he arrived at Don Humbert's house in a state of extreme debilitation. A liveried butler hired for the occasion opened the carriage door for him, but Nicolau's cane got caught between his legs when he tried to put his foot on the carriage step, and the manservant had to lift him down bodily and then retrieve his top hat from the gutter. Nicolau handed his hat, cane, and gloves to a maid in the hall. It was the maid Efrén Castells had seduced, and she was feeling just then the first symptoms of her pregnancy. "Everybody looks at me as if I was something that just crawled out of a hole," he thought, noticing her scowl. "Or a freak in a sideshow."

He was the first to arrive, his North European punctuality not having succumbed yet to Spanish laxity. Not even the lady of the house was ready: she was in her bedchamber scolding her maids, couturiere, and hairdresser, heaping insults on them all without rhyme or reason. Don Humbert did the honors in a salon that was too big for the two of them. He apologized lightheartedly for his wife's absence: "You know what women are like." Nicolau asked anxiously if Margarita would be late, too. "She was feeling a little under the weather this afternoon," said Don Humbert, "and is not sure she'll be able to join us for dinner. She begged me to apologize to you on her behalf." Though Nicolau knew such behavior was unpardonable, he covered his face with his hands and began to weep. Don Humbert, seeing his guest's distress but not knowing what to do, pretended not to notice. "Come along with me," he said. "We have plenty of time, and I would like to show you something interesting."

He led Nicolau to his study and showed him the mechanical telephone he had just had installed. It was very rudimentary and served only to communicate with the room on the other side of the inner patio. The telephone consisted of a simple wire with a horn at either end. In each window a pane of glass had been replaced by a thin spruce board; the wire ran through the center. When the wire had to turn a corner, it was suspended by threads, since contact with an object had to be avoided for the message to be successfully transmitted.

When they went back to the salon, the lady of the house was there, wearing a long dress, a welter of jewelry, and a penetrating wallflower scent. Her beauty, which had opened doors for her in her youth, was now well-padded but not entirely gone. She flirted, all milk and honey, with Nicolau, sometimes coy and seductive, sometimes effusive and theatrical, calling him "my dear boy." "All this humiliation," he thought, "and I won't even get to see her tonight"; he fought to hold back his tears.

The arrival of other guests rescued him from the embarrassing situation. This time Don Humbert had made certain of the presence of a few other guests in his home. "He's young and has always lived abroad," he had said to his wife. "He won't know the difference." The guests were a corrupt councillor who owed Don Humbert his job, the only job he could hold given his lack of ability; a gentleman, supposedly a marquis, who had fallen on hard times and whose gambling debts Don Humbert had taken on years ago in a moment of inspiration, needing him to lend a touch of class to his gatherings; the marquis's wife, Doña Eulalia "Titi" de Rosales; one Father Valltorta, an ecclesiastic with extremely bushy eyebrows and a penchant for the bottle; a lecturer in medicine whom Don Humbert paid to forge medical reports and certificates; and the lecturer's wife. It was to this sorry circle that Don Humbert had been reduced by Barcelona society.

To their polite remarks Nicolau replied laconically, but soon everybody was engaged in conversation and he was left in peace. Only the hostess urged him from time to time to eat more, but he did not touch the dainty morsels that appeared on his plate.

When dinner was over, they all went to the salon again. There was a grand piano there. Since the hostess, aware of his musical ability, would not take no for an answer, he was finally prevailed upon to play. He plowed reluctantly through a few Chopin études he knew by heart. When he turned to acknowledge the applause, though having no illusions about its sincerity, he was rooted to the spot: she was there.

Margarita was wearing a simple organdy gown with a broad scarlet band around the waist. The only ornament was a wrought-silver brooch at her breast, holding a flower in place there. Her copper hair was done up in a plait. She came over to the piano and murmured an apology for her absence at the meal: she had had a dizzy spell that afternoon but had recovered sufficiently to make an appearance. He believed her.

"I heard you play," she told him. "I didn't know you were an artist." "A poor amateur," he said, going red. "Is there any particular piece you would like me to play for you?" She leaned over the piano, pretending to look at the sheet music. He felt the warmth of her body, her bare arm reached past his cheek, and his mouth went instantly dry with the desire to kiss it. "Did you receive my letter?" she whispered in his ear. "Tell me, for the love of God, were you not given the letter I sent to your hotel?" Pretending to be absorbed in the keyboard, he said, "Yes." "Well, then," she asked, "what is your answer? Can I trust in your generosity?"

It took a superhuman effort for him to reply. "I am no longer in control of myself," he said. "I cannot sleep, I cannot eat, I feel ill all day. When you are not with me, there is a pain in my chest, I struggle for air, I think I'm going to die." "Well," she insisted, "what is your answer?" "She didn't hear a word I said," he thought.

The retired General Osorio y Clemente, ex-governor of Luzon, was hit by three bullets from a revolver fired from a closed carriage as he emerged from the Church of San Justo y Pastor after hearing Mass. He fell dead on the paving slabs of the square. A bunch of yellow flowers, tossed out of the carriage window, landed near the body. Later, eyewitnesses related the most curious aspect of the incident: the deceased's Filipino manservant, on hearing the first shot, took to his heels and ran to one end of the square; there he squatted, inserted a curved stick about a foot long into a hole in the ground, opened the iron manhole cover, and disappeared for good into the sewer system below. The police later stated that this was proof of his role in the crime. Others said that from the time his master received the turtle, the Filipino had begun to plan his flight, pinpointing and memorizing the locations of all the manholes in the city. That he carried that curved stick, which he had fashioned himself, wherever they went.

A few days prior to this incident, Señor Braulio suddenly felt uneasy. "This is some premonition," he thought as he looked at himself in the mirror. He had put on weight over the years; now when he dressed as a woman, he looked like a matron. He had, furthermore, grown a short mustache in the Teutonic style, which made him appear more ridiculous than sensual. But those who formerly laughed at him now shook their heads, seeing in his behavior symptoms of senility, or possibly a softening of the brain due to the battering he received when he went on his sprees.

The case of the Danish boxer Andersen, very much in the news then after his recent visit to Barcelona, came to mind. For many years this boxer had taken on champions from France, Germany, and the United Kingdom, and always lost after a thorough thrashing. Now he was being led from city to city; in Barcelona he was exhibited, in a cane-and-canvas shed erected in the Puerta de la Paz, as a case worthy of scientific interest, or so the posters read. In fact, under the cover of this scientific interest unscrupulous promoters were exploiting his misfortune. The man had become a child again: he shook a rattle in his massive paws and drank milk from a baby bottle. Payment of one real allowed one to ask him questions; for one peseta one could go through the motions of a boxing match with him. He was still a strapping figure of a man, with a mighty chest and biceps, but his movements were slow, his legs hardly able to bear the weight of his body, and he was almost blind, although only twenty-four years old.

This, of course, did not apply to Señor Braulio, who was in excellent health; only his looks had suffered a little, through age and the retirement Onofre had forced upon him. But his eccentricities and sudden changes of mood had become more pronounced.

He was worried about Odón Mostaza. Having money but no occupation, the ruffian was leading an increasingly dissolute life. Whenever Señor Braulio admonished him, Odón would retort: "You've peddled your ass all over La Carbonera, and now you come preaching at me." "That's how I lost my wife and my daughter," the former hotelier would sigh. "Two poor innocents had to pay for my wantonness."

One day Odón heard that Onofre wanted to see him; he went straight to his office. The two old friends met with much hugging and back slapping. "We haven't seen each other for ages," said Odón. "Ever since you turned respectable, nobody can get near you. Ah, what times we had! Do you remember when we took on Joan Sicart?"

Onofre let him talk, listening with a smile, but finally said: "It's time to do battle again, Odón. We can't rest on our laurels. I need you." The ruffian beamed a wolfish smile. "Thank God for that. The old weapon was getting rusty. What's the story?" Onofre lowered his voice: "An easy job. I've got it all worked out—you'll like it."

When the appointed day arrived, Odón set out very early, took a hackney carriage, and was driven to the edge of the city. When they reached a certain spot, he pulled his revolver on the coachman and told him to get out. A thug appeared from behind a bush, bound the man firmly with a rope, stuffed tow into his mouth to gag him, blindfolded him with a rag, and gave him a blow on the back of the neck that left him unconscious. The thug then put on the coachman's cape and climbed onto his seat. Odón got back into the carriage, closed the curtains, and removed the false beard and dark glasses he had been wearing to prevent the coachman from identifying him later. He bought a bunch of lilies in the Ramblas, as Onofre had instructed. So strong was the scent of the flowers in the closed carriage, Odón thought for a moment he would throw up. Meanwhile, he made sure his revolver was in good working order.

The church-tower clock was striking the hour when the carriage reached the square. Only a small group of the faithful came out from Mass, since it was a workday. Odón drew back the curtain a little and poked the revolver out. When he saw the ex-governor and his Filipino servant emerge, he took aim calmly, let him come down the steps, and fired three times. Only the Filipino reacted immediately. The carriage set off again. Then Odón remembered the flowers, banged on the roof of the carriage to tell the driver to stop, took the bunch of lilies from the seat, and hurled it out the window. By then sounds of shouting and running could be heard: everybody was taking cover.

A few days later, policemen from the criminal-investigation department arrested him as he was coming out of a brothel where he had spent the night. Since he knew he had an alibi, he put up no resistance; he greeted the officers with mock affection. "Enjoy yourself while you can, Mostaza," the sergeant said. "This time you're paying for what you've done." Odón puckered his lips and blew kisses at him, which infuriated the sergeant. The other officers, who knew his reputation, did not take their eyes off him for a second; they trained their muskets on him in case he made a move. Some of them were very young; even before they joined the force, they had heard of Odón Mostaza the gangster. Now they were bringing him handcuffed before the judge. When the judge asked him where he had been on such-and-such a day at such-and-such a time, he answered confidently, reeling off the lies he had worked out with Onofre. The judge repeated his questions, and the scribe wrote down the answers, which were the same. "Are you trying to pull my leg, too?" the judge finally asked.

"Your Honor should save his little tricks for thieves, socialists, anarchists, and queers," said the gangster. "I am Odón Mostaza, a professional with many years of experience, and I will say no more." But when the interrogation began all over again, as if the judge was deaf or an imbecile, he added, "Is Your Honor trying to make a name for himself at my expense? I would point out that others have tried it before; they all wanted to be the one who put Odón Mostaza behind bars. And they all made fools of themselves."

The judge's name was Acisclo Salgado Fonseca Pintojo y Gamuza; he was thirty-three, round-shouldered, with a thick neck, a bushy beard, and a pale complexion. He spoke slowly and raised his eyebrows in surprise whenever anybody said anything to him. "Tell me where you were on such-and-such a day at such-and-such a time," he repeated.

Odón lost his temper. "Let's get this comedy over with," he shouted in the courtroom, not caring if he was overheard by others awaiting trial. "What do you want from me? Money? I have no intention of giving you any, Your Honor. I know that business: I give you a hundred today, and you want a thousand tomorrow. Forget it. You have no proof, no witnesses, my alibi is airtight. Besides, everybody knows that the ex-governor was killed by a bunch of Malayans."

"What ex-governor?" the judge asked, perplexed. "What Malayans?" It took them a while to explain to Odón that he was accused of the murder not of ex-governor Osorio but Nicolau Canals i Rataplán, a young man he had never heard of.

On the morning of the day of the crime, a man wrapped in a cape and wearing a wide-brimmed soft hat had passed the *comptoir* of the Gran Hotel de Aragón so quickly that the receptionist had been unable to intercept him. The receptionist sent several members of the hotel staff and two policemen who were patrolling the Ramblas, very busy at that time of day, after the intruder, but he was never found. Some said he had climbed down on the outside of the building from one of the upper floors, that for that purpose he had under his cape a rope with a grappling iron. Others, pointing out that no passer-by had seen anything of the sort, were convinced it was an inside job. The only trail the man left was the body of Nicolau Canals i Rataplán, who had been stabbed three times; any one of the wounds would have been sufficient to kill him. The following day Nicolau was buried in the family mausoleum beside the mortal remains of his father, likewise a murder victim. His mother did not attend the funeral. He was the last descendant of that line of the Canals family.

Now the judge produced the soft hat and the cape. While Odón was in the brothel, the police had searched his house and found those garments, as well as a switchblade knife on which there were still traces of blood despite its having been washed. Odón denied everything, repeating the tale of the turtle, the chicken, and the pig. "The accused," said the judge later in his summation, "is plainly delirious." They made him put on the hat and cape in the presence of the hotel receptionist, whom the judge had summoned. The garments fitted Odón perfectly, and the receptionist identified him as the man who had run past his *comptoir*.

Odón bribed a courtroom attendant to take a message to Señor Braulio: "Damned if I know what's going on, but whatever it is, it's fishy." Señor Braulio went to see Onofre. "We'll get the best criminal lawyer in Spain," said Onofre. "Wouldn't it be better to settle the thing privately," asked Señor Braulio, "before it becomes too official?"

The lawyer was named Hermógenes Palleja or Pallejá; he said he came from Seville and had just joined the Barcelona bar, intending to set up practice here—though in the end he did not. Most of the witnesses for the defense this lawyer called never showed up: they were loose women, who disappeared when the court police went in search of them. Having no papers and being known only by their sobriquets, they were able to cover their traces easily. The three that did appear in the witness box made a poor impression on the court. They showed off their legs, winked at the public benches, used indecent language, and giggled for no reason. When replying to the prosecutor, they said, "Yes, honey," "No, sweetie," and so on. The court president had to call them to order several times. All three stated that they had been with the accused on the morning of the day of the crime, but when cross-examined by the prosecutor, and even by the defense, they became confused over dates, times, and men, and finally took back what they said.

Odón, who had never set eyes on these trollops before and could see how damaging to him their testimony was, asked to have a word with his lawyer. But the lawyer, saying he was too busy, did not visit Odón in his cell in the Palace of Justice, the same building near which, ten years ago during the World's Fair, Odón first met Onofre Bouvila, the man on whom he now pinned all his hopes.

But Onofre seemed unconcerned. Whenever Señor Braulio, at his wits' end after following the case all day from his bench among the crowd that packed the court, went to see him, Onofre was not available, giving some excuse. Or, if Señor Braulio was allowed in, Onofre quickly changed the subject.

The prosecutor asked for the supreme penalty for the accused, and the court finally pronounced its sentence: Odón Mostaza was condemned to death. "Patience," said his lawyer, "we shall appeal." And he did so, but missed legal deadlines or presented his appeals to the higher courts so carelessly that they were rejected on formal grounds.

Alone in his cell, the ruffian was in despair. He stopped eating and scarcely slept; whenever he did, he was assailed by nightmares and woke up screaming. The guards laughed at him, and sometimes entered his cell and cruelly beat him. Finally a change took place in the prisoner: he saw that through the crime that he had not committed he must pay for all his crimes that had gone unpunished. In this he saw the hand of the Almighty, and from being a jeering disbeliever became pious and humble. He asked for the prison priest, to whom he confessed his countless sins. The memory of his past life, that morass of vice in which he had disported himself for so many years, made him weep disconsolately. Although he received absolution from his confessor, he dared not appear in the presence of his Maker. "Trust to His infinite mercy," the confessor urged. Odón now wore a purple habit and a gray cord hanging from his neck.

Señor Braulio paid another visit to Onofre. He fell to his knees on the carpet and crossed his arms on his breast. "What's this nonsense?" Onofre asked. "I won't stir from here until you hear me out," Señor Braulio answered. Onofre rang a bell, and as soon as the secretary's head appeared around the door, told him, "We are not to be disturbed." When the door closed, he lit a cigar and settled back in his chair. "Now, tell me what all this is about."

"You know why I am here," Señor Braulio said. "He is a wicked man, but he is also your friend. In times of danger he was always at your side. You have never known a more loyal man. Nor I," he added in a broken voice, "a more handsome one."

"What are you driving at?"

"I can understand why you wanted to teach him a lesson. I'm sure he has learned his lesson. I'll answer for his conduct in the future."

"What more do you want me to do? I got the best lawyer in Spain, I knocked on every door, I tried to get His Majesty's pardon. . . ."

"Onofre, don't tell me that. I've known you for many years. You were a little whippersnapper when you first came empty-handed to my boardinghouse. I know you orchestrated this whole thing because you have an evil heart, because you are willing to sacrifice anything and anyone to get what you want, and because deep down you always envied Odón Mostaza. But this time you have gone too far, and you will have to put things right, whether you want to or not. Look at me here: on my knees to save that poor wretch's life. My heart, like the Madonna's, is pierced with seven daggers. Do it for his sake or do it for mine."

Seeing Onofre impassive, he sighed and got to his feet. "All right," he said, "if that's the way you want it. I've made a few inquiries lately, and know that Garnett and you, with Don Humbert's help, have doctored the contracts signed by Osorio, and that now all Osorio's assets in the Philippines are practically yours. I also know that people in your employ recently bought a turtle, a hen, and a pig, and had sizable parcels delivered through the mail. None of this will exonerate Odón of the crime he is charged with. Quite the contrary—any investigation into Osorio's death will reveal his guilt—but you cannot kill a man twice, and Odón is as good as dead now. Others could go down with him, though. You know what I'm getting at."

Onofre, still smiling, puffed away calmly at his cigar. "Don't be that way, Señor Braulio," he finally said. "As I told you, I've done everything humanly possible for my friend Odón. Unfortunately it didn't pan out. On the other hand, while seeking the release of one prisoner, by pure chance I obtained the release of another. Here in this drawer I have a signed copy of your daughter Delfina's reprieve. Believe me, it took a lot of influence and money to obtain it. The authorities refused to grant it at first on the grounds that public safety comes first, a view I personally happen to share. Now, happily, it is all fixed. It would be a great shame, would it not, if this reprieve were not to go through?"

Señor Braulio bowed his head and left the office without saying another word; tears streamed down his cheeks.

In the chapel for the condemned, two members of the Archconfraternity of the Precious Blood of Jesus Christ Our Lord brought in that brotherhood's crucifix, illuminated by six candles. In accordance with the archconfraternity's rules, they wore tunics and capes, black leather belts, rosaries, and a shield, their emblem, sewn on the breast. This archconfraternity, whose task it was to succor the prisoner in his last hours and then to take charge of his body in the absence of relatives, had been established in Barcelona in the year 1547 in the Most Holy Sacrament Chapel, commonly known as Blood Chapel, in the Church of Nuestra Señora del Pino.

Odón Mostaza was praying, hunched over, his forehead on the cold, damp floor. He was in an isolated part of the prison, where he could be visited only by the appropriate authorities, the prison doctor, priests and members of the archconfraternity, and, through a special clause in the law, by a notary "in the event the condemned desires to make a will or oral deposition." Silence reigned in the prison: exercise periods had been canceled, as had all other activities "that might disturb the proper spirit of recollection." Already gathered in the yard were those persons who were to be present at the execution, namely, "the judicial secretary, representatives of the government and judiciary, the warden with such prison officers as he should designate, the priests and members of the charitable association succoring the condemned, and three citizens designated by the mayor." Executions had not taken place in public since the royal decree of November 24, 1894. This provoked sharp criticism. Thus we read: "The death penalty in Spain has lost its instructive character, gaining nothing in return, since descriptions of executions in the press not only excite idle curiosity but also lend the criminal a romantic aura."

Now the three citizens were attentively watching the executioner, who was making sure that the garrote was in good working order. This instrument consisted of a high-backed chair fitted with a tourniquet with a halterlike metal bow at one end; applied to the condemned's throat, it caused death by strangulation. His Majesty Don Fernando VII, by a royal warrant of

April 28, 1828 "to mark the happy occasion of the birthday of the queen," had abolished hanging as a death penalty, declaring that executions from then on would be by *"garrote ordinario* for criminals from among the common people, *garrote vil* for heinous offenders, and *garrote noble* for gentlemen." Those of the first category were taken to the place of execution on horseback and wearing the *capuz*, a kind of cape with a hood worn over other clothing and normally used in mourning. Those condemned to *garrote vil* were led to execution on asses, or dragged if the sentence so indicated, and without the *capuz*. Finally, those condemned to *garrote noble* were led on a saddled horse with a black caparison. These distinctions were not observed, of course, when executions ceased to be held in public.

When his cell door opened, Odón did not lift his face from the ground. Four hands under his arms raised him. He murmured, "Lord have mercy on my soul," over and over, to shut out other thoughts. Once outside, he opened his eyes and saw the brothers of the archconfraternity leading the way, bearing the crucifix that had been in the chapel. He saw the white, cloudless sky of the dawn and asked himself what it mattered to him now whether the sun shone that day or thereafter.

At the far end of the yard he saw the garrote, the group of witnesses, and the executioner, who stood back a little. One of the witnesses threw a cigarette on the ground and stubbed it out with his foot. Seeing an open coffin made of dark wood with its lid propped against the wall, Odón went weak at the knees, but the guards on either side held him up. "Let it not be said of me . . . ," he thought, straightened, and lifted his head. "You may let go," he wanted to say, but only made a wheezing sound. "Under the circumstances, not bad," he joked to himself. Every step he took without collapsing seemed a triumph to him.

His sack tunic was dragging behind him. They had dressed him in this garment when he went into the chapel. By law these tunics were black, except for those of regicides and parricides, which were yellow with matching birettas. The tunic resembled a cassock, and when he saw himself in it, he felt humiliated. "Up to now I always chose my own clothes," he joked with the jailers. Had his execution been postponed a few months, he would have had no grounds for complaint, for the use of this tunic for those condemned to death was abolished by a law passed on April 9, 1900.

He sat in the chair and allowed himself to be strapped down. The crucifix was brought to his lips, and he kissed it, eyes closed. He did not notice somebody discreetly motioning with his hand.

Afterward, the deed of execution was drawn up and signed by all present. The brotherhood members removed the body, crossing the arms over the chest in the coffin, put a silver-plated rosary in the hands, closed the eyes, and smoothed down the hair, which had been ruffled by a breeze. When they saw him laid out, the brothers whispered among themselves: "Indeed, in Barcelona there was no man more handsome than he."

At the same time, at the other end of the city, the side door of the women's prison opened to let out Delfina. Señor Braulio was waiting for her by a closed carriage drawn up outside the somber walls. They hugged each other, tears in their eyes. "How thin you are, my daughter," said Señor Braulio after a while. "And you, Father, you are trembling. Are you all right?" she asked. "It's nothing, my dear," said the ex-hotelier. "The excitement, perhaps. Come, get into the carriage, let's go home. How thin you are! But never mind, I'll take care of you. You'll be surprised to see how much things have changed with me."

A month after Odón Mostaza's execution, Onofre once more asked Don Humbert for his daughter's hand in marriage, which this time was granted forthwith and without reservations.

CHAPTER FIVE

1

The nineteenth century, which had been ushered in by Napoleon Bonaparte on 18 Brumaire 1799, was now drawing to a close, with Queen Victoria on her deathbed. Outside the royal bedchamber once thundered the hoofs of the Imperial Guard horses, and in the streets of Europe the cannons of Austerlitz, Borodino, Waterloo, and other, similarly famous battlegrounds. Now all that could be heard was the shuffling of looms or the purring and backfiring of the internal-combustion engine. As centuries go, it had been comparatively sparing in wars, but not in new discoveries: a century of marvels.

Now humanity was crossing the threshold into the twentieth century with a shudder. The greatest changes were yet to come, but people were already weary of change, apprehensive, not knowing what disruption the morrow would bring. There was no shortage of visionaries imagining what the future would be like. Electric energy, radio, the automobile, aviation, and advances in medicine would change the world radically, they said.

Nature would be tamed; the human mind would bring chance under its control and do as it pleased with it; there was no obstacle man's ingenuity would not surmount; people would be able to change size and sex at will, travel through the air at unheard-of speeds, become invisible whenever it suited them, learn a foreign language in two hours, and live for three hundred years or more. Highly intelligent beings from the moon, the planets, and other, more distant celestial bodies would come and visit us, measuring their inventions against ours. The world would be an Arcadia inhabited by artists and philosophers, where nobody would have to work. Others predicted nothing but calamities and tyrannies. The Roman Catholic Church reminded anyone willing to listen that progress did not always follow the path laid down by God's will as expressly manifested in the sovereign pontiff, whose infallibility had been proclaimed on July 19, 1870.

The church was not alone in its aversion to progress: the majority of the world's rulers shared its misgivings; they saw in change the subversion of all principles, the end of their era. Only the kaiser took a different view: delighted with the fifty-ton cannons being churned out at the Krupp factory, he thought, "God bless progress if it permits me to bombard Paris."

In such fashion the years came and went. One evening in the month of August 1913, Onofre Bouvila's thoughts, as he stood on a wharf in Barcelona, were occupied by precisely this theme of time and its flight. He was supervising the unloading of certain crates whose contents were not on any bill of lading. The customs officials had been alerted and their blindness purchased for a scandalous sum, but he wished to leave nothing to chance. As he watched the ship docking, he recalled the day he had come to this same dock in search of a job. At that time nearly all the boats were sailing vessels, and he was still a child; now he watched the smokestacks against the fading light of that end-of-summer evening, and he was nearly forty. He stood, august and alone, watching the boats tying up.

A clerk came to tell him that the crates were about to be lifted from the bilge. "Has the packaging been damaged in any way?" Onofre asked absently. According to information from various sources, there would soon be a war; anyone able to supply the market with weapons would therefore make an immense fortune in a short period of time. Onofre had arranged for prototypes of guns, shells, grenades, flamethrowers, and so on to be smuggled into Spain. His agents were already stalking the chancelleries of Europe. The idea was not his alone: he would have to make allies and enemies, watch out for traps, and destroy competitors. Also he would have to trust spies acting for the future warring nations, spies who were already infiltrating Barcelona, as they were infiltrating every other city in the world.

"Why am I doing all this?" Onofre thought. His first son had turned out to be an imbecile. Born at the turn of the century, under the best of omens, the child soon gave evidence that he would never be normal. Now he was vegetating in the Pyrenees, in the province of Lérida, in the care of a religious institution to which Onofre gave generous financial support. The second son was stillborn. Then came two girls. His love for his wife, which had withstood so many trials before, did not survive these repeated failures. Abandoned, she became fat, consoling herself with cakes and chocolate all day long; somebody was always offering her sweets in the hope of winning her husband's favor.

He was wealthy and powerful, yet still an outcast. The city's leading figures admired him, not for how he had amassed his money but for the way he spent it. Money for them was an end in itself, not a means to obtain or accomplish anything. It never occurred to them to use it to take the reins of the country into their own hands, to shape the government according to their own theories. If at times they entered the arena of politics, they did so reluctantly. They served Madrid as good administrators, efficiently, with no scheming, even when this worked against the best interests of the Catalonia they had previously defended, or even against their own best interests. Perhaps deep down, though considering themselves separate from Spain, they could not completely do without Spain. Or perhaps everything happened too quickly: they had not been given time to establish themselves as a class, as an economic entity. And now they were unable to influence the course of history.

Onofre could hear the straining of the ships' rigging, the creaking of their timbers, the lapping of the water against their hulls. Many of these ships were transporting his merchandise to and from the Philippines and other points; some were owned by him. None of this had served to redeem him from his obscure origins in the eyes of society. People went to see him when they needed him, but his name was always forgotten on their invitation lists.

A year before, a group of leading city gentlemen presided over by his old acquaintance the Marquis of Ut came to see him, announcing their visit with great ceremony. The majority of those present had had dealings with him before, often illegal ones, but, having once eaten from his hand, they now pretended that they hadn't and went through the ritual pantomine all over again.

"To what do I owe this honor?" he asked them. Each was busy offering his seat to another, deferring interminably. "You speak. . . . No, no, you do the talking, you do it so much better than I. . . ." Onofre waited patiently, studying their faces. Some had been members of the World's Fair board of directors, potentates in the days he slipped into the fairgrounds at the crack of dawn to hand out anarchist pamphlets and sell hair restorer. Most of those board members had died in the interim: Rius y Taulet shortly after the World's Fair closed its doors in 1899; in 1905, Nanuel Girona i Agrafel, who had been the event's royal commissary, paying for the cathedral's new façade out of his own pocket and founding the Bank of Barcelona; Manuel Durán i Bas in 1907, etc. The survivors were all old men; none of them suspected that the man who was now eyeing them with irony had seen them pass in parade when he was a child hiding behind a pile of cement bags.

"We have come," they told him, "because we know of the depth of your love for Barcelona, this city you so honor with your presence and your activities, and also because we are well aware of your generosity."

"How much is it this time?" he asked sardonically.

"We have been advised by the Ministry for Foreign Affairs," they said, not at all offended, being thick-skinned old birds, "that a person of royal blood, a member of a reigning house, will soon visit this city. The visit is private in character, and consequently from the official standpoint there is no budgetary allowance for it, as you will no doubt appreciate. On the other hand, we cannot allow, as the ministry itself has pointed out, in line with the sentiments of His Majesty the King, may God preserve him—we cannot allow, we repeat, this illustrious visitor to go without fitting token of our hospitality. In short, the cost of the maintenance and entertainment of the illustrious visitor and retinue is to be defrayed by ourselves."

Onofre asked who the visitor was. After much hesitation they told him, in the strictest confidence, that it was Princess Alix de Hesse, granddaughter of Queen Victoria, now better known as Alexandra Feodorovna, wife of His Imperial Highness Tsar Nicholas II. This information left Onofre cold: he had not the slightest interest in the Romanovs, considering them a pack of fools. His interest had been kindled, however, by the careers of the maximalist conspirators, Lenin, Trotsky, and others; he was kept abreast of their moves by his informers in London and Paris, where they were at the time, and had occasionally thought of financing their hotheaded schemes with a view to future business dealings.

The present meeting struck him as absurd. "Why should I help these people?" he asked himself. Though many of them were regarded as among the sharpest of financiers, they saw only what was going on under their own noses, completely ignorant of what was happening in the world outside their offices; they knew nothing of the world of the wretched, the mad, and the blind living and reproducing in the darkness of the back alleys. But Onofre knew that world well, and recently he had sensed the beat of revolution there.

"Leave everything to me," he said.

All the way down the stairs they made speeches to express their gratitude. A long line of carriages was at hand to convey them back to their residences on Paseo de Gracia. The carriage hoods and the horse blankets gleamed in the drizzle; a yellowish halo formed around the gas streetlamps and the lanterns of the coaches. Onofre waved to them from the doorway. "My entire fortune will be inherited by my daughters," he was thinking, "and the scoundrels who get them into bed. It serves me right for having married an idiot."

The tsarina and her entourage came ashore incognito in the Puerta de la Paz. The drizzle had stopped a few hours earlier. Reflected in puddles on the ground were the tops of luxuriant banana trees, whose branches stirred in the damp breeze. "A nasty day to be welcoming Her Imperial Highness," muttered the Marquis of Ut. He and Onofre were smoking in his carriage, a mahogany brougham drawn by four English horses. Behind them an army of hackney carriages and long wagons hired for the occasion were waiting to take the entourage to the suites reserved for them in the Ritz.

Onofre made no reply to the marquis's remark. Two days before, he had received a letter signed by Joan Bouvila. He assumed it was from his father, but as he read it, he saw it was from his brother, whose existence he had forgotten. Joan wrote that their father was on his deathbed: "Make haste if you want to see him alive."

Onofre had not seen his father since the short visit home he made in the autumn of 1907 on the occasion of his mother's funeral. At the wake he noticed young Joan's absence. His father told him the boy was doing his military service in Africa, where there was always trouble brewing with the Arabs. When they got back from the cemetery and were at last alone, the *americano* said, "I don't know what will become of me now." Onofre said nothing. His father looked at the room, untidy after all the visiting, as if half expecting his wife to reappear from behind a piece of furniture. "I didn't even know she was ill," he went on after a while. "She walked a little bent over and had no appetite, but if there were other symptoms, I didn't see them. One evening I came home and found her dead on that little chair, the one she used, next to the stove; the water in the pot wasn't boiling, so she couldn't have been dead long, yet when I took her hand, it was as cold as ice." While the *americano* spoke, Onofre opened doors and rummaged around. Like most peasant women, his mother never threw anything away, and the house was filled with useless junk. Onofre found pieces of old bedspreads, kitchen pots with no bottoms, and a broken distaff riddled by termites. "There are important affairs requiring my attention in Barcelona," he said. "I must leave."

Getting off the train in Bassora, Onofre had stupidly asked after Uncle Tonet. Somebody had finally told him the trap driver died years before. Onofre had hired a calash, which now stood waiting for him outside the door, chickens and hens all around it. Their clucking and the buzzing of the blowflies deepened the silence. "I've been thinking," the *americano* said, seeing that his son was doing nothing to encourage him, "that I could go with you to Barcelona. You know I never was much for country life. I'm more the city type, and now that I'm on my own again . . ." Onofre consulted his watch, took his hat and cane, and moved toward the door; his father followed him. "You know I've been around, I'm not just any old yokel," he said. "I'm sure you could find a job for me, I could help you in some modest way in your business dealings. And if I was working, I wouldn't be a financial burden." Onofre went outside, his eyes glued to the calash.

The coachman, nodding in the middle of a swarm of flies

in the shade of a fig tree, stood up when he saw Onofre come out and hurried to his carriage. "At your orders, sir," he said. A broad-shouldered man with close-cropped hair, he had fought in Cuba under General Weyler. "You are so busy," said the *americano*, "I could spend time with your children." "Joan will soon be back from Africa," Onofre said as he climbed up. "When he returns, everything will be back to normal. I'll pull strings in Madrid to have him demobilized without delay." The driver untied the reins, released the brake, and raised his whip. The *americano* clutched his son's leg: "Onofre, don't leave me alone. I can't live alone, I don't know how to look after myself, I won't get through the winter sitting by the fire with nobody to talk to. Please, for my sake." Onofre put his hand in his inside jacket pocket, took out all the money he had on him, and without counting it held it out for the *americano*. "With this you can live in comfort until Joan gets here." The *americano* would not take the money. "Come on, Father, take it," Onofre said impatiently. "I'll send more when I get to Bassora." The *americano* let go of the leg in order to take the money. Onofre motioned vehemently to the coachman and they set off at a trot.

A face appeared in the window of the Marquis of Ut's carriage. "Don Onofre, could you spare a moment? We caught some fellow snooping around here."

"What's going on?" the marquis wanted to know. The man outside, plainly one of Onofre's agents, did not reply.

"You stay here in the carriage in case Her Highness arrives," Onofre said to the marquis. "I'll go and see what this is all about and then come straight back."

He got out and followed the man, who held his oil lamp high to light the way. Picking their path between coils of rope and puddles, they came to a group of people: one man was being beaten by five others. He had lost his glasses in the scuffle. "That's enough," Onofre ordered. "Who is he?" "We don't know," they answered. "We've searched him, and he's not armed."

Onofre turned on the infiltrator and asked him how he had managed to get onto the docks.

"It wasn't hard," said the other, smoothing his jacket. It was clear from his accent that he was not a foreigner. Neither did he appear to be a Menshevik, a Nihilist, or anybody else with an interest in harming the tsarina. When Onofre asked him who he was and what he was doing there, he said he was a journalist and gave the name of the newspaper he worked for. "I was walking along the Ramblas when I noticed all the preparations. I guessed that somebody important or dangerous was arriving, so I slipped through the cordon and hid in here. Unfortunately I was spotted and given some very rough treatment. And just what do you intend to do with me now?" he added defiantly.

"Nothing, nothing at all," said Onofre. "You were only doing your duty as a journalist. In this particular instance, however, I would ask you not to reveal anything you have seen. I will compensate you, of course, for any damages resulting from this unfortunate incident." And from his inside jacket pocket he took a wad of banknotes, counting out three and offering them.

The journalist refused: "I do not accept bribes, sir."

"This is a simple gesture of good will," said Onofre. "I have a special interest in the affair."

"Which will be duly recorded in my article," threatened the journalist.

Onofre smiled. "That is up to you. I would have preferred to establish more amicable relations with you. I have always been on good terms with the press. I am Onofre Bouvila."

"Onofre Bouvila?" exclaimed the journalist. "Forgive me, Señor Bouvila. How could I have guessed? I lost my glasses accidentally. . . . Please, forget what I said and rest assured that my lips are sealed."

Onofre's business dealings had been commented upon in the press for the first and last time in September 1903 over some murky development scheme involving the port of Barcelona. Nothing came of it, yet some people made a lot of money in the process. After he read the article, Onofre had a note delivered to the journalist responsible: "I would like to have a little chat with you." To this the journalist replied with another brief note: "Name the time and place, as long as it's not at dawn in San Severo"— a clear allusion to the trap Onofre set years ago for Joan Sicart. Onofre did not take offense. "You are not that important," he replied. "Come and see me in my office. I am sure we can reach some agreement." The following day, the journalist showed up.

"Name the price for your silence, and let's get this over with," Onofre said when they were alone. "I have no time to waste." "Who says I'm for sale?" retorted the journalist with the hint of a smile. "If you were not for sale," Onofre said, "you would not have come." The journalist scribbled some figures on a piece of paper and passed it to him; it was an exorbitant sum, intended to anger him—sheer provocation. "You undervalue yourself," said Onofre, smiling. "I had a higher figure in mind: here you are." He took a bulky envelope from a drawer and handed it to the journalist. The latter glanced at the envelope's contents, remained silent for a moment or two, then without saying anything put on his hat and left the office. At the first street corner he came to, four men seized him; they took the envelope and also the money he had put in his pocket for his own needs before leaving home that day. Then they broke both his legs.

After the journalist left, apologizing, Onofre began to walk back to the Marquis of Ut's carriage, but just then the retinue moved. The long wagons passed by him, to the sounds of glass clinking and hardware rattling; he had to jump onto some sacks piled on the wharf to avoid being flattened by these heavily laden carts. Goats poked their heads out of a window, he felt their beards brush his face and caught a whiff of their foul breath. "What in hell are goats doing here?" he asked, raising his voice over their plaintive bleating. The muzhik who was looking after them explained in a language Onofre could not understand. Finally a character with swollen features, dressed as a hussar, shouted to him in bad French that His Highness the Tsarevich, who was accompanying his mother on this journey, did not trust the milk put in his tea in foreign countries. Even the forage for the goats came in bales from the distant steppes. The tsarina's favorite furniture had been brought along, too, her bed, her mirrored wardrobes, her divans, her piano, and her bureau, 106 trunks of clothing and many more boxes of shoes and hats.

Onofre had to wait for the whole procession to pass before he could leave his refuge. Eventually he found himself alone on the wharf: with all the uproar, nobody had stayed behind to wait for him. His shoes, spats, and trouser legs were covered with mud; even his frock coat had been splashed. He found his top hat buried in a pile of manure, and there it stayed.

Onofre got into a hackney carriage on the Ramblas and went home; there he changed as quickly as he could while the fastest tilbury in his stable was being prepared. Even so, he arrived at the Ritz after the banquet began, the banquet he had organized and paid for himself. He hurried to the head table, where he saw the tsarina, the tsarevich, Prince Yussupov, and other illustrious guests surrounded by their Catalan hosts.

But at the table there was no chair free, no place set for him. The Marquis of Ut got up and whispered in his ear, "What are you doing standing here like a half-wit? Your place is over there, at table number three." Onofre protested: he wanted to sit beside the tsarina. "Don't talk nonsense," the marquis whispered, alarm all over his face. "You are not nobility—do you wish to offend Her Imperial Highness?"

Onofre recalled all this as the cranes hoisted, from the ship's deck, the fearsome German howitzers and cannons of a size that had never been seen on any battleground before: they were anti-aircraft guns that he had managed to obtain from the French headquarters at great cost. As he looked at those bizarre crates, he felt a glow of satisfaction—a rare sensation, for he spent most of the year in a state of boredom. At night, in his home, shut up in the library and surrounded by hundreds of books he had no intention of ever reading, he would smoke his Havanas and recall nostalgically those riotous nights when he and Odón Mostaza, whose death he now regretted, watched the dawn through the steamed-up windows of some house of pleasure. Surrounded by empty bottles, leftover food, cards, dice, naked women sleeping curled up against the walls, and garments scattered all around the room, the pair lay exhausted and satisfied, with the dazed innocence of youth.

2

In Madrid, His Excellency Mohammed Torres was perspiring profusely. Accustomed to enjoying the Atlantic breeze on the flowery patios of his Tangier palace, he found the Palacio de Oriente stifling; he had stopped off here on his way back from Paris, where he had had a meeting with Clemenceau. His musk perfume made Don Antonio Maura ill. Until now the sultanate had maintained a precarious independence, thanks to the rivalry between France and England, but Germany was seeking to install naval bases on the Moroccan coast and open up markets for German manufactured goods. Faced with this new situation, the two rival powers signed a pact in April 1904, and now France was planning to take over Morocco, converting it into an extension of Algeria.

His Majesty Don Alfonso XIII, who was listening with interest to the lamentations of the sultan's minister for foreign affairs, thought the solution simple enough. "Just put your foot down," he suggested.

"Your Majesty is most perceptive," said the emissary. "But we cannot renounce the protectorate of a great power without putting at risk the throne and even the head of my lord, His Majesty the Sultan Abdul Assis."

"What is your opinion, Don Antonio?" asked the king, turning to the prime minister. Don Antonio Maura was in a quandary: maintaining a Spanish presence in Africa meant continuing to live over a hornet's nest, not advisable for an impoverished country still licking its wounds after the recent colonial disasters. Relinquishing that presence, however, would be tantamount to losing the last traces of prestige in the family of nations. He outlined all this succinctly to His Majesty. "Well, who cares?" replied the king. Don Antonio took him aside, leaving Mohammed Torres to admire, on the wall, a monumental diptych in which Judith and Salome seemed to compete with each other, as to whose trophy was bloodier. Swollen tongues protruded from the livid mouths of John the Baptist and Holofernes. He remembered that the Prophet had forbidden all pictorial representations of the human form.

The king and the prime minister returned from their tête-à-tête. "His Majesty was in favor of abandoning Morocco to her fate," said Don Antonio, "but I have managed to dissuade him." "His Majesty's acumen is proverbial," the sultan's foreign minister said, performing the salaam three times.

"I have also brought him up to date on other factors relating to this matter," said the prime minister, placing his hand on his heart. "Now that Cuba has been lost, the army is idle, and idle officers are always dangerous. In addition, I mentioned the business of the mining concessions and Spanish investments in that territory."

His Majesty Don Alfonso XIII, who was eighteen years of age at the time, slapped him on the back. "We'll give old Raisuli a run for his money," he said.

Now, five years later, the mothers of the recruits bound for Africa were demonstrating again, as they had at the time of the Cuban war, in the railroad station; they sat on the ties to block the train's path. Some ladies from a Catholic association who came to the station to distribute crucifixes among the troops urged the engineer to drive the train right over them. "No, the little tykes back there might not take kindly to seeing their mothers sliced up like that," the engineer replied. The mothers were yelling "Down with Maura!"

It was a clammy Monday in July 1909 when the Marquis of Ut hurried to the house of Onofre Bouvila. "We're done for," he exclaimed, his hair disheveled, his tie undone. "The provincial governor refuses to declare a state of emergency, the mob is ruling the streets, the churches are all ablaze, and Madrid, as usual, has left us high and dry."

Onofre extended to him an embossed leather box full of Havanas. "Nothing will come of it. At worst your palace might be burned down. Is your family out of the country?"

"They're spending the summer on the coast at Sitges," said the marquis.

"And your palace, is it insured?"

"Of course."

"Well, there you are. Take my advice: go and spend a few days with your wife and children."

"I was considering that, but it's impossible: I have a board of directors' meeting tomorrow," said the marquis. After a moment's thought he added, "I must have been out of my mind to stay on."

Onofre poured two glasses of amontillado. "Excellent for calming the nerves," he said. "To your health." From the street came the roar of cannon fire. "Could that be the revolution?" he wondered. He recalled those distant days when he prophesied revolution to the World's Fair workers. He was young then and penniless and hoped what he predicted would never come to pass; but now that he was rich and no longer young, he could not help feeling a flicker of hope. "At last!" he thought.

"And to yours," said the marquis, raising his glass. He downed

260

the wine in one gulp, belched, and wiped his mouth with the back of his hand. Onofre admired the aristocrat's freedom. "He doesn't have to prove anything," he thought.

"And what do you think of all this?" the marquis asked him.

Onofre lit a Havana and inhaled with evident pleasure. "I have no board meeting, and yet I haven't left. Nor do I intend to leave Barcelona. What are you afraid of?" he said, seeing the marquis's furrowed brow. "A handful of derelicts with no arms and no leaders? Let them play out their game. The only card they have is our fear." His thoughts went back to the demonstration he had joined more than twenty years ago; he remembered the Civil Guard, their horses and sabers, the cannons loaded with grapeshot. He kept those memories to himself. "Suppose for a moment they somehow triumph," he went on, gazing out the window. In the intensely blue sky of that summer afternoon, a column of smoke was rising. It was in the Raval district: maybe the Church of San Pedro de las Puellas was in flames, or maybe the Church of San Pablo del Campo. "Do you know what would happen? They would come and beg us to help them. After a few hours, there would be complete chaos—they would need us more than ever. Remember Napoleon." The marquis laughed in spite of himself.

Onofre drew back from the window prudently: a company of soldiers went by, their musketoons over their shoulders, some carrying shovels and others picks. He wondered where they were headed, equipped like that—it was supposed to be the workers who were building barricades. "The time has not yet come," he added, sitting in his armchair again. "But one day it will, Ambrosi, and not so far off that you and I shall not live to see it. On that day universal revolution will break out, and the present bourgeois order, based on private property, exploitation, and oppression, will disappear. Not a stone will be left upon a stone, first in Europe, and then in the rest of the world. With the cry of 'Peace for the workers, freedom for the downtrodden everywhere, and death to tyrants,' all states and churches will be destroyed, and all institutions, be they religious, financial, or social, so that the millions of human beings who today live muzzled, enslaved, tortured, and exploited will be delivered of their keepers and benefactors, official and unofficial. And at last they will fill their lungs with the clean air of liberty."

The marquis stared, wide-eyed in disbelief. "What are you saying?"

Onofre burst out laughing. "Nothing. I read that in a pamphlet that came my way a long time ago. I have an unusual memory: I remember everything I read, word for word. My wife and the girls are in La Budallera," he added, "my in-laws' place. Stay here for dinner. You won't be able to go to the club today, whatever happens."

They were having dinner when they became aware of a growing rumble: the floor shook, the chandeliers swayed, the glasses tinkled, and the plates on the table danced. They sent the butler to find out what was going on; he returned and told them that a regiment of cuirassiers were marching down the street, their drawn sabers resting on their epaulets.

"Perhaps," murmured the butler, "the situation is more serious than my master believed."

"You will have to stay the night," Onofre said to the marquis, who nodded in agreement. "I can lend you one of my nightshirts—I hope it will fit."

"Don't trouble yourself," said the marquis, looking out of the corner of his eye at the maid who was clearing the table. "I have my own ideas about how to keep warm."

All night long the cannons boomed, interspersed with the rattle of machine guns and the isolated shots of snipers. The following morning, when they met in the dining room for breakfast, there were dark rings around the eyes of the Marquis of Ut. The newspaper had not arrived. The butler informed them that the shops were not open. The city was at a standstill, and all communication with the outside world was cut off.

"It won't last long," Onofre said. "Is the pantry well stocked?"

"Yes, sir," said the butler.

"How awkward," said the marquis. "Besieged by the mob like this, and unprepared . . ." He stared at the maid, who was serving coffee; she blushed and looked the other way. "Could you lend me a little money?" he asked Onofre.

"Whatever you need. But why?"

"To reward this delightful creature." The marquis indicated the maid with his thumb. "By the way, I suggest you send her packing."

"Why?"

"Unimaginative in bed."

Onofre saw fear in the maid's face. She could not have been a day over fifteen; though she had just arrived in the city from her village, her features and manners were refined, and for that reason she had been assigned to serve at table and not given more menial work. He knew that if he dismissed her, as the marquis suggested, her only options would be the brothel or starvation.

"What's your name?" he asked her. "Odilia, sir." "Do you like it here, Odilia?" "Yes, sir," she said, "very much, sir."

"In that case, what we shall do is this," Onofre said, turning to the marquis. "You keep the money, since you were not satisfied, Odilia stays here, and I double her wages. What do you think?"

He was not acting out of generosity, or out of self-interest, for he did not believe in human gratitude: he was only demonstrating to his guest that he did as he pleased in his own house. The marquis stared for a few moments, then roared with laughter.

Thus elapsed the week that was later to be called "the tragic week." They played cards and spent long hours chatting. The marquis was a priceless source of information for Onofre: there was no high family with which he was not connected and whose secrets he did not know. It was easy to prize the information from him: he liked nothing better than to relate anecdotes in vivid detail. For Onofre these stories were a keyhole through which he could spy on that dusty and rather sad world whose doors would always be closed to him. Then, at night, after dinner, they would send the butler up to the sun roof; if he reported that there was no danger, they would go up there to smoke their cigars and drink their brandies, leaning on the balustrade. Eventually, weary of this, they sent a humorous note to the provincial governor: "Put an end to this situation—we are running out of cigars." It had been a pleasant week; Onofre thought he had found a friend. Now, as he watched the marquis sitting at the head table next to the tsarina, he realized that that had been an illusion.

A red silk baldachin bearing the Romanov coat of arms had been spread over the table; the salon walls had likewise been covered with silk. Plaster-of-Paris sculptures specially made for the occasion stood in each of the four corners. With the chandeliers and candelabra, there were four thousand beeswax candles to light the salon. The cutlery on all the tables was silver, and gold on the head table; the plates were Sèvres porcelain.

Seeing this splendor, the exact cost of which he knew, Onofre recalled the "tragic week." Brooding, his spirit far removed from the feast around him, he was startled by the deep voice of the man sitting beside him: "It is about the revolution that you think," he heard the man say, and looked at him for the first time. The man was about forty, tall and thin, with roughly chiseled peasant features that were not displeasing; his tangled beard went halfway down his chest. He wore an indigo cassock, which made him look even taller and thinner, and he gave off a pungent smell of vinegar, incense, and sheep.

From this and from the man's penetrating, distracted gaze,

Onofre guessed that he had been put next to one of those monks—ignorant, stubborn, cunning, superstitious, fanatical, and abjectly servile—who wormed their way into the entourages of the powerful. The monk's name, Onofre later learned, was Grigori Efimovich Rasputin and he was enjoying the tsarina's protection because he had cured the tsarevich's hemophilia when the doctors gave up. Extraordinary things were told of him: that he had hypnotic and prophetic powers, that he could read minds and perform miracles at will. And his influence was to grow, until it tyrannized the court; he would control appointments and honors; careers would be made or ruined, depending upon him—until at last a plot led by the same Prince Yussupov who was now sampling traditional Catalan dishes in the Ritz culminated in Rasputin's assassination in 1916. Shortly after, as the monk had predicted, would come the revolution and the demise of the Romanovs in the fortress of Ekaterinburg. But at the time of the tsarina's trip to Barcelona, that influence was only just beginning to assert itself.

Rasputin told Onofre how a few years before, he had witnessed the lamentable Bloody Sunday. Standing on a third-floor balcony of the Winter Palace, he was holding the Grand Duchess Anastasia in his arms, she being little more than a baby, and holding the tsarevich's hand, too; from the neighboring balcony, the Grand Duke Sergei was teasing the children. The Grand Duke Sergei was at the time the most influential man, enjoying the complete confidence of Tsar Nicholas. (In February of that same year, an anarchist named Kaliayev hurled a bomb at the coach in which Sergei was traveling. All that was left of the coach, the horses, and the grand duke was a pile of smoking debris.) From a second-floor window the Grand Duke Vladimir, in consultation with his military staff, was deciding, minute by minute, what was to be done. "Let us not be rash," he said. When the demonstration spilled into the square, he let it advance toward him. "What are your demands?" asked the tsar. "A constitution, Your Highness," they answered. "Ah," said the tsar. The Grand Duke Vladimir gave the order to open fire on the crowd, and the demonstration was over in a matter of minutes. "That's the way to do it," said the grand duke. More than a thousand bodies were left in the square. The monk regretted not having been able to take charge of events that day. "I know how to avoid the revolution," he said. He ate voraciously, like an ogre. Onofre felt an inexplicable attraction for this madman.

"Onofre, is that you?"
Onofre looked at the man calling to him on the station platform: a rustic face prematurely wrinkled, sunken eyes, thin hair. "I am Joan," said the man. The two brothers shook hands coldly. Joan Bouvila was twenty-six now. Their father had died the night before. "It's a pity you didn't arrive in time," Joan said. "He was asking after you till the very end."

Onofre made no reply. The calash driver who had taken him from the station to his home a few years previously, at the time of his mother's death, approached him: he remembered him well, he said, after all that time, and wanted to be the first to offer him his services. "We can walk," said Joan. "It's only around the corner." Onofre gave the driver a tip. "For your good memory," he said. Joan looked askance at that gesture.

The mortuary chapel was in the nuns' oratory in the old-age home in Bassora, a solid-looking building with brick walls and a slate roof; all the windows were barred, and the garden was enclosed by a high fence. On both sides of the home were apartment houses, the inhabitants of which stood at the windows watching Onofre walk up the garden path.

"I don't know how they found out you were coming," said the mother superior, who welcomed them at the gate. "Do not be surprised by all this attention," she added in a confidential tone of voice. "All your poor father did in his rare moments of lucidity was talk to everyone about you. Sister Socorro, who took care of him ever since he came to our center, can tell you that. Isn't that so, Sister?" She turned to a little nun with an oval face and very white, almost transparent skin, who had joined them in the dim room. The nun lowered her eyes in the presence of Onofre and his brother. "On such occasions he always said the same thing," the mother superior went on, "that you would come for him. He firmly believed you would turn up at any minute. Then, he said, he would go with you to Barcelona, where you would both live in comfort and luxury. Some of the other old men, in their gullibility, ended up envying him and bearing him a grudge. Your father was a man of a very lively imagination."

As she spoke, they walked down long deserted corridors, with closed doors on either side. The tiles on the floor were so clean, they reflected the statuettes along the way like the surface of still water. Rounding a bend, they came upon a hefty nun scrubbing the floor on her knees, wearing a gray apron over her habit. The scrubbed floor gave off an acrid smell. When they arrived in the chapel, Onofre looked gloomily at the drawn face he saw in the coffin. Lit by the wavering flames of two long candles, that impassive parchment face replaced all his previous memories. "You can close it up now," he said.

"During his stay with us," said the mother superior, "he did make a few friends here. They would like to be present for the prayers for the dead, if you would permit them." Two nuns brought in a group of elderly men, who dragged their feet as they walked. Actually, some of them had not known the *americano*, but they joined that sad huddle so as not to miss the entertainment. All were dressed in rags. "We depend on charity, so our circumstances are straitened," said the mother superior.

When they were getting ready to go to the graveyard, Sister Socorro tugged at Onofre's sleeve. "Come," she whispered. "I have something to give you." He let himself be led to a narrow door that was painted blue. The nun opened the door with a huge key that hung from a ribbon attached to her habit, reached into a dark closet, and emerged with a half-made basket in her hand. "We teach the men to weave," she told him. "Your father was making this. His skill was not great. The truth is, he was already very ill when your brother brought him here, almost a year ago. He paid for the wicker, so really it belongs to you."

On the way back from the cemetery, Onofre took his brother to the restaurant where many years ago he and his father met Baldrich, Vilagrán, and Tapera. The two brothers ate their soup in silence. While they were waiting for the next course, Onofre said, "I meant to come, but it was impossible. I was dining with the tsarina."

"I don't know what a tsarina is," said Joan, "but there's no reason for you to apologize to me."

"Naturally I'll reimburse you for the funeral," said Onofre.

"I've been thinking about selling the land," said Joan, as if not hearing what his brother said. "To do that I will need your signature." He looked steadily at Onofre. "Then I'll go to Barcelona—wait, don't say anything," he blurted, seeing his brother about to speak. The look in his face reminded Onofre of their mother. Between the two of them they had emptied the wine carafe, although Onofre had taken only a few sips.

"Don't raise your voice," he said. "Everyone is listening."

"Let them listen!"

Onofre smiled. "You are not so clever as you imagine. Calm down and listen to what I have to tell you." He clapped his hands and asked the waiter to refill their carafe. "I know what you're thinking. We may be strangers, but we're not that different. You're sick of working the land, sick of the country. Of course." He passed him the wine, noting that Joan drank mechanically, and that as he drank, the sparkle gradually left his sunken eyes. "The land is of no use, I know that very well. The money is in the forests. That's what we're going to busy ourselves with from now on, the forests. There's no work in a forest: it grows by itself. All you have to do is to keep watch, so nobody comes first and takes away the wood. They're paying an arm and a leg for wood in the cities. The forest will be the source of our wealth."

"I don't know what you're talking about," Joan said. "The forests belong to everyone. No one owns them." But he lowered his voice. He could not escape Onofre's influence, either. Now that they were face to face, the hatred that had been building over the years seemed to fade into the background, and its place was taken by a mixture of curiosity and greed.

"Up to now they have belonged to everybody," said Onofre. "In other words, to nobody. But if the whole valley became a municipality instead of a parish, whatever wasn't private property would be public land, under the control of the municipal administration, which means the mayor. . . . Would you like to be a mayor, Joan?"

"No," Joan answered.

"Well, now, perhaps you will change your mind on that point."

This conversation, in which Onofre for some reason tried to win over the brother he hardly knew and in whose eyes he read only resentment, ended up costing Onofre a lot of money and trouble, as he now remembered.

The sudden appearance of two armed customs men startled him. They touched the peaks of their caps. "Beg your pardon, Don Onofre," they said. "We were looking for a consignment of tobacco."

He had not seen Joan again since that day of the burial: he had not been present when Joan was made mayor, nor did he know how his brother was managing. At regular intervals the wood and the cork so abundant in the mountains of that region arrived in his warehouses in Pueblo Nuevo. "And this," he thought, "is all the family I have, by blood—Joan, an imbecile of a son, and two snobs for daughters. Only a fool cuts his roots."

Onofre and his brother went their separate ways as soon as they finished eating. Their relations remained cold, but they had reached an agreement. As Onofre strolled by himself through the streets of Bassora, Joan set off for home at half past two, while there was still plenty of daylight ahead. Onofre's train, however, did not leave until eight o'clock. Bassora, which had so dazzled him as a child, now struck him as boring and ugly; the air stank, and the passers-by he met were uncouth. "The soot has got into their brains," he thought. Without any intention or awareness on his part, his steps took him to a street with colonnades on both sides. He located a particular building, went up to the second floor, and knocked; the door was opened by a kindly-looking, stooped lady. He asked her if a taxidermist had ever lived there. She invited him to come into the hall. Yes, she told him, the taxidermist he referred to was her father; he was indeed still alive, though very old, but had not been practicing his trade for several years. Both of them, father and daughter, lived on his savings, modestly but without hardship.

When he was shown in, Onofre asked the taxidermist if he remembered having stuffed a monkey a good many years back, to which the man immediately replied that he did. In the course of his professional life, that monkey was the only one he had ever had occasion to stuff. It had been a hard job, he remembered, since he had not been familiar with the anatomy of monkeys, and since, in addition, the specimen had been a small one, with very fragile bones. The taxidermist had put a lot of effort, many hours, into the challenge, and had been proud of the result. But then months went by with no sign of the monkey's owners. The taxidermist remembered the gentleman, too, despite the intervening years: he was dressed in white with a straw hat and a cane, and had a little boy with him. "You can see my head is still clear for one of my age," the old man concluded. "Father, don't tire yourself," said the woman. In an aside she explained to Onofre that her father got excited easily and then could not sleep until well into the night.

"What became of the monkey?" Onofre asked, ignoring the daughter's entreaty. The old man made an effort to remember. He had kept it in a cupboard for a while to protect it from the dust. Then, feeling sure nobody was going to come and claim it after so much time, he had put it on a shelf in the workshop, as a display. "And then?" The taxidermist shook his head. His daughter came to his aid. "Yes, Father, Señor Catasús took it, don't you remember?" "Ah, yes," said he. Señor Catasús and his brother-in-law used to bring big game from their hunting for the taxidermist to stuff: they were his best customers. "Never anything less than a roe deer," he said, "and sometimes a wild boar." They saw the monkey and took a fancy to it. Since it had sat on that shelf for years, he saw nothing wrong in giving it to them.

The Catasús family lived on the outskirts of the town. The calash driver, whom Onofre met at the hackney line near the station, said he knew the place. At the house, Onofre handed the maid his visiting card. As he waited in the hall, he thought, "Foolish decisions can have dire consequences. I should give up this sentimental nonsense now, while there's still time."

Catasús himself came out to greet him. He was a breezy, jovial, satisfied-looking man in his sixties. "Bouvila," he said, "such an honor!" He had heard so much about him; they had mutual acquaintances; and was it true that Onofre had arranged a banquet in honor of the tsarina? "Out here in the provinces these things always cause a stir," he admitted, laughing freely and openly. But to what did he owe the pleasure of this visit? "A private matter," Onofre said, and outlined it briefly. "No doubt you find it absurd that I should take such an interest in this monkey." "Not at all," replied Catasús sympathetically. "But I'm afraid I cannot have the pleasure of gratifying your wish." He told him how his brother-in-law, one Esclasans, the owner of a distillery, seeing the monkey one day at the taxidermist's, took it into his head to baptize a whiskey with the name Monkey Liquor. Esclasans persuaded the taxidermist to give him the monkey, intending to use it to advertise the product, but the lawyer looking after his affairs in Barcelona wrote to inform him that such a trade name was already registered; there was an aniseed drink on the market with the same name. For a while the monkey served as a toy for the children; when they grew up, it was left in the attic; finally, thoroughly moth-eaten, it was thrown out.

"It is remarkable, even so," said Catasús as he finished his tale, "that after all this time you were able to reconstruct the story of that monkey in its entirety." He glanced at the pendulum clock, as if wishing to get rid of his guest but not knowing how to go about it. Onofre, too, was groping for a polite way of taking his leave. "But I see there are over two hours left before your train departs, and the station is just around the corner. Do come in and join us in a modest snack. As you can see, we are having a little family reunion."

Onofre let himself be led into the spacious dining room with its coffered ceiling and oak furniture, where twelve or thirteen people sat. He did not pay much attention to the introductions Catasús made. Some of the guests were Catasús's sons and their wives; others were not as closely related. The last person to whom Onofre was introduced was a quaint character named Santiago Belltall.

"Santiago is an inventor," said Catasús. From the derisive edge Onofre thought he detected in his host's voice, and from the winks he received from those present, he guessed that the man was one of those poor or luckless souls who end up becoming the buffoons of their families. Santiago Belltall, whose name would be connected with Onofre's in history, was twenty-eight at the time but looked twice as old: he had the half-starved, worn-out face of a man who has given up eating and sleeping over some obsession. His mop of greasy straw-colored hair, his bulging watery eyes, his long nose, his wide mouth with narrow lips and big teeth, all added to his comical appearance; his old woolen jacket, darned and redarned, his frayed and gaudy tie, the trousers that were not quite long enough, and the hemp shoes did not do a great deal to inspire respect, either. It was obvious that he lived on the charity of others, yet he hardly touched the buns and sweets within reach on the table.

Their eyes met. For a moment Onofre thought of that other young man, whom he had never actually known, who emigrated to Cuba with a headful of fantasies and came back with his spirit broken but his fantasies intact. This new face was fleetingly superimposed on the face of the one whose burial Onofre had just attended. An illogical idea flashed through his mind: "I came looking for a nonexistent monkey and found this idiot instead."

Catasús began telling the story of the monkey; his account was interrupted by one of the people at the table, who declared that monkeys were uncommonly intelligent animals. He had read in a travel book that the ancient Egyptians, even though they did not believe in God, worshiped monkeys. Another gentleman said he had it on good authority that, in contrast with ancient Egypt, in China and Japan people ate monkey meat and considered it a delicacy. A third remarked that somewhere in South America people ate caymans and snakes. A fourth said that that must be Chile. One of his aunts, he explained, had married a wool merchant, and the couple emigrated to Chile. His wife corrected him, saying that the relatives he had in mind emigrated to Venezuela, not Chile. It was a sorry state of affairs, she added, that she had to remember such things, when they were his relatives and not hers, except by marriage. The gentleman who had brought snakes into the discussion told how to cook them: once the serpent was dead, it was cut with a handsaw into pieces about six inches long; then the pieces were sewn at the ends with needle and thread and fried in fat or oil like a sausage. A lady complained of white patches on her skin. Another lady recommended she take the waters at Caldas de Bohí. A boy added that he had been told that the streets of Paris were packed with automobiles, and that it was a common sight there to see the bodies of dogs, cats, and even donkeys flattened under the wheels of those vehicles. The vogue of the automobile, observed an elderly gentleman, who had until then remained aloof from the conversation, would bring sorrow and ruination to many a family. Almost all present were in agreement on that point. Catasús said that nevertheless one could not stand in the way of progress.

Thus they whiled away the afternoon. Onofre said nothing. He observed Santiago Belltall, who also was silent, out of the corner of his eye. Unlike Onofre, he made not the slightest effort to show interest in what was being said: he was thinking his own thoughts. From time to time his eyes took on an unexpected light, and then he looked quite dangerous, but nobody noticed. At other times his face darkened and filled with sadness.

Suddenly a child entered the dining room. No more than three or four years old and still dressed in a frilly smock, the boy ran over to his mother, hid his head in her lap, and burst into loud sobs. The mother finally managed to get him to tell her, between hiccups, why he was crying.

"María hit me," he said.

With his chubby hand he pointed at the door, which he had left open. From where he was sitting, Onofre could see, in a bare, round hall lit by a skylight, a thin and gawky girl. She was wearing a short, threadbare skirt that did not cover her skinny legs in dirty stockings. He knew immediately who she was. Noticing that she was being observed with such great interest, the girl threw a look of defiance at him. Despite the distance, he saw that her eyes were caramel-colored. Santiago Belltall got up and went to his daughter. Though it was bad manners, Onofre, too, got up and stood by the door to overhear the exchange between father and daughter. Catasús came up behind him.

"Do not worry, Bouvila," he said. "This happens every time they come. She isn't entirely to blame. María is seven and beginning to see things too clearly. It's a difficult age."

"And the mother?" Onofre asked. Catasús shrugged and narrowed his eyes. "The least said, the better," those gestures conveyed.

A sharp noise made them turn around. Belltall had just slapped his daughter. "A violent man," Onofre thought. The girl struggled to hold back her tears.

Pale, the inventor came back into the dining room and mumbled an excuse, getting his words mixed up to the merriment of those present. Onofre, who was at his side, put a hand on his shoulder and felt the man's collarbone in his palm. "Take the girl out of here," he whispered in Belltall's ear. The inventor glared fiercely at him, but Onofre replied with a quiet smile. "Easy, now," was the unspoken message. "You don't make me laugh, but you don't frighten me, either. I could have you killed, but I've chosen to take your side." He slipped his visiting card into the other's jacket pocket. Belltall, unaware of this, tore himself free, grabbed the girl, and headed for the opposite door, dragging her unceremoniously behind him.

Onofre took advantage of this to leave, too. He thanked Catasús for his hospitality. On his way to the station, Onofre's carriage passed the inventor and his daughter, who were speaking heatedly. Unobserved by either of them, he turned and watched them until the carriage went around a corner.

Now several million men were preparing to slaughter one another in the trenches at Verdun and the Marne, and Onofre was doing his best to make sure they would have the means to do so. A year had gone by since that meeting, and he had forgotten all about Santiago Belltall and his daughter. The cranes lowered the guns onto the wagons; the tarpaulins covering them were tied down onto the side rings. A team of eight mules dragged them from the wharf to Bogatell. Men with torches led the way, while others guided the mules, pulling at the bridles, and others guarded the cargo with pistols in their hands.

4

The streets of Paris were no longer packed with automobiles, as Catasús's nephew had said; they were now dark and ominously silent. The war had been raging for four years; all the menfolk were mobilized, the factories were still, the fields lay uncultivated, and every last head of cattle had been sacrificed to feed the troops. Without their colonies and the supplies arriving from neutral countries, the warring parties would have had to start laying down their arms, beaten by starvation, until the last one left, the one whose provisions and munitions had held out the longest, could proclaim itself master of the world.

Over this appalling situation many people in Barcelona gleefully rubbed their hands. Now anyone who had something to sell could get rich overnight, become a millionaire in the twinkling of an eye, in one glorious instant. The city seethed: twenty-four hours a day, with never a pause in the markets of La Lonja and El Borne, in consulates and legations, in commercial offices and banks, in clubs and restaurants, in salons, dressing rooms, foyers, casinos, cabarets, hotels and inns, in sinister back alleys, in a deserted church cloister, in the bedroom of a perfumed and panting prostitute, offers and counteroffers were made, prices snatched out of thin air, bids made, bribes hinted at, threats hurled, and the seven deadly sins all harnessed to the making of money. Money went from hand to hand so swiftly and in such abundance that paper took the place of gold, words the place of paper, and pure imagination the place of words. Many believed they had made fabulous sums, and many believed they had spent them, and their beliefs had little to do with reality. At poker, baccarat, and *chemin de fer*, both real and fancied fortunes changed hands several times in the space of a few hours. The most exotic delicacies, things previously unavailable in Spain, were consumed casually—caviar sandwiches were taken to bullfights—and every adventurer, gambler, and *femme fatale* worthy of the name paid a visit to Barcelona.

Only Onofre Bouvila seemed indifferent to this heady boom. He rarely showed his face in public. Wild rumors circulated about him: raking in all that money had driven him mad; he was seriously ill; he was following the war blow by blow and had offered to buy the Hapsburg throne from the emperor if Austria lost; he had financed the uprising that had deposed the Tsar of Russia, and that for this maneuver Germany had deposited one hundred kilograms in gold bars for him in a Swiss bank and given him the title of archduke.

None of this was true. A private army of agents and informants was keeping him up to date on what was happening on the battlefields and in the high commands, but the war had ceased to interest him. He saw dark clouds on the horizon. He said that the worst was still to come: revolution and anarchy. In his imagination, he saw arising from the smoking ruins of Europe a vengeful mass ready to rebuild society on the basis of order, honesty, and justice in the distribution of wealth. He considered Western civilization his personal property and despaired at the thought of its annihilation. But perhaps he was destined to prevent such a thing from occurring, perhaps he had been singled out to play that historic role. "It is unthinkable that my life should have been a succession of remarkable events all for nothing," he told himself. Under the worst possible circumstances he had managed to become the richest man in Spain and possibly one of the richest in the world. Now he believed himself chosen for a higher mission; he saw himself as a new messiah, and in that sense he could indeed be said to have gone mad.

Leaving his business operations to prosper by inertia, Onofre devoted his days and nights to forming a plan to save the face of the earth from chaos. At his disposal he had his money, his indomitable energy, his unscrupulousness, and a lifetime of experience. All he needed was a galvanizing idea that would pull all this together. Since no idea was forthcoming, his moodiness grew: for no reason at all he would strike his subordinates with his cane, and his wife and daughters hardly ever saw him. At last, on November 7, 1918, two days before the proclamation of the Weimar Republic, the idea for which he had been casting about in his reveries crystallized before his eyes in the most unexpected fashion.

Señor Braulio's health never recovered from the blow it received over the death of the man he loved. He went into complete retirement, living with his daughter Delfina in a modest little two-story house with a garden, situated in a quiet street in the former town of Gracia, now fully absorbed into urban Barcelona. Only rarely did either of them leave the house. Every morning Delfina went to the Libertad market and did her shopping almost without saying a word: she pointed to what she wanted and paid without haggling. The saleswomen, knowing nothing of how she had terrorized another market in bygone days, considered her a model customer. In the evening, father and daughter would appear arm in arm in the Plaza del Sol, amble slowly around the square under the acacias, and go back home without responding to the greetings and kind words some of the people in the neighborhood called out to them—partly to be sociable, and partly hoping to strike up a conversation that would throw a little light on the mystery of the couple. After their stroll they would lock the garden gate with padlock and chain. Lights could be seen in the windows of their house for a few hours thereafter, until about ten. They received no visitors, no mail, no newspapers or magazines, and never set foot in the parish church.

It was common knowledge that Señor Braulio had a lot of money, which at his death—which could surely not be far off— would go entirely to his daughter. This made Delfina a good match, a tempting quarry for fortune hunters. But the few who made advances came up against a barrier of such silence and indifference that they quickly gave up.

For Delfina the years now passed with the inexorable, icy slowness of a glacier. People said she was waiting for her father to die before entering a religious order; her money would then be signed over to that order. "And when the convent gates close behind her," they added, "we'll have lost forever our chance to find out who she is and what tragedy blighted her life."

Toward the end of October 1918, the couple stopped appearing in the Plaza del Sol. The gossip, after slumbering for years, revived again: the poor man was ill; he would soon die; he was sinking fast; he had death written on his face. Or perhaps it was she who was ill. A doctor arrived in a cabriolet. Delfina herself came out to unlock the gate. "Ah, so it *is* the old man, as we thought," said the busybodies. Then two more doctors came to the house. "They're conferring," people deduced. Then followed a procession of specialists, nurses, and general practitioners. Delfina continued to go to the Libertad market every morning. The saleswomen asked after her father, expressed their wishes for his speedy recovery, but Delfina pointed to what she wanted, paid, and left without saying a word.

The month of October and the first week of November went by in this state of uncertainty. A new and restless rhythm had replaced the former tranquil routine of the house and its two occupants. At last the neighbors were rewarded for the time they had spent waiting. A wonderful automobile appeared. They immediately recognized the man who emerged from it, having seen his photograph continually in the press. But what connection could there be between the all-powerful magnate and that retiring, obscure couple. "She sent for him," somebody said, but nobody was listening: they had all gone to have a closer look at the automobile. Its seats were of red leather, the travel blankets were sable, the horns and headlights were solid gold. The chauffeur wore a gray dustcoat with an astrakhan collar, the lackey a green dress coat with gold braids.

The house could not be seen from the gate: nobody had pruned the trees or weeded the garden. In that garden stood a palm tree, a laurel, several cypress trees, and a hundred-year-old almond tree that was almost a fossil. To the right of the almond tree was a muddy pond, and above the pond a blackened, chipped dolphin overgrown with weeds, from whose mouth not even a trickle of water came forth. Around it a throng of dragonflies of all colors darted. In contrast with the garden, the house, seen from outside, seemed clean and tidy; there were no ornaments or pictures on the walls, no curtains on the half-open windows. But this appearance was deceptive: deeper inside, dust and decrepitude were everywhere. Cobwebs had taken over every corner, moths devoured the repulsive, dirty laundry, and cockroaches, growing fat on the putrid leftovers of meals, bred by the thousands every day in the larder. An appalling symbol, this, of Delfina's deterioration.

"I didn't send for you, it was my father. He wanted to see you one last time," she said in the dimness of the hall, her face hidden by a thick veil. She did not want him to see her face until she had revealed the truth to him. She looked like a ghost. Onofre regretted not being armed, cursed himself for having left behind in the automobile the lackey who carried weapons in his stead. "But nobody forced you to come," Delfina added. "You must have had your own reasons for agreeing to this meeting." He could think of no reply to that. "Go on up and see him. Don't be afraid. There's a nurse with him. I'll wait for you here."

He went up a flight of stairs, went to the only open door on the landing, and inside saw a bed with a canopy; on the bed lay Señor Braulio. In the violet light of a shaded lamp the man's face took on a whiteness like that of flower petals. The nurse was snoring in a large armchair.

Onofre did not need to go over to the bed to see that Señor Braulio had been dead for several hours. He walked around the room. At the far end, opposite the bed, was a lacquered dressing table with ivory inlays on which stood various jars of creams, cosmetics, tweezers, an eyelash curler, and a collection of combs and brushes. Hanging from the frame of the oval mirror was a black lace mantilla. In the top drawer Onofre found a tortoise-shell comb. During the last years of his life, Señor Braulio boasted that he had been the model for Isidro Nonell's famous portraits of gypsy women. Now Nonell was dead and the truth of that claim would never be known. Beside the comb was a razor-sharp knife: between primping and murder this ill-starred life had steered its course.

Onofre felt a hand on his shoulder and nearly cried out. "I didn't hear you come in," he gasped. Delfina did not answer. "He was already dead when you sent for me, wasn't he?" he asked, but again received no answer. "And this nurse, what did you give her a dose of?"

"The last time we saw each other," Delfina began, "I said that one day I would tell you a secret. Now I can reveal that secret, since we will never meet again: with my father dead, why would we?"

"I don't know what you're talking about," Onofre said. A long silence ensued.

The secret had dominated her thoughts during the painful years of imprisonment and later, in the gray years of voluntary seclusion; it had been the one thing that kept her going. Now she could see he did not remember her promise and had never felt the slightest twinge of curiosity about it. Of all his possible reactions that she had elaborated upon in her imagination, creating an entire novel in her mind based on variations on that single moment, this was the only one she had not considered. In that silent room she summoned up once more the scene with which she had spent her entire life, like a well-worn print. The way he tore the frayed nightshirt that she had washed and ironed every day for that occasion. The sight, on her mattress, of his naked, perspiring body and the evil glint in his eye, as the spring dawn in the year 1888 filtered wanly through the smudged window-panes of her attic room.

She had been awaiting his visit for months, and this was her whole secret. She had loved him since the moment he crossed the boardinghouse lobby. During those months she had heard his stealthy steps on the landing of the floor below; she had got up every night and left her room, unable to sleep, unable to bear the interminable wait, and had to conceal herself whenever her father went out on a binge. She remembered, now, the feel of his hands on her waist and the roughness of his lips. She had almost fainted when he sank his teeth into her. Then, in prison, she watched time efface the bruises on her thighs and calves, and felt that she would die of desire and sorrow.

His scheming to make her his own had been unnecessary; she would have surrendered to him at once had he only asked. It was she who hurled Beelzebub out the attic window, eliminating the only obstacle between them. She had chosen this moment to reveal her secret to him; then she would be his again, for an instant. Afterward, she would take her own life, using a powerful poison which she kept in her pocket. "With it I shall put an end to my miserable existence," she decided. But one simple sentence had brought this edifice crashing down. The first time, she had hoped to give herself to the man she loved, but had been brutally violated, robbed of her chance to surrender to him; now, thirty years later, the confession of her passion had been choked again— this time by his indifference.

She lifted her veil with both hands. "You haven't changed," she said.

But Onofre's mind was elsewhere—on Germany. That country, which he had favored, was on the point of surrendering, in ruins. Over two million Germans had been killed in the war, and another four million had been wounded, incapacitated for any kind of work. There was much sedition; a few days before, German sailors at the Kiev naval base had mutinied; the socialists had proclaimed an autonomous republic in Bavaria; Rosa Luxemburg and her Spartacists were sowing the seeds of disorder, creating soviets; and the moderates were negotiating the armistice behind the back of the kaiser, who had taken refuge in Holland. The Holy Empire lay drained and exhausted, like Señor Braulio on his deathbed. Onofre alone had the strength and the means to reanimate that corpse, a victim of its own history and of the rash heroism of its leaders.

Delfina's suffering, in comparison, was unimportant, an annoyance. The memory of their night together, which was turning to dust between her fingers, for him was only a vague anecdote. But he noticed in her eyes a brilliance, a delirium, as of some cataclysmic impulse repressed—and it was in that instant that his idea crystallized.

Impatiently he tore the veil off; the tulle drifted slowly to the floor. By the light of the lamp beside the deceased, he studied her face intently. With trembling fingers she began to undo the clasps of her dress. When she was down to her petticoat, she looked up to see what he was doing and found him plunged in thought. "What do you want to do with me?" she asked. He smiled enigmatically.

Several years before, the Marquis of Ut showed up unexpectedly at his house to put an out-of-the-ordinary proposition to him: "How would you like to be pissed on by a giant dog?" It was a cold, unsettled winter's night; it had been raining on and off, and the gusty wind set the rain drumming against the windowpanes. Onofre had withdrawn into the library, as was his custom. Logs were burning in the fireplace; the marquis's shadow cast by the bright flames grew as he drew closer to the fire to warm himself. He was wearing tails and his shirt had coral buttons.

"All right," Onofre had answered. "Give me ten minutes to get ready."

Out in the street, the marquis's coach was waiting. They crossed to the other end of the city in the rain and pulled into a little square where two streets merged, the Plaza de San Cayetano. There was nobody about, and the houses, their windows shut tight against the weather, looked uninhabited. The postilion jumped down from his white horse, landed with both feet in a puddle, then led the horse and carriage to a large wooden door, on which he rapped with the butt of his whip. A few seconds later, a peephole was pulled back, sending a beam of light into the street. The postilion said something, listened to the reply, and motioned back to the coach. The Marquis of Ut and Onofre got out and hurried to the door, picking their way between the puddles and the water streaming from the gutters onto the square below. The door opened for them, then promptly shut behind them, leaving the postilion outside. The two men muffled their faces in their cloaks to conceal their identities before taking off their top hats.

They were in a hall lit by torches; on the whitewashed walls were damp patches and torn strips of what had once been posters. Above the opening at the far end of the hall, which led into a murky passageway, a monumental bull's head could be seen: the animal's nose gleamed, moist, but one of its glass eyes was missing. The man who had let them in was about fifty years old; he hobbled as if one leg were shorter than the other. In fact, his limp was the result of an accident at work: a machine had broken his hip some twenty years ago. Now, unfit for work, he earned his living by the most diverse means. "Your excellencies are just in time," he said, no trace of irony detectable in his solemnity. "We are about to begin."

Following him down the dark passageway, they emerged into a square room lit by bluish flames spurting from gas jets in the floor. The jets marked out a semicircular area, a kind of stage, for which they served as footlights. There were several men in the room, all cloaked; some made furtive Masonic signs, which the marquis returned furtively. The guide leaped over the little flames and took the center of the stage, nearly burning a trouser leg on account of his limp, which occasioned uneasy chuckles from all present. The guide then cleared his throat and said, "Most worthy gentlemen, if there are no objections, let us begin. After the show, my daughters will serve refreshments." He hopped back over the barrier and disappeared behind a curtain, whereupon the lights went out and the room was left in darkness.

A beam of grayish light cut across the darkness from one wall to the other, falling on the whitewashed upstage wall, revealing a vague shape, blurred, resembling one of the damp patches in the hall. The patch began to move, and murmurs were heard from the audience. The patch gradually assumed a recognizable form, a fox terrier as large as the entire wall. It seemed to be studying them with the same curiosity as their own in studying it. It was like a photograph, but moved as a real dog moved, its tongue lolling, its ears pricked, its tail wagging. Then the dog turned its profile to the audience, raised one of its back legs, and began to piss. The gentlemen in the room rushed for the door to avoid getting drenched.

There were bumps, collisions, and falls before the lights came back on and order was restored. Now the guide's daughters were on the stage, three very young and quite comely girls, wearing dresses that revealed their chubby arms and fine ankles. But their appearance was greeted with little enthusiasm: the show had disappointed the gentlemen, and neither the prettiness of the girls nor the boldness of their attire made up for that. Few refreshments were ordered, and the take for the session was meager.

As with many other modern breakthroughs, the paternity of cinematography is disputed. Several countries today take credit for this popular invention. After its promising first steps, however, came disenchantment, which was due to a misconception. The first viewers did not confuse what they were seeing on the screen with real life (as the legend, invented *a posteriori,* would have us believe); rather, they believed they were seeing photographs in motion. This led them to think that with the movie projector any image could be set in motion. "Soon before our astonished gaze the *Venus de Milo* and the Sistine Chapel, to mention only two examples, will come to life," we read in an 1899 scientific journal. An article that appeared in a Chicago daily that same year recounts the following: "Then Mr. Simpson the engineer did something quite remarkable: with the aid of a kinetoscope, to which we have already referred in these pages countless times, he managed to endow his own family photograph album with motion. The astonishment of friends and relatives knew no bounds as they saw Uncle Jasper, who was buried in the church cemetery many years ago, stroll leisurely around the dining-room table in his greatcoat and chimney hat, or Cousin Jeremy, who died heroically in the battle of Gettysburg."

In August 1902—i.e., three years later—a Madrid newspaper reported that a businessman from that capital had reached an agreement with the Prado Museum entitling him to present the ladies portrayed in Velázquez's *Meninas* and Goya's *Maja Desnuda* in a variety show. The retraction the same newspaper published the following day did not stem the flood of letters for and against that project, and the debate was still going on in 1903. But then the real nature of cinematography was generally known: a by-product of electric energy, a curiosity with no practical application.

For a few years cinematography led a larvalike existence, confined to establishments such as the one in the Plaza de San Cayetano, to which the Marquis of Ut had taken Onofre; its only function was to act as a lure for customers whose real interests lay elsewhere. Then it became thoroughly discredited. The handful of establishments that opened in Barcelona had to close down after only a few months: they were frequented only by tramps who availed themselves of the darkness to take a nap with a roof over their heads.

The lame man sheltering in the doorway from the rain, which had been getting heavier over the past few hours, held an oil lamp in his right hand, and from time to time raised it over his head and waved it slowly. In the flash of lightning that lit up the Plaza de San Cayetano, he saw the trees bent by the wind, and the pavement submerged under a torrent of opaque water. He also saw, in the middle of the square, two black horses pawing the ground in their fright at the raging storm. Two men got out of the carriage. Lighting the hall with his oil lamp, the man led them to the same room in which, a few years before, he had shown the pissing dog film. Now his projector lay gathering dust in a corner of the basement of his house; he dragged it out on rare occasions to show obscene films he acquired God knows how, which pleased the marquis and a few other degenerate types who later described them as "educational."

The projection room had been restored; it had a garnet plush sofa, a ceiling lamp with iridescent glass beads, leather armchairs, marble pedestal tables, and an upright piano with bronze candelabra. The man's oldest daughter, who had grown to a serene, plump beauty, would play that piano with languid fingers; the second daughter showed a special aptitude as a pastry cook; the youngest was not good at anything in particular, but her features still retained the freshness of adolescence.

"It's a terrible night," said the man. "I wouldn't be surprised if there was flooding. I had the salamander stove lit: the room will warm up in a few minutes. If you like, please help yourself to the buns my second daughter just took out of the oven."

Onofre declined the offer, but his companion was less fastidious; by a combination of signs and guttural sounds that terrified the lame man, he indicated that he would gladly accept. While

Onofre's companion satisfied his hunger, the lame man hobbled off to answer a furious banging on the front door. "Come in, sir," they heard him say at the far end of the passageway, "the other gentlemen are here already." This third guest, whose gait Onofre recognized at once, entered the room wrapped up in his cloak.

"Gentlemen," Onofre began, "since we are not expecting anybody else, I think we might unmask ourselves. I can vouch for the discretion of all present." And he unbuttoned his cape at the collar and tossed it on the sofa. The other two followed suit: they were the Marquis of Ut and Efrén Castells, the giant from Calella. After they had exchanged greetings, Onofre said, "I have taken the liberty of summoning you on this infernal night, since what I am going to show you has something infernal about it. Something of the divine, too. . . ."

Efrén interrupted. "Get to the point," he threatened, "or I'll finish these buns and go have my dinner."

Onofre smiled. "I assure you this is eminently practical. But it needs a prologue. I'll do my best to be brief. You are both aware of the situation in Europe. . . ." He described the desolate panorama that had recently been preoccupying him. The marquis said he couldn't care less what happened to the rest of Europe. If France and England disappeared from the map along with their inhabitants, he would be the first to celebrate the event. Onofre argued that the era of nationalism was over, that times had changed. The marquis lost his temper. "What is this now, socialist international propaganda?" Seeing that tempers were rising, Efrén intervened. With his mouth full of marzipan and pignolia nuts, it was impossible to make out what he was saying, but his size inclined them to calm down.

"The war is now coming to an end," Onofre continued. "But what will become of us? We have created an industry for which suddenly—overnight—there will be no demand. What does this mean? It means bankruptcy for companies, factories closing, unemployment, not to mention the inevitable unrest and assassinations. You will say we have faced these problems before and solved them. I am telling you that this time things will reach an unprecedented pitch. The unrest will not be contained by frontiers: it will be universal, it will be that revolution about which we have heard so much."

The oldest daughter was playing the piano, and the marquis was nodding off to the rhythm of a barcarole. The youngest daughter reclined on the sofa; she had put her feet up on the pedestal table, which exposed her silk stockings to the knee.

"And to weigh us down with these prophecies you bring us here, of all places?" Efrén asked. Onofre smiled without answering: he knew that it was only in a place of this nature that the Marquis of Ut would come to such a meeting.

"You may amuse yourself," he said to the giant. "We have time."

Efrén motioned to the girl, and together they disappeared through a portiere of wooden beads threaded on long strings that concealed the door of a dimly lit chamber. The rattling of the beads roused the marquis. He asked where Efrén was. Onofre pointed to the portiere and winked. The marquis stretched and said, "And what do we do till he gets back?"

"We can talk," said Onofre. "When he gets back, I'll tell you both about the plan I have. It's important that he goes along with it, because he will be running all the risk involved without realizing it. So you and I have to act as if we were in agreement. He must think all three of us are in this together; he must not suspect that he is a mere instrument in our hands. Should there be any differences of opinion, we can sort them out between the two of us in private, as we have always done."

"I get it," said the marquis, who loved conspiracies. "But what the devil is this plan all about?"

"Later," said Onofre. At that moment the giant from Calella re-emerged, followed by the girl. The marquis stood up. "Back in a minute," he muttered, then took the girl by the arm and dragged her off toward the portiere. Efrén flopped down in his armchair and lit a cigarette.

"Why did you send for that effeminate clown?" he asked, poking his chin at the seat the marquis had just vacated.

"His collaboration is essential if our plan is to work," replied Onofre. "Just make it look as if you're behind me. If he sees us united, he won't object. Any differences of opinion between us two can be sorted out later in private, the way we've always done."

"You can rely on me," said the giant. "But this famous plan, what does it involve?"

"Shh!" said Onofre, rolling his eyes toward the chamber door concealed behind the beads. "Here he comes."

His Holiness Pope Leo XIII decided to take a stand against certain attitudes that had been flourishing under the guise of progress and that his predecessor, His Holiness Pius IX, had tolerated. With that end in mind, he shut himself up in his chambers and told the captain of the Swiss guard, on duty that night, that he did not wish to be disturbed. He wrote until dawn and gave to the world the encyclical *Immortale Dei*. This was in the year 1885. Now, more than thirty years later, Onofre Bouvila remembered the Sunday when he heard that encyclical read out in the San Clemente parish church. In keeping with the importance of the text, it was read first in Latin. The faithful—all the valley folk, men and women, grownups and children, the sick and healthy—listened standing up, their heads bowed. Then they sat down on the wooden benches, which always resulted in an unholy racket, since the benches were not screwed down to the floor and their legs were of different lengths. With silence finally restored, the rector—that same Don Serafí Dalmau at whose hands Onofre had received the waters of baptism—read the infallible text of the encyclical again in Spanish (the use of Catalan had not yet been introduced in ecclesiastic rites, so that many people in Catalonia believed that both Spanish and Latin were divine languages) and tried, unsuccessfully but exhaustively, to expound its meaning.

Onofre's mother was sitting beside him. For Mass she had put on her Sunday best: a black flower-patterned dress that he now saw superimposed on the reports from the Western Front, informing him of the ravages of German submarines in the Atlantic and of the entry of the United States of America into the war. Onofre the child touched her hand and asked what all the reading was about. "Something the pope wrote to us," his mother told him. "And we must obey him in everything he says in it." "A letter?" he asked. She nodded. "Did Uncle Tonet bring it?" "Of course, who else?" his mother whispered. "And did the pope send it specially for us?" he asked after a while, when the question formed in his mind. "Don't be silly," his mother told him, "he sent it to the whole world. He doesn't know anything about us, not even that we exist." "But he loves us just the same," Onofre said, repeating what the rector had literally pounded into him. "Who knows?" was his mother's reply.

It was nine years since her husband had gone off to Cuba. But that was not what was on Onofre's mind then (and still less now, as he remembered it). He knew that the pope lived in Rome; beyond that his geographical knowledge had to be supplied by his imagination. He thought of Rome as an incredibly distant place, an inaccessible castle atop a mountain a thousand times higher than those surrounding his valley. One could get to it only by crossing a desert mounted on a horse, a camel, or an elephant. These images came from the illustrations in the books used in Sunday school. That from such a place the holy father had sent a letter to the humble parish of San Clemente, of whose very existence he was unaware, amazed Onofre at the time.

Now, Onofre the adult was filled with the same amazement. "That is power!" he muttered under his breath, alone in his office.

Only that omnipresent power could stem the tide of rebellion threatening the world. But it was the exclusive preserve of the church, and the church seemed asleep, aimlessly adrift with no-body at the helm. Yet only the church could reach the most insignificant corners of the globe; in the most isolated, wretched hovel there would be a holy text nailed to the wall, an invocation that took acceptance and obedience for granted. And all that, he thought with admiration, had been accomplished by a carpenter twenty centuries ago, with a handful of lowly fishermen from Galilee. Even now, with all the information Onofre had at his fingertips, he could not have found Galilee on the map if his entire fortune depended on it. And later, others had tried to repeat Christ's performance: Julius Caesar, Napoleon Bonaparte, Philip II. . . . They all suffered ignominious defeat, having put their trust in military force, disdaining the religious force, which could hold together by invisible bonds thousands of millions of particles that otherwise would fly off in all directions, losing themselves in infinite space or colliding with one another. But now he, Onofre Bouvila, had a new strategy: to grow, from the seed of religion, a mighty tree with countless branches and count-less roots.

The lame man's youngest daughter was crying in the kitchen. During the course of that night she had had to cater to the de-pravity of the marquis four times, and nine times suffer the mighty gorings of Efrén Castells. This resulted in bleeding and sharp pains; her oldest sister had to leave the piano and take over in the chamber. The middle sister meanwhile cooked more buns, since the giant had already consumed fourteen kilograms of them. Daybreak could be seen through the window, a leaden, rain-sodden sky.

Despite the frequent interruptions, Onofre was able to un-fold his plan completely. Neither the marquis nor Efrén under-stood it, or the part they were supposed to play in it. Both had serious doubts as to their friend's sanity. But they said nothing, afraid of unleashing again the torrent of high-sounding words which they had already endured for hours. There were black rings around the marquis's eyes, but Onofre was full of smiles; staying up all night seemed to agree with him. Now the negotiations began, and he knew that he would get his way.

Thus he set in motion the most ambitious project of his life—his biggest failure, too. It would get off to a bad start, and everything would go wrong that could go wrong. Eventually his friends and allies would abandon him, and he would find himself alone once more.

5

A row of automobiles was lined up in the back street: the winter sun sparkled on their radiators, and an occasional white cloud wandered across their mirrorlike fenders. The automobiles advanced a few yards, stopped for a moment, then advanced another yard or two. When they came to the end of the street, they turned right, into another back street, even narrower than the first and darker, a street the sun had never seen. There, they finally stopped in front of an iron door. A doorman in a frock coat, top hat, and gold buttons opened an automobile door, took off his top hat when its occupant emerged, bowed, closed the door, put his hat on again, lifted a whistle to his lips, and blew. At that signal, the chauffeur at the wheel moved on, and the next vehicle pulled up to the door. And so on. When the first automobile reached the end of this second back street, it turned right again and took another side street, which led into a square. There all the cars, having delivered their occupants, waited under the acacias to be summoned back by the whistle. A wine bar on one of the corners of the square had set out tables and chairs, and sunshades with blue, yellow, and red stripes whose fringed edges were ruffled by the breeze. Glasses of beer or wine with soda were served to the chauffeurs, along with stuffed olives, pickled anchovies, boiled potatoes with paprika, and marinated sardines. As the automobiles gradually filled the square, the number of chauffeurs taking their morning apéritif grew. By half past twelve there was no room left, not for one more automobile, not for one more chauffeur.

Meanwhile, the gentlemen, helped out by the ceremonious doorman, were led from the iron door to their seats by young ladies whose appearance was striking—but striking not on account of youth or beauty. They wore perfectly straight dresses that descended from braided straps at the shoulder, like cylinders, showing neither bust nor waist. White-sequined, the dresses came to an inch above the knee; thus not only the arms of these young ladies were fully exposed—from their shoulders to the tips of their fingernails—but also their legs: long, muscular legs, more appropriate to a racing cyclist than to a lady worthy of the title. Added to this, a motley kind of makeup, as if applied in separate daubs, and a short, limp hairdo held in place by a silk ribbon almost an inch wide.

The gentlemen rolled their eyes upward and made the sign of the cross. "Did you ever see anything like it?" they said among themselves. "With that getup I don't know what to make of them. Good Lord! These days you can't tell a woman from a man. If things go on like this . . . What can you do, that's fashion for you. . . . Well, all I say is this: if I ever see my daughter in that kind of outfit, I'll . . . No good will come of it. . . . Time will tell." The general verdict was that the business had got off to a bad start. Now the Marquis of Ut regretted having lent his name to such a venture, and rued the day he gave in to Onofre's persuasion.

Neither the marquis nor Onofre was to be seen at that moment in the hall. Officially it was Efrén Castells who assembled everyone there, and he who had to face the music. The giant from Calella was highly regarded in Barcelona society: he was earnest in what he did, prudent in difficulty, and punctual when it came to paying. Never involved in scandal, financial or otherwise, he was held to be an exemplary family man. His weakness for the fairer sex was known (indeed, his feats in this field were legend), but that was simply attributed to the exuberance of his nature. He was free with his money without being prodigal, did charitable works without ostentation, and had become a respected art collector. Now, using this prestige, he was putting it at risk. "I wouldn't want to be in his shoes," muttered the marquis, and Onofre nodded in agreement. They both watched what was happening down in the hall from behind a lattice screen in their box. The seats were nearly full.

It was beginning to dawn on those below that they were in a theater, having entered from the back, through the stage door. "What are we all doing here?" they wondered. "A private performance? In the middle of the day? What the devil . . . ?" Two spotlights converged on the stage. Standing in front of the curtain was Efrén Castells. In that pre-eminent spot, and wearing a tuxedo, he looked even bigger than he was. Some joker began singing an improvised version of a well-known song, "The giant is in a tuxedo," and everyone joined in, laughing. "This is going to be a farce all the way," muttered the marquis from his observation post. "In his place, I'd have died of embarrassment by now." Onofre smiled. "His skin is thicker than you think." He remembered Efrén shilling for the hair restorer he used to sell, and then receiving a peseta for his collaboration. "Now it's just the same," he thought, "it's always just the same."

With his mighty voice Efrén had no difficulty obtaining silence when he saw they were tiring of the song. Unable to think of any follow-up to their joke, they were willing to listen. "Friends," he began. "You all know me. I'm a simple man. There isn't one among you who can deny that in my dealings I always put friendship before profit. I did not gather you here to ask you for money. . . ." Now they were all exchanging wary glances.

(Onofre winked at the marquis: "I told you he would know how to tame this bear." "The important thing is getting the bear to dance," replied the marquis.) ". . . Nor do I wish to waste your valuable time with idle talk. I'm not the eloquent, long-winded type. All I ask is a few minutes of your attention. You will see something you've never seen before, but in the future you will see it thousands, hundreds, dozens of times. . . ." ("Thousands, hundreds, dozens?" said the marquis. "Numbers were never his strong point. Just let him do it in his own way.") ". . . Today the privilege of this exclusive event is yours and yours alone. And you know what that means in the business world, but there's no need to thank me for it now. I'll say no more for the moment. Now the lights will go out. Don't be afraid—everything is under control. Stay in your seats, please. I'll be back later to explain what this is all about. Thank you for your attention."

As he hurried off the stage, the curtain was drawn aside by an electric motor, revealing an enormous screen with no visible seams, made of a material that appeared to be neither cloth nor metal but, rather, a combination of the two, like asbestos. Then the lights went out and the assembled guests heard a machine whining and a piano being played behind the screen.

"They're going to show us a movie!" exclaimed a voice from the audience.

"If it's the dog one, I'm leaving!" somebody shouted. The uproar drowned out the piano as the first images took shape on the screen.

The scene was a humble dwelling, little more than a hut, and the only light was a candle. Against the back wall of this room was a narrow, unmade bed; in the middle stood a table and four chairs; on the table were a sewing basket, balls of yarn, reels of cotton, scissors, and remnants of cloth. Everything bespoke a life full of toil and hardship. This caused great mirth in the audience. Sitting at the table, with her back to the viewers, was a woman dressed in black, middle-aged and slightly plump.

Her shoulders shook, her disheveled head drooped, conveying her suffering. "What she needs is a nice cup of tea," somebody shouted, to general guffaws. ("May God have mercy on us," muttered the marquis. "Pull yourself together," snapped Onofre.) On the screen the woman raised her arms toward the roof of the hut, tried to stand up, but fell back into the chair, as if her joints gave out, or her will, or both. The laughter increased; whatever gesture the woman made, it fueled the hilarity.

Efrén burst into the screened-off box where Onofre and the marquis were sitting. His eyes were wild. "Onofre, for the love of God, tell them to stop the movie right now!"

"If anybody so much as dreams of doing that, I'll have him shot," said Onofre, teeth clenched.

"But can't you hear the scoundrels laughing?" said the giant. Like that of the woman in the film, his great body was racked with sobs.

Onofre grabbed Efrén by the lapels of his tuxedo and shook him as hard as his inferior strength allowed. "Since when did you lose your nerve?" he railed at him. Then they realized that the laughter was dying down. They went over to the lattice screen and looked out anxiously: the troubled woman had finally got up from her seat and had turned round. Her face filled the screen. The audience fell silent. As Efrén Castells had announced, they were seeing for the first time what the whole world would see for years: the grief-stricken face of Honesta Labroux.

Physically she could hardly have been less attractive. At that time, when the charms of the fine-figure-of-a-girl, all sinuous curves, were being eclipsed by the vogue for the androgynous, narrow, pruned-back slip-of-a-girl, she had a full, heavy, somewhat mannish body, ordinary features, and was affectedly prim and coy. Her dress, like herself, was common, vulgar. Yet from 1919 to 1923, when she retired from films, her photograph would appear in the newspapers almost every day, along with stories and gossip about her; all the illustrated magazines did features on her (which she never authorized) and interviews with her (which she never gave) to increase their sales. The twenty kilograms of correspondence delivered to her daily contained declarations of love and marriage proposals; there were also heart-rending pleas, macabre threats, vile obscenities, and oaths binding the writer to suicide if he did not obtain such-and-such a favor, etc.

To elude the siege of admirers and psychopaths, she changed address frequently and never appeared in public. Indeed, very few could boast that they had seen her in the flesh. A rumor circulating at the time had it that she was kept under lock and key around the clock, and allowed out only to go to the studio for filming, early in the morning, tied up and gagged and with a sack over her head, so that not even she knew where she lived or where she went. "The price of fame," people said.

The aura of mystery around her, and the secrecy surrounding her real identity and her past, lent a certain plausibility to the twenty-two full-length films in which she starred during her brief, meteoric career. Only fragments of those films have come down to us, and in very poor condition at that. The films were all practically identical. But this, for the moviegoers, was a virtue; any departure from the formula immediately provoked expressions of anger in the house, and sometimes violence. Honesta Labroux gaped, tossed her head, and gesticulated hopelessness while Mark Anthony was losing the battle of Actium on her account and an asp that looked like a stuffed sock was poised to strike her bulging breast; or while her lover was dying of tuberculosis and a band of diabolical Orientals laced her drink with narcotics so they could sell her into a sultan's harem; or while an alcoholic husband beat her with his belt after announcing that he had staked and lost her honor at the gaming table; or while a cowboy revealed to her, as he stood on the scaffold, that she was really his mother. In these films the men were cruel, the women heartless, the priests fanatical, the doctors sadists, and the judges implacable. But she would forgive them all after endless saccharine agonies.

"But who could possibly like such nonsense?" the Marquis of Ut exclaimed when he read an outline of the plot of the first feature film, which his studios were later to duplicate *ad nauseam*.

Onofre had shut himself up in his study and worked for days and nights conceiving it all—situations, scenes, sets, costumes—to the last detail. His wife, concerned and curious, tried to enter and found the door locked. Alarmed, she knocked. "Onofre, it's me. Are you all right? Why don't you answer?" She began to pound on the door with her fists. The servants appeared, drawn by the commotion. Seeing them around her, she shouted, "Onofre, open up or I'll have the door broken down!" His calm reply was, "I have a revolver in my hand and will shoot the first person who dares to disturb me again." "But, Onofre," she insisted, even though she knew he was perfectly capable of carrying out his threat, "you've had nothing to eat or drink for two days." "I have everything I need," he said.

A maid, asking for permission to speak, informed the lady of the house that at her master's command she had brought a two weeks' supply of food and drink to the study, plus a few changes of clothing and all the chamber pots the local dealer had in stock. The master had told her that she was not to breathe a word of this to anyone and that he did not wish to be disturbed on any account whatsoever.

The lady of the house bit her lip and said, "You should have reported this to me before." She thought she detected sarcasm in the maid's voice and a hint of defiance in her black eyes.

"She can't be more than fifteen or sixteen," she thought, "and already she's acting as if I were the maid and she the lady." Onofre's wife felt constantly that people were laughing at her behind her back. "Sure as heaven he's carrying on with this one," she thought. "I'll bet she smells of garlic and curd and he prefers that to the French perfumes and bath salts I use day in, day out. I'll bet they get into bed and cover their heads with the sheets to intoxicate themselves on the body odor they have after all that pounding away like two steam engines. And they probably do it over and over again, like the night he came into my room through the window, climbing up the wall of my father's house. I'll bet he's told her all about it, and they've laughed at my expense till the early hours of the morning. I should send her packing without further ado." But she did not dare. "The maid would know why she was dismissed and insult me in front of the other servants, and tell everyone, and I would be a laughingstock. And he would only get her an apartment somewhere and go see her every evening, and spend the night with her, telling me he has to stay up all night working, as he has done so often." Thinking in this fashion, she did not see that it was this very cowardice that had made her lose his love.

The same maid came to tell her, two weeks later, that the master was emerging from his seclusion. Onofre's wife was having her midmorning coffee with her older daughter and the dressmaker when the maid came in with this news. By then she had forgotten her jealousy and thought, "This girl is very loyal— we shall have to see about rewarding her."

Mother, daughter, and dressmaker hurriedly lumbered like three hippopotamuses down the hall. When they reached the study door, Onofre had just come out. For two weeks he had not washed, shaved, combed his hair, or changed his clothes. He had slept and eaten little. He looked wasted and moved falteringly, as if just awakened from a trance or some deep, poignant dream. An intolerable stench came from the study, wafting down the corridors like a lost soul.

"Agustí, prepare my bath," he said to the butler, as if unaware that his wife, his daughter, and the dressmaker were standing there. He held a bundle of papers covered with writing, full of corrections and words crossed out. The maid running up with buckets and mops to make the study fit again for human habitation were stopped in their tracks by an imperious gesture. "No need to clean up—we are moving," he said.

Now Honesta Labroux was giving life to the plot that had prompted the misgivings of the Marquis of Ut. To the marquis's statement that he did not know who could possibly like such nonsense, Onofre had darkly replied, "Everybody."

Indeed, the spectators were now weeping. Those hardened men of business could not hold back their tears. They said afterward that this was due only to the magic of Honesta Labroux. We shall never know the nature of that magic. Pablo Picasso, in a letter dating from much later on, states that the woman's influence lay in her gaze, in her mesmerizing eyes—which seems to support an unconfirmed rumor recorded by some of his biographers: that Picasso actually met her in person; that, bewitched by her, he abducted her in a laundry truck (aided and abetted by Jaume Sabartés) and took her to the village of Gòssol, in Berguedà; that he brought her back to the studio safe and sound a few days later, during which time he made several sketches and began an oil painting, which works initiated his famous so-called blue period.

A still more improbable story, reported by one magazine, was of Honesta Labroux's meeting, several years before, with Victoriano Huerta. This wily general had usurped the presidency of Mexico after ordering the assassination of Francisco Madero and Pino Suárez. When the uprisings led by Venustiano Carranza, Emiliano Zapata, and Pancho Villa obliged him to abandon the presidency and escape from Mexico, he went to live in Barcelona. A quarrelsome drunkard, he spent his time in the seedy bars of the city's red-light district, the *barrio chino*. When he was sober, he busied himself with schemes for his return. German agents, planning a maneuver to divert the attention of the United States from the war in Europe, decided to use Huerta as a decoy. Huerta, with the money he had accumulated during his brief months as president and deposited in the vaults of a Swiss bank, bought arms and ammunition from Onofre Bouvila. But Onofre alerted the North American government of the sale, and the cargo was intercepted in Veracruz harbor, an operation that involved a landing of the marines and many casualties in the civilian population. When the arms were returned to Onofre, he sold them over again to Carranza, now fighting his former allies Villa and Zapata.

According to the magazine, it was during this period that Honesta Labroux danced for Huerta one night. Immediately captivated by her, he offered her incalculable sums of money and promised to re-establish a monarchy upon his return to Mexico so that he could have her crowned empress, like the hapless Carlota. But she refused. This scene took place in the traitor's suite at the Internacional, the hotel that had been built in the incredibly short time of sixty-six days to accommodate visitors to the 1888 World's Fair. The ceiling and the walls of the suite had several bullet holes; the hotel management had issued a stern warning to Huerta because of this, and also because he abused the staff and didn't pay his bills. On the night of their rendezvous, he was said to be in his bare feet and with his fly undone; underneath his shirt, also unbuttoned, could be seen a yellowish vest with moth holes in it. Little wonder that Honesta Labroux did not take him seriously.

Both stories are probably apocryphal. Picasso did go to Gòssol in 1906 to spend a few months, and Victoriano Huerta died an alcoholic in a prison in El Paso, Texas. But at the time in question, Honesta Labroux's career was not yet launched by Onofre, and her screen name had not even been invented: she was still living in seclusion in a modest house in Gracia, waiting for her father to die so that she could surrender herself for the second and last time to the man of her life before ending it.

She was dissuaded from carrying out this melodramatic act by the very man whose actions, many years before, had driven

302

her to such desperation—dissuaded not by his words but by the same evil, icy stare that in the boardinghouse attic had subjugated her, terrorized her, and forced her to commit the worst crimes. Her mother had died that night, and of the anarchist cell that she had betrayed, most of the members had perished in the ditches of Montjuich—all this was on her conscience.

The pain and suffering in her sulphurous eyes did not escape Onofre's notice. He also knew that from the mid-nineteenth century on, the Industrial Revolution had made a profound change in man's notion of time. Formerly, time had not been strictly marked out: if circumstances called for it, a person might work for days and nights on end without stopping, or be idle for a similar period. Entertainments, such as harvest festivities, might go on for one or two weeks. A sporting, bullfighting, or theater event, or a religious occasion, or a parade could last five, eight, ten hours; participants would stay for the duration, or leave, or leave and come back later, as they pleased.

Now all that had changed: every day work started at the same time and stopped at the same time. A person's life could be easily predicted from childhood to old age; it sufficed to know what he did, what his trade was. This made life more comfortable, eliminating a good many nasty surprises and resolving many uncertainties. A schedule, a philosopher could exclaim, was destiny. Now nothing was left to chance or the inspiration of the moment. Regularity, punctuality was everything. The tired horse had to be given the whip, or the eager horse reined, so that the wagon would arrive at its destination on schedule, neither a little before nor a little after. So much importance was attached to punctuality that some politicians based their campaigns on it. "Vote for me, and I will be punctual," they told the electorate. Foreign countries were no longer extolled for their landscapes, works of art, or hospitality, but for their punctuality. Countries that previously almost nobody visited were now deluged by tourists wishing to see for themselves the vaunted punctuality of their citizens, offices, and public transportation.

This change could not have taken place on such a scale without electricity, whose continuous, invariable current guaranteed regularity and punctuality in everything. A streetcar powered by electricity no longer depended on the health or mood of a mule to keep to its schedule.

But entertainment and leisure activities still lagged behind business and transportation. A bullfight could last many hours. If a particular bull, full of resolve or wile, succeeded in goring all the horses that came one by one into the ring, a Sunday bullfight could run into Monday. In 1916 in Cadiz there was a famous bullfight that began on Sunday and ended the following Wednesday, with the result that the shipyard workers, absent without leave, lost their jobs. After some rioting, during which a few convents were burned down, the workers were rehired, but it had become clear that things could not go on like this.

Before Onofre's reunion with Delfina, before she stripped to her petticoat and threw herself in his arms and gazed at him with the sulphurous eyes that were to switch his thoughts onto a very different track, the idea had crossed his mind several times that cinematography could be the new entertainment humanity was looking for. Cinematography had three advantages that made it ideal: it ran on electricity, it allowed no audience participation, and its contents were not subject to change. "To be able to put on a show that is always identical, that begins and ends exactly at the times indicated!" he thought. "To have the audience seated in darkness, in silence, as if asleep, as if dreaming a collective dream!" That was his ideal. "But no, it's too good to be true, it would never work." Having seen the dog film and a few others besides, he was forced to agree with the pessimists. Nobody went to see a film unless it was immediately followed by something else—folk dances, sack races, a young bull let loose, or barbecued lamb chops. But others were thinking along the same lines as Onofre. In 1913 the first movie conceived as a complete show in itself was filmed in Italy. Called *Quo Vadis?*, it ran to fifty-two reels and took two-and-a-quarter hours; it was never shown in Spain, for a reason so peculiar it is well worth a digression.

The year 1906 saw the debut, in a Parisian variety theater, of a dancer who was later to win international acclaim; she was Dutch and her name was Gertrud Margarete Zelle, but she passed herself off as a priestess from India and adopted the name Mata Hari. Like all dancing girls of her kind, she received a good many propositions, but none so extraordinary as the one put to her by a gentleman on a summer night in 1907. "What I am going to ask you to do," he said, twirling his waxed mustache, "is something that nobody has ever asked you before." Mata Hari's head appeared above the folding screen behind which she had cast off the organdy tunic, silver belt, amethysts, and turquoises that made up her costume. "I do not know if I will be exotic enough for you, darling," she said in her Dutch-accented French. The gentleman lifted his monocle to his left eye when she emerged from behind the folding screen. His visit had been preceded by six dozen roses and a diamond necklace. Now she was wearing the necklace as a sign of acquiescence, and a kimono with a dragon embroidered in black and gold on the back. Thus arrayed, she sat before the circular mirror of her dressing table, a mirror in which princes, bankers, and marshals had seen their eyes glowing like embers with lust. Languidly she removed her sacred rings, some carved like human skulls, and placed them in a sandalwood box.

"And what it is you want of me? Can it be mentioned out loud?" she asked coquettishly. "In your ear," he said, drawing so close that the edge of his mustache tickled her cheek; in his eyes burned not desire but cold calculation. "I represent the German government," he whispered. "We would like you to spy for us." This conversation soon reached the ears of the intelligence agencies of England, France, and the United States. Before long, Mata Hari's fame as a spy eclipsed her fame as a dancer; contracts flooded in from all over the world, and she was in demand even more than Sarah Bernhardt, a state of affairs that would have seemed unthinkable only a few years previously. The rivalry between the two stars was the talk of all Paris. Thus, when in 1915 Sarah Bernhardt had to have a leg amputated, she was reported to have remarked, "Now at last I'll be able to dance as gracefully as Mata Hari." In Barcelona Mata Hari appeared only once, at the Teatro Lírico, and scored more of a success with the audience than with the critics.

Eventually the Allied secret services decided to get rid of her, and they set a trap for her. A young staff officer pretended to fall for her charms, as so many others had done before him; he showered her with presents, and they were seen together everywhere—riding in the Bois de Boulogne, having lunch and dinner in the classiest restaurants, sitting together in a box at the Opéra, going to the races at Longchamp, etc. She never asked him how he could afford such a life style on his modest officer's income; perhaps she assumed that he had other sources of income as well, or perhaps she did not think about it at all, returning his feigned love with genuine love. What other reason could there be for a spy as experienced as she was to swallow such conventional bait?

One night, as together they lay in that bed between whose sheets the war had suffered so many victories and defeats, he suddenly announced that he had to leave for a week, or maybe two. "I cannot be without you that long," she said. "Don't go." "My country expects it of me," he said. "Your country is here, in my arms," she replied. He ended up revealing to her the nature of the mission that was tearing him away from her side. He had to go to Hendaye, just over the border in France; there he was to intercept a film the Bulgarians were trying to smuggle to German agents stationed in San Sebastián. With the film safely in his hands, the German agents would be captured and shot on the railroad platform.

He had barely finished speaking when she hit him on the

head with a little statue of Siva, the cruel god, the destructive principle; the young officer slumped on the floor, his face covered with blood. Believing she had killed him, Mata Hari threw a *renard argenté* fur coat over her nightgown, put on a toque and long rubber boots, and got into the black twenty-four-horsepower Rolls-Royce that belonged to her (along with three other automobiles and a two-cylinder motorcycle, all given to her by highly placed officials from France and other countries—and paid for out of taxpayers' money).

As soon as she had gone, the officer sprang lightly to his feet and went over to the window; from there he sent signals to the two agents stationed outside the house. He was not dead, not even wounded: prepared for such an eventuality, the French secret service had replaced all the heavy objects in the room with rubber copies and had given the officer several capsules of red ink to suggest profuse bleeding.

Now the Rolls-Royce was speeding through the snowbound fields of Normandy. The railroad track ran alongside the road. In the distance Mata Hari glimpsed a horizontal column of smoke: it was the train heading for Hendaye at full steam. The chase was followed from the air by a plane carrying the dashing officer and three agents. After almost suicidal acceleration, the automobile managed to gain ground, and drew alongside the freight car in question. The intrepid spy stood on the Rolls-Royce's running board: she had torn strips from her nightgown and used them to tie down the steering wheel, and had also wedged a stone over the accelerator. She wrote with her lipstick on the windshield: *Adieu, Armand!*—the name of the man she thought she had sacrificed in the course of duty. She leaped from the running board and seized with one hand the iron railing at the rear of the freight car. From there she saw the Rolls-Royce plunge off the road and finally come to a halt in a field. This Rolls-Royce, which miraculously suffered no damage in the adventure, can still be seen in the little Musée de l'Armée in Rouen.

Once inside the freight car, and by the faint beam of a dark lantern, Mata Hari tried to locate the film he had spoken of. She thought she would find a couple of feet of celluloid, no more than a dozen frames. Instead she found several stacks of cylindrical cans—the fifty-two reels of *Quo Vadis?* When the agents burst into the wagon, they found her cut and bruised, her hands bleeding; the wind howling in the open door had carried away her helmet and was playing havoc with her curly hair. She had managed to throw twenty of the fifty-two reels out onto the track, where they were soon buried in the snow. And so the film never reached its destination and could not be shown in Spanish theaters. The war had brought production to a standstill all over Europe, and such films would no longer be made.

Now it was up to Onofre Bouvila to resuscitate the film industry, but he could not decide how to go about it, until chance once more placed Delfina in his path.

To the accompaniment of distant thunder, the downpour returned; it lashed the shutters and drummed on the skylight over the kitchen. In the kitchen the lame man's daughters had fallen asleep against the warm wall, all three entwined in a tender embrace. Meanwhile, in the hall, the three guests were still at their discussion.

"You're mad," Efrén told Onofre. Efrén was the only one who could speak to him like this with impunity.

Onofre ran his fingers gently over the photographs he had produced from his jacket pocket and placed on the table for the others to see. "Believe me, these photographs do not do her justice," he told them. "I knew that from the start. I made her put on twenty kilos, hoping that that might give her a little more . . . how should I put it . . . physical presence."

He took her to the estate at Alella, which he had rented exclusively for that purpose; the estate suited his plans, for it was surrounded by a high fence of thick cypress trees. He told her she had suffered much and needed a good rest. "You've been looking after your father, God rest him, for years. Now it's time somebody looked after you." Delfina did not know how to react to this approach: she had spent a long time in prison, then had lived in absolute seclusion, devoted, as he had said, to the care of her sick, simple-minded father. Unaccustomed to being in charge of her own life, she could imagine no alternative to blind obedience but death.

When Onofre took her to the house, there was already a chauffeur on duty, and a cook and a chambermaid. It did not strike her as odd that there was no automobile to go with the chauffeur, or that these members of the domestic staff had taken over the principal residential floor, whereas she was relegated to the room upstairs. "They are completely dependable," he told her. "I have given them their instructions, so they know what to do. There's no need for you to worry about anything—just do as they suggest." The only reaction that occurred to her was to thank him. She thought, "This must be what it is like being married to him."

During the months that followed, she simply said "Thank you" to everyone who addressed her. In the mornings the chambermaid would wake her up and bring her breakfast in bed: a sausage omelette, cold cuts, mashed potatoes, toast with olive oil, and a liter of hot milk. Then she would dress her and leave her out in the garden, to recline in a large wicker armchair in the shade of a mimosa. Delfina's shoulders would be covered with a bright-yellow angora shawl: butterflies and bees would make for this shawl, drawn by the color. Then she would have lunch and take a siesta. She would wake up as the sun went down, and would be served tea or cocoa with buns. Afterward she would go for a short walk around the garden, followed at a discreet distance by the chauffeur.

On one of her first days there, she tried to get this chauffeur talking. "Didn't Onofre say whether he was coming out to see me?" she asked. The chauffeur looked her up and down before answering. "If you are referring to my master," he said haughtily, "he is not in the habit of informing me of his plans, nor do I tell my master what he is to do." "That puts me in my place," she thought, thanked him, and continued her stroll. On another occasion she started to part the cypresses forming the fence to look out onto the road, but the chauffeur shoved her back. This bothered her less than not knowing whether Onofre would be coming out to see her.

In fact, he was not coming out, because he was locked in his study writing the script for the film in which she was to star. While he was thus occupied, his men went on fattening her up. At night they gave her a powerful drug to make her sleep. She did not realize that she was eating to excess: after starving in prison, she had lost all sense of proportion, of moderation. Had they given her a lump of bread, a little moldy cheese, and a herring or a piece of cod in brine, she would have seen no cause to object, but the Pantagruelian feasts she was made to eat were also acceptable to her. She did not know that one had choices in life and the right to exercise them now and then—her will had been annihilated. Perhaps that was why she went on loving him, too.

Eventually she decided to send him a letter, telling him what she had not been able to express in her dead father's presence. When she finished it, she gave it to the chambermaid, begging her to mail it as soon as possible. That night in the kitchen the staff began to read the letter, whose contents they did not understand. They were three ruffians, often drunk, tired of one another's company but unable to be alone. The chauffeur fornicated alternately with the chambermaid and the cook. At times, when he had drunk too much, he would fornicate with both at once. On such occasions the two women fought over him, pulling each other's hair, scratching and biting like animals. The shouts and the general racket that accompanied these orgies would sometimes rouse Delfina. Since she was still under the effect of the sleeping medicine, she would not fully awake but imagine herself still in prison, where for years she had been wakened every night by infernal screams.

"That fateful night," she wrote in the letter that never reached Onofre, "I dreamt I heard screaming, and also felt an urge to scream, but kept it down. The scream has remained bottled up inside me, and I've heard it every night since. I do not tell you this as a reproach, for it is not only a scream of pain—it is also a scream of joy. But whether of pain or joy, it ruins my sleep, my peace. I expect no peace now but in death. Yet I do not want to make a show of valor when I have none. I cannot lie to you: at times, at difficult moments, I have felt like renouncing all that is great in my destiny—namely, having loved you. But that is not meant as a reproach, either. If you were not the way you are, if you had acted differently, my life would have been different, too, and there is nothing that frightens me more than the thought that even one instant of my life could be different, because that would mean that at that instant I would not love you as I love you. I do not envy anyone, I would not change places with anyone, because no one can love you as much as I love you."

As the servants read this letter, several wine stains appeared on the paper. "What will our master do," they said, "if he sees these stains?" To escape detection, they threw the letter into the fire.

The Marquis of Ut said, "It's time I was on my way." He struggled to his feet, his joints aching because of the late hour and the rain. "That's all you have to say?" said Onofre. The marquis consulted his watch and frowned; he thought about it and decided that his presence was not really required anywhere else at the moment. "I suppose I can stay on to the end," he sighed. Onofre smiled gratefully. "Sit down and tell me what's worrying you."

The marquis rubbed the stubble on his cheek. "There's

something I don't understand." Fatigued, he had difficulty concentrating, but he had difficulty concentrating at the best of times. He looked at the photograph of Delfina: a dolled-up matron standing against a background of cypresses and staring into space with a vacant expression. He put down the photograph, chewing his lip.

"Out with it, now," said Onofre patiently.

"What's my role in all this?" asked the Marquis of Ut.

Perhaps if all businessmen knew that sooner or later they were bound to die, economic activity the world over would come to a standstill. Fortunately that was not the case with the Marquis of Ut. A Freemason, a libertine, and a meddler, he was politically an archconservative; his total lack of convictions carried great weight in the country's most reactionary circles. These circles, comprised of aristocrats, landowners, and a few army men and clergymen, wielded over the nation's political life a decisive but passive influence: they never intervened in anything except to prevent changes from being introduced. They merely let people know that they were there, warning them that awful things might happen if their immobility was threatened in any way. They supported no ideology and took a dim view of any attempt to argue their position. One did not need to defend what was the natural order of things. "Let others justify themselves," they would say. "We have no need of justification, for we are right." Any innovation, even if it was in their own interests, horrified them, and giving way to it was seen as a form of suicide.

Onofre knew from experience that it was impossible to discuss things with them. From time to time he had suggested to the Marquis of Ut the expediency of introducing some reform in some area or other, for the sole purpose of avoiding greater evil later on. The marquis invariably lost his temper. "Why do you want to change the world? Who do you think you are, God Almighty? Let things be. You are rich and nobody lives forever: you look out for yourself, and let those that come after us look out for themselves!" His reasoning was not sound, but it was unshakable. That these subversive proposals came from Onofre only confirmed the marquis in his opinion of him. "When all is said and done," he would tell him, "you're an upstart, a peasant who was allowed to make a bundle of money. Now it's gone to your head, you want to have a say in things, you want to be *heard*—isn't that right?"

This impertinence from a man who never refused his hospitality and who owed him many favors and substantial sums of money aroused Onofre's admiration and envy. He could not be offended by the marquis. "Why are you all so headstrong?" he would say gently, by way of reply. "With your inflexibility you will only bring about your own destruction." To which the marquis would react by ranting and raving like one possessed, warning him that his patience was coming to an end and that if the conversation continued along these lines, he would be obliged to challenge him to a duel. At such moments the marquis would have made no bones about killing Onofre. Since for the marquis and his kind the existing order was a natural one, any disorder was a disease that had to be removed by any means.

"Louis XVI said the very same thing when they told him what was happening in the streets of Paris," said Onofre, smiling. But the Marquis of Ut, unruffled, replied that the French were all dogs and he didn't give a damn what happened to one of that nation. "Not even the king?" Onofre countered. "Certainly not," said the marquis, standing up. "Let no man bring up the House of Orléans in my presence, and if the conversation continues along these lines, I shall be obliged to send you my seconds. So now you know."

By this time there were new developments to be taken into account. What had happened in Russia, in Austria-Hungary, or indeed in Germany could not be dismissed. Only profound, bold changes could allow things to go on as before.

"And these profound, bold changes come down to this?" said the marquis. "Making films with that walrus?"

Onofre still smiled; he was not yet ready to reveal the full extent of his plans to the marquis. "Trust me," he said. "All I ask is this: don't send the troops out into the streets. Tell your people that I am not a madman and that I am acting in good faith. Give me a period of grace: I will show you what I can do. But during this period there must be calm in your ranks. If a few little disturbances occur, let the masses enjoy themselves, look the other way—it's all part of my plan."

"I cannot commit myself that far," said the marquis, blinking with fatigue.

"All I'm asking," Onofre said, "is for you to have a word with your people about this. Will you do it, for old times' sake?"

"Let me think it over," said the marquis. Onofre could not ask for more, and so he did not insist.

And now the theater was full of the Marquis of Ut's peers, and he, Onofre, and Efrén were watching the audience reaction from the screened-off box.

"It seems to be going well," said the giant from Calella.

Onofre nodded. Once again his intuition had proved right.

When she was taken to the film studios, Delfina had offered no resistance and shown no curiosity; they could just as easily have taken her to any other place. These film studios had been built between San Cugat and Sabadell, not far from the present-day site of Barcelona's Universidad Autónoma. Building costs had been high, and the technical equipment had had to be imported from several different countries. Two pioneers of Catalan cinematography took part in the project, Fructuoso Gelabert and Segundo de Chomán. Neither of them, however, wished to direct the film Onofre had conceived: to them the project seemed preposterous. Finally an old out-of-work photographer had been hired, a surly man of central European extraction called Faustino Zuckermann.

The choice proved a wise one: this man immersed himself fully in the project from the start. He was tyrannical with Delfina, making her cry for one reason or another at every filming session. An alcoholic, he was given to sudden attacks of uncontrollable rage. At such times it was wise to stay away from him. A wardrobe girl had had three fingers of one hand broken by him, and a porter had had a chair smashed over his skull. The atmosphere of fear created in the studio by this man pleased Onofre: he knew that from it would arise a more delicate, sweet-smelling flower.

The results were long in coming. Barcelona's technology was still tremendously backward in this field. The first film took three months at the laboratory stage. When it was finally developed, it was clearly useless: some sequences were too dark, others so bright they hurt the eyes; in some, amorphous ocher stains swam across the screen, while in others the action was somehow reversed—the characters walked backward, filled their glasses with a liquid from their mouths, etc., and some walked on the ceiling and some walked on the floor.

This did not upset Onofre. He ordered the film burned and everyone to start over. When told that Faustino Zuckermann was not fit for work, that he could not stand up, Onofre said, "Then he can direct sitting down." A style that many famous directors were later to imitate. Everything had to be made from scratch for the second filming, since the sets and costumes from the first had all been burned, too—a measure insisted upon by Onofre himself, so that nothing of what was happening in the studios would leak out. Secrecy was essential.

Finally they came to tell him that the second film was ready, and could be viewed, if he so wished, in a projection room at the studios. On hearing this, he dropped everything and was driven out there in an automobile with tinted windows. The film was the one that now had the audience of notables, assembled thanks to the Marquis of Ut, in tears. When that first, private showing was over, Onofre sent for Zuckermann. The old photographer reeked of red wine and raw onions, and his breath seemed to come from the bowels of the earth.

"My congratulations," Onofre said. "Everything I wanted is there: the hopes and fears of humanity." The bloodshot stare Faustino Zuckermann fixed on him with the persistence of the drunkard convinced him of the rightness of his choice: "They are two of a kind," he thought. "The same yearning and the same desperation. Soon this light that shines deep in their eyes will go out—turning first to embers, then to cold ashes—but it will be fixed forever on film."

CHAPTER SIX

1

The man who came out to meet Onofre Bouvila was past the age when physical appearance owes more to circumstances than to the passing years. He had not a single hair on his head — a spherical head, the color of dark clay. His features were small, his eyes a very pure blue. Dressed in striped cotton trousers held up by a string tied around his waist, a loose flannel shirt, and canvas shoes, he leaned on a knotted stick as he walked. Thrust under the string that served as a belt was a knife so large, it looked unreal. Close to his heels walked a little dog, a repulsive creature with an oversized head, a very short tail, and feeble-looking legs. The dog never took its eyes off its master, and he in turn often looked down at it, as if seeking its approval for what he was doing or saying.

"This way, sir," the man said. "The path isn't in good repair, so watch your step."

Onofre followed the man and the dog. The chauffeur who had brought him to this clearing in the woods began to follow, too, but Onofre motioned him to stay behind. "And do not worry if it is a good while before I get back."

The chauffeur sat down on the automobile's running board, put his peaked cap beside him, and began rolling a cigarette as the two men and the dog disappeared into the woods. Despite his years, Onofre's guide picked his way nimbly between the roots, stones, and undergrowth, while Onofre had to stop frequently to disentangle his jacket from the brambles. Each time, the old man would come back, cut away the offending bramble with his knife, and apologize profusely to Onofre, who had already written off the jacket.

The film industry he created in 1918 reached its zenith, its glory, just two years later. After that, things began to go wrong. In 1923, to everyone's dismay, Onofre handed over to Efrén Castells, with whom he had been in partnership from the start, his share of the business and announced his retirement not only from the film industry but from all his other business operations, too. His close friends or, in the absence of anybody who could claim such a relationship, those who had frequent dealings with him were less surprised by the decision. They had seen a change in him from the day he moved to his new house. It was no accident, they thought, that the move had coincided with the beginning of his most ambitious project.

"This used to be the tradesmen's entrance," said the old man. "Forgive my showing you in this way, but the going is easiest here, and it doesn't involve climbing over the fence."

Onofre had looked at hundreds of houses, but was totally unprepared for what he found here. This mansion, situated in the high part of La Bonanova, had belonged to a family whose name was sometimes Rosell (Catalan) and sometimes Roselli (Italian). The house itself had been built at the end of the eighteenth century, although little of the original structure was left standing after the extension work carried out in 1815. The garden, too, dated from that year.

318

This garden, Romantic in conception and somewhat bizarre in its final realization, covered some eleven hectares. The southern part of the garden, to the left of the house, contained an artificial lake fed by a Roman-style aqueduct from the river Llobregat. The outflow from the lake formed a canal that circled the garden and passed in front of the house, and on it one could go boating in a skiff or a punt under the shade of the willows, cherry trees, and lemon trees growing on both banks. There were several bridges across the canal: the three-span main bridge built entirely of stone, which led directly to the front entrance of the house; the one known as the "water-lily bridge," a little smaller than the first and with a pink marble parapet; the "Diana bridge," named after the statue to that goddess, which had been brought from the ruins at Ampurias and which now presided over the bridge; the "covered bridge," in teak; the "Japanese bridge," which together with its reflection in the water made a perfect circle; and so on.

Various kinds of exotic and colorful fish were let loose in the lake and the canal, and several extremely rare species of butterfly were brought from Central America and the Amazon and acclimatized by a process involving tremendous trouble and a degree of scientific knowledge almost unheard of in the Catalonia of the time.

Then, in 1832, after the Rosell family's trip to Italy, where grottoes were in vogue and whence the family originally hailed—or where they had settled at the time of Catalan rule in Sicily or the kingdom of Naples (when the family name underwent the change mentioned above), and to which country the offspring of the Barcelona branch of the family periodically went when they reached marriageable age (which strategy eventually led to the dismemberment of that branch)—a grotto was added to the garden, and one much admired in its day. The grotto consisted of two chambers, the first spacious with a vault ten meters high and curious formations of stalagmites and stalactites exquisitely fashioned in plaster and porcelain, and the second, even more extraordinary, small in size and entirely without ornamentation, but situated at the side of the lake and below the water level, the lake bottom being observable through a section of the wall that had been replaced by a sheet of glass fifty centimeters thick. Through this glass one could see, when the sun's rays penetrated as far as the bottom of the lake, the algae and the coral, the shoals of fish, and a pair of giant turtles brought from New Guinea that had survived the change of habitat and lived, as they are wont to do, to a ripe old age, surviving until well into the twentieth century, although they never bred.

"My father," said the man, "was a huntsman in the service of the Rosell family. Then, when he went deaf, he was made gamekeeper. It could be said, sir, that I was born into the family's service."

Apart from these marvels, the garden had innumerable nooks and crannies, pavilions, summerhouses, shrines, greenhouses, and mazelike avenues in which the walker could lose his way without fear, around whose bends he might unexpectedly encounter the equestrian statue of the Emperor Augustus or the frown of Seneca or Quintilian on their respective pedestals, and through whose hedges he might hear clandestine conversations or see passionate kisses exchanged in the moonlight. On the grounds, on the seven terraces carved out of the hillside, pairs of peacocks and Egyptian cranes lived out their lives.

"First I was Señorita Clarabella's page," said the man, "being six years old at the time. Señorita Clarabella was thirteen or fourteen then, if my memory serves me correctly. Although she spoke several languages fluently, she always addressed the servants in Italian. We never understood the orders we were given. My job, in any event, was simple enough: walking her seven lapdogs. Seven dogs, sir, all thoroughbreds, all different—you should have seen them."

The house had three stories, each occupying twelve hundred

square meters; on the front façade—facing southeast, toward Barcelona—there were eleven balconies on each of the upper floors, and ten great windows and the entrance door on the ground floor. The balconies, windows, transoms, glazed doors, skylights, miradors, and fanlights made a total of 2,006 panes of glass in the house, so window cleaning would be a nonstop activity.

This glass was now all broken, the interior devastated, and the garden a jungle. The bridges had collapsed, the lake was empty, the grotto caved in, and all the exotic fauna devoured by the beasts of prey and the rats that were now masters of the estate. The skiffs and carriages were nothing more than firewood in the doorless sheds, and the Rosell family escutcheon had been worn away by the elements to illegible verdigris on the main door's frieze.

"Tell me what happened," said Onofre. They had crossed the bridge at some risk to life and limb and were standing before the main entrance. The man sat on a stone lion that had no head or tail, and his dog lay down at his feet. He rested his chin on his hands, which he had crossed over his stick, and sighed deeply.

"Although it was the custom of the Rosell family, sir, as is well known, never to marry within Catalonia," the man began, "which stirred up some resentment here, as if being born on the same soil and under the same sun made a person less eligible, they were not a haughty family, no, sir, quite the contrary. It was a rare day I did not see some visitor as I was coming back in the evening after exercising the dogs—two hours, sir, they had to be walked, even in the hot summer months, over there, in the shade of those poplars, which are taller now than they were then, of course, since many years have passed."

He spoke in long sentences, as if remembering aloud, but now and then he would fall silent, lost in thought. During such moments he would go red like a schoolboy; his skin, naturally ruddy, would turn one shade darker, almost to indigo. Then he would shake his head and, lifting one hand off the pommel of his stick, point to those wild fields as if he could see people walking and carriages coming and going across the grass. "And then, with the visitors in view, you can imagine the trouble I had holding back the dogs, all playful and excited, straining at the leash, and sometimes they overpowered me, small as they were, because I was small, too, and dragged me across the soft lawn, much to the delight of the visitor who saw this comical scene before his coach went over the bridge and the gate opened wide to receive him."

Onofre left the man to his memories and entered the hall. The light poured in through the shutterless, curtainless windows. There were dry leaves all over the floor. A few objects had survived the looting—a brightly colored ball, a bronze vase, a chair—but the absence of furniture was painfully evident. He thought of all the things that filled a house; many of them required much time to fabricate and assemble. If one translated that into man-hours, a mansion such as this represented several lifetimes of labor, and its destruction rendered those lives a useless investment. He was roused from these dark financial reflections by the voice of the man, who had quietly joined him to continue his account.

"And the fiestas, sir, the garden parties and the carnivals!" With the ferrule of his stick he moved aside some of the leaves on the floor, revealing a foot and a girlish calf in a mosaic. Had he continued, he would probably have bared a mythological scene as large as the hallway floor itself, but that would have required several hours' work. He left the leaves alone and returned to the fiestas as they walked from room to room.

Naturally he had not been allowed to take part in those fiestas, which generally were evening affairs, but he would slip out of his bedroom in his nightshirt, barefoot despite the night chill, and hide where he could see without being seen. The servants, having their hands full, took no notice of a little brat like him.

Swifts had made their nests in the coffered ceiling of the mirrored salon, and mice ran along the moldings. Seeing this, the old man fell into a sad silence. When he spoke again, he did so quickly, as if wishing to get this painful visit over and done with.

"One summer day, sir," he said, "one terrible summer day, as I came back from my evening walk with the dogs, I found the house in a great commotion and everybody stunned and confused, which made me think, at first, that another big party was being prepared. But that was not possible, because we had just had two big parties, the San Juan garden party and the visit of the San Carlo theater company from Naples that Señor Rosell had invited, asking them to do, for his family and a few close friends, *Le Nozze di Figaro* by Mr. Mozart, which was a lot of trouble, because the singers had to be put up and looked after, as well as the choir, the orchestra, and the theater staff, some four hundred people, not to mention the instruments and costumes—so it was hardly likely that we were going to take on an affair of such proportions for a good while. And yet here I saw a battalion of bricklayers, carpenters, plasterers, and painters—the bare minimum, in short, you needed to prepare for a reasonably decent party.

"Excited, I ran inside, followed by my seven dogs, looking for somebody who could tell me what was going on, and finally found a pantrywoman who I suspect was related to me, since marriages within the domestic staff of a house were not uncommon, which, I might add, sometimes led to quaint situations, such as the woman who was my first-cousin-once-removed being also my first cousin, or one of my mother's brothers being also my nephew, and so on. Anyway, this pantrywoman to whom I suspect I was related, who might even have been, now that I think of it, my mother, since my father, on those rare occasions when he came out of the forest, slept with her, which of course proves nothing—she was plucking a pheasant between her knees and told me that that same afternoon a rider had come, wrapped in a cape and with a felt tricorn on his head, and that he had leaped from his still madly galloping horse and, not bothering to tie it up or hand the reins to the groom, who, wakened by the clatter of hoofs on the bridge, was coming to assist him—which oversight the horse took advantage of to have a nice dip in the canal—whispered a password in the butler's ear, at which the doors were thrown open before him and a speedy meeting with Señor Rosell arranged. My master then ordered the necessary preparations to be made for a grand ball that very night—that very night, mind!—in honor of an illustrious guest, whose name, however, was not disclosed to the staff.

"Right away the emissary set off again, and hard at his heels other messengers, from us, carrying invitations. 'But who can it be?' I asked the pantrywoman, probably my mother, with the curiosity of my tender years, but she replied that it was a secret, and that even if she told me, I would be none the wiser, because the name would mean nothing to me, but I nagged so, that in the end she gave up and said that the person in whose honor all those preparations were being made was none other than Duke Archibaldo María, whom the Rosell family had been supporting for many years as pretender to the throne of Spain."

Few dry leaves had found their way to the second floor. But here the dirt was deeper, seeming to come from the floor itself. "What an incredible amount of filth can build up," Onofre thought.

"To support a candidate to the throne was not, in those days, like having a favorite bullfighter, for example. No, sir, it was a risky business, it could get a person in trouble. Now, this Duke Archibaldo María, the one who would be visiting us, had promised in some unreadable document, some sort of 'edict' promulgated in Montpellier, to grant Catalonia limited independence, like India's in the British Commonwealth. And on that vague promise, sir, the Rosell family staked their lives and fortune. Now, the pretender to the throne's unexpected visit posed an awful dilemma for the household, since on the one hand the guest had to be wined and dined as befitted his possibly future rank, but on the other hand the visit had to be kept secret at all costs, seeing as the authorities had put a price on his head. This, as you can imagine, apart from the short notice, put the family's imagination, breeding, and *savoir-faire* to the test."

The floor here was covered with tiny fragments of porcelain, which crunched underfoot. Onofre picked up one of these chips and studied it closely. It was from a Sèvres or Limoges set of china capable of providing for no fewer than two hundred guests and including soup tureens, gravy boats, serving platters, and fruit bowls. "If the dining room is downstairs, how did this china end up here?" Onofre asked. The old servant, lost in his recollections, made no reply. He continued:

"As soon as we set eyes on the man, we knew that he would bring us no good. Duke Archibaldo María was forty-five at the time and had always lived in exile. His furtive, rootless life had made him debauched, immoral. As he crossed the bridge, he fell off his horse, he was so drunk. I am sure he never noticed the skiffs on the canal, in which the servants were holding candelabra and candlesticks to create moving patterns of light. His aide-de-camp, a fellow named Flitán, had something of the gypsy about him; he leaped from his saddle with the ease of a circus rider, helped the duke to his feet, and led him to the parapet, over which His Highness vomited, while Señorita Clarabella, acting on her father's instructions and with the motions her dancing master had taught her all afternoon, gave him the most graceful curtsy and, on a checkered silk cushion, a copy of the key to the house in gold, with a white lily. . . . It was an extremely warm summer night, sir, terribly close, sir, the duke had not shaved for days or washed for months, and his clothes gave off a sour smell. Thick mucus dangled from his nose when he laughed, and you could see that his teeth were half rotten. Never was a royal house more sorrily represented. He hefted the key appreciatively in his hand, tossed it to his aide-de-camp, dropped the lily on the ground, and pinched Señorita Clarabella's cheek. She blushed, curtsied again, and ran and hid behind her mother."

To the third floor they took a staircase whose banister had been reduced to a few sticks jutting from the steps. When they reached the top, the old man, who until then had moved slowly, heavily through the house, dawdling in each room, gave a little hop and stood in front of Onofre, as if to block the way.

"This was where the bedrooms were," he explained, although he had said nothing about the functions of the other rooms. "Our masters' bedrooms, I mean," he added hastily. "The domestic staff, naturally, slept in the attic, the hottest part of the house in summer and the coldest in winter, but, on the other hand, from there you had the best view of the estate. My bedroom was a little apart. Sleeping with Señorita Clarabella's seven dogs, I did not have to share it with other servants, as was the usual practice, which meant that I was spared practical jokes and acts of sodomy—not completely, of course, but most days yes. I think I can say that while I lived here, I was subjected to practical jokes and acts of sodomy no more than once a week, which very few in my position can claim, sir. The rest of the time I was left alone, and would sit on the windowsill looking at the stars, or looking in the direction of Barcelona, hoping to see some fire, since otherwise the city was all in darkness. Then along came electric lighting and all that changed, but by that time there was nobody living in this house. Come now, sir," he said suddenly, tugging at Onofre's sleeve, "let's go up to the attic and I'll show you where my room was. The rooms here are of no interest whatsoever, believe me."

The attic ceiling had fallen in in several places, and one could see the sky. Through these holes, bats zigzagged in and out. The bats not zigzagging were asleep, hanging upside down from the rafters. Large rats scurried across the floor, their stiff fur bristling. The man gathered his little dog up in his arms, to protect it.

326

"That night, I couldn't sleep," he went on, resuming his tale. "The dance music played by the orchestra drifted up to my room. I was looking out the window and saw, below, on the far side of the bridge, on the esplanade that used to be there, by the faint light of the stars that filled the sky that summer night— that terrible summer night, sir—the carriages in which the guests had come, all steadfast supporters of the duke, and beyond them, on the hillside, countless little lights moving slowly like a swarm of lazy glowworms. But they were not glowworms, sir, no, they were lanterns being used to light the way for General Espartero's troops, because he had been informed by some accursed traitor of the duke's presence and was now surrounding the estate. And the only one who saw this trap was your humble servant here, an an innocent child of six, who knew nothing of treachery and war."

The old servant wiped his eyes with a checkered handker-chief, then wiped the little dog's eyes, too, though it squirmed at this. Putting the handkerchief back in his pocket, he continued:

"I listened to the music until sleepiness began to get the better of me, and I got back in bed. I don't know what time it was when I woke with a start. The dogs were padding nervously around the room, scratching at the doors and whining, as if they smelled a nameless peril in the air. Outside, the night was dark. I looked out the window and saw that both the carriages and the glowworms that had entertained me before were gone. I lit a stump of a candle and, barefoot in my nightshirt, slipped into the hall, not letting the dogs out, for it wouldn't do if they escaped and went running all over the house, which seemed all asleep.

"Down that very stairway you see before you, sir, I crept to the floor below. I don't know what possessed me to do that. Suddenly a hand grabbed my arm and another my mouth, so I could neither run nor call for help. I dropped the candle, which was immediately picked up. The person holding me, I saw, was Duke Archibaldo María himself, and the one who had picked up the candle, with which he now illumined his diabolical face, was

Flitán, and the villain had a dagger clenched between his teeth. 'Fear not,' the duke whispered in my ear, breathing so much alcohol into my face that I nearly fainted. 'Do you know who I am?' he asked me. My answer, a weak nod, satisfied him, because then he said, 'In that case, you know that you must obey me in all things.' He asked if I knew where Señorita Clarabella's bedroom was. Another nod provoked a rapid exchange of glances and leers between the two men, the significance of which was entirely lost on me. 'Lead me straight there,' said the duke, 'for Señorita Clarabella awaits me. I have a little message for her,' he added with an uncouth laugh that his aide-de-camp echoed.

"Naturally, I obeyed. At her door they gave me back the candle and told me to return at once to my room. 'Go back to sleep, and tell no one what has happened,' the duke warned me, 'or Flitán will cut your tongue out.' I ran to my room as fast as my legs could carry me, not once looking back. But at my door I stopped, because this encounter bothered me in a way I did not understand. At the other end of the attic hall was the pantrywoman's room, which she shared, as I explained before, with other maids. I tiptoed there, went over to her bed, and shook her. She half-opened her eyes and gave me an angry look. 'What the devil are you doing here, you little brat?' she muttered, which made me think that perhaps she was not my mother after all, in which case I could expect nothing but a whipping. But I replied, 'I'm frightened.' 'All right, then,' she said. 'Stay if you like, but not in my bed. Don't you see I have company tonight?' And she put her finger to her lips and pointed to the man who was snoring beside her and who was not, by the way, my gamekeeper father, which doesn't prove anything either way, of course, so I lay down on the matting at the foot of the bed and began to count all the chamber pots I could see from there.

"Again I was awakened, the pantrywoman was shaking me. All the maids, and all the men that for whatever reason were also in the room, were rushing here and there to find their clothes.

328

When I asked what was happening, the only explanation I got from the pantrywoman was a smack. 'Enough of your questions, and let's get out of here right away,' she said. She threw a fichu over her nightgown and left the room, dragging me along behind. The staircase thundered as the servants all hurried down to congregate in the basement. There we saw the master and the mistress. Señor Rosell was still in evening dress, and in his right hand he held his drawn saber, and his left arm was around Señora Rosell's shoulders while she wept all over his shirt. I heard him murmuring, 'Alas for Catalonia!' I looked all around me to find Señorita Clarabella in the crowd, but my small size made it impossible. People near me said that General Espartero's troops had just crossed the bridge and would soon break down the front door.

"As if to confirm that statement, a tremendous pounding began above us on the ground floor. I hid my head in the forest of knees around me. Señor Rosell said calmly, 'Make haste, no dallying now, for our lives are at stake.' We all went into a storeroom where I had seen beans, lentils, and chick-peas kept in light-colored wooden barrels with iron hoops around them. I was amazed that so many people could fit in such a small space. But as I drew nearer, I saw a trapdoor in the floor of the storeroom. Normally concealed beneath the barrels, it was now open, letting us all descend into a secret passage, known only to the owners of the house, a way of escape in case of siege, as was now the case. The pantrywoman, possibly my mother, beckoned to me, and I would have followed her, sir, if I hadn't suddenly remembered the seven little dogs still shut up in my room. 'I must go and get them,' I told myself, 'or Señorita Clarabella will be very angry with me.' Without giving it a second thought, I turned around and ran up the four flights from the basement to the attic."

Onofre went over to the window and looked down. The thicket and the bushes had overgrown the estate's boundaries: now a green mass went from his feet to the edge of the city. The villages that the city had been absorbing one by one could be clearly made out; the Ensanche, with its trees, avenues, and luxury homes; farther down, the old quarter, with which, even after all these years, he still identified; and finally the sea. On either side of the city, smokestacks belched into the dark evening sky. In the streets the lamps were being lit one after another, to the unhurried rhythm of the lamplighter.

"I am not interested in the rest of your story," he said curtly, giving the old man a peremptory look over his shoulder. "I'll take the house."

2

By pure chance or cosmic design, the collapse of Onofre Bouvila's film empire coincided with the completion of the reconstruction of the mansion he had acquired. With great tenacity, heedless of all considerations of time, energy, and expense, he had the entire interior of the house gutted and rebuilt exactly as it had or should have been. With no description or plan to help in this task, he let himself be guided only by the dictates of logic and the uncertain memory of the old man with the little dog. He listened with infinite patience to the opinions of the architects, historians, decorators, cabinetmakers, artists, dilettantes, and charlatans who filed in and out. To solve the problems that arose at every turn, the experts offered conflicting opinions; Onofre, hearing their opinions, for which they were handsomely paid, chose the course he found most appropriate, never letting himself be swayed by his own personal preferences.

He watched as the house gradually rose again, along with its garden, stables and sheds, the lake and the canal, the bridges and the pavilions, the flower beds and the vegetable garden. Inside, the floors and ceilings were either restored or, where time had gnawed away at the works of man until they were beyond recognition, invented anew. Onofre distributed the fragments of porcelain and glass among his agents and sent them to the four corners of the earth to find exact copies. These men, who only a few years before had covered those same foreign cities selling artillery shells and bombs to the highest bidder, now found themselves ringing the doorbells, in damp side streets, of goldsmiths, silversmiths, and antique dealers. Painters and sculptors from distant studios and attics were summoned, and restorers from art galleries and museums. A fragment of a vase no larger than the back of one's hand made the journey to Shanghai two times. He had horses from Andalusia and Devonshire harnessed and yoked to a replica coach built specially for him in Germany.

People thought he was mad, that he had taken leave of his senses; nobody knew what drove him. Practicality, convenience, and economy were ignored in his single-minded quest: each thing had to be exactly as it had been before, in the day of the Rosell family—whose survivors, curiously, he made no attempt to trace. Whenever anyone asked him how he, who had tried to replace the religion of his fathers with movies, could now go to such lengths to re-create a thing that was at odds with progress, a thing upon which progress itself had turned its back, Onofre would only smile.

This colossal project lasted several years. One day, at the mansion, a decorator told Onofre that he had searched unsuccessfully for a majolica statuette of no great value; he had heard that perhaps in Paris, at such-and-such an establishment, one might find the thing, but the decorator had decided against going to any further trouble over a statuette that in his opinion was not worth it. Onofre obtained the address of the establishment in Paris, had the decorator dismissed, got into the automobile that was waiting for him on the bridge, and said to the chauffeur, "To Paris," having never left Catalonia before, not even to go to Madrid, where so many of his business deals were always pending.

On the way to Paris he dozed now and then in his seat. When they crossed the border, since there was a nip in the air, he went to buy a traveling blanket to cover his legs, but they would not sell him one: he had no French money on him. He continued without the blanket as far as Perpignan, where a bank provided him with the cash he needed and gave him a letter authorizing him to draw any sum wherever and whenever he pleased. After Perpignan it began to rain, and rained for the rest of their journey. They spent the night in the first town they came to, and the following morning set off again. When they arrived in Paris, they went directly to the address given him by the decorator, found the majolica statuette, and bought it for next to nothing.

With the statuette in his possession, Onofre had the chauffeur drive him to the nearest luxury hotel, and there he took the *suite royale.* He was having a bath when the manager came in, dressed in a tailcoat, with a gardenia in his lapel. He had come to ask if Monsieur Bouvila desired anything in particular. Onofre ordered his evening meal to be served there in the suite, and his chauffeur, occupying a room on a different floor, to be supplied with female companionship. "He has a long day ahead of him tomorrow," he remarked. The hotel manager assumed an understanding air. "And monsieur?" he went on. "Would not monsieur also like a little companionship?" "Discreet and accommodating," Onofre said, trying to imagine what the Marquis of Ut would require under the circumstances. The manager raised both arms. *"C'est la spécialité de la maison!"* he exclaimed. *"Elle s'appelle Ninette."* When Ninette came to the suite later, she found Onofre on the bed fully dressed and sleeping soundly. She took off his shoes, undid his waistcoat and shirt collar, and covered him with the counterpane. As she moved to turn out the light, she saw on the bedside table an envelope on which he had written: *Pour vous.* Inside there was a wad of banknotes. Ninette put the envelope back on the bedside table, turned out the light, and quietly left the suite.

"Travel is boring and does not broaden the mind, whatever they say," he thought the following day. The hotel manager suggested he might save time by returning to Barcelona in an airplane: there was as yet no regular service between the two cities, but if money was no object, something could be arranged. His chauffeur drove him out to the airport, and Onofre struck a deal with a Belgian pilot and hired a biplane. The chauffeur left for Barcelona by road, and Onofre and the pilot boarded the airplane. Unfavorable winds took them to Grenoble. From there they managed to get to Lyon, where they refueled and drank several cognacs in the airport bar to warm up. As they crossed the Pyrenees, they narrowly escaped a serious accident. Finally they landed in the Sabadell airport, safe and sound. To his great surprise, Onofre saw that Efrén Castells and the Marquis of Ut were waiting for him by the runway.

"Good of you to meet me," he said. They shouted something, but he could not hear: all those hours flying had left him temporarily deaf. He also staggered as he walked: the giant from Calella practically had to carry him. "How did you find out I would be arriving today?" Onofre asked. They had looked for him everywhere, had traced him, through the various banks, to Paris, and from there the hotel manager had informed them by telegraph of his movements: *Bibelot acheté monsieur baigné Ninette deçue monsieur volé.*

Now the three of them were heading for Barcelona in Efrén's automobile. Efrén, sitting on the folding seat, told the chauffeur to step on it. Onofre asked what had happened. "Something important," said Efrén. "Thanks to you and your stupid joyride, we've already lost valuable time." He spoke with a seriousness not typical of him.

"Let's put on our hoods," said the marquis. He pulled out from under the seat a rectangular inlaid wooden box, and from this took three black pointed hoods adorned with the Maltese cross. With the hoods on, they had to sit hunched up to avoid crushing the points against the automobile's roof. At the lower slopes of the Tibidabo hill, the automobile stopped outside a large red brick house with false towers, battlements, and gargoyles. Two men with gowns over their shoulders opened the gate and closed it again after them. The marquis, Efrén, and Onofre got out at the main door, rushed up the marble steps, taking them two at a time, and entered a circular high-ceilinged hall, their hurried steps ringing out as they crossed it.

Doors opened and closed, servants in breeches and white sateen masks bowed, indicating the way, and they emerged into a room with a long narrow table in the middle, at which several hooded men were seated. The marquis, Efrén, and Onofre sat down on the three unoccupied wooden chairs. The man presiding asked in a harsh voice, "Is everybody here now?" He was answered by a general muttering in the affirmative. "Let us begin, then," said the chairman, making the sign of the cross. All present followed suit, after which the chairman said, "To this extraordinary chapter have come representatives of our brothers in Madrid and Bilbao, whom I have the honor and pleasure of welcoming to Barcelona." Another general murmur followed. Then the chairman struck the table with his gavel and went on: "I assume you are all aware of the situation."

By 1923 the social situation had deteriorated to the point, according to some, of no return. Onofre did not share this pessimism. "We have always lived in a social crisis," he said. "That's the way the country is." He believed that the problem wasn't really serious. "Let nature take its course," he said. "Everything will sort itself out, with a minimum of violence." Confused and troubled times suited them well—he had, after all, got where he was by turning such conditions to his advantage. The Marquis of Ut and his brethren, however, took the opposite view: they had inherited their position of superiority and lived in constant fear of losing it. Any measure was justified to them if its aim was the preservation of stability. Now they were losing sleep over the specter of Bolshevism. "Ah," thought Onofre when the discussion came around to that, "if Bolshevism were to triumph here, as in Russia, I would be a Lenin." He had unbounded confidence in his ability to master any storm.

This, however, he could hardly say to the Marquis of Ut and his brethren. "One would have to be a complete ass to let things get to such extremes," was his only comment.

"The present situation is like the fable of the camel and the tent," said the marquis, raising his voice. "The lower classes ask for something and we give it to them. The next day they ask for something else and we give that to them, too, and so on until they take up arms, put us to the slaughter, and stick our heads on posts."

This analysis was greeted with murmurs of approval. The hooded man next to Efrén said that the worker was stepping out of line and that the moon and the stars weren't enough for him now. "What he wants is to chop off our heads, rape our daughters, burn down our churches, and smoke our cigars." All the hooded men began thumping on the table with their fists.

When finally the noise stopped, Onofre spoke up again. "I know what the workers want. What they want is to become bourgeois. And what is wrong with that? The bourgeoisie have always been our best customers. . . . " There was a disapproving rumble. Onofre did not care what happened to the working class, but he did not like being contradicted: he decided to make a stand, even though he knew that the decision had already been made. "Look," he said, "you all think the worker is a tiger crouching to spring at your throats, a beast to be kept at bay by whatever means. But this is not so: the worker is a human being like us. Give him a little money, and he'll run to buy what he himself produces, and production will spiral upward at a tremendous rate—"

One of the hooded men interrupted to say that he had heard

that economic theory before. "I didn't understand it, but it struck me as pernicious. Then I learned that it came from England— say no more." Another remarked that this was not the time to discuss economic theories. The Marquis of Ut added that the situation reminded him of the fable of the donkey that played the flute. Onofre spoke again: "If we meet the worker's demands within reasonable limits, he will be eating out of our hands, but if we are unyielding, what will keep him from violence?"

"The army," said a man who had not spoken until then, in a full voice that Onofre thought he recognized. "The army is there precisely for emergencies, when the fatherland is in danger." Onofre dropped the pencil he had been fiddling with; as he bent to pick it up, he looked under the table and saw that the speaker was wearing high boots. "This means trouble," he thought. "I know who he is." "When there is chaos," the hooded man went on, "the army must impose order, discipline, for chaos endangers the fatherland." There was conviction in his voice, as well as a certain obstinacy that brooked no argument. A respectful silence ensued.

"I suppose this means," Onofre finally said, "that we will have to dig into our pockets."

From the railroad-car steps the general turned to take his leave of those who had accompanied him to the station. When he saw the entire platform full of hooded men, he rubbed his eyes in disbelief. "Surely this can't be *delirium tremens*," he thought, "not yet." Then he remembered what he was doing and why the hooded men were there. He straightened up as the train whistled.

"Gentlemen, if they do not make mincemeat of me first, tomorrow I shall be ruling Spain," he said solemnly. The men smiled behind their hoods: they had telegraphed their banks and were reasonably confident of the success of the coming coup d'état. There were no travelers or porters on the platform; the station had been cordoned off by the infantry, and mounted troops were patrolling the city. Machine guns and light artillery had been positioned in the working-class districts and in the city's nerve centers. Silence reigned in Barcelona.

As he left the station, Onofre asked Efrén for a lift home, since he had no automobile with him. The giant from Calella hesitated before saying, "By all means. Jump in." Onofre gave a sigh of relief: he did not like the idea of being gunned down on the station steps. Once inside the automobile, he felt relatively safe. "For a moment I thought you were going to leave me high and dry," he admitted. The giant answered, "We're friends." They took off their hoods and looked at each other. Onofre felt a pang, remembering the bear he had met at the World's Fair as he looked at the sagging features of the financier, now bald and prematurely aged. "I suppose I haven't fared much better," he thought, smoothing down his hair with his fingers.

Efrén suggested that he lie low for a few days. "Primo de Rivera is not a bloodthirsty man," he said. "If it was up to him, there would be no bloodshed. And most likely everything will go well and the change will scarcely be noticed. But it's possible," the giant went on, his face clouded not so much by worry as by the effort involved in making such a lengthy statement, "that he'll meet some resistance when he gets to Madrid—not from the people but from other military men with the same desire for power as himself. Even a civil war is possible. You are very powerful, and Primo knows now he cannot count on you. You were not very prudent tonight," Efrén rebuked him. "I don't know why you had to come out with all that nonsense."

"Because it is what I think," said Onofre, looking at his friend tenderly, "and because I'm too old to go on keeping things under my hat. But you are right this time: I'll go to France. I was just in Paris: an awful place, but I can get used to it if I have to."

"They won't let you over the border," said Efrén.

"The plane I came in won't be leaving until early morning.

If later this evening you could take me to Sabadell, you would be doing me a great favor."

"I'll take you straight to Sabadell. We shouldn't waste time. One of Primo's men might already be looking for you."

"Maybe," Onofre replied, "but let's stop at my study first: you and I have a couple of matters to attend to there."

In front of his house, he got out of the automobile and said to the giant, "Fetch my father-in-law, will you? Get him out of bed and drag him by the scruff of the neck if necessary. He's on his last legs, but we need a lawyer."

Onofre entered the house as quietly as possible, not wishing to wake his wife and daughters; the very thought of a tearful parting put him on edge. "It'd be worse still if they got it into their heads to follow me into exile," he thought as he groped for the bell rope. He tugged at it until the butler appeared in night-shirt and nightcap. "No need to get dressed," he told him. "Light the fire in my study." The butler scratched his neck. "The fire, sir? But it's only the beginning of September!"

While the butler lit some tallowed torches with a match, Onofre removed his jacket, rolled up his sleeves, took a revolver out of a drawer, and checked to see that it was loaded. He placed it on the table and dismissed the butler. "Get me some coffee, but try not to wake anybody. I don't want to be interrupted. And one more thing," he said, calling back the butler. "Don Efrén Castells and Don Humbert Figa i Morera will be arriving soon. Show them straight into the study."

As soon as he was alone, he began opening drawers and file cabinets, taking out papers, flicking through them, and either putting them back or throwing them on the fire. From time to time he prodded the ashes with the poker. A pendulum clock struck twelve somewhere in the house. The butler came in to announce the arrival of Efrén and Don Humbert.

"Show them in," Onofre said.

His father-in-law was in tears. He had thrown a dark coat

over his striped pajamas. Since his wife had died Don Humbert had gone a little soft in the head: he no longer knew what was going on around him. "Onofre, Onofre, is it true what this big brute is telling me? That the García Prieto government is about to fall and you have to go to France or you'll be shot?" he asked as he came in. "Good Lord above, and my daughter and my granddaughters, what's to become of them? I'd been saying to my wife, God rest her, that we should never have let our little dear marry you, she'd have been much better off with that hunchback, do you remember him, Onofre? Such a polite and shy young man who lived in Paris—what was his name?"

Onofre calmed his father-in-law. "Everything is all right. The field marshal for Catalonia set off for Madrid a few hours ago. The garrisons of Catalonia and Aragón are supporting him. Now we must wait and see what happens in Madrid. If he meets with opposition, there might be war, but I think it's really all settled: neither the staff officers nor the king will stand in his way. The cream of the nation is behind him," he said without irony. "I am on their side, and they ought to know that," he added sadly, "but they do not trust me. In fact, they fear me more than they do the working class." He lit a cigar thoughtfully and said, "I should have foreseen all this long ago."

On October 30, 1922, the blackshirts made their famous entry into Rome. Now, a year later, on September 13, 1923, Don Miguel Primo de Rivera y Orbaneja was trying to follow in Mussolini's footsteps. Not being able to count on the support of millions of followers, he had to turn to the army. "That is the difference between the two," said Onofre. "Primo is not a bad man, but he is none too clever, and, like all such men, he is suspicious and timid. He won't last long. But while he does last, I must keep out of the way. Don Humbert, take a seat at the table, and pen and paper, and draw up a contract: I wish to transfer my businesses to Efrén Castells here present."

"What madness is this?" exclaimed Don Humbert. The butler knocked and entered with the coffee Onofre had ordered, but had taken it upon himself to add two cups to the tray, should Don Efrén and Don Humbert care to join him. "It would appear you are in for a long night," he murmured. Rumors had already reached his ears. Tension was spreading through the streets like fog; carrier pigeons were darting across the sky. The leaders of subversive movements sought shelter in the city's underground sewage system. At intersections of stinking tunnels, anarchists, socialists, and Catalan nationalists met, recognized one another by the greenish light of their respective lanterns, and moved on, exchanging few words.

"It's the only way to avoid confiscation," said Onofre.

"But what you're asking is impossible—how can we put a value on all you own?" Don Humbert protested.

"The value doesn't matter," said Onofre. "The important thing is for it all to be in safe hands."

After calculating and arguing for a while, they agreed on a sum in pounds sterling, which the giant from Calella promised to transfer the next day to one of the bank accounts Onofre had in Switzerland. Don Humbert sobbed as he drew up the agreement. Several times he stopped and said he felt as if he were witnessing the dismemberment of the Ottoman Empire, a recent event that had sorely grieved him. He had always had a special feeling for that empire, which was strange, considering that he did not know where it was or anything else about it, but for him the Ottoman Empire meant pomp and magnificence.

Onofre urged him to get on with the job at hand. "It will soon be daybreak, and I am supposed to be far away by then. I entrust to you the task of taking the contract to the notary and having it stamped," he told his father-in-law. "The care and safekeeping of my family I entrust to both of you," he added in a neutral tone, which did not prevent Don Humbert from bursting into tears again. At last the document was signed by both parties, and by Don Humbert and the butler as witnesses. When that was done, Efrén took Onofre to Sabadell.

The automobile was now gliding through the empty streets. It was getting light, but the lamplighters had not dared to come out, so the streetlamps were still lit, as if it were the middle of the night. They saw only a little boy loaded down with newspapers. He had been ordered to deliver them as usual, so the nation would be informed of what had happened in Madrid a few hours ago. The military had acclaimed Primo de Rivera, the government had presented its resignation to the king, and the king had charged Primo de Rivera with the task of forming the new Cabinet. On the front page was the list of generals making up the Cabinet and the announcement that all constitutional guarantees had been temporarily suspended. Most of the remaining pages of the newspaper were censored.

At the airport they had to wait a while before the pilot showed up. He was upset: between the hotel where he had spent the night and the airport, he had been stopped eight times by as many different patrols. Finally the Civil Guard had escorted him to the plane. "*Parbleu, on aime pas les belges ici,*" he exclaimed irritably when he saw Onofre. Onofre told him he wished to return to Paris with him, which was much to the pilot's liking, since he had not been looking forward to making the journey back alone. Efrén and Onofre embraced each other, and Onofre climbed into the aircraft, which took off without further ado.

They had been flying for half an hour when Onofre told the pilot to bear a little to the left. That was not the way to Paris, the pilot said. "I know," Onofre replied, "but we are not going to Paris. Do as I say, and I'll pay you double."

That argument convinced the pilot. The plane now circled a mist-filled valley in the mountains. As they descended, Onofre gave the pilot instructions: "Watch out, there are some very tall holm oaks on that slope. More over that way—let's see if we can follow that river," etc. Eventually they spotted, between the banks of mist, a recently used threshing floor. When the plane touched down, a flock of blackbirds who had been pecking at the sheaves took flight. These birds were so numerous, they blocked the sun for a moment. Onofre handed the pilot an IOU that could be cashed at any French bank, jumped to the ground, and from there gave the pilot directions to get back on course. Without stopping the engine, the pilot turned his machine around, accelerated along the threshing floor, and took off, leaving a whirlwind of dust and bits of straw in his wake.

An hour later, Onofre approached the door of the house in which he had been born. A farmer was living there now with his wife and their eight children. In answer to his inquiries, Onofre was told that the mayor lived in a new house next to the church. He thought he recognized the farmer and his wife, but they did not recognize him.

3

His knock was answered by a woman about thirty years old, her face intelligent, coarse but not unattractive. A kerchief on her head kept the dust off, and in her left hand was the duster she had been using. Had his brother got married without telling him? The woman's look was more wondering than guarded. "That means he hasn't told her about me," he thought. Out loud he said, "I am Onofre Bouvila." The woman blinked. "Joan's brother," he added. "Señor Joan is asleep," the woman told him, "but I will let him know that you are here." It was clear from her tone that she was not Joan's wife. "His mistress, perhaps," Onofre thought. "She doesn't look like an unmarried woman, either. Possibly a young widow." Since she had left him standing at the door, he went into the hall. Over the archway was a glazed tile in a frame with the words "Ave Maria." The hall had a dusty smell, owing, no doubt, to the woman's housework. A lamp, a wrought-iron umbrella stand, and four straight-backed chairs were its only furnishings. Four doors opened off the hall, two on either side. The woman knocked on one of them, saying, "Señor Joan, your brother is here." She spoke quietly, though not in an attempt to avoid being overheard. A voice replied from inside the room. The woman listened attentively, her ear to the door, then turned to Onofre: "He says he's getting up, and would you kindly wait for him." A slight motion of her duster indicated the dining room, visible at the far end of the hall.

In the dining room was a square table on which stood a ground-glass lamp. The chairs were lined up along the walls. There was also a dark sideboard, a side table with a white marble top, and a salamander stove. This last item was made of iron, but it had glazed pottery sections that lent an air of prosperity to the dining room. Hanging on the wall over the side table was a picture of the Last Supper carved out of wood. Opposite the archway a double glass door led to a rectangular patio, with a small privy at the end. A magnolia and an azalea were growing on the patio. The kitchen was to the right. Everything had a clean look, neat and cold. As Onofre was taking all this in, the church bell rang, so close that he jumped. The woman, who had been watching him from the hall, stifled a snigger.

"I suppose it's just a matter of getting used to it," he said. She shrugged. "Do you live in this house?" he asked. She gestured to one of the doors. It was not the door at which she had just knocked, but that proved nothing.

At that moment his brother appeared in the hall. Shoeless and wearing a worn pair of cord trousers and a loose-fitting navy-blue shirt only half buttoned, he scratched his head with both hands and passed through the dining room without saying anything, as if he hadn't seen either his brother or the woman. He went out onto the patio and shut himself in the privy. The woman meanwhile went to the kitchen to fill a metal bucket with water from the tap. Even though Onofre had recently spent the night in one of Paris's most elegant hotels, seeing running water in his village gave him a sense of material well-being. When the bucket was full, the woman took it by the handle and carried it into the hall. Then she went back to the kitchen and began lighting the fire with sticks, coal, matches, and a straw fan. "How slow everything is here," Onofre thought. In half the time he had spent in this house already, he could have transacted several business deals. "Yet time here has no value." His brother emerged from the privy, doing up his fly. He washed his hands and face in the bucket of water, then took the bucket and emptied it in the privy. He came back into the dining room, while the woman went to the patio to get the bucket.

"Did you come by car?" Joan asked his brother. "By airplane," said Onofre, smiling. Joan looked at him for a moment, lips pursed. "If you say so, it must be true," he said, sighing. "Have you had breakfast?" Onofre shook his head. "Nor have I," said Joan. "As you can see, I just got up. I went to bed late last night." But he did not explain why he had stayed up late. A smell of toast came from the kitchen. The woman brought in a board with a selection of cold meats and a hunting knife stuck in the board. Seeing that food on the table, Onofre felt a painful emptiness in his stomach and realized that he had not eaten for many hours. "Go ahead," Joan told him. "Make yourself at home." Onofre wished this home were indeed his home. After so many years of striving, he had come full circle, he was back at his starting point. From the kitchen the woman brought in a plate full of toast. On an earthenware dish she then brought in a salt cellar, several cloves of garlic to rub on the toast, and a cruet of olive oil to pour on it. Finally she brought in a bottle of red wine and two glasses. The wine loosened Joan's tongue, moving him to a loquacity that was new to Onofre.

When their breakfast was over, it was nearly noon. Onofre could barely keep his eyes open. His brother said he could have one of the bedrooms; although the subject had not come up, they knew that Onofre would be staying for an indefinite period. The room he was given was the one the woman had pointed to before, when he asked her if she lived in the house. He lay turning that over in his mind until he fell asleep. That room contained an old rustic chest of drawers which had belonged to his mother. The sheets smelled of soap.

The days passed, and Onofre lived as the fancy took him: he ate and slept when he felt like it, went for long walks in the country, chatted with people or avoided them, and nobody bothered him. His presence in the village quickly ceased to be a secret. They had all heard of him. They knew he had gone to live in Barcelona years back. It was said that he became a rich man there, but that did not impress the local people. The story of Joan Bouvila the father was known, and if that man went off to Cuba and came back claiming he had a fortune that turned out to be nonexistent, why couldn't the son be up to the same tricks?

Their skepticism was to Onofre's liking, and he cultivated it. Besides, they might be right to think him penniless: Efrén and Don Humbert might well have taken advantage of his absence to strip him of all he had. Don Humbert could have doctored the contract, as he had done at Onofre's instigation years before with the properties of Osorio, the ex-governor of Luzon. "It was Osorio's turn then, now it's mine," he said philosophically. His brother sneered. "A lifetime of toil for this," he said. "Had I been a road sweeper or a beggar," Onofre replied, "I'd have toiled just the same."

Only now was he beginning to see the true brutality of the world in which he had moved with such confidence and ease. The cynicism of his youth was replaced by the grim pessimism of maturity.

"You were always an idiot," his brother said. "Now at last I can tell you that to your face."

Onofre remained indifferent to such remarks. He took interest only in unimportant things: a stove going out in a corner of the room, a cloud crossing the rectangular patch of sky framed by the patio, the sound of steps out in the street, the smell of burned wood, the distant barking of a dog. But sometimes his stoicism gave way suddenly to indignation: he would then revile his brother. These outbursts did not disturb Joan: in an alcoholic stupor, he was lucid only two or three hours of the day, at which time he did his municipal business at the town hall astutely and dishonestly. The villagers had resigned themselves to this state of affairs: concluding that it was progress, they did their best to keep well clear of it.

Joan Bouvila had never tried to make anything of his position other than a way of living without working, but even in such a small place, political realities eventually forced him beyond that modest aim: he now found himself at the head of the pillars of the community. These pillars were more numerous than Onofre at first thought: the rector, the doctor, the veterinarian, the pharmacist, the schoolmaster, and the owners of the local store and tavern. Since Onofre had left it, the village had grown considerably. These leading lights, each in his own way, now attempted to win Onofre's confidence. They bowed and scraped despite his clear contempt for them. A night did not pass without a visit from one of these small-time villains. This was a source of great aggravation for the rector, a young little priest—dull, greedy, and hypocritical—who had railed from the pulpit against the woman living with Joan. Now, because of the presence of Onofre in the same house, he found himself obliged not only to go along with all the rest, but also to be always on his best behavior. Onofre and his brother enjoyed discomfiting the rector.

"Look, Father," Onofre would say, "I've read through the Gospels many a time, and nowhere did I see it written that Jesus Christ had to work for his living—what kind of teaching is that?" Assaulted by such blasphemy, the little priest would bite his lip, lower his eyes, and plan a merciless revenge. Onofre, who could read the man's thoughts with no difficulty at all, could barely keep from bursting into laughter.

The pharmacist and the veterinarian were keen on hunting, and between them they had several greyhounds, other pedigreed dogs, and half a dozen shotguns. Sometimes they invited Onofre

346

and Joan to join them on their outings. Since Joan was almost always under the influence, being in his company with a shotgun was dangerous indeed.

As for the owner of the village store, he received a few newspapers every week, brought to him in the van that now covered the route between the village and Bassora. Through them Onofre followed the course of the political events that had led to his exile. The papers, obtaining their information secondhand, from other papers, gave out-of-date and often false news. This apparently did not trouble their readers. Besides, politics took the back seat in these papers, which headlined local events and the weather.

Such an inversion of values irritated Onofre. After a while, however, he began to find sense in it. Did he not hold futile now everything that before had seemed so important to him? He would meditate thus in moments of peace and quiet, when he managed to avoid the fawning parasites who besieged him. He resorted to the hiding places of his childhood. Some of those spots no longer existed; some might still be there, but he could not find them; and some were inaccessible to a man of his age. Those that he did visit were small and wretched; it had been his child's imagination that had turned them into places full of danger and wonder. This depressed him.

Only the stream preserved the enchantment it had in his memory. He had gone there almost every day with his father after the latter's return from Cuba. Now, too, a day never went by that Onofre did not sit on a stone there and watch the water run and the trout leap, and listen to those clear sounds that seemed always on the point of becoming words.

The smell of the country also went to his head. In the city, smells, like people, were individual, aggressive; smells would compete—the stink of a factory, a lady's perfume, and so on. But here all smells blended to form one, with which the air was imbued: here breathing and smelling were the same thing.

The path to the stream was already covered with dry leaves,

and multicolored mushrooms grew around the tree trunks: it was autumn.

These impressions of nature raised vague memories in Onofre, images that darted across his mind like shadows of birds in flight. He had a recurrent daydream: the hand of his mother or his father trying to guide him toward a brighter, safer spot. But the hand never quite reached his.

In one of the drawers of the chest in his room he found a piece of coarse wool that his mother had used as a shawl. The wool, hard and rough to the touch, smelled of damp and dust. Sometimes Onofre took the shawl out and spread it over his knees. He would sit like that for hours, absentmindedly stroking the shawl.

One day, on his way back from the stream, Onofre saw a man sitting with his back against a tree trunk. The man seemed to be asleep, his head drooping over his chest, but there was something wrong about his posture that made Onofre leave the path and go up to him. From the cassock it was plain that this was the rector. Onofre knew before he reached him that the little priest was dead. A closer examination revealed that his death was not due to natural causes: somebody had shot him in the chest with a shotgun. Around the wound the cassock was stiff with coagulated blood. There was also blood on the right hand, the forehead, and the cheek, although no wounds were there; after being hit, he had probably lifted his hand to his chest and then to his face—then died.

Although Onofre was by no means unaccustomed to violence, chancing upon the crime upset him greatly. That it was he who discovered the body he took as a bad omen, or else a plot trying to connect him with the murder. In any case, the inner peace he had found in the village was irremediably broken.

He ran to his brother's house. His brother was sitting in the dining room drinking wine, while the woman was preparing supper in the kitchen. When he got his breath back and told his brother what had happened, Onofre observed that the woman was leaning against the jamb of the kitchen door, listening attentively. And there was an exchange of glances between her and his brother that did not escape Onofre's notice.

Since the day of his arrival, he had spoken to the woman on a number of occasions and had learned without surprise that it was she who ran the house. Almost every night, after she put Joan to bed, his drunkenness rarely allowing him to reach the hour of midnight conscious, the two of them, Onofre and the woman, would sit in the dining room or, if the night was warm and not too humid, out on the patio, which in the evening was redolent of azaleas, and converse, sometimes well into the night. The woman was no intellectual, but had the feminine faculty of knowing things that men, however hard they might try, could not grasp. She saw through appearances to the raw reality, and now passed this on to Onofre. He learned, thanks to her, that underneath the harmony prevailing in the village seethed base passions and age-old hatreds, envy, treachery. The peasants in the valley were cold, emotionless beings who would let their old parents starve, kill their children, and torture their pets just for the pleasure of it. He found all this difficult to believe, attributing it to the general resentment he could observe in her; nor did he rule out the possibility that such grim gossip was part of a deliberate plan she had.

In any event, what she told him only added to his uneasiness. Sometimes, following his brother's example, he sought in the bottle the repose that his mind seemed stubbornly to deny his body. On one such occasion he awoke in his bed at cockcrow and found to his horror that the woman was sleeping peacefully at his side. He could not remember what had happened the previous night. When he woke her and asked, she made a face but did not answer. He told her to leave, then spent a while turning this development over in his mind. Had he made advances? Or had he been tricked? He couldn't help admiring the woman's courage, and was beginning to feel an attraction to her, which was much more worrisome than a moment of indiscretion caused by alcohol. There was nothing remotely spontaneous in the woman's behavior, nothing innocent: she knew full well where she stood in that house and how it was all viewed down in the village. Yet she was not a scheming, calculating person, either: she merely made the best of the few advantages she had, playing her cards with the coolness of the professional gambler who knows that his survival depends on chance as much as skill.

Onofre still had not got to the bottom of the relationship between the woman and his brother. She was a widow whose need had impelled her to enter Joan's service, but the rest was shrouded in mystery. His brother's alcoholism seemed to rule out the carnal element in the relationship. Yet, if that were so, why perpetuate, for all the village to see, the damaging appearance of cohabitation? "Unless she's patiently waiting for the chance to snare him," Onofre thought. "She knows he'll fall for it sooner or later, and then she'll be the mayoress and get her revenge for all these years of humiliation. Ah, we poor people have only two alternatives: honesty and the pain of humiliation, or wickedness and the pain of guilt." Such were the thoughts of the richest man in Spain.

Later Onofre found out that the woman's husband had also met a violent end. But, however much he pressed her, she would not go into the details of that matter. The revelation set off all kinds of conjecture in his mind. Perhaps she was not altogether above suspicion in her husband's death, even though she did not seem to have gained anything from it in material terms. Or perhaps his own brother had been involved in the crime and was now indissolubly bound by it to that woman.

After the incident of waking up and finding her next to him, Onofre became more uncomfortable than ever in that house. He told himself that she, by sleeping with him, was only seeking to force his brother into resolving the ambiguity of their relationship. But this logical explanation did not still Onofre's growing fear that he was the victim of some plot.

Now the glances exchanged between Joan and the woman after hearing of the rector's murder seemed to have a strange significance. When Onofre pointed out to his brother that the rector's death from a shotgun wound limited the list of suspects to the pharmacist and the veterinarian, the only ones who had firearm licenses, Joan laughed: there was no house in the valley that did not hold a small arsenal of illegal weapons. This observation worried Onofre: now tongues would wag, and he might be implicated. His baiting of the rector was common knowledge; their arguments had never been serious in nature, merely a pastime on his part, but the gossips could easily exaggerate their significance, and a mutual hatred could be assumed. Moreover, any suspicion falling on him would be supported by the notorious ill-will that had existed between the rector and the woman: this possible ramification of the case established another link between Onofre and her.

Onofre was not in fact worried about being accused of a crime he had not committed: he had dodged too many accusations of crimes he did commit to lose sleep over the death of a little country priest. What bothered him was the thought that this crime would not have happened had he not been there, that it was he who had given the criminal the idea of framing him. In his search for peace Onofre had brought discord and violence to the valley; he had poisoned the atmosphere. He could not escape his destiny: having started out along the road of evil, he had no choice but to follow it to its end.

The next day Onofre left the village in the van that had brought him from Bassora. The rector's body was discovered that morning, but nobody dreamed of making him stay in the village or of questioning his right to leave; to Onofre's way of thinking, that was proof that they all thought he was guilty. His brother bade him farewell as blankly as he had welcomed him; his dull eyes were the eyes of a complete derelict. Nor did the woman show any feeling over Onofre's departure, but her eyes had the dryness that long weeping and the deepest despair produce. "Could it actually be that she loved me, and all the rest was the product of my overwrought imagination?" he wondered as he rode off in the van.

4

When he went back to his house, Onofre found his family in a state of great agitation. They had been looking for him desperately for days. Believing him to be in Paris, they had telephoned the Spanish consulate and embassy there, and all the better hotels, and had even contacted the French authorities. The reason for this surprising solicitude was that a young man of pleasing appearance and very good family had asked for the hand of their younger daughter, who had just turned eighteen. "There they are, fighting over my spoils already," Onofre thought with a sigh. He had expected such fortune hunters. He gave instructions to have the suitor summoned to his study that same afternoon, then withdrew to rest.

The butler woke him to announce a visit from Efrén Castells. The giant burst into the office with a briefcase full of papers: he had come to talk business, a prospect that made Onofre's heart sink.

"It was a good thing you disappeared—they were after your blood all right," said Efrén. For a few days not even he had felt safe. Mysterious automobiles had ridden the streets in the middle of the night. But eventually everything had returned to normal.

The giant opened his briefcase and began pulling out papers. "I came to show you what I've been doing. . . ." Onofre stopped him with a wave of the hand: "There's time enough for that." But Efrén insisted on bringing him up to date; the financial situation in which they both found themselves was peculiar.

"At first they wanted to take it all away from you," said the giant. "Then they saw the contracts we had signed and didn't know what to do. They were furious." Those same men, who would not have thought twice about killing him, had been paralyzed by a handful of legal documents. "They called all their lawyers to a general meeting and spent several days and nights discussing the situation; they could not see where to stick the knife in. Desperate, they asked for my collaboration. I stood firm. We reached an agreement in the end: I continue running your businesses; they, in return, respect my independence. But I need your consent to this agreement; it all hangs on that now." The giant waited.

"I have been retired, haven't I?" said Onofre.

"Looks like it," said Efrén.

At eight o'clock, the suitor turned up, all flustered, in Onofre's study. Looking frail and none too intelligent, he did not appear to be either a thoroughgoing rascal or an honest man. Onofre's approach was cordial; this cordiality, unexpected, confused the suitor. His father had told him, "Whatever happens, don't lose your composure, and if he insults you or says unpleasant things about our family, take no notice." Now, the suitor had no idea what to say or do.

Onofre was adrift, too. Shortly after Efrén had left, his father-in-law had called. Don Humbert gave him the same advice as the giant from Calella. "The best policy is to put up with it patiently. Take it as a well-deserved holiday, devote yourself to family life, domestic pleasures, eating well." Then Onofre's daughter and wife had come in. "Father told me all about it," his wife said. "I'm glad you've decided not to be upset." He detected satisfaction in her voice: if this setback brought him closer to the family, she welcomed it. His daughter went straight to the point. "Be kind to him, Father," she said. "I love him with all my heart. Now my happiness depends entirely on you."

Onofre recalled these words as he looked at the suitor. "He'll be putty in her hands, a lapdog. Perhaps that's what she wants. She's old enough to have figured things out. Very well, then, I'll give my consent, and earn the gratitude of the whole family. Soon the house will be crawling with grandchildren. . . . Perhaps my father-in-law is right and it's time for me to make the most of domestic life," he thought. But out loud he said, "I am categorically opposed to this absurd marriage and forbid you to see my daughter again. If you try to contact her or any other member of this household, family or staff, I'll have my men break every bone in your body. I believe I have made myself clear. The butler will show you out."

This encounter did much to restore Onofre's good spirits; he even found it in himself to say a few kind words to his wife later on. "Don't fret. If they love each other truly and he's worthy of her, he'll ignore my threat. Then I'll arrange a big wedding and see that they never want for anything. But I think we will hear no more of the boy. Believe me, dear, he would never have made the girl happy. There are plenty more where he came from. Come now, that's enough crying, run along and console her. You'll see how quickly she gets over it."

But, apart from such occasional entertainment, family life held no interest for him. He devoted all his time to the mansion, whose reconstruction had been suspended when he left. This tremendous project was finally completed in the middle of December 1924, shortly after his fiftieth birthday. The garden, no longer a jungle, had regained its former harmony. Newly varnished skiffs bobbed on the canal; the curved necks of swans were reflected in the lake's limpid water. Inside the house, doors opened and closed softly, lamps sparkled in the mirrors, freshly painted cherubim and nymphs smiled from the ceilings, carpets muffled one's footsteps, and the shining furniture caught the redundant light that filtered through the curtains.

The time had come to move. Onofre's daughters did not want to leave the city. "Who will come to see us in that godforsaken place?" they said. "As long as I'm rich," he replied, "they'll come. They would come even if we lived in hell." The truth was that his wife and daughters were afraid of being isolated with him, who tyrannized them and seemed to take pleasure in making them suffer. The mansion itself unnerved them. Although the renovation was perfect, there was something disturbing in that perfection, something both pompous and demented in that excessive fidelity to a past that was not their own. Those imitation paintings, vases, clocks, and statuettes, which were neither gifts nor heirlooms, whose presence there was not the result of finds or fancies, and which had no personal history behind their acquisition other than a cold and thoroughgoing will, were all false and oppressive.

Once the noise of the building had died away and the bricklayers, laborers, plasterers, and painters had left, the mansion took on a funereal solemnity. And at dawn it even had a sinister aspect. This pleased Onofre. There he could live as he pleased, neither seeing nor hearing his wife and daughters for weeks on end. He never ventured out for a stroll in the garden, and rarely left the rooms he had set aside for his own exclusive use. He received nobody, and despite his prediction, nobody came to see him.

A few months after the move, his two daughters left home. The younger was the first to go. With the help of her grandfather, Don Humbert, who adored her to such an extent that he was prepared to incur the wrath of his son-in-law, she moved to Paris, where she married a Hungarian pianist who had uncertain prospects and was twice her age. Together they wandered from city to city, hounded by creditors. The older daughter, following her sister's example, joined a congregation of lay missionary women who busied themselves with education and medicine in remote corners of the earth. After several years in the Amazon, near Iquitos, trying the best she could to reconcile the practice of obstetrics with the immoderate consumption of whiskey, she was arrested by the Peruvian authorities. Several government officials had to be bribed, and the victims of her negligence, vice, and ignorance compensated. Thereafter she lived in a peaceful, alcoholic haze in a suite at the Ritz in Madrid, until her death in 1981.

Onofre watched with indifference as his family dissolved. His wife spent the entire day and part of the night in the chapel on the second floor: she had boxes of ice-cold truffles and liqueur-filled chocolates sent up to her there and devoured them compulsively as she lost herself in a labyrinth of novenas, triduums, stations of the cross, adorations, the forty hours, octaves, and vigils.

The house was really deserted; it took on a phantasmal life. Noises would be heard at night in empty rooms, and the next morning cupboards would be in different places and carpets would be rolled up. There was actually nothing supernatural in this: it was the servants expressing their resentment. "Let's drive the mistress crazy once and for all," they said, and in the dark banged saucepans, dragged furniture around, and thumped chairs against walls.

Onofre paid no attention to this; he had taken to going out every night. With his chauffeur and bodyguard he frequented the most infamous dives; fleeing elegance, he sought the company of thugs and whores. He was trying to recapture the Barcelona of his lost youth. But he did not feel at home in the city's wretchedness; he felt only repugnance for those filthy, airless dens, those sweaty, pestilent beds in which he would awaken with a start. The cheap wine, the watered-down champagne, and the cocaine did not agree with him. Often he vomited in the street or in the car on his way home at daybreak. He knew that all the charlatans, smugglers, and whores wanted was his money. When his chauffeur practically carried him out of some brothel, the whores who had welcomed him with euphoria and lust would scowl bitterly, for their pimps took with violence the money he had showered on them, and their greed remained unsatisfied. He knew this, but told himself that he was paying for the right to breathe once more the port air, the smell of saltpeter and oil and the fruit rotting in ships' bilges, as if he still belonged to that world.

One night he woke in a tiny room whose walls were covered with gray wallpaper that had once been orange; dangling from the ceiling, a light bulb flickered. His feet and hands were like ice, and he felt an unpleasant tingling in his ribs. He realized that he was dying. A whore screamed at his side, one whose face he did not remember seeing before. With a great effort he grabbed her wrist: he knew that if she escaped, she would take everything he had on him and not tell anyone. She would leave him there to die. "I'll promise her the world," he thought, but the words stuck in his throat, choking him. "A nice place to die," he thought. "What a scandal it will be. . . . But what am I saying? I don't want to die, here or anywhere else." The whore pulled free, picked up her clothes scattered around the floor, and ran out with them in her arms. "It's the end," he thought, alone. He heard shouts in the hall before he lost consciousness.

But everyone did the right thing. The whore ran and told the chauffeur as soon as she was dressed, and he, fearing he would be held responsible, in turn hurried off and fetched Efrén Castells. When the two men entered the house of ill repute, the women and their pimps had done their best to dress Onofre; but they had not been able to make him take a sip of cognac, even after trying to pry open his mouth with a spoon handle. Efrén rewarded them for their services; even the two night watchmen present received a share; everyone was pleased and swore to keep the thing quiet. It was four in the morning when they got him into bed and notified his wife. She rose to the occasion, behaving in a thoroughly ladylike fashion: accepting impassively the improvised, improbable story Efrén stammered out, she set the entire domestic staff in motion.

In a few hours, the mansion was teeming with people: doctors and nurses were there, as well as lawyers with their

clerks—in case the outcome proved fatal—and stockbrokers, real-
estate agents, tax officials, consuls and trade attachés, gangsters
and politicians trying to be anonymous, journalists and columnists, and a great number of priests ready to administer the appropriate sacraments: confession, Communion, and extreme unction.
This throng now roamed around the garden and the house, in-
vestigated the sheds, poked in cupboards, opened drawers, rooted
through closets, fingered works of art and damaged—accidentally or on purpose—various objects of value. The newspaper
photographers set up their tripods and cameras in the middle of
rooms and put spots in people's eyes with their magnesium flashes.
The servants accepted bribes, divulging real or imaginary family
secrets to the highest bidder. There were impostors, too, passing
themselves off as close associates of the sick man; from these,
inexperienced journalists and businessmen obtained—or, rather,
purchased—incredible lies, which caused prices to fall on various
stock exchanges.

Onofre knew nothing of all this: thanks to the medicines he
had been given, he felt that he was floating in mid-air. There
was no pain, and he did not feel his body at all, only the persistent cold in his hands and feet. "If it wasn't for that, I would feel
great," he thought. Something in this well-being took him back
to his earliest childhood. He lost all sense of time. People came
in and out of the room, doctors examined him, nurses gave him
pills, food, injections, and blood tests, and attended to the natural
functions. The periodic visits from his wife, who spent her brief
moments alone with him weeping at his bedside, the sudden appearance of men who had managed to wangle their way in to
ask some posthumous favor of him, who urged him to make his
peace with the Lord, who asked him for some essential piece of
information concerning a commercial transaction of the utmost
importance, or who wanted to hear from his lips the secret of his
success—all seemed to him fictitious figures, characters sprung
from a children's picture book.

"What does this mean?" he asked himself. "Who are all these people? Why are they here?" Then his mind would transport him dizzily through a limitless space, to the shore of some scene from his past, which he would relive in painful precision. The scene would then fade slowly away, like cigarette smoke in the warm air of a room, and all that would remain was the fear of death. "How can it be that there is absolutely nothing I can do to avoid so horrible a thing?" He felt that his life was about to be extinguished as one turned out a light, with the flick of a switch, and that he would disappear forever, and he burst into tears—but nobody knew this, for his face was fixed as a mask, serene and full of fortitude.

But there were pleasant visions, too. In one of these, he was in a place of diffused light, and saw a man coming toward him, a man he recognized. "Father, it's been such a long time," he said, happy for this reunion. The *americano* smiled. He was exactly as he was the day he returned from Cuba with his drill jacket, his Panama hat, and the monkey in the cage, except that he now had a long and well-kept beard. "And the beard, Father, why the beard?" Onofre asked. The *americano* shrugged, then opened his mouth and moved his lips slowly, but said nothing. Onofre held his breath, expecting his father to reveal something transcendental at any moment. But his father only closed his mouth again and smiled a melancholy smile.

"Perhaps this is what being dead is really like," thought Onofre with a shudder. "There is no change, no pain, but no happiness, either. Death is the absence of everything, the blankness on my father's face. That is why his company, which at first made me glad, now only fills me with sadness. Which indicates that I am not dead," he observed afterward, "or I would not be thinking as I am. But I can't be alive, either, or I would not have had this vision. I must be in an in-between state, with one foot in the grave, as they say in the world I am about to leave. What wouldn't I give to live again! I do not ask to start over: that is impossible, and anyway I'd certainly do everything I did before. No, all I ask is to go on living—I'll settle for that. Oh, if I could live again, I would see everything very differently."

5

"I'm not sure we're doing the right thing, letting you see her," the nun said. "That is, letting her see you."

"Then you know who I am?" he asked.

The nun pursed her lips and looked at him coldly. There was no ill-will in that look—only caution.

"Everyone knows who you are, Señor Bouvila," she said quietly. Her face revealed her character: unselfish, kind, patient, strong, etc. "The poor woman has suffered much. Now, most of the time, she is at peace. Occasionally there are relapses, but they last only a few days. During those relapses she believes she is a queen and a saint."

Onofre nodded. "I am acquainted with her condition," he said. He had actually found out recently. Over the interminable months of his convalescence, over that period in which his life, snatched from the clutches of death, had seemed to hang by a thread, they had kept the truth from him. "Any upset could prove fatal," the doctors said. But they could not keep him from finding out eventually.

One autumn day, when he was turning the pages of an old magazine as he sat with an alpaca blanket over his legs by the bay window in the salon, he saw the report on the wedding. At first its significance was lost on him. A maid took away the magazine—he had dropped it on the floor—and drew the curtains to keep the afternoon sun off his face. When she left, he rested his cheek on the antimacassar, which smelled of fresh basil, and dozed. Any activity tired him, and he slept frequently. This time, however, he woke with a start. Judging by the sunlight on the marble floor, he could not have been asleep long. For some reason, he was uneasy. "Could it have been something I saw in the magazine?" he wondered. He rang the little bell that was always at his side; the maid and the nurse hurried over with looks of concern. "There's nothing the matter with me, for Christ's sake," he snapped at them. "I just want to see that magazine I was reading a while ago." While the maid went off to fetch the magazine, the nurse, a lean, sour-faced woman, took his pulse.

"That's my wife getting her revenge on me with these viragos," he had told Efrén when the latter came to visit him. "What do you want, then," the giant had answered, frowning, "some pretty young thing to give you another attack?" And, looking around to make sure nobody was listening, he had added, "You should have seen yourself when I took you out of that whorehouse."

"Stop checking to see whether I'm alive or dead," Onofre grumbled, wrenching his wrist from the nurse's hand, "and clean my glasses for me with that wad of cotton sticking out of your pocket." His eyes and the nurse's locked defiantly for a moment. "It's come to this," he thought. "Here I am, crossing swords with old maids." He ordered her to draw back the curtains and leave him in peace.

With feverish haste he searched and found the report on the wedding. "I am very happy," the star told the magazine reporter. "James and I will spend most of the year in Scotland. He has a castle there." She met James, an English aristocrat, on a transatlantic cruise. "It was love at first sight," they both said. They had kept their engagement a secret to avoid being hounded by the press. During those few months, he had sent a white orchid to her room every day; it was the first thing she saw when she opened her eyes. The wedding would take place this autumn, in a place they would not reveal. "Then we are going on a long honeymoon to exotic lands," she informed them. "I am very happy," she repeated, and announced that she was retiring from the movies.

"Where is she?" Onofre fired his question at Efrén that afternoon.

"She's as well off as she can be," the giant, upset, assured him. "It's a pleasant place, it doesn't look like an asylum. Don't glare at me that way, Onofre, for God's sake. You would have done the same. What else could we do?" He told him how things had gone from bad to worse after the film studios changed hands. Honesta Labroux would take orders from nobody but Onofre; but he had gone for good. Now a film that before took four or five days to shoot needed whole weeks. The problems grew and grew.

Eventually she tried to kill Zuckermann. One day, when he had been more than usually cruel to her, she took a pistol from her bag and fired at him. The pistol was an old relic—God knows where she got it—and blew up in her hand: it was a miracle she wasn't hurt. After that incident, everyone agreed that she had to be locked up. Onofre nodded darkly. With Honesta Labroux gone, the film industry he had created began to decline. They tried other actresses, but without success. Now just breaking even on a film was difficult, whereas before they had been raking in the profits. Moviegoers preferred films from the United States, films featuring Mary Pickford and Charlie Chaplin. The company decided to close the studios and import foreign films. "Let *them* beat their brains out and risk their money," Efrén said. Onofre drew the alpaca blanket up to his chest and shrugged: it was all the same to him.

"Come," said the nun suddenly. Onofre followed her into a medium-sized room that was simply furnished, clean, and comfortable, but had a distinct whiff of illness and decay. The delicate light of a winter noon was coming through the window; it was cold. Three men of indeterminate age were playing cards around a table underneath which was a stove; two of the men wore berets, and all three had scarves wrapped around their necks.

On another table, which was covered with a blue cloth and pushed against the wall, there was a crèche screen: the mountains were cork, the river tin foil, the vegetation bits of moss, and there were clay figures of odd sizes. Beside the table was an upright piano covered with a tarpaulin.

"The patients made this crèche themselves," the nun said. Hearing that, the three men looked up from their game and smiled at Onofre. "On Christmas Eve, after Midnight Mass, we have a community supper—in other words, their families and close friends can come, too, if they wish."

Onofre noticed that all the windows had bars. They left through a different door, which led into another hallway. At the end of it, the nun stopped.

"Now you will have to wait here a moment," she said. "Men may not enter the women's wing without warning, and vice versa. We can never quite be sure of their state of dress."

The nun left him standing there. He searched his pockets for a cigarette, even though he knew that was a pointless exercise: the doctors had forbidden him to smoke. It occurred to him to go back to the other room and ask the card players for a cigarette. "They'll have something by way of a smoke, and they don't seem dangerous," he thought. As he turned this over in his mind, he looked at his reflection in the hall window. He saw an old man, bent over, pale, wrapped in a black overcoat with an astrakhan collar, and leaning on an ivory-handled cane. His other hand held a soft hat and gloves. A comical figure.

The nun's return ended this distressing contemplation. "You may come in now," she said.

Delfina had aged, too. In addition, she was alarmingly thin, reminding Onofre of the short-tempered chambermaid of years ago. Nobody would have recognized in her the world-famous actress. She was wearing a thick woolen dressing gown over her flannel nightgown, woolen socks, and rabbit-skin slippers. "Look who's come to see you, Señora Delfina," the nun said. Neither these words nor his presence met with any reaction—she was staring at some distant point beyond the wall. There was an uncomfortable silence.

The nun suggested they go for a walk, just the two of them. "It isn't that warm today, but you'll be all right in the sun," she said. "Go out into the garden—the exercise will do you both good." In the nun's eyes a film star could not be much better than a prostitute; if she was willing to let them go out alone, therefore, it must have been that their common decrepitude conferred a new purity on them, Onofre thought as he led Delfina down the hall toward the garden.

This took time. Delfina walked very stiffly and slowly, as if her every movement was the result of a carefully thought-out decision that involved risk. "That's half a step," she seemed to be saying. "Well, now I'll try another half." At this snail's pace, the garden, which was not big, seemed enormous. "Come now, Delfina," Onofre finally said, wearied by her exasperating slowness, "let's sit a while on that bench." But when they sat side by side on the stone bench, the need for conversation became imperative. The trees had lost their leaves, and moss was growing on the asylum wall. He asked her how she was, if she was in pain, if they treated her well, if she needed anything. She made no reply, but went on staring straight ahead imperturbably, apparently unaware of where she was or who was with her. "So much has happened," Onofre said quietly, "and yet nothing has changed. We're both the same, don't you think? Except that life has taken from us the little we had."

A blackbird alighted on the gravel, stayed there a while, then flew away. Onofre went on: "Do you remember when we first met, Delfina? I don't mean the exact moment. It was in 1887, a different century. Just think: Barcelona was a little town, there was no electricity, no streetcars or telephones. It was the time of the World's Fair. Did you know there's talk of having another one? Maybe we should get up to our old tricks again, what do you think? Oh, I was lonely then, a bundle of nerves. In that respect I haven't changed. But I had you then. We never got along very well, but I always knew you were there, and that was enough for me, even though I didn't realize it at the time."

She sat completely still. "A statue of ice," he thought. "She was always a statue of ice, except for the night I held her in my arms." He took her by the hand, and it was cold. "Here," he said, "put on my gloves." He took them off and put them on Delfina; she neither cooperated nor resisted. He was surprised that the gloves fit, but then remembered that she had always had big hands. "With those hands she clutched my shoulders desperately," he thought. "You can keep the gloves," he said.

Looking up, he saw the three men who had been playing cards; they were at the window, watching the couple on the bench. He let go of Delfina's hand. She put that hand on her other hand. "I'm talking like this," he continued, "because I was at death's door. I was afraid. I don't mind telling you that: you were the only person who understood me. You knew why I did what I did. The others don't, not even the ones who hate me. They have their ideologies, their theories to explain everything, to justify everything, success as well as failure. I don't fit in the system. Not that they hold against me the things I've done, or my ambition, or the means I used to climb higher and get rich. Because that is what we all want, and they would have done the same in my circumstances, if they had had the courage. And yet I've lost. I thought that by being evil I would have the world at my feet, but I was wrong: I am evil, but the world is more evil still."

In the spring, he received a letter signed by a nun, perhaps the same nun who had escorted him the day he went to the asylum, which informed him of the death of Delfina. "Death came to her in her sleep," said the letter. He was being notified of this sorrowful event, though he was neither a relative nor a close friend, "given the special affinity between yourself and the

365

deceased." Although she had not spoken since the day he visited her, it was not going too far to say that "she died, so to speak, with your name on her lips." In the deceased's room had been found some sheets written in her hand, probably a letter intended for him, together with "other writings of an intimate and lewd nature that we thought best to destroy."

Delfina's letter went as follows: "The reality surrounding us is only a painted curtain. On the other side of this curtain, there is not another life, it is the same life. The beyond is only that other side of the curtain. When our gaze falls on the curtain, we do not see the other side, which is the same. When we finally understand that reality is nothing more than an optical illusion, we will be able to pass through the painted curtain. When we pass through the painted curtain, we will find ourselves in another world, which is the same as this one. In that other world live those who have died and those who have not yet been born, but we do not see them, because we are separated from them by the painted curtain we mistake for reality. Once one passes through the curtain one way, it is easy to pass through it the other way, too. One can live on this side and on the other side, but not at the same time. The best time for passing through the painted curtain is dusk, and for coming back, dawn. Other methods don't work. It is no use making invocations, no use praying. On the other side, the ridiculous division of matter into three dimensions does not exist, and those who have not yet been born think that the dead are their mothers and fathers."

After this, the handwriting became illegible.

CHAPTER SEVEN

1

Though not as big as the Cullinan or the Excelsior, or as celebrated as the Koh-i-noor (mention of which is made in the Mahabharata) or the Great Mogul (property of the Shah of Persia) or the Orloff (which graces the Russian imperial scepter), the Regent was held to be the most perfect diamond. It came from the legendary mines of Golconda and had belonged to the Duke of Orléans, who pawned it in Berlin during the French Revolution. Recovered from the hands of the pawnbroker, it was set in the hilt of Napoleon Bonaparte's sword.

Onofre Bouvila was holding the Regent in the palm of his hand the night Santiago Belltall came to see him; with a magnifying glass he was admiring its purity and brilliance. Retired from active life on account of the dictatorship of Primo de Rivera, he had decided to invest his fortune—the money Efrén Castells had transferred to Switzerland for him—in the international diamond market. His agents now were forging their way into the mountains of the Deccan and the jungles of Borneo, and haunting the taverns and brothels of Mina Gerais and Kimberley. Without meaning to, Onofre was once again becoming one of the richest men in the world. He could easily have overthrown Primo de Rivera by then, taking his revenge for the wrongs done him, but he felt no inclination to do so: he had always viewed politics with contempt and wanted no part of it.

Ennui had set in. "Time passing just brings me closer to death," he thought as he looked at the diamond. Delfina's death in 1925 was followed by that of his father-in-law, Don Humbert, at the beginning of 1927, and then by that of his brother Joan— in somewhat murky circumstances—at the end of that year. In each of these deaths Onofre sensed a bad omen. Besides, he saw no need to fight a dictatorship that was on its way out anyway. Following Mussolini's example, Primo de Rivera had created a monolithic party called Unión Patriótica. When he founded it, he thought its ranks would be swelled by leading figures of various political persuasions, that in its bosom the cream of the nation would be reconciled. He managed to attract, however, only the hangers-on of the former regime and a handful of young political opportunists. The army eventually disassociated itself from the dictator it had acclaimed only a few years before, and the king himself was desperately casting about for a way to remove him. Plot followed plot, from inside Spain and from without. Primo de Rivera retaliated with imprisonments and deportations, but he was not bloodthirsty and had no desire to kill anybody. Only the opposition's impotence, plus administrative corruption and the people's understandable dread of any change, kept him in power, which he clutched like a man possessed. He had governed not that badly. In a short period of time he had stimulated public spending projects, thereby palliating the mass unemployment and modernizing the country, which had been good for the people.

The favorable balance sheet of his term in office made all the more incomprehensible to him the isolation in which he now found himself. When he saw that he had lost the support of the Crown, he attempted to seek that of Onofre Bouvila; through the Marquis of Ut, still faithful to Onofre, he tried to make overtures of peace, but it was too late.

Santiago Belltall, whose name was to be associated with Onofre forever, was forty-three years old the evening he went to see Onofre. Although his attire was of the poorest quality, he was reasonably presentable, for he had had a bath and a shave that day, and some well-meaning person had given him what could charitably be called a haircut. This sprucing up reinforced his scrounger's appearance; only the sharp eyes in the worn-out face saved him from being wholly ridiculous. When the butler informed him that his master received no one who had not been given an invitation, Santiago Belltall produced from his pocket a crumpled, yellowed visiting card. "Señor Bouvila gave this to me himself," he said. "I think it is equivalent to an invitation." The butler examined the card with a perplexed frown. "When did my master give it to you?" he asked. "Fourteen years ago," was Santiago Belltall's deadpan answer. "If it was an invitation, it would seem you have played rather hard to get," the butler remarked. "What did you say your name was?" Santiago Belltall gave his name—"although I shouldn't think Señor Bouvila will remember me." The butler, somewhat at a loss, scratched his head, but finally decided to inform his master of the presence of this disreputable person; he did not like to disturb his master, but knew of the latter's soft spot for strange characters. In this instance he was right. "Show the man in," Onofre said.

Though it was a warm night, there were logs burning in the study fireplace. Santiago Belltall felt choked by the heat. "I am surprised," he said, a touch of flattery in his voice, "that an important man like you should remember an insignificant man like myself." Onofre smiled disdainfully. "If my memory were as bad as you and other simpletons seem to think, I would not be where I am today." As he said this, he raised his right fist. For a moment Santiago Belltall thought Onofre was going to strike him, but it was not a threatening gesture. "It was fourteen years ago when we met," Santiago Belltall said. "Not fourteen, fifteen," Onofre corrected him, "in nineteen hundred and twelve, in Bassora. Your name is Santiago Belltall, you are an inventor, and you have a daughter called María, a wayward child. What have you come to sell me?"

Santiago Belltall was left tongue-tied: this cool superiority made nonsense of the speech he had been preparing and rehearsing for hours. He blushed. "I see I was wrong to come here," he muttered. "My apologies." But Onofre's sarcastic smile turned his timidity into rage: he jumped to his feet and made for the door. "It's your loss," he shouted.

"What is my loss?" asked Onofre with sardonic calm. The inventor came back and faced the powerful financier: now they were eye to eye, equals. "A wonder," the inventor said. Onofre opened the hand he had kept closed until that moment. Santiago Belltall stared at the facets of the Regent, whose brilliance speckled the damask dressing gown Onofre was wearing. "What wonder can compare with this?" Onofre murmured.

"Flight," the inventor replied immediately.

By the second decade of the twentieth century, aviation had indisputably "come of age." Nobody doubted the ascendancy of these machines, heavier than air, over the other forms of airborne transportation. Not a day passed without some new feat in the headlines. There were still a few problems, however. The least of these problems, strange as it may seem today, was safety: there were not many accidents, and only a small percentage of those that did occur were serious or fatal. Most accidents were due not to mechanical failures but to pilots who showed off their machines and their skill by performing such aerobatics as flying upside down, looping the loop, and going into nose dives. The quick reflexes required of pilots in those early days were such that they were necessarily very young (fifteen was the ideal age for test pilots) and therefore reckless.

Thus we read in a Barcelona newspaper of 1925 the following: "Since in Paris and London those pilots dubbed 'daredevils' by certain sensationalist tabloids rival one another in an exploit that consists in flying under the bridges of the Seine and the Thames respectively, with the predictable spate of dunkings, and since Barcelona, having no river, has no bridges, our pilots, in the teeth of the express prohibition of the municipal authorities, have invented a stunt along similar lines and one even more hazardous: they bank their aircraft to the perpendicular and, as if threading a needle, pass between the towers of the Sagrada Familia."

As they carried out this tour de force, the chronicle goes on, an aged man of starved and shabby appearance could be seen standing at the top of one of those towers shaking his fist, as if attempting to bring down the irreverent aircraft with one swipe as he hurled curses at the pilot.

The protagonist of this dramatic scene (which years later was to inspire a similar scene that has since acquired classic status in the film *King Kong)* was none other than Antonio Gaudí i Cornet, then in the last months of his life. There was something allegorical in that unequal confrontation: the modernism of the famous architect was being challenged by a movement in Catalonia called *noucentisme.* Gaudí's modernism looked to the past, especially the Middle Ages; the new modernism, materialist and skeptical, set its sights on the future. The followers of *noucentisme* jeered at Gaudí and his work, mocking it in caricatures and acerbic articles. The aged genius, embittered, lived alone in the crypt of the Sagrada Familia, which had been turned temporarily into his workshop. Surrounded by colossal statues, rosettes, and scrollwork that could not be fixed in their appointed places because of a lack of funds, he slept in his clothes, which were soon reduced to tatters, and all day breathed that cement-and-plaster-filled air.

In the morning he would do his exercises, hear Mass and go to Communion, eat a handful of hazelnuts with alfalfa or berries for breakfast, and then lose himself in that anachronistic, impossible project.

Whenever anybody came to visit the temple or a group of curiosity seekers passed by, he would leap from the scaffolding with an agility surprising in a man of his years, and with hat in hand beg for money like a tramp, in order to be able to continue his work, even if only for another day or two. For one peseta he would toss a hazelnut into the air and catch it in his mouth after doing a back somersault. His face, burning with enthusiasm, would become transfigured. Sometimes he would have to be dragged from a pit of freshly mixed mortar. In private, among his friends, he was unable to hide his pessimism. "I am at war with progress," he told them, "and fear I am losing." Eventually he was run over by a streetcar at the crossroads of Calle Bailén and the Gran Vía and died in Santa Cruz Hospital.

A more serious problem for the aeronautical engineers was the range of their machines. "What use is flying if it takes you nowhere?" they said. Aircraft were fitted with large fuel tanks, but so large, they weighed down the craft to the point where takeoff became impossible. Fuselages were lightened to compensate for this, until pilots flew literally sitting on tanks of highly flammable fuel. Now they feared burns as much as crashes. The quality of the fuel also improved: oil was refined, and mixtures were produced that increased performance.

These experiments bore fruit: on May 21, 1927, Charles Lindbergh, an American aviator, made a nonstop solo flight from New York to Paris. The possibilities opened up by his feat were limitless. Shortly afterward, on May 9, 1928, an Englishwoman, Lady Bailey, left Croydon in a Havilland Moth fitted with a hundred-horsepower engine. Going by way of Paris, Naples, Malta, Cairo, Khartoum, Tabora, Livingstone, and Bloemfontein, she arrived in Cape Town on April 30; she rested there a while and began her journey back on May 12; after stopping at Bandundo,

Niamey, Gao, Dakar, Casablanca, Malaga, Barcelona, and Paris again, she landed in Croydon, eight months after the beginning of her journey, on January 10, 1929.

In Spain, too, the aeronautics industry was not left behind. The Moroccan war had fueled its development, as the Great War had done for the other countries of Europe. In 1926, Franco, Ruiz de Alda, Durán, and Rada, aboard the *Plus Ultra,* made the trip from Palos de Moguer to Buenos Aires between January 22 and February 10. That same year, Lóriga and Gallarza flew from Madrid to Manila in a sesquiplane between April 5 and May 13, and the *Atlántida,* flown by Llorente, went from Melilla to Spanish Guinea and back in fifteen days, from the 10th to the 25th of December.

Each flight was a step toward a future full of promise, but each step brought new problems: compasses went mad when the planes crossed hemispheres; traditional maps did not meet the requirements of the navigators; altimeters, cathetometers, barometers, anemometers, radiogoniometers, etc., constantly became obsolete, and not only instruments but clothing and food, too, had to be updated. One had to be able to forecast atmospheric changes with precision, for a gale or a dust storm could prove fatal to an aircraft and its crew. A train or an automobile could always stop when taken by surprise meteorologically, and a boat could weather the storm, but a plane hundreds of leagues from the nearest airport and with limited reserves of fuel—what could it do? Engineers racked their brains; they studied the anatomy of certain flying insects, who could land with enviable skill on the tiny surface of a pistil. Landings were difficult, because they could not be made at speeds less than a hundred kilometers per hour. In planes, thrust and lift were not independent of each other. . . .

Onofre listened absently to the confused explanations of the inventor, then pushed the buzzer. When the butler came in answer, he told him to put a few more logs on the fire.

"I see my proposal has not convinced you," Santiago Belltall said when they were alone again. Onofre, wakened from his abstraction, looked at the inventor as if seeing him for the first time. "It doesn't interest me," he said coldly. "Not that the idea does not have merit," he added, seeing the anguish in the inventor's face: the attention he had shown at first had evidently raised the man's hopes. "Sometime in the future I myself may even . . ." he added wearily, but did not bother to finish the sentence.

Over the week following this interview, news of Santiago Belltall reached Onofre's ears on several occasions. The inventor was offering his project to other people; he also approached business firms and government offices. All he had to show for his trouble were words of encouragement and vague promises. "We will study the matter," they told him. Through his men Onofre learned that the two Belltalls, father and daughter, lived in a sublet apartment on Calle Supúlveda. According to the neighbors, neither was quite right in the head, and they hadn't a penny to their name. Onofre decided to wait.

One leaden afternoon, the butler announced a caller; echoes of thunder were rumbling in the distance. "A young lady, sir, and she says she would like a word with you in private." A shiver ran down Onofre's spine. "Show her in, and see to it that I am not disturbed," he said, turning his back on the door as if wishing to hide his agitation. "Wait," he added as the butler went to carry out his orders. "Tell the chauffeur to remain on duty and to have a car ready at all times."

Seeing that no further orders were forthcoming, the butler proceeded to the hall. "Be so good as to come this way," Onofre heard him say. "My master will receive you."

The woman could not avoid a shudder, either. "I know what's going to happen," she thought as she followed the butler. "I hope to God that's all that happens."

Onofre recognized her as soon as he saw her, as if the years between that first, brief meeting and now were only a few minutes. "As if I'd dozed for a moment, and a lifetime went by," he thought. She said, "I am María Belltall." "I know who you are," he said. "It is very warm in this room," he added, to fill the silence. "I always have a fire lit. I was ill a few months ago, and the doctors insist on heat. Have a seat and tell me why you've come."

She hesitated. Since she was wearing a very short skirt, the position she would have had to assume in one of those deep arm-chairs would have been awkward, even ridiculous. At that time, skirt hems, which had lifted off the tops of shoes in 1916 to begin their slow climb up the calf, had reached the knee; there they would call a halt until the sixties. This shortening of the skirt produced panic in the textile industry, the backbone of Catalonia. Their fears proved unfounded, however: although dresses did re-quire less material in the making, the size of feminine wardrobes grew greatly, for women were taking increasingly active roles in public life, in work, in sports, etc. Fashions changed in every-thing: bags, gloves, footwear, hats, and hairdos. Jewelry was little in evidence, and fans were out for the time being. When she crossed her legs, sitting, Onofre could not help noticing her trans-parent stockings.

"I hope you do not think," María Belltall began, "that my father sent me. We are not working as a team, despite what people say. All I know is that he came to see you—to offer you his latest invention, probably. I have only come to tell you this: my father is not the charlatan or idiot you might have taken him for, judging by his appearance. He is a real scientist—self-taught, admittedly, but knowledgeable in his field, a tireless and honest worker, and a man of talent. His inventions are not wild fantasies or crazy schemes. I know that it's one thing to say this and an-other to prove it, and why should you believe me, his daughter? My coming here really was madness. It's just that things are not going well for us. They never have, but now our situation is desperate. We can't pay the rent, we can't make ends meet. I won't pretend: I've come to plead with you. Father is getting old, but that isn't really what's worrying me. I can work, I can provide for both of us. It's time he had a chance, a success, so he doesn't have to face old age feeling his life has been wasted."

As she said this, she got up and paced the carpet. From his armchair Onofre saw between her legs the logs burning on the fire. Finally she sat down again and continued, more calmly. "I have turned to you, because I know you are the only person who can help my father. You are a man who knows how to take risks. The fact that you gave him your card years ago proves that you do not shrink from the unknown or the new. Ever since that day," she added, blushing slightly, "I remembered your gesture. All I ask is that you reconsider. Whatever my father offered you, do not reject it out of hand. Get an expert to examine the plans, consult technicians in the field, ask for their professional opinion, let them say whether it is worthwhile or not."

She broke off suddenly, breathless with anxiety, afraid that he would simply turn her out, but even more afraid that he would now propose a humiliating quid pro quo. She was aware of this risk and had accepted it. What frightened her was the form it might take. Onofre looked hard at her. She remembered his looking at her the same way when she was a child. Then, she had felt ashamed, ashamed of her gawkishness, her ragged clothes, the poverty in which she and her father lived. Meanwhile Onofre was thinking, "I remembered those eyes as being caramel-colored, and now I see that they are gray."

2

A recent legend goes like this. One fine day, in the first few years of this century, the devil whisked a Barcelona financier from his office to the top of Montjuich hill. It was a clear day; the man could see all Barcelona from the port out to the Sierra de Collcerola, and from the river Prat to the Besós. Most of the 13,989,942 square meters constituting the Cerdá scheme had by now been built; the new Ensanche district had reached the edges of the neighboring villages (those villages whose inhabitants in days of yore amused themselves by watching the people of Barcelona crawling like ants in the little streets of their tiny city, squeezed between its walls and in the lugubrious shadow of the Citadel). Smoke from the factories formed a curtain of tulle that drifted in the breeze; through this curtain the emerald-green fields of the Maresme could be glimpsed, the golden beaches, and the calm blue sea dotted with fishing boats. The devil began, "All this shall be yours if you prostrate yourself at my feet and—" But the financier did not let him finish: accustomed to striking quick business deals every day in the chambers of La Lonja, he found this offer advantageous and without hesitation signed on the dotted line.

The financier, whether obtuse, myopic, or deaf, had not grasped clearly what the devil was offering in exchange for his soul. He thought the deal was for the hill itself, the one on which they were standing. No sooner did the vision vanish and he awoke from his dream than he began to think up ways of making money out of that hill. Montjuich was—and is—quite steep, but also an agreeable, leafy place; at the time, orange trees, laurels, and jasmines grew there. When the infamous castle that crowned it was not showering shells, grapeshot, and bombs on the city below for one reason or another, the people of Barcelona would spend time on the hill: its fountains and springs were the setting for family picnics and for maids and soldiers.

After much thought, the financier finally had a brainstorm: "Let's organize a World's Fair up here on Montjuich, a World's Fair as successful and as profitable as the one in 1888." By then the deficit from the last event had just been settled, at great sacrifice, and the city remembered only the celebrations and the splendor. The mayor's reaction was enthusiastic, though a little envious ("What a great idea—why didn't I think of it first?") as the financier outlined his plan. A subsidy was granted forthwith.

Montjuich was fenced off to the public; trees were cut down, springs made canals or blocked off, slopes leveled, and foundations laid for what would be palaces and pavilions.

As on the previous occasion, stumbling blocks appeared. The outbreak of the Great War and, as always, the unresponsiveness of the Madrid government brought work to a halt. On his deathbed, through the intercession of Saint Antonio M.ª Claret, the financier managed to save his soul from the clutches of the wicked one, but the fair did not revive. Twenty years were to pass before the public-spending policy of General Primo de Rivera injected new life into the scheme. Now not only Montjuich but the entire city had to be prepared: many buildings were pulled down, and the streets dug up to lay the underground lines for the Metro, which work resembled the trenches of the war that had originally prevented the fair.

Thousands of workers were involved in the project; there were laborers and bricklayers from all over the peninsula, particularly from the south. They arrived in jam-packed trains at Barcelona's Francia Station, which had recently been extended and refurbished. The city, of course, could not handle this avalanche. Having no accommodations, the immigrants set up house in hovels known as *barracas*. Whole districts of *barracas* sprang up overnight on the outskirts of the city, on the lower slopes of Montjuich, on the banks of the Besós—infamous communities dubbed La Mina, Campo de la Bota, and Pekin.

The most disturbing feature of this *barraca* phenomenon was its air of permanence: the immigrants plainly did not intend to leave. Hanging in the windows of their wretched hovels were curtains made out of scraps of old rags; in front of each *barraca,* whitewashed stones marked out vegetable gardens, and old oil cans were pressed into service as flowerpots for red and white geraniums, parsley, and basil. To remedy the situation, the authorities encouraged—granted subsidies for—the construction of large blocks of "low-cost" apartments. In this housing it was not only the rent that was cheap: the building materials used were of the poorest quality, the cement was mixed with sand or rubble, the beams were sometimes rotten ties discarded by the railroad companies, and the interior walls were made of cardboard.

These apartments formed satellite towns beyond the reach of the city's water, electricity, telephone, and gas lines. Nor were there schools, health facilities, recreation centers, or greenery of any kind. Since public transportation was also unavailable there, the men went to work on bicycles. Barcelona's steep streets exhausted the cyclists, and some even expired when they got to work. (The women and children preferred tricycles, which were safer and more comfortable, though heavier and less practical.) The appliances and plumbing in these "low-cost" homes were so defective that fires and floods were everyday occurrences.

The daily press of the time is an abundant source of illuminating news items, such as the following: "Yesterday evening Pantagruel Criado y Chopo, from Mula in the province of Murcia, a twenty-six-year-old assistant bricklayer currently employed on the site of the World's Fair's German Pavilion, after an argument with his wife and mother-in-law, punched the wall of his kitchen. The wall collapsed and Pantagruel Criado found himself in the bedroom of his neighbors, Juan de la Cruz Marqués y López and Nicéfora García de Marqués, to whom he made ungentlemanly remarks. During the course of the subsequent dispute, all the other walls on that floor were knocked down, and the occupants of the apartments joined in the altercation." Or this headline in 1926: "Child Killed As Upstairs Neighbor Flushes Toilet."

To those living in *barracas* and "low-cost" homes we must add the so-called subtenants. These were people given the use of a room in a regular apartment (always the worst room) by its legal occupants, together with limited bathroom and kitchen privileges, in exchange for the payment of a subrent. In Barcelona, subtenants totaled over a hundred thousand in 1927.

Upon this foundation of misery, bitterness, and humiliation, Barcelona was building the fair that was to astonish the world.

Far from Montjuich, in her chapel blackened by candle smoke, Saint Eulalia looked upon this panorama and thought, "What a city, my God." Indeed, it could hardly be said that Barcelona had been kind to Saint Eulalia. In the fourth century A.D., when she was only twelve, she was first tortured and then burned at the stake for refusing to worship pagan gods. Prudentius tells how, when the saint died, a white dove flew from her mouth, and snow fell and covered her body. For this reason she was for many years the city's patron saint; later that title was passed to Our Lady of Mercy, who still holds it. As if the demotion were not enough, it was later determined that Saint Eulalia, virgin and martyr, to whom Barcelona had supplicated for several centuries, had in fact never existed: she was only a copy, a plagiarism, of another Saint Eulalia, who was born in Mérida in the year 304 and burned along with other Christians during the persecution instigated by Maximian. "The saints are thumbing their noses at us, that's what things have come to," the people of Barcelona said to one another. Finally even the existence of the Saint Eulalia from Mérida—the authentic Saint Eulalia, whose feast we celebrate on December 10—was called into question.

The statue to the false saint now occupied a side chapel in Barcelona Cathedral, and there she meditated on what was taking place around her. "Things can't go on like this," she said to herself one day. "As sure as my name is Eulalia, I must do something." She asked Saint Lucía and Our Lord of Lepanto to cover her absence miraculously, stepped down from her pedestal, went out into the street, and strode purposefully to the town hall, where the mayor received her with mixed feelings. On one hand, he was pleased to be able to count on the support of a saint, but on the other hand he was not sure how her intervention would go down with the people. "Calamity, Darius, awaits thee and thine!" Saint Eulalia scolded. Darius Rumeu i Freixa, the Baron de Viver, had been mayor since 1924. "When I took over, the whole thing was already well under way," he said. "If it had been up to me, the fair would not have been approved."

This mayor was not—and could not have been—an impetuous man like his illustrious predecessor Rius y Taulet: Barcelona was now a huge and complex city. "It's all Primo's fault, with his mania for public spending," he said, "a popular policy for which we all have to foot the bill, whether we like it or not. It's because of him, too, that our city is crawling with immigrants, infested with the dregs from the south." Suddenly remembering that the saint herself came from the south, he hurriedly added, "Don't get me wrong, Eulalia, I don't have anything against southerners. We're all equal in God's eyes. It's just that it breaks my heart to see the wretched conditions in which those hapless creatures live. But what can I do about it?" Saint Eulalia shook her head slowly, sadly. "I don't know," she said at last, "I don't know." She sighed and added, "If only we could get Onofre Bouvila in on this!" But he was not available just then.

"Perhaps I should accompany you, sir," his chauffeur suggested.

Calle Sepúlveda opens onto the Plaza de España, which now had been turned into an awesome crater: work for the World's Fair had begun there, and from it Avenida Reina María Cristina led past half-built palaces and pavilions. In the center of the square, a monumental fountain was being built, with the new Metro station beside it. Many thousands of workers were involved in the construction. Some of them, who had no *barraca* or gloomy "low-cost" apartment to go to, spent the nights on the streets near the square, exposed to the elements, the more fortunate wrapped in a blanket, the less fortunate in newspapers. The children slept huddled up to their parents or brothers and sisters; the sick propped themselves up against the walls of the houses to await whatever relief the new day might bring. Far off, the glow of a bonfire could be seen, and the shadows of those gathered around it. Wisps of smoke hugging the ground brought the smell of food; in a corner a guitar played.

Onofre told the chauffeur to stay by the car. "I'll be all right," he said. He knew that these pariahs were not violent. Wrapped in a black overcoat with a fur collar, a top hat, and kid gloves, he walked calmly down the middle of the street. The people looked on more with surprise than hostility, as if he were part of some show. Finally he stopped outside a house, a plain house devoid of all ornamentation, and rapped repeatedly on the door with the knocker. Holding up a coin for whoever it was that peered through the spyhole had the desired effect; the door was promptly opened.

Once inside, Onofre talked in a whisper with the old lady who let him in. This old lady, laughing noiselessly, had not a single tooth in her head. He started up the stairs while the old lady, bowing gratefully, held an oil lamp to light his way. After the first landing, however, he had to proceed by feel. This did not slow him down or make him lose his sense of direction: he still retained his old night-owl ways.

At last he stopped on a landing and struck a match; by its brief light he made out a number and knocked on a door, which was soon opened by a skinny, unshaven man in a worn dressing gown and dirty, creased pajamas. "I have come to see Don Santiago Belltall," Onofre said. "This is no hour for visiting," the man retorted. He began to shut the door, but Onofre kicked it open, with the end of his stick hit the man in the ribs, and threw him against the china umbrella stand, which fell over and smashed to pieces. "I did not ask for your opinion," Onofre said without raising his voice. "Go and tell Don Santiago Belltall to come out and then remove yourself from my sight." The skinny man struggled to his feet, tying his dressing-gown cord, which had come undone, then without a word disappeared behind a curtain dividing the foyer from the rest of the house. Shortly thereafter Santiago Belltall came through the curtain, apologizing profusely:

"I was not expecting a visitor, and certainly not such an important one. The conditions I live in . . ."

Onofre followed the inventor down a dingy corridor to a small room. All it had for ventilation was a miserable little window looking onto a closed-in yard; the air was close. There were two metal beds, a little table with two chairs, and a lamp; the subtenants, father and daughter, kept their clothes and other belongings in cardboard boxes along the walls. These walls were covered with blueprints the inventor had pinned up. Maria Belltall sat at the table. By the feeble light of the lamp, she was darning a sock, using a wooden darning egg. To keep out the cold and the damp, she had thrown a knitted shawl over her ordinary old-fashioned woolen dress; knitted stockings and felt slippers completed her pitiful attire. The outfit emphasized her slenderness and the pale complexion which makeup had hidden at their meeting a few days previously. Her pallor contrasted with the redness of her nose—the chronic sniffles of all the people of Barcelona. When he entered the room, she looked up from her darning for a moment, then lowered her eyes again; her eyes now had that caramel color he remembered from the distant past.

"Forgive this mess," the inventor said, moving among the furniture and adding, with his nervousness, to the chaos of the room. "If we had known that you intended to honor us so, we would have taken, at least, all this paper off the walls. But I haven't introduced you to my daughter. My daughter, María. María, this gentleman is Don Onofre Bouvila, of whom I spoke. A few days ago I went to his house to make a proposal to which he was kind enough to give his attention."

A glance passed between María and Onofre that would have been enough to arouse anyone's suspicion, but the inventor did not notice. He took his visitor's hat, stick, gloves, and coat, carefully placing them on one of the beds. Then he pulled a crate over to the table, offered Onofre the free chair, and sat on the box, clasping his hands, ready to listen to whatever his visitor had come to tell him.

Onofre, as was his way, got straight to the point. "I have decided to accept your proposal." With a motion of his hand he stopped the expressions of gratitude welling up in the inventor once he got over the initial shock. "By this I simply mean that I consider it a reasonable risk to place at your disposal a sum of money that will enable you to carry out the experiments you described. Naturally, there are conditions. These conditions are precisely the reason for my coming here."

"I am all ears," said the inventor.

If the Baron de Viver, who was a monarchist, received visits from Saint Eulalia, then General Primo de Rivera, who had stopped being a monarchist out of spite, was visited now and then by a crab with a Tyrolean hat. Deserted by all, but loath to part with his power, the dictator now pinned his hopes on the Barcelona World's Fair. "When I took over here, Spain was an overgrown bear garden, a country of terrorists and scroungers. In just a few years I transformed it into a prosperous, respectable nation; there are jobs and there is peace, and this will be abundantly evident at the World's Fair. Then those who today criticize me will have their fill of humble pie."

The minister of development ventured an observation: "This project of Your Excellency's, magnificent though it is, unfortunately demands an expenditure that is beyond our means." This was true: the national economy had suffered a dreadful decline over the previous few years; reserves were exhausted, and the peseta's exchange rate in foreign markets was laughable.

The dictator scratched his nose. "The devil take it," he muttered. "I thought the Catalans would pay for the fair. A race of misers!" He gritted his teeth.

With exquisite tact the minister of development pointed out to him that the Catalans, quite apart from any virtues or defects they might have, did not want to spend another peseta for the greater glory of a man who abused them at every turn. "What if we deport the hostile elements?" asked Primo de Rivera. "There are several million of them, General," said the minister for internal affairs. The minister of development was well pleased that it was a Cabinet colleague and not he who said this. Primo de Rivera thumped the table with both fists. "The whole Cabinet can go jump in the lake!"

But he was not really angry, for he had just had a bright idea to save the day. "All right," he said, "here is what we'll do: we'll subsidize another World's Fair in another Spanish city: Burgos, Pamplona, it doesn't matter." Seeing the ministers' stunned faces, he gave them a cunning smile and added: "We won't have to spend much on that. When the Catalans get wind of it, they'll run to their banks and spend like crazy to make sure the Barcelona Fair is the better of the two." The ministers had to agree it was a good idea. Only the minister of agriculture dared to raise an objection: "Somebody will tell." "And that man shall be deported, so help me!" roared the dictator.

Work on the Barcelona World's Fair was now proceeding at full tilt, and once more debt was gnawing away at the municipal patrimony. Montjuich was the open wound in the city's economy. The mayor and others not properly enthusiastic about the idea, all those who opposed that squandering of resources, were pushed aside to make way for men faithful to Primo de Rivera. Among this latter group were speculators who took advantage of the confusion to feather their own nests. Newspapers could publish only praise of what was being done; if they criticized, the issues were confiscated and the editors fined.

Montjuich was transformed into a magic mountain. Already standing were the Palaces of Electricity and Magnetism, Textiles, Industrial Arts, Film, Graphics, Construction, Labor, Communications, etc. Designed several decades before, these buildings now appeared unsightly, affected, and in poor taste. Beside them, in contrast, the foreign pavilions sprang up; they had been designed recently and represented the latest trends in architecture and aesthetics. "If other fairs have been devoted to one theme, such as Industry or Transportation, this present one could well be dedicated in its entirety to Vulgarity," wrote a journalist in 1927, shortly before he was exiled to Gomera. "Quite apart from the question of our financial ruin, we will be displaying ourselves before the world as a bunch of Neanderthals," he concluded. These discordant voices, however, did not shake the fair's promoters in their resolve.

While these events were taking place in connection with the World's Fair, Onofre Bouvila, on a hill separated by the whole city from Montjuich, was soliloquizing in the garden of his mansion. "What? Me, in love? At my age? No, it's impossible. . . . And yet, yes, it is possible. Yet who would have guessed!" He smiled, but then his smile disappeared and a frown took its place. "Why do I find that insignificant woman irresistible? Physically she is not unattractive, but she is no beauty, either. And even if she were, why should I fall for her like this? I never lacked for beautiful women, women who could bring traffic screeching to a halt when they crossed the street. Of beauty for sale, I bought the best. Yet, when it comes down to it, I never felt anything but contempt for them. This one, on the other hand, makes me feel humble. When she speaks to me, smiles at me, or just looks at me, I feel grateful."

Perhaps, he reflected, this humility would redeem him. "I can't deny that on occasion I have behaved in a manner less than orthodox, that there are pages in my life history for which I will be called to account. Though I never killed with my own hands, people have died because of me. And others were made unhappy. How terrible to think of all this now when it is too late to be forgiven!" As the full enormity of his sins was brought home to him, he fell to the ground as if struck by lightning.

There was no breeze. The sun, gleaming on the still surface of the lake, made the swans dazzling white. In Onofre's troubled mind they were emissaries from the Supreme Being delivering a message of mercy and hope. "There shall be more rejoicing in heaven over one sinner who repents than over ninety-nine who have no need of repentance," they seemed to be reminding him. Deeply moved, he buried his head in the grass and mumbled, "Forgive me, forgive me." Before the eye of his conscience, as if from the turning pages of a photograph album, accusing faces filed past: Odón Mostaza; Don Alexandre Canals i Formiga and his son, the poor Nicolau Canals i Rataplán; Joan Sicart and Arnau Puncella; General Osorio the ex-governor of Luzon, and his wife and daughters, too; Delfina and Señor Braulio; Onofre's father and mother, and even his brother, Joan. All these and many others, whose faces he had never seen and never would see, he had sacrificed to his ambition and his thirst for vengeance; they suffered so that he could enjoy the momentary, bittersweet taste of victory. "How can heaven forgive the monster I have been all these years?" he thought, feeling tears well up behind his tightly closed eyelids.

Suddenly he felt a tap on his shoulder. Knowing he was alone in the garden, he dared not open his eyes; it might be an angel, an angel with a sword of fire. When finally he looked, he saw that the tap had come from a swan's beak. Puzzled by the presence of the unknown creature that lay huddled near the lake, the swan had come up on the grass and approached him, perhaps delegated by the others, to investigate.

Onofre sat up suddenly, and the swan took fright and beat a hasty retreat. Seen from behind, its waddling was ludicrous; its squawking made an ugly sound. Indignant at having cringed before such an inelegant animal, he caught up with it before it could reach the safety of the lake and gave it a mighty kick. The bird described a parabola in the air and fell headfirst into the water, where it remained, its tail sticking up, as the water gradually stilled and the white feathers the swan had lost on the way settled on the surface.

Onofre shook the blades of grass from his clothes and resumed his walk. He left the pleasant, tidy lawns and entered the woods. Reaching the edge of the woods, he stopped to observe the activity going on not far away. There was a circus tent, with people dressed like mechanics going in and coming out all the time. At the mouth of the canvas tunnel that served as the entrance to the big top, to which remnants of streamers and pennants were still attached, stood two armed guards. Onofre knew that beyond the tent, though hidden by it, were sheds housing special generators that supplied energy to the electrical equipment that was buzzing and screeching inside the tent. Naturally it would have been simpler and much less costly to have obtained that energy from the electric company, but this would have made it impossible to keep the operation secret. The generators were purchased in various countries through dummy corporations created for the purpose, smuggled into Catalonia, and surreptitiously brought here part by part and assembled. Similarly, the coal that fed them had been delivered in small consignments and was now stored in depots buried under the lawns, the woods, and the lake. The complex machinery necessary for the project had also been assembled secretly.

Hiring the staff now working there had been a trickier matter. Whereas the flood of immigrants allowed laborers to be recruited with complete discretion, the disappearance of specialists, technicians, and engineers from their posts and the public eye was much more difficult to explain. That problem had to be solved on an individual basis, case by case. Some were hired abroad. Some, in Spain, were brought out of a retirement into which various circumstances had forced them. Some were sent false offers from American universities; those accepting received shortly afterward first-class tickets for a liner across the Atlantic; when the ship left Spanish territorial waters, these important engineers were brought out of their cabins at gunpoint and forced into a speedboat that took them back to land. There they were driven to the mansion, where the reason for the kidnapping was explained to them as well as the nature of the work they were being asked to undertake—and for which they would be royally paid. The happy ending to their adventure delighted them all.

This recruitment method, however, was slow, complicated, and expensive. The only bargain, among the expenses for the project, was the tent, whose size was just right for the job; they bought it from a circus whose members had been decimated in the south of Italy by an outbreak of cholera. The only survivors—a bearded woman, a lady horseback rider, and a strong man—were obliged to disband the troupe and sell their equipment as best they could. Now these three characters, who had had to be hired and brought along to show how to erect the tent, were wandering around the mansion in their tights, tutus, and sequins, practicing their skills to the surprise if not alarm of those around them.

Onofre was recalling all this when he saw María coming out of the tent. She wore a free-flowing pink skirt so short that it did not cover her knees; the folds of the cloth, moreover, showed the outline of her thighs as she walked. This drew the stares of the mechanics. "I must have a word with her about that," Onofre thought, fuming as he looked at the mechanics and then back at her. Squinting in the sunlight, she stopped for a moment at the opening of the tent, then pushed her hair in place with her fingers and put on a broad-brimmed hat. Then, for no apparent reason, she began walking toward the woods in his direction. "She mustn't see me," he thought, concealing himself completely behind a holm oak.

During the months in which María Belltall and her father had been living in the mansion, Onofre had exchanged only two or three words with her—that everyone should know that his sole interest was the father's project. Indeed, he had endless discussions with the inventor, whose instructions directed the growth of this strange industrial complex. Santiago Belltall and his daughter lived in one of the hunting lodges built long ago in the garden and which was entirely separate from the house. Their quarters were comfortable but not luxurious, since that would have made all too plain Onofre's true motive, the real reason behind his embarking on yet another wild venture at his age. He never set foot in that house—whose furniture and decor he had chosen in every detail—since the Belltalls moved in; a messenger would summon the inventor to the library when it was time for one of their meetings.

The secret nature of the project meant that nobody involved could leave the estate, so Onofre knew that she was always there, that, although she did not yet belong to him, she did not belong to anyone else, either. The two of them were living side by side on his property. This sufficed him for the time being. He spied, as he was doing now, on all her movements.

"Strange," he thought as he crouched behind the holm oak, admiring her graceful walk, her slimness, her poise. "When I was young, with a lifetime ahead of me, everything seemed urgent. Yet now, when time is running out, I am never in a hurry. I have learned to wait. I find meaning only in the waiting. Now, however, things are coming to a head."

Onofre recalled visiting the World's Fair site the day before. His visit had coincided with that of the Marquis of Ut, whom he had not seen for a long time. The marquis, on the World's Fair board of directors, was Primo de Rivera's right-hand man there. It was he who received instructions from Madrid and carried them out behind the mayor's back. In exchange for this loyalty, he enjoyed absolute impunity for the shady deals he pulled off on the side.

When the marquis saw Onofre, he frowned: the friendship that had once existed between the two had turned into resentment and mutual mistrust. Both, however, kept up appearances in public.

"Well, well, you're looking fine," exclaimed the marquis, embracing Onofre. "I heard you went through a bad spell, but I'm pleased to see you completely recovered. And as young as ever!"

"You don't look so bad yourself," said Onofre.

"If you only knew, if you only knew . . ." said the marquis.

They walked arm in arm, picking their way between ditches and piles of rubble, crossing excavations over planks that sagged. The marquis pointed out the palaces, pavilions, restaurants, toilets, etc. With pride he directed Onofre's attention to the Stadium site. This building, a later addition, covered 46,225 square meters and would be used for sports events.

Ever since fascism caught on in Europe, all governments were encouraging participation in sports and attendance at sports competitions. They were emulating the Roman Empire. Now it was victory in sport that marked the greatness of a nation. Sport was no longer solely for gentlemen of leisure or a privilege of the rich; it was the best form of recreation for city dwellers. Politicians and thinkers hoped, in this way, to improve racial characteristics. "The athlete is the idol of our time," said the marquis. Onofre could not deny it.

Then they visited the Greek theater, the Pueblo Español, and the extraordinarily intricate maze of tubes, cables, dynamos, and nozzles that were to feed and set in motion the illuminated fountain. This fountain would be the main attraction, the most spectacular and most commented-upon thing of the fair, as the magic fountain had been in the previous fair. It was situated on the hillside in such a way as to be visible from any point in the fairgrounds; it had a basin fifty meters across holding thirty-two hundred liters of water, and several jets that would handle three thousand liters propelled by five 1,175-horsepower pumps and illuminated by thirteen hundred kilowatts of electricity, enabling the whole to change constantly in shape and color. This fountain and the smaller fountains lining both sides of the fair's central boulevard would use in two hours as much water as that used by the whole of Barcelona in one day. "Tell me, when and where was such a marvel ever seen before?" the marquis asked. Onofre had to admit that it was marvelous. So much agreement awakened the marquis's suspicions. "What did the old fox really come for?" he wondered. "Why is he suddenly so agreeable?"

The Marquis of Ut had no way of knowing that, two weeks before, a strange delegation had shown up in one of the coordinating offices: a lady and a gentleman, elegantly dressed, circumspect, and speaking with a foreign accent, told the official that they represented an international manufacturing corporation. The official had never heard of its name but could not doubt its authenticity after seeing the documents they produced without waiting to be asked. He was surprised, however, to note that protruding from the veil covering the lady's face was a bushy beard. Naturally he refrained from making any comment on this. The gentleman, meanwhile, who hardly opened his mouth, watched the official with an unsettling ferocity. The official later recalled that the man had an unusually robust build. But these details caused no suspicions in the official: since he had been appointed to that post, he had dealt with a great many foreigners, and was accustomed to strange countenances and behavior.

The official asked if he could be of service. They replied that they wished to obtain the necessary permits to install a pavilion at the World's Fair. "Our company intends to display its machinery and products," said the lady. "There will also be wooden panels or sliding doors with a chart showing the company's organization," she added. The official told her that foreign companies could participate only through the pavilions of their respective countries. "If we were to let one company in," he said, "we would have to let others in, whoever applied. Organizing a World's Fair is a complex business, a huge undertaking, and we cannot make such exceptions." And he pointed to a book on the table, the catalogue of exhibitors, which had 984 pages. The gentleman picked up the book and tore it in half with no apparent effort. "I am sure we will be able to smooth out all the difficulties," said the bearded lady, opening and closing her black handbag. The official, seeing that it was stuffed with banknotes, realized it would be a good idea to keep his mouth shut.

The pavilion of this unknown company was now rising on a spot initially allotted to the Missionaries' Pavilion, which was moved to another spot. The new pavilion, taking on the shape of a circus tent as work progressed, was situated in the Plaza del Universo, right next to Avenida Rius y Taulet. This was an excellent location, allowing access to the back door of the pavilion from an empty lot (which is today Calle de Lérida) in total secrecy. A few sinister-looking characters were always standing around in the vicinity of the pavilion to ensure that nobody came too close; their appearance discouraged not only curious passersby but also the fair's supervisors from carrying out their duties. But none of this was known to the Marquis of Ut, or else he simply failed to connect it with Onofre Bouvila and his visit to the fair.

Now the latter, concealed behind a holm oak, thought: "Yes, everything will work out as I have planned. Nothing can go wrong. She is too beautiful, and I am too clever and powerful. Ah, how she moves, what a bearing! One glance is all you need to see she was born to be a queen. Yes, it will work like a dream—it must." And he looked superstitiously at the sky: despite his optimism, he thought he could detect in that blue, cloudless vault a sarcastic comment on the folly of his expectations.

Indeed, doom was in the air. By January 1929 the deficit caused by the Barcelona World's Fair had reached 140 million pesetas; the Baron de Viver saw a bottomless pit yawning at his feet. "This situation calls for drastic measures," he exclaimed. He doused his office with gasoline and was preparing to strike a match, when the doors were thrown open and in burst Saint Eulalia, Saint Agnes, Saint Margaret, and Saint Catherine. This time all four had come, stepping down from a romanesque altarpiece that can still be seen in the diocesan museum at Solsona. All four had met violent deaths and knew about these things: they took the match from the distraught mayor and made him see reason, knocking out of his head the foolish ideas he had entertained in his despair. In addition to contemplating suicide, he had considered starting a riot. "Primo de Rivera's days are numbered," they told him, and reminded him of the fable of the toad that went on puffing itself up until it burst. "Besides, there's one thing about riots: we know how they begin, but we never know how they'll end," said Saint Margaret, whose feast day is celebrated on July 20. "Sit at the door of your house and you shall see the body of your enemy go past," said Saint Agnes, whose day falls on January 21.

The mayor promised to wait and not do anything rash. Which was the wisest course to take then: by now nobody believed in the state Primo de Rivera sought to create, and everybody had had enough of his dictatorship, which was threatening to produce chaos and looked as if it might end in revolution. His public-spending program had led to an intolerable level of inflation, and the peseta was constantly dropping in value. Only the lack of another general with ambitions prevented an insurrection. On top of that, on February 6, with three months to go before the opening of the World's Fair, Queen María Cristina died of angina pectoris. It was she who, as queen regent, had inaugurated the '88 fair, which everybody now remembered with nostalgia. Her death was considered a bad omen. It was also said in Madrid that the queen, from her deathbed, had advised her son to get rid of Primo de Rivera soon. That could hardly have failed to make an impression on the monarch.

It was in this atmosphere that the day of the fair's inauguration finally came.

"You should go to bed, Father. Tomorrow we have a very busy day ahead of us. You will need all your strength," said María Belltall.

The inventor got up from his armchair, where he had been smoking his after-dinner pipe. Instead of heading for the bedroom, as his daughter had suggested, he went to the door. "Father, where are you going?" she asked. Without replying, Santiago Belltall left their hunting lodge. Although it was natural enough that he should be abstracted on that particular night, she decided to go with him: over the years she had acquired the habit of never letting him out of her sight. Before leaving, she grabbed a shawl, because the night was chilly; outside in the garden, the gusty wind brought hints of rain to come. "Not rain," she thought, "anything but rain."

She saw her father walking out of habit toward the tent; he had been doing so every night, never going to bed without first visiting the tent. He would then have to be scolded back into the lodge.

On this occasion, however, the visit was purely symbolic, since the machines and the fuel had been taken to Montjuich and the contraption entirely reassembled there. The man who was still standing guard at the tent entrance (though now there was no reason to) greeted him amiably: "Good evening, Professor Santiago." The inventor nodded absentmindedly. The guard said, "Tomorrow's the big day, isn't it, Professor?" The inventor started and asked, "What was that you said?" The guard rested the butt of his musketoon on the lawn and smiled: "The big day. Let's hope to God everything goes well."

"How odd," the inventor thought as he went into the tent. "They are all excited on the eve of the event, they feel they are a part of it, even this thug, whose role could scarcely have been less scientific or more at odds with the spirit of our undertaking.

His happiness, too, seems to hang on its success." For his part, the guard was thinking: "Not the friendly type, but without a doubt a real man of science. Of course he's weighed down by cares. And his daughter—what a doll!"

All that remained inside the tent were a few tools scattered here and there, some empty crates, and bits from the ninety-two tons of shavings that had been used to pack highly delicate equipment. The desolation of the scene was depressing. "Here I am, having just realized my life's ambition, and I feel dejected," thought Santiago Belltall. The interminable years of struggle now seemed happy years to him: then, he had lived on hope. Or, rather, he had sacrificed his life to hope. Had the sacrifice been worthwhile?

The guard's voice interrupted this meditation. "Good evening, Señorita Belltall," he heard the man say. "It's María coming to bring me back," he thought. "She has been the greatest victim of my madness. I put my dreams of glory before her well-being. Instead of my tending to her needs, she tended to mine. Because of me, her life has been nothing but renunciation, humiliation." He noticed his daughter's shadow out of the corner of his eye, by the dull light of the oil lamps in the tent. "Even now, at this very moment, she is here because of me, looking for me to tell me I should rest."

"Father, you should be in bed now. It's late, and there's nothing more we can do here," said María. "You can see for yourself—everything is in Montjuich. Even the engineers have left."

This was true: as their tasks came to an end, the workmen and technicians had been dismissed one by one. Onofre sent the aerodynamics experts home with the promise of a handsome reward if they kept their lips sealed. Now the only people still involved in the project were Santiago Belltall and a Prussian military engineer, a ballistics expert with whom Onofre had had frequent dealings during the Great War and whose assistance had turned out to be indispensable.

396

"María, there's something I'd like to tell you," said the inventor.

"It's too late, Father. You can tell me tomorrow."

"Tomorrow will be too late."

This dialogue was interrupted by the entrance of a man into the tent, the butler from the mansion. On Onofre's orders, he had gone to the hunting lodge and, finding it empty, came here.

"My master awaits you in the library," he said.

Santiago Belltall sighed. "I had better not keep our benefactor waiting," he said to his daughter, and then, to the butler, "I will join you in a moment."

The butler shook his head. "I beg your pardon, sir, it is not you but Señorita Belltall whom my master awaits." The inventor and his daughter looked at each other in surprise. "Go on, then, my girl," he said at last. "I'll go straight to bed, don't worry."

"Perhaps I should stop at the hunting lodge for a moment to change my clothes," thought María Belltall.

He said nothing, he did not even raise his head when the butler announced her presence. "Show her in, then shut the door and leave us," he said quietly. "I will not be requiring your services again tonight." Alone with him, not knowing what was expected of her, she went up to his table. When she was near, Onofre said, "Look, María, do you know what this is?" He had never called her by her first name before, and this did not escape her notice. (The wind beat at the windowpanes. "Will it rain tomorrow?" he thought.) "It is the Regent," he said, "the most perfect diamond in existence. It is mine. With it, I could buy whole countries. And yet it fits in the palm of the hand—look." He put the diamond in her hand and made her close her fingers over it. She had glimpsed flashing facets; it was as if the diamond had a fire within it. "Everything has a price," he said. She opened her hand; he took the diamond, wrapped it in a white handkerchief, and put it in his dressing-gown pocket. The slight tremor in his lips suddenly ceased. "I would like to know the nature of your feelings," he said. "If all you feel for me is gratitude or fear, then say nothing." María Belltall shut her eyes. "For twenty years I have lived only for this moment," she breathed in a ghost of a voice.

Santiago Belltall woke up covered with sweat. He had dreamed he was losing his daughter, that he would never see her again. Lighting the lamp by his bed, he looked at the clock and saw it was four in the morning. The wind had died down and the sky was clear; it was still dark, but a gray line was beginning to form on the horizon, gradually making the stars pale. "It will be a fine day, thank God," he thought, but that did not help his uneasiness. "Something's wrong," he said. He got up and left the room in his pajamas and bare feet.

The hunting lodge was all in silence. Seeing his daughter's bedroom door ajar, he looked in. Her bed was untouched, she nowhere to be seen. "How can that be?" he wondered. "Has she still not come back from her talk with Bouvila?" He went over to the window and looked toward the house; no lights were on. "What can be going on there now?" he wondered. Without wasting seconds to put on shoes or clothes, he went outside. His way through the garden was blocked by three men: one of them was the guard who had greeted him at the tent entrance; another was the muscleman who had been acquired with the tent; the third, whom he did not remember having seen before, was an old man with reddish skin, blue eyes, and a clumsy little dog. This old man seemed to be in charge.

"Be so kind as to follow us, Señor Belltall," he said, "and do not raise your voice, please. We must act discreetly and swiftly."

"Who the devil are you," exclaimed the inventor, "to give me orders? What is the meaning of this?"

"Do not excite yourself, Señor Belltall," answered the man with the little dog. "We are only doing as Señor Bouvila asked. Your daughter has come to no harm."

"My daughter!" growled the inventor, clenching his teeth and shaking a fist at the old man. "Why should my daughter come to harm, you accursed old goat?" As he said this, he tried to break away, but the circus Hercules, seeing what was coming, gripped him firmly by the arms. Santiago Belltall began shouting at the top of his voice, "Police! Police! I'm being kidnapped!"

"Nobody can hear you here," said the old man with the little dog. "But in the house you must be quiet, or you'll wake everyone. Please do not force us to use the chloroform."

This warning brought him back to his senses; he thought it best to remain silent. "Could it be," he wondered, "that my daughter and I have been mere pawns all along, in a game whose rules we know nothing of?" The most fearsome answers came crowding into his head, but his mind rejected them with the desperation of one who awakens from a marvelous dream into harsh reality. Meanwhile, the sky had turned red; over the city hung scarlet strips, with something of the glow of a great fire. "What's this? Is all Barcelona going up in flames?"

The striking and grandiose daybreak was being contemplated simultaneously by his daughter. "You'd think the horizon was on fire," she murmured. "Hell has come to pay us a visit." She was standing next to the library's bay window, wrapped in one of its dark-red velvet curtains. Looking back inside, she saw her clothes scattered over the carpet; with a shudder she fixed her gaze once more on the ominous sky. "What will become of me now?" she thought. There was a shout. "What was that?" she asked.

Onofre had just finished dressing and was lighting a cigar with studied calm. Before replying, he blew out the match, dropped it in the ashtray, and took several puffs. "I don't know, a servant, a muleteer whipping his mule, what does it matter?" The shout came again, and María shuddered once more. "It's my father," she said. "It's your imagination," he replied. "You're on edge." "Please pass me my clothes: I must go and see what's happening," she pleaded.

He did not budge, but looked at her through the cigar smoke, his eyes half closed, dwelling on the sight of her exposed shoulders and neck, her vulnerability, her tousled hair, and the fitful breathing that jerked the folds of velvet.

"I will never let you go," he said at last, and thought: "I will not let you abandon me. I love you, María, I've loved you madly ever since that first moment. For twenty years, without realizing it, I've loved you."

"And my father," he heard her asking, "what will you do with him?"

"Nothing bad," he said.

"Where is he now? What are your men doing to him?" she insisted.

"They are taking him somewhere safe. Don't worry, do you think I would do anything to upset you?" He smiled. Just then there was a knock at the door. "Cover yourself," he told her. "I don't want anyone to see you." Raising his voice, he said, "Come in." The door opened a little, and the head of the old man with the dog came through the crack. "Everything under control?" The old man nodded silently. "Very well," said Onofre, "we'll be on our way in a minute."

When the old man disappeared and the door was closed, he strode toward the table. "You can come out now," he said. "Come on, get dressed, we have no time to lose." Seeing her hesitate, he added tauntingly, "Very well, I won't look. Why this modesty now?"

While she picked up her clothes here and there, he turned his back, which did not mean he did not watch her out of the corner of his eye—lest she try to run away or attack him with an object, but she did nothing of the sort. Meanwhile, he took a letter from the table drawer, signed and folded it, put it in an envelope, scribbled something on the envelope, licked the gummed edges to seal it, and placed it in a conspicuous spot on the table. Then he turned toward her; she was fastening the loops of the garters around her thighs. "Ready?" She nodded. "Then let's be on our way!" he said.

Hand in hand they went out into the hall. As they began their descent down the staircase to the lower floors, he put a finger to his lips and whispered, "Shh! It wouldn't do to have my wife wake up." They tiptoed to the front door. There the butler was waiting, a jacket over his arm. Onofre removed the dressing gown and put on the jacket the butler held out for him. Then he reached into the dressing-gown pocket and took out the handkerchief in which the diamond was wrapped, put it in his jacket pocket, and slapped the butler's shoulder: "You know what to do." The butler said he did indeed. "Take care, sir," he added in a voice that betrayed no emotion. Without replying, Onofre took María's hand again. In the garden the grass was damp with dew. At the far end of the bridge, against the red backdrop of daybreak, an automobile was waiting. Onofre and María got into it. "You know where to go," he said to the chauffeur. Its headlights piercing the mist, the automobile drove off.

However much local public figures danced attendance on him, however far the city's leading lights went with their off-color jokes, and even though the occasion had been declared festive by decree, His Majesty Don Alfonso XIII would not crack a smile. Having settled into the Pedralbes palace, he was recalling in vivid detail the terrible events of twenty-three years before.

He was young at the time and had just married Princess Victoria Eugenia of Battenberg. Despite the drizzle, the crowds thronged in the streets of Madrid to see the procession go by. The august couple, leaving the church of San Jerónimo, where their nuptial ceremony had taken place, proceeded to the Palacio de Oriente in the royal coach. As they went down Calle Mayor, a bomb, hurled from an apartment, fell in front of the coach and exploded. They got the fright of their lives but were not injured. Alfonso XIII turned to his bride. "Are you all right?" he said.

Her dress was spattered with the blood of spectators and of the soldiers who had been escorting them. Princess Victoria Eugenia nodded calmly and said simply, in her native English, "Yes." Between thirty and forty people died in the bombing. When they got to the palace, the monarchs hurriedly changed their clothes. In the folds of his cape Alfonso XIII found a finger; he quickly stuffed it in his trouser pocket before his wife saw it. Then, during the wedding reception, he surreptitiously passed it to the Count of Romanones. "Here," he said, "flush this down the toilet." "Your Majesty," the count exclaimed, "it is the mortal remains of a Christian." "Then have it buried in the Almudena, but get it out of my sight," said the king.

As the nobility and the diplomatic corps danced, several thousand policemen scoured every corner of Madrid for the would-be regicide. After a few days they found the man's body in Torrejón de Ardoz. He had been stopped by a guard on a private estate; realizing that the game was up, the fugitive first killed the guard and then himself. Some aspects of this version of events did not quite add up, but everyone, in a hurry to forget the incident, readily accepted it. The man's identity was soon discovered: Mateo Morral, son of a manufacturer from Sabadell, near Barcelona. He had been a teacher or an administrator in the Ferrer Guardia Modern School.

From that time on, Alfonso XIII considered the Catalans a hostile people, hotheaded and unpredictable. Now, in the Pedralbes palace, he kept his hunting shotguns at the head of the royal bed. "Just in case," he said to his wife. Nobody could rival him with a shotgun. When he went hunting—and he did so often—he took three guns. With these he could bring down two partridge before him, two overhead, and two behind. Only George V could rival him in this respect. Even so, the king slept poorly that night. He got up before anyone came to rouse him and stood at the window watching the dawn: the sky was ablaze. "Magnificent," thought the king. "But what does it mean?"

In another part of the city, General Primo de Rivera was also searching the sky for signs. "No doubt about it," he said to himself, "an aurora borealis: there are calamities in store. And here I am sitting like a stuffed puppet." He had not slept well, either, and was feeling a little confused. He sent an aide out for coffee. When the aide came back, he found the dictator wrestling with his boots. "Allow me, General," he said, going down on his knees. Primo de Rivera poured himself a cup of coffee and lifted it to his lips. "One afternoon," he said, "it was a good while ago, in Tangier, I went to a tavern . . . for no special reason . . . you know, just to have a quick one. . . . Anyway, when I went in, who do you think I saw there?" The aide shrugged. "I have no idea, General." "Come on, guess," said the dictator. The aide scratched his head. "I can think of no one, General," he said finally. "Just say the first person that comes into your head," the dictator insisted. "But you'll never guess," he added with a smile. He took a sip of coffee and heaved a sigh. "Nothing like a good strong cup of coffee to start off the day!"

In the distance a bugle blared; it was followed by a drum roll, and finally a brass band began rehearsing a march. "Always the same thing, and always off-key!" grumbled the dictator. "Where are my medals?" The aide held out a dark wooden box with a crown carved on its lid, which belonged to his uncle, the first Marquis of Estella. Primo de Rivera opened the box and examined the medals with a mixture of pride and nostalgia. "Well, then, so you're not going to tell me who I met in that tavern in Tangier?" he asked his aide. The aide stood to attention before speaking. "Buffalo Bill, General," he said. Primo de Rivera's mouth fell open: "Well I'll be damned! How did you know?" The aide, blushing, stammered, "Forgive me, General, it was an accident, I swear to God." "No need to apologize, my man," the dictator said soothingly, "you've done nothing wrong."

The Baron de Viver was also getting ready to fulfill his obligations, although inwardly he was seething. The previous day, in his office in the town hall, he had received a visit from the royal family's head of protocol, who had shown him unintelligible plans and peremptorily given him instructions. "What impudence!" the mayor fumed, alone in his house. "Telling me what to do, and where and how and when. Who do they think they are? This is my city, gentlemen!" In his top hat, gesticulating, he paced in circles in his dressing room.

"And this organization, whose idea was it?" he asked the air. "First His Majesty, then the royal family, then Primo de Rivera and his ministers, then the royal commissary for the fair, the reverend bishop, the honorable ambassadors and legates . . . and me, where do I come in? Bringing up the rear?" He rushed to the door, grabbed the knob as if to leave, froze, let go of the knob, and continued pacing. "No," he said to himself, suddenly calm again, "this isn't due to chance, ignorance, or incompetence. It's a premeditated insult to me, to my position, and therefore to the whole city of Barcelona." The insult to Barcelona enraged him again, and his soliloquy took on manic tones. "I will have my revenge, by the Lord God Almighty I will have my revenge. In the middle of the inaugural ceremony I'll drop my pants and piss on their shoes, and let them shoot me then if they dare!"

This fit was soon over, and he sank into sadness. "And what right have I to say that the city is represented in me? Am I not, rather, the least of its servants, the humblest of its administrative staff? I did not even compete in a public examination for the post—it was Primo de Rivera himself who appointed me." Now at last the sun broke through the clouds, and the glorious dawn was over. The ruddy glow dissolved, and in its place sparkled the calm blue sky of a spring morning. "What is life?" the mayor asked himself with a bitter sigh.

His Majesty Don Alfonso XIII was putting on his gloves as he walked through the salons and halls of the Pedralbes palace, following a chamberlain toward the main door. "What a production!" he thought. "Such a huge palace for us to spend a couple of nights in." His great strides obliged his retinue to trot along behind him. Only the queen could keep up with no apparent effort, and even talk to him as they walked. "You know," he said to her, "this is the second World's Fair I have inaugurated in Barcelona. At the first, I was only two years old, a toddler. Of course, I remember nothing of it, but my mother told me stories." His childhood memories were always official ones: since his father, Don Alfonso XII, had died before he was born, he was King of Spain at the moment of his birth. The midwives and nurses waiting on his mother had curtsied before slapping his bottom to make him cry. "When one is forty-five, it's the second time around for everything," he said, stepping into the armor-plated berline that was to take them to Montjuich.

Primo de Rivera said, "You can talk yourself blue in the face, but I assure you that the man you saw was an impostor." "If you say so, General," said the aide, "but the poster said, as plain as day, 'The one and only Buffalo Bill.'" "Buffalo Bill died in 1917," said the dictator. "This show you saw, were there Indians in it?" Their automobile was crossing Barcelona at full speed. It was late, and they were hurrying to get to the fairgrounds before Their Majesties. If Their Majesties had to wait for the dictator, the delicate political balance of the nation could be destroyed. The aide's face lit up. "Indians? Absolutely, General. And how they yelled, the bastards."

"H'm . . . and cowboys?"

"Cowboys, too, General."

"You're sure? Cowboys lassoing things?'"

"As sure as I'm sitting here, General."

Along the way was an unbroken but not very deep line of people. A few passers-by joined the line at the last moment, drawn by the sirens of the motorcyclists who were clearing the way for the dictator. Nobody, however, applauded or waved handkerchiefs. Many, hoping it was the king, refrained from voicing their disappointment only because of the heavy police presence.

"And was there a stagecoach?"

The aide blinked. "A stagecoach? What stagecoach, General?"

"Aha!" exclaimed the general.

He was nearly dumped on the automobile's carpeted floor when the driver stamped on the brake. He looked out the window and saw it filled with smiling faces. "We've arrived and, thanks be to God, His Majesty is still on his way." When the general got out of the automobile, he was greeted by bows and cheers.

Lost among the swirling mass of personages around him, on tiptoes and craning his neck, the Baron de Viver fixed his eyes—eyes reddened by sleepless nights and rage—on his mortal enemy. "He doesn't look well," he thought. "I could swear he was ill." And immediately all his hatred for the dictator evaporated. A cannon roared, then another, and another, until the official salvos were finished. The castle batteries were saluting the arrival of the king in Montjuich. The Baron de Viver was swept along by the crowd toward the National Palace, where the opening ceremony was to take place. From the palace, a sea of heads could be seen in every direction. When the ceremony was over, the monarchs went out onto the balcony and the people cheered. A few, anonymous in the crowd, booed Primo de Rivera.

The Marquis of Ut, detecting in this the imminent fall of his protector, elbowed his way to the king's side in an attempt to regain his favor. With a theatrical gesture, he swept the magnificent panorama spread before those on the balcony. "Behold, Your Majesty, what Catalonia has to offer you: her men, her ingenuity, and her toil," he intoned grandiloquently.

"And her anarchists," said the king, who recalled Mateo Morral. The marquis groped for a reply, but found none.

But then something unexpected attracted the attention of the monarch and all present. To the right of the balcony, at the far end of the Plaza del Universo, next to Avenida Rius y Taulet, was a circular pavilion strangely reminiscent of a circus tent. Unlike the other pavilions, this one flew no flag or insignia of any kind—a detail that had gone unnoticed until then. Now a persistent purring sound was coming from it, a noise like an airplane engine, increasing steadily. Soon the noise was a terrible din that drowned out the murmurings of the crowd. Those in charge of the fair did not know what to make of this: there were so many officials, no one knew what their various functions were. Who was responsible? The officials exchanged nervous, questioning glances.

Finally, seeing that the roar was not abating and that nobody was doing anything about it, Primo de Rivera himself began issuing orders left and right. After a while the following forces set off for the pavilion: a detachment of the Municipal Guard under the command of Don Alvaro Planas Gasulla; a squad of the Badajoz infantry regiment commanded by Captain Don Agustín Merino del Cordoncillo; a company of Civil Guard under the command of Captain Don Angel del Olmo Méndez; a squadron of security-forces cavalry under Captain Don Antonio Juliá Cebells; a company of local security forces commanded by Lieutenant José María Perales Faura; a squadron from the Montesa cavalry regiment led by Commander Don Manuel Jiménez Santamaría; a detachment of local police led by Sergeant Don Toás Piñol i Mallofré; and an unspecified number of plainclothes policemen.

Over two thousand men were now attempting to push their way through the crowd, which was beginning to panic. Many remembered the bloody assassination attempts of recent years, the Corpus Christi procession bombing, and, believing themselves in a similar situation, struggled to reach safety by whatever means. Human avalanches began, even more dangerous than bombs. For some unknown reason, a shot was fired, and this was followed by shouting and screaming that usually precede famous disasters.

Up in the balconies of the National Palace, crammed with

officials, all eyes were on that strange pavilion, whose walls had begun to vibrate, as if the whole building were some giant explosive device. The policemen, guards, and soldiers advancing toward it were stopped by the crowds surging frantically in the opposite direction. "Shameful!" exclaimed with one voice those responsible for the event. "A disgrace to the city!" They could picture what newspapers the world over would be saying the next morning, or even that same day in special editions: "Barcelona Tragedy." And, below that headline, "Insufficient security measures due to the negligence of . . ." and there each official saw his own name in print.

But now the roof of the pavilion, powered by a hydraulic mechanism, was opening, as if made of sliding panels, and a rush of hot air rose in a column above the pavilion, visible because it caused the light to shimmer, and the column went up as far as the eye could see. At last the roof panels withdrew entirely into the walls, making the pavilion a cylinder open at the top, like a cannon, and a machine emerged and soon was clear of the pavilion, suspended in space without wires, as if it were a planet. It could be seen from everywhere within the fairgrounds, and even from outside it. The crowd, struck dumb at first, burst into exclamations of wonderment.

The contraption, oval in shape, was about ten meters long, and four wide at its widest point. (These dimensions were estimated on the spot and even today are a matter of controversy: they could not be verified, since neither the craft nor the plans for it were ever seen again.) The rear half was of smooth, shiny metal; the front half, of glass protected by ribs of steel or pliable wood. The two halves were joined by a band half a meter wide, which bore several hundred lighted bulbs that enveloped the craft in a halo of light. The rear half contained the motor, which drove it and kept it hovering, and the front half was for the passengers, whose silhouettes could be vaguely made out through the cloud of dust rising with the craft.

The crowd was rapt at the sight of this prodigy, and even His Majesty the King dropped his posture of disdain and whistled in admiration. All, to a man, wondered what it could be. "No doubt about it," some said, "it's the Martians. They've chosen our very own Barcelona to display to the world the marvels of their superior knowledge. This will have everybody in Paris, Berlin, and New York grinding their teeth with envy."

At that time nobody doubted the existence of beings on other planets. The tallest tales circulated on this score, and scientists appeared to be in no hurry to pour cold water on them. These extraterrestrials, representations of whom seemed to have been entrusted exclusively to comic-strip illustrators, were invariably portrayed with the body of a man and the head of a fish. Mostly they went naked, which gave no offense, since no reproductive organs were shown and their skin was green. If they wore anything by way of clothing, it would be jerkins and breeches. The detail of the nose in the form of an ear trumpet was not incorporated until the 1940s, when the cinema, in alliance with the microscope, was able to show highly magnified images of mosquitoes and other insects. Visitors from other worlds had an intelligence far beyond that of earthlings, but their intentions were peaceable and their character naive.

The craft, rising above the domes of the National Palace, described a semicircle and began to descend slowly over the magic-fountain basin. It was observed then that the crew were men of flesh and blood, and the machine a type of ornithopter or helicopter—i.e., a vertical-takeoff aircraft. They had been the subject of experimentation in recent years, but the results had been none too encouraging until now.

On April 18, 1924, the Marquis of Pescara managed to take off and land vertically at Issy-les-Moulineaux, but the distance traveled had not been great: a mere 136 meters. The Spanish engineer Juan de la Cierra had invented, the year before, a less ambitious but more efficient craft called the autogyre, a conventional aircraft in every respect (wings, tail, ailerons, fuselage), to which was added a free-spinning multibladed screw propeller. The propeller turned on an axis situated on top of the fuselage and was powered by the wind displaced by the craft in flight. When the engine was turned off and the plane plummeted, the passage of air caused the propeller to rotate with greater speed, which slowed the fall. Once a few other problems were overcome, such as friction, stability, and so on, the autogyre turned out to be a safe and viable invention: during the 1930s it covered the Madrid-Lisbon route nonstop.

But from the autogyre to vertical takeoff and the ability to hover in mid-air there was still a giant step. This step had now been taken by the craft flying over the World's Fair site. The machine ascended and descended as the crew pleased, hovering at any height, like a ceiling lamp, and moved sideways without jerking or shuddering. This was amazing, but even more amazing was that it could carry out these and other maneuvers without propellers.

4

On the wasteland around the fair whole shantytowns of *barracas* had sprung up; out there, thousands of immigrants lived as best they could. Nobody knew who had arranged the *barracas* in such a way as to form streets, or who had laid out those streets into regular blocks. At the doors of some of the shacks were wooden crates inside which rabbits or chickens were kept; the lids of these crates had been replaced by sheets of gauze through which one could see the animals huddled inside. At the doors of other huts, starved dogs lay dozing.

The automobile pulled up to one of these doors, and Onofre and María got out. The dog gave a grunt as they passed it, and a disheveled woman dressed in rags appeared from behind a sack curtain hanging from the lintel. The shack consisted only of four panels of wood set in the ground, with nails sticking out everywhere. The light of dawn filtered through its cane-and-palm-leaf roof. When they entered, the woman let the curtain fall back into place, then stared at Onofre like an imbecile. She had evidently been asleep. "And your husband," he said, "why isn't he here?" The woman put her hands to her hips and threw back her head. "He went away yesterday evening and hasn't come back yet," she answered with a contemptuous smirk. "All the money you give him he spends on liquor and whores," she added, glancing at María. "That's his business," said Onofre. The sack curtain shook as the dog came in. It sniffed with its wet muzzle at María's legs and sneezed.

"Well, what are we waiting for?" Onofre asked María, whose hand was still in his. The disheveled woman got down on her knees, scraped aside the dirt with the edge of her hand to reveal a trapdoor, and lifted it by tugging at a metal ring. From the hole in the floor, steps cut in the bare earth led downward. Onofre took a few coins from his pocket and held them out for the woman. "Hide them where your husband won't find them," he advised her. The woman's mouth twisted into a smile: "And where might that be?" She looked around at her hovel. But Onofre was already making his way down the steps with María behind him.

They walked, lighting the passage with a dark lantern, until after a hundred meters or so they came to another stairway, similar to the first. At the bottom of it there was another trapdoor, which opened when he knocked three times with the handle of his lamp. They were now inside the pavilion. The pavilion had no doors or windows: this trapdoor was the only access to it. The man who opened the trapdoor for them was advanced in years and pink-complexioned; he wore a white lab coat over his town clothes. When he saw Onofre, he frowned and pointed to his wristwatch, as if saying, "You are late."

Onofre had met him during the Great War; the man was

then a respected military engineer, a ballistics expert. The defeat of the Central Powers left him out of work; for ten years he eked out a living teaching physics and geometry in Tübingen, in a Marist Brothers' school. There, at the beginning of 1928, he received a letter from Onofre inviting him to move to Barcelona "to participate in a project in your field." The money necessary for his moving expenses would be made available in a Tübingen bank. "I regret I cannot be more specific, but the nature of the project demands secrecy," the letter had ended. That kind of talk reminded the Prussian engineer of old times. He took the train in Tübingen and arrived in Barcelona after four days and five nights of nonstop travel, during which his habitual ill humor was not improved. When Onofre explained everything to him, showing him the plans, the engineer hurled his glasses to the floor and jumped up and down on them: "This project is insane, the man who dreamed it up is insane, and you are even more insane— you are in fact the most insane person I've ever met." Onofre smiled and watched him let off steam. The engineer's life in the Tübingen school, he knew, had been purgatory: the pupils had called him "General Boom Boom" and played all manner of vicious practical jokes on him.

It was thanks to this engineer that Santiago Belltall's wild ideas were given scientific form. The Prussian turned the inspired ravings of a genius into a flying machine. For his part, Onofre needed all his patience and ingenuity to settle the quarrels that kept flaring up between the Catalan inventor and the Prussian engineer; without Onofre the collaboration between that pair would not have borne fruit.

The craft occupied the center of the pavilion, mounted on scaffolding as intricate as a lace mantilla. Outside, the cannons roared, announcing the monarchs' arrival at the fairgrounds. "Finish up," called the engineer. Several men in blue coveralls were working, each carrying out his separate task. Nobody spoke or took breaks for a quick smoke or a drink: the Prussian engineer had instilled Prussian discipline into them. These were the elite among mechanics, the kind that would not take their eyes off the job even when María Belltall passed by.

She now understood why Onofre had brought her here. She pulled away, but he held on to her firmly. He saw terror in her eyes. "She doesn't trust her father's invention," he thought, "and she takes me for a madman. Maybe she's right."

They now had the entire World's Fair at their feet. "How strange," Onofre thought. "When I see it all from up here, it looks unreal. Perhaps poor Delfina was right, that the world is really an illusion. Well, now, let's drop a little and have a look at their faces." He worked the levers on the control board to make the craft lose altitude. The crowd was calm again, watching these maneuvers with fascination. "Look, it's Onofre Bouvila!" people said when the craft was close enough for them to recognize the crew members. "It's him, all right. And the girl with him, who is she? A young thing, pretty. But look at that short skirt! Shameless slut!"

Such comments were exchanged with an affection bordering on worship. The stories circulating about Onofre's fabulous wealth and the methods he had used to amass it had made him a popular figure. When he was out in the streets, people would stop and look — discreetly but intensely, as if trying to read in his face confirmation or denial of the rumors they had heard. They would ask themselves, seeing his unassuming, ordinary figure, "Can it be true that in his youth he was an anarchist, a thief, and a gangster? That he was an arms merchant during the war? That he had famous politicians in his pocket, even whole Cabinets? And that he did all that alone, single-handed, starting from scratch, armed only with his courage and his cunning?" And they wanted to believe that it was all true: in him the dreams of every man were realized, in him a collective revenge was achieved. If he had been a crook, what did it matter? What other choice did a man have in this country? And so they cheered him when they recognized him, giving the ovation they had been giving the king to him.

"Look, they are cheering me," Onofre said to María, who scarcely dared to open her eyes. "People are really good, you know," he added, raising his voice to make himself heard over the engines. "You'd never believe what they'll put up with without complaining!" As he said this, he pushed a button, which opened a hatch in the rear of the craft; dozens of doves flew out. There were gasps of delight at the sight of this; the king himself gasped.

Satisfied at the effect produced, Onofre made the craft advance slowly toward the balconies of the National Palace, which were packed with public figures, and stopped just a few meters away. Now he could see all their faces clearly, and they his. "Look," he said, "it's the king. Long live the king! Long live the queen! Long live Don Alfonso XIII!" he shouted, though he knew that nobody could hear him except María. "And there's Primo de Rivera! Go jump in the lake, you old drunkard!" Excited, he pointed out the faces he knew to his companion. "See that tall fellow, head and shoulders above the rest? That's Efrén Castells—the only true friend I ever had. Well, maybe I had more than one, but the others are all gone. But enough, let's get away from here, we've seen all there is to see."

He pushed a lever as far as it would go, and the craft shot upward and backward. Now the whole city was at their feet, the Sierra de Callcerola, the river Llobregat and the Besós, and the immense, luminous sea. "Ah, Barcelona," he said with emotion, "how beautiful you are! And when I think what it was like when I saw it for the first time! . . . The country began right there, the houses were puny little things, and these teeming suburbs were just villages," he said. "There were cows grazing on the Ensanche—you can't believe that, I suppose. I lived over there, in a little back street that is still just the way it was then, in a boardinghouse that closed down centuries ago. All kinds of characters lived there, too. There was a fortune-teller who read my future one night. I don't remember a word of it." "And even if I do," he thought, "what difference would it make? That future is already my past."

Those following the trajectory of the craft from Montjuich, and those drawn out onto their balconies or sun roofs by the noise of its engines, saw how the flying machine changed course and headed out to sea, as if caught by a sudden west wind. Far from the coast it dipped, climbed again for a moment, then plunged into the sea. The fishermen who had been fishing near there at the time told how they had watched in terror as the craft loomed overhead. They had no idea what the thing was. Some thought it was a meteorite, a ball of fire coming at them. Yet they could not say for sure whether the craft had been on fire or whether the blaze had simply been the sun reflected off its metal-and-glass surface. All agreed, however, that right before it fell, the engines suddenly cut out. The roar stopped, and the lapping of the waves restored the peace of the sea. It seemed, they said, as if time stood still. Then the craft hit the water like a cannonball.

Those who went out to the spot where they thought they had seen the craft go down found no debris, not even an oil slick or gasoline floating on the water. They disagreed as to the exact point of impact. The navy immediately dispatched several ships to the area. Some countries offered to help, to participate in the salvage operations. Actually, they were interested in recovering the flying machine to learn its secret. But divers came up empty-handed, and radar showed nothing but a sandy bottom. A storm forced them to discontinue the operation, and it was never resumed.

Since the bodies did not turn up, prayers for the dead had to be said in the cathedral. Afterward wreaths were tossed into the dark waters of the harbor, whence the current swept them out to sea. The newspapers published the usual obituaries, paragraphs full of rhetoric. Expurgated biographies of Onofre Bouvila appeared, for the edification of the reading public. The consensus was that a great man had left the world. "The city owes him a perennial debt of gratitude," said one newspaper. "He symbolized more than anyone the spirit of an epoch that has to some extent passed away with him," said another. "The 1888 World's Fair marked the beginning of his career, and this fair of '29 its end," observed a third.

The fair of '29, which Onofre had enlivened with his spectacular exploit, was showing signs of turning into a spectacular failure. In October of that year, four months after the opening, the New York Stock Exchange crashed. Overnight and out of the blue, the capitalist system was tottering. The crash was followed by bankruptcy for thousands of firms. Their representatives came running to the pavilions and palaces of the fair and hurried away with the exhibits before the sheriffs could get there with their seizure warrants. Many exhibitors committed suicide, jumping from the office windows of Wall Street skyscrapers. To keep the pavilions from being emptied, which certainly would have made a bad impression, the Spanish government substituted each item removed with whatever was at hand. Soon there were pavilions no better than flea markets.

Under such dire circumstances, new rumors concerning Onofre Bouvila were not given the attention they would otherwise have received. These rumors said that he had not died at all, that the accident had been faked, and that he was living comfortably in some distant land in the company of María Belltall, at whose side he had at last found true love and in whose arms he spent his days and nights.

To support this romantic theory, several bits of evidence were enlisted. Well before the accident, Bouvila had arranged things in such a way that it proved impossible to locate not only the craft but also the plans for it and the men who had built it. When army sappers finally managed to break into the mystery pavilion through a hole in its concrete wall, they found on the ground only the planks that had been used as scaffolding for the craft. Eventually the trapdoor was discovered, but the passage from it led merely to an abandoned shack. It was also suspicious that Bouvila should have had on his person the Regent, the perfect diamond, when the accident took place. This, along with the events of that year, made some venture the theory that Bouvila was behind the collapse of the world economy, although nobody could say what motive he would have had to act thus.

All eyes then turned to his widow, but no enlightenment came from that quarter. The mansion was sold to the Barcelona County Council, which took no interest in it; through their indifference it gradually deteriorated, until it returned to the ruin it had once been. Bouvila's widow moved to a chalet in Llavaneras that formerly belonged to the ex-governor of Luzon, General Osorio y Clemente. There she remained in the strictest seclusion until her death on August 4, 1940. She left a few documents, but the letter Bouvila had placed on his study desk before leaving for Montjuich eleven years before was not among them. Little by little, these and other, similar rumors died; no fresh evidence came to light to revive them, and other, more pressing matters now occupied the minds of the people of Barcelona.

Meanwhile, the World's Fair was languishing. Public opinion openly jeered at the organizers and indirectly, through them, at Primo de Rivera's government. Despite the censorship, nobody shrank from making comparisons between Barcelona's two World's Fairs: the fair of '29 was sharply criticized, while the fair of '88 was praised to the skies—people preferred not to recall the problems it had caused in its day, the wrangles and animosities, the deficit with which it had burdened the city. Now the Baron de Viver was sorry he had not taken a firmer line. "For this farce, this travesty that will make fools of us all, we have mortgaged our city," he lamented. He soon resigned. Primo de Rivera, too, who had been the driving force behind the fair, pinning so many hopes on its success, finally had to admit that his situation was untenable, and that he was unpopular. In January 1930 he tendered his resignation, and the king accepted it with no attempt to hide his satisfaction. Primo de Rivera immediately went into voluntary exile in Paris, where he lived only a few months, dying on May 16, 1930, a few days before the first anniversary of the opening of the Barcelona World's Fair. Four years later, Alfonso XIII himself abdicated the Spanish throne and went into exile. These events were followed by others of no less importance. Some were joyous, some grim. Later, both the joyous and the grim combined in the collective memory, forming a chain, a graph, that led inexorably to war and holocaust. Later still, as people looked back over their history, they concluded that the year Onofre Bouvila disappeared from Barcelona marked the onset of a distinct decline in the city.